SOCIOLOGICAL
METHODOLOGY
🌿1993🌿

SOCIOLOGICAL METHODOLOGY
1993

VOLUME 23

EDITOR Peter V. Marsden

ADVISORY EDITORS Gerhard Arminger

David J. Bartholomew

Kenneth A. Bollen

Richard T. Campbell

John Markoff

Adrian E. Raftery

Nora Cate Schaeffer

Ronald Schoenberg

Michael E. Sobel

Judith Tanur

An official publication by Blackwell Publishers for

THE AMERICAN SOCIOLOGICAL ASSOCIATION

FELICE LEVINE, *Executive Officer*

Library of Congress Catalog Card Information
Sociological Methodology. 1969–85
San Francisco, Jossey-Bass. 15 v. illus. 24 cm. annual. (Jossey-Bass behavioral science
series)
Editor: 1969, 1970: E. F. Borgatta; 1971, 1972, 1973–74: H. L. Costner;
1975, 1976, 1977: D. R. Heise; 1978, 1979, 1980: K. F. Schuessler;
1981, 1982, 1983–84: S. Leinhardt; 1985: N. B. Tuma

Sociological Methodology, 1986–88
Washington, DC, American Sociological Association. 3 v. illus. 24 cm. annual.
Editor: 1986: N. B. Tuma; 1987, 1988: C. C. Clogg

Sociological Methodology. 1989–1992
Oxford, Basil Blackwell. 4 v. illus. 24 cm. annual.
Editor: 1989, 1990: C. C. Clogg; 1991, 1992, 1993: P. V. Marsden
"An official publication of the American Sociological Association."
1. Sociology—Methodology—Year books. I. American Sociological
Association. II. Borgatta, Edgar F., 1924– ed.

HM24.S55	301'.01'8	68-54940
	rev.	
Library of Congress	[r71h2]	

British Cataloguing in Publication Data
Sociological Methodology. Vol. 23
1. Sociology. Methodology
301'.01'8

ISBN 1-55786-464-0
ISSN 0081-1750

Typeset by Huron Valley Graphics, Ann Arbor, MI
Printed by Edwards Brothers, Ann Arbor, MI

CONSULTANTS

Paul D. Allison
Gerhard Arminger
David J. Bartholomew
Mark P. Becker
Richard A. Berk
William T. Bielby
Hans-Peter Blossfeld
Kenneth A. Bollen
Phillip Bonacich
Ronald L. Breiger
Charles Brody
Richard T. Campbell
Charles Cappell
Aaron Cicourel
Clifford C. Clogg
Thomas A. DiPrete
Patrick Doreian
Scott R. Eliason
Barbara Entwisle
Glenn A. Firebaugh
John Fox
David B. Grusky
Jacques A. Hagenaars
David R. Heise
Jan Hoem
Michael Hout
Gudmund Iverson

Guillermina Jasso
Tony Lancaster
Kenneth C. Land
Robert D. Mare
J. Miller McPherson
N. Krishnan Namboodiri
J. Zvi Namenwirth
W. Russell Neuman
Robert Nash Parker
Trond K. Petersen
Adrian E. Raftery
Karl Reitz
Nora Cate Schaeffer
Ronald Schoenberg
John Skvoretz
Herbert L. Smith
Michael E. Sobel
Aage B. Sørensen
Philip J. Stone
Judith Tanur
Jay Teachman
David Thissen
Peter G. M. van der Heijden
David L. Weakliem
Robert Philip Weber
Christopher Winship
Lawrence Wu

CONTENTS

CONTRIBUTORS

Gerhard Arminger, Department of Economics, Bergische Universitat Wuppertal, Germany

William G. Axinn, Department of Sociology and Population Research Center, University of Chicago

Kenneth A. Bollen, Department of Sociology, University of North Carolina at Chapel Hill

Kathleen Carley, Department of Social and Decision Sciences, Carnegie Mellon University

Clifford C. Clogg, Department of Sociology and Population Research Institute, Pennsylvania State University

Katherine Faust, Department of Sociology, University of South Carolina

Linton C. Freeman, School of Social Sciences, University of California, Irvine

Guang Guo, Department of Sociology and Carolina Population Center, University of North Carolina at Chapel Hill

Daniel H. Hill, Survey Research Institute and Department of Economics, University of Toledo

Charles F. Manski, Department of Economics, University of Wisconsin

Arland Thornton, Survey Research Center and Department of Sociology, University of Michigan

Kwok-fai Ting, Department of Sociology, University of North Carolina at Chapel Hill

Stanley Wasserman, Departments of Psychology, Sociology and Statistics, University of Illinois at Urbana/Champaign

Douglas R. White, School of Social Sciences, University of California, Irvine

Kazuo Yamaguchi, Department of Sociology, University of Chicago

INFORMATION FOR AUTHORS

Sociological Methodology is an annual volume on methods of research in the social sciences. Sponsored by the American Sociological Association, *Sociological Methodology*'s mission is to disseminate material that advances empirical research in sociology and related disciplines. Chapters present original methodological contributions, expository statements on and illustrations of recently developed techniques, and critical discussions of research practice. *Sociological Methodology* seeks contributions that address the full range of problems confronted by empirical work in the contemporary social sciences, including conceptualization and modeling, research design, data collection, measurement, and data analysis. Work on the methodological problems involved in any approach to empirical social science is appropriate for *Sociological Methodology.*

The content of each annual volume of *Sociological Methodology* is driven by submissions initiated by authors; the volumes do not have specific annual themes. Editorial decisions regarding manuscripts submitted are based heavily on the advice of expert referees; each article submitted for consideration is read by two or more editorial consultants. Criteria for evaluation include originality, breadth of interest and applicability, and expository clarity. Discussions of implications for research practice are vital, and authors are urged to include empirical illustrations of the methods they discuss.

Authors should submit four copies of manuscripts to the Editor (see below). Manuscripts should include an informative abstract of not more than one double-spaced page and should not identify the author within the text. Submission of a manuscript for review by *Sociological Methodology* implies that it has not been published previously and that it is not under review elsewhere.

Inquiries concerning the appropriateness of material and/or other aspects of editorial policies and procedures are welcome; prospective authors should correspond with:

Peter V. Marsden, Editor
Sociological Methodology
Department of Sociology
Harvard University
630 William James Hall
33 Kirkland Street
Cambridge, MA 02138

Electronic mail address:
SOCMETH@ISR.HARVARD.EDU

PROLOGUE

𝕏𝕏𝕏𝕏𝕏𝕏𝕏𝕏𝕏𝕏𝕏𝕏𝕏𝕏𝕏𝕏𝕏𝕏𝕏𝕏

Sociological Methodology 1993 is the twenty-third volume in an annual series initiated in 1969. It begins with an in-depth essay on
methodological strategy that focuses on the problem of assessing the
adequacy of the information available for addressing a research question. Later chapters deal with such problems as coding textual materi-
als, representing complex social network data, ascertaining the
goodness-of-fit of covariance structure models, and analyzing cross-
classifications that include ordered variables. The final three chapters contribute to the literature on methods for the study of event-
history data.

In the introductory chapter of *Sociological Methodology 1993*,
Charles Manski presents an extensive discussion of problems of *identification* in the social sciences. Manski argues that many substantive
disputes in disciplines like economics and sociology revolve around
identification problems. These arise whenever assumptions based on
theory or the results of prior research, together with newly gathered
data, do not yield information sufficient to enable an analyst to
discriminate between alternative claims about a phenomenon. Identification problems are more fundamental than statistical ones, in
Manski's view; larger samples and more efficient techniques of estimation cannot compensate for limited knowledge about the phenomenon to be studied.

Sociologists are most familiar with identification problems in
the setting of linear structural equation (or covariance structure)
models, where extensive attention has been devoted to the condi-

tions under which data from a sample together with a priori restrictions on model parameters are sufficient to imply unique parameter estimates. Manski's chapter discusses identification problems in a wide variety of other settings. His analyses of identification problems start by exploring what can be known in the absence of any prior assumptions; as he proceeds, he successively adds prior information and examines what can be learned as such assumptions are imposed. His approach assumes abundant sample information, setting aside problems of statistical estimation that are present when sample sizes are limited.

Manski begins with prediction problems in regression analysis, showing that identification problems arise when an analyst predicts the value of a dependent variable for values of an independent variable that lie outside the range sampled in a data set. Such projections become possible only when global assumptions about the form of a regression are imposed. He then turns to the selection problem, which occurs when the dependent variable is not observed for certain values of an independent variable. Here, Manski's approach to identification problems yields substantial dividends, for he demonstrates that quite weak assumptions suffice to place bounds on the values of many quantities of interest, even when point estimates of those quantities are not identified. Moreover, the breadth of those bounds is proportional to the amount of missing data.

The final sections of Manski's chapter address identification problems present in models that attempt to capture sociological phenomena such as reference group effects and the effects of intentions on behavior. His discussion of reference group effects demonstrates the difficulty, in the absence of prior information, of distinguishing between internal social influences or "endogenous social effects" and external influences or "contextual effects." Similarly, "ecological" effects cannot be separated from "correlated individual effects." The discussion in this part of the chapter makes it clear that analysts cannot ascertain the channels through which such effects operate from data on outcomes alone.

Chapter 2, written by Clifford C. Clogg and Gerhard Arminger, is a commentary on Manski's chapter. While commending Manski for his insights into what analysts can hope to learn from a body of data, Clogg and Arminger argue that researchers must also give due attention to problems of statistical estimation. They suggest that it will often be fruitful to begin by imposing enough assumptions to make it possible to estimate a model, and successively relaxing them, instead of taking Manski's "top-down" approach. Indeed, proceeding according to the Clogg/Arminger strategy will often be necessary given the typical numbers of observations in the data bases that social scientists study. Clogg and Arminger suggest that the bounds Manski establishes through mathematical analysis will often be unduly wide, and that they could be appreciably improved through the introduction of prior information. Clogg and Arminger also emphasize that the resolution of identification problems may require attention to other important methodological issues. For example, research designs such as experiments and quasi-experiments may aid in isolating a phenomenon for study by holding fixed some factors that have to do with competing explanations.

Chapter 3, Kathleen Carley's "Coding Choices for Textual Analysis: A Comparison of Content Analysis and Map Analysis," discusses the preparation of textual data. Such data are of interest to a wide variety of social science disciplines, and readying them for analysis entails a number of complexities. As always, coding decisions depend in part on the analyses that are contemplated. In this regard Carley contrasts *content analysis,* which examines the frequency with which concepts occur in texts, with *map analysis,* a term that covers a number of specific procedures that extract concepts and the relationships among them, thus studying the context in which concepts are used. Carley suggests that map analyses are better able than content analyses to capture differences in meaning between texts.

Chapter 3 points to eight important coding decisions that must be made in the course of coding data for content analysis, ranging from the decision to delete information judged to be irrelevant to the development of translation rules for generalizing concepts that a researcher decides to treat as equivalent. Additional issues arise for a map analysis; Carley points to four new coding choices here, having to do with such things as definitions of relationships among concepts and the inclusion of implicit social information in the map of a text.

Carley's chapter illustrates the different inferences that emerge from content analyses and map analyses by way of brief examples that demonstrate cases in which, for instance, content analyses indicate that texts are identical while map analyses demonstrate appreciable distinctions among them. She also shows how different coding choices can influence the degree of similarity found between one text and another. Toward the end of her chapter, Carley distinguishes between different map analytic techniques—based on semantic structures, proximity of words to one another within a text, or "story-line" structures—and examines a related approach to textual analysis known as concordance analysis. The chapter concludes by sketching open issues in the analysis of texts, arguing that there is much progress yet to be made in the development of procedures for comparing and contrasting coded texts. Carley's discussion of coding and analysis issues for textual analysis is general, but she exemplifies it with the aid of a specific software package for textual analysis (MECA) that she has developed.

In Chapter 4, "Using Galois Lattices to Represent Network Data," Linton C. Freeman and Douglas R. White illustrate a new method for creating visual representations of "two-mode" networks. The diagrams that have long been used to picture social networks use points to represent actors (or other units) and lines to represent social relations among the actors. When the actors are of one type only (e.g., people or organizations) the data are "one-mode," and the usual representations suffice.

Many social network data of interest, however, involve relationships between entities of two types; for example, one may examine the positions taken on issues by political candidates (for example, see James Beniger's chapter in *Sociological Methodology 1982*) or the memberships of persons in groups, as in studies of interlocking directorates (for example, see Philip Bonacich's contribution to *Sociological Methodology 1972*). In this case one has two-mode network data. The usual graphical representations do not serve well for this case because they are unable to distinguish the two distinct types of entities. Moreover, two-mode data–relating, say, persons to events–induce two other structures, one relating events to one another and the second relating persons to one another; the usual graphical representations do not exhibit these readily.

Freeman and White suggest that Galois lattices provide a basis for presenting all of these features of two-mode network data. Their chapter shows how this pictorial representation can display the event-actor, actor-actor, and event-event relationships in such data. Moreover, these diagrams allow them to identify classes of events and classes of actors, to identify different actors as core or peripheral to sets of events, and to locate actors who are involved in integrating persons across sets of events. A very rich set of implications, then, follows from the lattice representation.

Chapter 5, Kenneth Bollen and Kwok-fai Ting's "Confirmatory Tetrad Analysis," is about the assessment of goodness of fit and the isolation of possible specification errors in structural equation or covariance structure models. Tetrads are differences of products of pairs of covariances, and restrictions embodied in structural equation models often imply that certain tetrads vanish–that is, take on values of zero. In fact, early research on factor analysis noted such implications. More recently, vanishing tetrads have been used in exploratory efforts to specify models properly; see the chapter in *Sociological Methodology 1988* by Clark Gilmour, Richard Scheines, and Peter Spirtes.

Bollen and Ting, however, use tetrads for purposes of testing a prespecified model. They present three methods for locating the vanishing tetrads implied by a model, and they discuss methods for determining a set of nonredundant tetrads. They then give a test for assessing a hypothesis that one or more tetrads is zero. This test, which does not require iterative procedures, is valid under quite general conditions; Bollen and Ting also discuss methods for assessing the power of their test.

Chapter 5 presents confirmatory tetrad analysis as a diagnostic approach that supplements rather than replaces the chi-square tests often used to assess the goodness of fit of structural equation models. Bollen and Ting note that one can test the vanishing tetrads implied by underidentified models. Further, some models that are nested in terms of implied tetrads are not nested in terms of restrictions on parameters; hence certain model comparisons that are difficult using the usual techniques can be undertaken readily using the Bollen/Ting approach. Several examples are used to illustrate the applications of confirmatory tetrad analysis.

In Chapter 6, Katherine Faust and Stanley Wasserman articulately describe, compare, and contrast correlation and association models for studying cross-classified data. Both of these techniques can be viewed as methods of intrinsic measurement. They induce scores for row and column categories of a cross-tabulation on the basis of the association between the variables; related methods are discussed by

Peter van der Heijden and Jan de Leeuw in *Sociological Methodology 1989*. Correlation models, also known under the term correspondence analysis, select scores that maximize the correlation between row and column variables. Association models choose scores by fitting log-linear and log-multiplicative models for various odds ratios. Both correlation and association models may induce multiple sets of scores, and multiple corresponding canonical correlations or measures of intrinsic association, for a given cross-classification.

Faust and Wasserman give particular attention to important restricted versions of correlation and association models. Restricted models may place constraints on the number of sets of scores and measures of association derived for a given cross-classification. Such models may restrict the row and/or column scores themselves; for example, one may hypothesize that the scores are equally spaced, that the scores are proportional to other a priori values, or that scores for pairs or sets of response categories are identical. Faust and Wasserman show how the use of statistical procedures facilitates inferences about the validity of these different types of restrictions.

The procedures discussed in Chapter 6 are illustrated with data on dyadic relations in social networks; Faust and Wasserman examine the association between expressions of liking and measures of both observed and reported interactions among members of a fraternity, and between friendship claims and communication among participants in a computer conferencing system. They find that several restricted correlation and association models describe these data well. In the examples presented, the two types of models yield rather similar inferences about the scores to be assigned to the ordinal measures studied, but in the concluding section of the chapter, Faust and Wasserman discuss conditions under which such inferences might differ.

Event-history or "hazard rate" models examine the rates at which events (e.g., entry into marriage or unemployment) occur in time, and the manner in which such rates vary over time or with covariates that describe heterogeneity among the units under study. They are suitable for studying longitudinal data bases that record the occurrence and timing of events. Major advantages of event-history methods, as outlined in Nancy Tuma's chapter in *Sociological Methodology 1982*, include the capacity to take account of "censored" observations—those for which an event takes place outside the period covered by observation—and to make use of covariates (i.e., explanatory variables) that change value over time.

Guang Guo, in Chapter 7, examines the problem of left-truncation in event-history analysis. A case is left-truncated when its exposure to the risk of experiencing an event begins prior to the period during which cases are observed. The problem posed by left-truncation is one of sample selection: high-risk cases in the same cohort as left-truncated cases will have experienced the event before the beginning of the observation period, and will not be included in the study at all; hence, without an adjustment for left-truncation, the sample studied will consist disproportionately of low-risk cases, and estimates of rates will be biased negatively.

Guo notes that the problems posed by left-truncation may be addressed in several ways. Under certain specifications of the rates at which events occur, left-truncation is not problematic; but such assumptions can be incorrect. Alternatively, left-truncated cases can be excluded from an analysis; however, this can mean that a large amount of the information available is neglected. In Guo's example, which focuses on rates of marital dissolution among women based on the Panel Study of Income Dynamics, nearly half of the cases would have to be removed if this approach were to be taken.

Guo then discusses a conditional approach to estimation for left-truncated event-history data that avoids many of the problems of other approaches. His technique requires data on the time at which a case first came to be at risk of experiencing the event; hazard rates of an event for such cases are estimated under the condition that the case does not experience the event prior to the beginning of the observation period. Guo argues that the conditional approach is well-suited to the event-history data studied by social scientists, because the retrospective surveys or archival sources often used to obtain such data will frequently yield information on the time at which a case first came to be exposed to risk. Moreover, the conditional approach requires information on time-varying covariates only for the observation period, and such information too is typically available to social scientists. Guo's empirical illustration of three implementations of the conditional approach—a piecewise exponential version, a discrete-time version, and a partial likelihood version—shows that it effectively addresses problems of left truncation.

In Chapter 8, "Competing Hazards with Shared Unmeasured

Risk Factors," Daniel Hill, William Axinn, and Arland Thornton study a problem that arises when a case's exposure to the risk of experiencing an event may end in two or more different ways. For example, death due to illness removes one from the risk of accidental death; similarly, entry into retirement removes one from the risk of being laid off or fired from one's job.

Hill and his coauthors note that a common approach to the study of competing risks, the multinomial logit model, involves the assumption that the different destinations that terminate a spell of exposure to risk are independent of one another. They suggest that this assumption may be inaccurate in many applications. Their own illustration deals with rates of entry into marriage or unmarried cohabitation from the state of being single; they suggest that shared unmeasured factors may predispose people toward marriage or cohabitation–that is, that these destinations are not independent.

As an alternative to the multinomial logit model, Hill and his coauthors suggest the use of the nested logit model. This groups the destination states that may end a spell of exposure into sets; the nested model asserts that destinations are uncorrelated between sets but permits them to be correlated within sets. In the spirit of Manski's chapter, Hill and his colleagues discuss the information needed to identify the nested logit model: Prior to analysis, one must know the grouping of destinations into sets and the covariates that affect the propensities to move toward different destinations. The authors discuss two different approaches to estimating the model, one of which can be implemented with widely available statistical software. Estimates for their empirical example indicate that entry into marriage and entry into cohabitation are affected by some highly correlated unmeasured factors, and that failure to take them into account can imply substantial biases in the estimated effects of measured covariates.

As noted above, one of the strengths of event-history approaches lies in their capacity to accommodate time-varying independent variables when predicting the rates at which events take place. Kazuo Yamaguchi's chapter, which concludes this volume of *Sociological Methodology,* examines a related problem. Yamaguchi is concerned with models in which the coefficients of covariates may change over time (the covariate values themselves may be constant or varying in time). His study of "varying parameter" models is related to several previous presentations in *Sociological Methodology*, but distinct in that he deals with longitudinal data. The chapter on multilevel analysis by William Mason, George Wong, and Barbara Entwisle, which appeared in the 1983–84 volume, examines parameters that may vary by context (e.g., country) in analyses of cross-sectional surveys, while that by Thomas DiPrete and David Grusky (in *Sociological Methodology 1990*) deals with the estimation of models including parameters that may vary over time, using repeated cross-section (or trend) studies.

Yamaguchi approaches this problem for event-history models by examining saturated models of hazard rates, under conditions where covariates are categorical. His method requires either that the measurement of time be discrete (as in Paul Allison's chapter in *Sociological Methodology 1982*) or that rates in continuous time be specified as constant within known time intervals. Among other things, these models provide a very clear illustration of how estimates of rates, and of the effects of covariates on rates, are related to observed data on the number of events taking place and the length of time that units have been exposed to the risk of an event.

By reparameterizing the saturated model using different specifications for the way in which effects of covariates vary with time, Yamaguchi is able to accomplish a number of useful analyses. He develops a test for proportionality of covariate effects (for multiplicative models in which parameters describe relative risks of experiencing an event) or additivity of covariate effects (for additive models in which parameters describe differences in absolute risks). He also shows how to examine the goodness of fit of various *un*saturated models for time-varying covariate effects. Yamaguchi illustrates these methods in a study of over-time variations in the effect of employment on entry into marriage by men.

ACKNOWLEDGEMENTS

I have received a great deal of help in assembling this volume of *Sociological Methodology*. Fifty-four editorial consultants read one or more manuscripts for this volume; their names are listed on page v. Their considered judgment and generous advice have been instrumental in developing many of the chapters that appear here, and I am deeply grateful to them.

At Harvard, Suzanne Washington has assumed principal responsibility for managing the *Sociological Methodology* editorial office; Katsch Belash and Rick Suarez have assisted her in this. Ruth Myott at Blackwell has taken over the task of shepherding the volume through the production process. I thank Ruth for her competence and for her patience in the face of some unavoidable delays. The chapters in this year's volume were copyedited by Stephanie Argeros-Magean.

Sociological Methodology is supported financially by the American Sociological Association, and I am delighted to acknowledge the Association's essential contributions to it. Harvard University has made many in-kind contributions to *Sociological Methodology* during my editorship, including office space, office equipment, accounting support, and other aid; for these too I am most appreciative.

Peter V. Marsden
Harvard University
March 1993

1

IDENTIFICATION PROBLEMS IN THE SOCIAL SCIENCES

Charles F. Manski*

The aim of methodological research in the social sciences is to learn what conclusions can and cannot be drawn given empirically relevant combinations of assumptions and data. Methodologists have long found it useful to separate inferential problems into statistical and identification components. Studies of identification seek to characterize the conclusions that could be drawn if the researcher had available a sample of unlimited size. Studies of statistical inference seek to characterize the generally weaker conclusions that can be drawn given a sample of positive but finite size. Statistical and identification problems limit in distinct ways the conclusions that may be drawn in empirical research. Statistical problems are most severe when the available sample is small. Identification problems are most severe when the researcher knows little about the population under study and the sampling process yields only weak data on the population. This chapter synthesizes some of my recent research and thinking on identification problems in the social sciences. Four problems are discussed: extrapolation of regressions, the selection problem, identification of endogenous social effects, and identification of subjective phenomena. These problems arise regularly in social science research and are the source of many substantive disputes.

*University of Wisconsin

This chapter was presented to the Section on Methodology, 1992 Annual Meeting of the American Sociological Association. The author has benefited from several discussions with Robert Mare and from the comments of Clifford Clogg, Peter Marsden, Yu Xie, and the reviewers.

1

1. INTRODUCTION

The members of our open society often express differing views on social policy. Disagreements presumably arise out of the conflicting self-interests and ideologies of the population, but normative differences are not the only contributing force. Many controversies reflect divergent beliefs about human behavior, specifically about the effects of government programs on behavior.

Consider, for example, the continuing debate about welfare. Perspectives on AFDC and other welfare programs appear in part to reflect beliefs about the way these programs affect marriage, fertility, and labor supply behavior. Almost everyone has an opinion on the matter, but the opinions vary widely.

Divergent beliefs about human behavior should, one might think, be reconciliable through empirical social science research. Yet social scientists rarely seem able to settle questions of public concern. During the past 20 years researchers have worked hard to learn how welfare affects behavior (see Moffitt 1992) and to evaluate the job training programs that aim to move welfare recipients into the labor market (see Manski and Garfinkel 1992). They have similarly worked to understand how neighborhoods influence their inhabitants (see Jencks and Mayer 1989), how the threat of punishment deters crime (see Blumstein, Cohen, and Nagin 1978), how school attributes affect student learning (see Hanushek 1986, and Gamoran 1992), and how early childbirth affects the lives of mothers and their children (see Hayes and Hofferth 1987). In these and so many other areas, progress seems painfully slow. Indeed, the cumulative research on a subject only rarely converges toward a consensus.

Why has empirical research in the social sciences so often failed to yield clear-cut answers to questions of interest? Perhaps the social sciences are immature. Or perhaps the questions that the social sciences address may just be hard to answer.

I believe the core problem to be the inherent difficulty of the questions facing the social sciences. The conclusions that one can draw from an empirical analysis are determined by the assumptions and the data that one brings to bear. In social science research, the available data are typically limited and the range of plausible assumptions wide; hence the generally accepted conclusions are necessarily weak. Disagreements about the determinants of human behavior, the nature of social interactions, and the consequences of public policy persist because researchers who analyze the same data under different maintained assumptions reach different logically valid conclusions.

Although the core problem of the social sciences is the difficulty of the enterprise, there is also a problem of immaturity. Many social scientists do not appreciate the core problem. Some seem not to recognize that the interpretation of data requires assumptions. How often do we see an empirical analysis that applies some conventional statistical method with little understanding of the assumptions needed to interpret the results in the conventional way? Some researchers understand the logic of scientific inference but nevertheless deny it when reporting their own work. The scientific community rewards researchers who produce strong novel findings and the public, impatient for solutions to its pressing policy concerns, rewards researchers who offer simple analyses leading to unequivocal policy recommendations. These incentives make it tempting for researchers to maintain assumptions far stronger than they can persuasively defend, in order to draw strong conclusions. When this happens, empirical research degenerates into the advocacy of "forensic" social science, where researchers sharing the same data but maintaining different assumptions argue about the interpretation of the data. With empirical resolution impossible, scientific inquiry is replaced by debate.

1.1 *Statistical Inference and Identification*

The aim of methodological research in the social sciences is to learn what conclusions can and cannot be drawn given empirically relevant combinations of assumptions and data. For at least a century, methodologists have used statistical theory to frame their studies (see Stigler 1986; Clogg 1992). One supposes that the empirical problem is to infer some feature of a population described by a probability distribution and that the available data are observations extracted from the population by some sampling process. One combines the data with assumptions about the population and the sampling process to draw statistical conclusions about the population feature of interest.

Working within this familiar framework, methodologists have found it useful to separate the inferential problem into statistical and identification components. Studies of identification seek to characterize the conclusions that could be drawn if the researcher had available a sample of unlimited size. Studies of statistical inference seek to characterize the generally weaker conclusions that can be drawn given a sample of positive but finite size. Statistical and identification problems limit in distinct ways the conclusions that may be drawn in empirical research. Statistical problems are most severe when the available sample is small. Identification problems are most severe when the researcher knows little about the population under study and the sampling process yields only weak data on the population.

Statistical problems contribute to the difficulty of empirical research but identification is the more fundamental problem of the social sciences. Increasing the sizes of our available data samples would enable us to sharpen the inferences we now make but would not enable us to make new kinds of inferences. New inferences require either new knowledge of the population under study or new sampling processes yielding data on different features of the population.

1.2 *Focus on Identification*

Beginning in the early 1980s, I have gradually devoted less time in my research and teaching to the study of statistical questions and more to the analysis of identification. I now find it natural to study inference in two stages. First, one determines what restrictions on the population of interest are implied by the available prior information and by the sampling process generating data. Second, one develops methods for estimating identified population features, usually by treating the sample as analogous to the population (see Manski 1988*a*).

This chapter synthesizes some of what I have learned about identification problems in the social sciences. Early on I found that effective study of identification requires an appropriate balance between generality and specificity. An overly general analysis may yield only sterile theorems stating that a given population feature is identified if some system of equations or extremum problem has a unique solution. An overly specific analysis may obscure basic ideas.

With these concerns in mind, I have chosen to discuss four identification problems that arise regularly in social science research and are the source of many substantive disputes. These are extrapolation of regressions (Section 2); the selection problem (Section 3);

identification of endogenous social effects (Section 4); and identification of subjective phenomena (Section 5). The first two problems are generic to science, while the latter two are more specific to the social sciences. I conclude (Section 6) by calling attention to several themes that arise in the course of considering these identification problems.

2. EXTRAPOLATION OF REGRESSIONS

The problem of extrapolating regressions is very familiar and so forms a good starting point for our discussions. A consideration of extrapolation also serves to introduce basic ideas of nonparametric regression analysis used repeatedly in Sections 3 through 5.

Informally, extrapolation is the prediction of a variable y given a specified value for another variable x, in the absence of data on the behavior of y when x takes this value. Formally, let $Y \times X$ be the space of logically possible values of (y,x). Assume there is a probability distribution on $Y \times X$ and that a random sampling process yields observations of (y,x). Suppose that, given a value of x_0 in X, one wishes to make the best prediction of y, in the sense of minimizing square loss. As is well known, the best predictor in this sense is $E(y|x = x_0)$, the mean regression of y on x evaluated at x_0. Extrapolation is the problem of identifying $E(y|x = x_0)$ when the regressor value of x_0 is logically possible but there is zero probability of observing x within some neighborhood of x_0.[1]

A point x_0 is said to be on the "support" of x if there is positive probability of observing x arbitrarily close to x_0; and it is off the support if there is zero probability of observing x within some neighborhood of x_0.[2] The identification of $E(y|x)$ on and off the support of x presents very different challenges. Minimal prior information about the population suffices to identify the regression on the sup-

[1]More generally, extrapolation is the problem of evaluating any regression at x_0. The modern statistical literature uses the term regression to refer not just to $E(y|x)$ but to any feature of the probability distribution of y conditional on x—for example, the conditional median or variance. So we speak of the mean regression, median regression, variance regression, and so on (see Manski 1991 for an exposition). The discussion of extrapolation in this section applies to all of these senses of regression, not just to the familiar mean regression.

[2]For example, suppose that x is uniformly distributed on the unit interval [0,1]. Then the support of x is the unit interval. Regressor values $x_0 < 0$ and $x_0 > 1$ are off the support.

port; indeed, the literature on nonparametric regression analysis shows that it is easy to estimate $E(y|x)$ on the support. On the other hand, extrapolation requires substantial prior information.[3] These matters are explained in Sections 2.1 and 2.2.

2.1. Identification and Consistent Estimation on the Support

There are two cases to consider. Suppose first not only that the point x_0 is on the support but that $\text{Prob}(x = x_0) > 0$. Then $E(y|x = x_0)$ is identified and can be estimated consistently given only the assumption that $E(y|x = x_0)$ exists and is finite. Given N observations labeled $i = 1, \ldots, N$, an obvious estimate is the sample average of y across those observations for which $x_i = x_0$, namely

$$\frac{\sum\limits_{i=1}^{N} y_i \, 1[x_i = x_0]}{\sum\limits_{i=1}^{N} 1[x_i = x_0]}. \tag{1}$$

(The indicator function $1[.]$ takes the value one if the bracketed logical condition holds and zero otherwise.) The strong law of large numbers implies that the cell average (1) is a consistent estimate of the conditional mean $E(y|x = x_0)$.

Now suppose that x_0 is on the support but that $\text{Prob}(x = x_0) = 0$. This is the situation when x has a continuous distribution with positive density at x_0. The cell-average estimate no longer works; with probability one, the event $x_i = x_0$ never occurs in the sample. On the other hand, one can estimate $E(y|x = x_0)$ by the sample average of y across those observations for which x_i is suitably near x_0–that is, by a "local average" of the form

---

[3]Throughout this paper, the term "prior information" is used in the classical sense to refer to restrictions that are known with certainty to be satisfied by the population of interest. Bayesian inference uses the term in a more general sense to refer to restrictions that may or may not be satisfied by the population; the researcher places a subjective probability on the event that the restriction holds. Beginning from subjectively probabilistic assumptions, Bayesian inference generates subjectively probabilistic conclusions about identification.

$$\frac{\sum\limits_{i=1}^{N} y_i 1[\rho(x_i, x_0) < \delta_N]}{\sum\limits_{i=1}^{N} 1[\rho(x_i, x_0) < \delta_N]}. \qquad (2)$$

Here $\rho(.,.)$ is any sensible metric measuring the distance between x_0 and x_i; for example, Euclidean distance will do. The parameter δ_N is a sample-size dependent "bandwidth" chosen by the researcher to operationalize the idea that one wishes to average over those observations in which x_i is near x_0.

This simple nonparametric approach to estimation of $E(y|x = x_0)$ works, in the sense of providing a consistent estimate, if

(a) $E(y|x)$ is continuous at $x = x_0$ and Var(y) exists.
(b) The bandwidth is tightened as the sample size increases.
(c) The bandwidth is not tightened too rapidly.

Of these conditions, only (a) requires prior information about the population and the required information is very weak indeed.

To understand why conditions (a), (b), and (c) suffice, suppose that δ_N is kept fixed at some value δ. Then as N increases, the strong law of large numbers implies that the estimate (2) converges to $E[y|\rho(x_i, x_0) < \delta]$—that is, to the mean of y conditional on x being within δ of x_0. If $E(y|x)$ is continuous at $x = x_0$, then as δ approaches zero, $E[y|\rho(x, x_0) < \delta]$ approaches $E(y|x = x_0)$. These two facts suggest that an estimate converging to $E(y|x = x_0)$ can be obtained by adopting a bandwidth-selection rule that makes δ_N approach zero as N increases. It can be shown that this heuristic idea succeeds provided that the variance of y exists and that δ_N does not approach zero too quickly. In particular, the rate at which δ_N approaches zero must be slower than $1/N^{1/K}$, where K is the dimension of the vector x. This condition ensures that the number of observations actually used to calculate the estimate (2) increases with the sample size N.

The literature on nonparametric regression analysis refers to (2) as a "uniform kernel" estimate. Further exposition of this and other nonparametric regression methods is found in Manski (1991) and in the opening chapters of Hardle (1990).

2.2 *Identification off the Support*

The local-average estimate (2) does not work when x_0 is off the support of x. Suppose that there is zero probability of observing x within some distance d_0 of x_0. Then the estimate (2) ceases to exist when one attempts to reduce the bandwidth δ_N below d_0.

The failure of the local-average estimate is symptomatic of a basic problem: In the absence of prior information, the distribution of y conditional on x_0 is not identified when x_0 is off the support of x. The random sampling process alone identifies the joint distribution of (y,x) but no more. When x_0 is off the support, the joint distribution of (y,x) does not constrain the distribution of y conditional on x_0.

2.2.1. *Local Smoothness Assumptions*
What kind of prior information does and does not identify the regression off the support? An important negative fact is that local smoothness (e.g., continuity or differentiability) assumptions on $E(y|x)$ do not suffice. Suppose that Var(y) exists and that $E(y|x)$ is continuous on all of X. Then $E(y|x = x_1)$ is identified and can be consistently estimated at every point x_1 on the support of x. But we have no information about the value of $E(y|x = x_0)$ at points x_0 off the support.

To understand why, let x_1 be the point on the support that is closest to x_0. A continuity assumption implies that $E(y|x)$ is near $E(y|x = x_1)$ when x is near x_1, but it does not tell us how to interpret the two uses of the word "near" as magnitudes. In particular, we do not know whether the distance separating x_0 and x_1 should be interpreted as large or small.

2.2.2. *Global Restrictions*
Identification off the support requires prior information that restricts the regression globally rather than locally. The traditional practice has been to assert a parametric model for $E(y|x)$–for example, a linear model

$$E(y|x) = x'b. \tag{3}$$

Suppose that the components of x are linearly independent, so that the parameter vector b is identified. Then (3) may be applied to identify $E(y|x)$ at all logically possible values of x, whether on or off the support. Weaker global restrictions allowing partial extrapolation appear in the literature on semiparametric regression analysis (see Manski, 1988b).

The problem with global restrictions, of course, is that the assumptions made about the form of the regression may be wrong. A model may fail either on or off the support of x. Failure on the support is detectable. The classical statistical theory of hypothesis testing was developed for just this purpose. Failure off the support is a qualitatively different problem as it is inherently not detectable.

Irresolvable disagreements arise when researchers hypothesize models that agree with $E(y|x)$ on the support of x but that behave differently off the support. Given a specified sampling process, there is no empirical way to discriminate among models all of which "fit the data." The only ways to judge the extrapolations implied by such models are by subjectively assessing the plausibility of the models or by initiating a new sampling process that gathers data at values of x where the various models yield different values for $E(y|x)$.

2.3. *Identification of Contrasts*

One often wants to contrast the regression at two values of x. Then the object of interest is $E(y|x = x_1) - E(y|x = x_0)$ for specified x_0 and x_1. This contrast can sometimes be interpreted as the "effect" on y of changing the regressor from x_0 to x_1 (see Section 3.4.2).

The discussion of section 2.1 applies if both x_0 and x_1 are on the support of x. Otherwise, the discussion of Section 2.2 applies to either or both of x_0 or x_1, as the case may be. There is little else of a general nature to say about identification of contrasts, but I would like to call attention to a familiar problem that arises when the vector of regressors is functionally dependent. An instance of this problem will be seen in Section 4.

Let $x = (w,v)$, where w and v are vectors. One is often interested in a contrast of the form $E[y|x = (w_1,v)] - E[y|x = (w_0,v)]$. That is, v is held fixed and w is varied between the values w_0 and w_1. Suppose that the regressor values (w_0,v) and (w_1,v) are both logically possible but that w happens to be a function of v within the population—say $w = f(v)$. Then (w_0,v) and (w_1,v) cannot both be on the support of x; at most, $[f(v),v]$ is on the support. Thus, functional dependence implies that identification of the contrast $E[y|x = (w_1,v)]$ $- E[y|x = (w_0,v)]$ requires global restrictions on the regression.

3. THE SELECTION PROBLEM

Some respondents to a household survey decline to report their incomes. Some women responding to a longitudinal fertility survey complete their childbearing after the survey is terminated. Some welfare recipients do not enroll in a job training program. These very different situations share the common feature that a variable is *censored:* a respondent's income, a woman's completed family size, or a welfare recipient's employment status after job training.

Social scientists constantly seek to draw conclusions from censored data. They routinely pose and try to answer questions of the form:

What is the effect of _____ on _____?

For example,

What is the effect of the AFDC program on labor supply?
What is the effect of schooling on wages?
What is the effect of family structure on children's outcomes?

All efforts to address such "treatment effect" questions must confront the fact that the data are inherently censored. One wants to compare outcomes across different treatments, but each unit of analysis, whether a survey respondent or an experimental subject, experiences only one of the treatments under consideration.

Whereas the implications of censoring were not well appreciated 20 years ago, they are much better understood today. In particular, methodologists have devoted substantial attention to the *selection problem:* the problem of identifying regressions from random samples in which the realizations of regressors are always observed but the realizations of outcomes are censored. The selection problem is logically separate from the extrapolation problem discussed in Section 2. The extrapolation problem follows from the fact that a random sampling process does not yield observations of y *off* the support of x. The selection problem arises when a censored random sampling process does not fully reveal the behavior of y *on* the support of x. So selection presents new challenges in addition to those faced in extrapolation.

Nature of the Problem.
To introduce the selection problem formally, suppose that each member of the population is characterized by a triple (y,z,x). Here y is scalar, x is a vector, and z is a binary variable taking the value of 0 or 1.[4] One draws a random sample from the population and observes all the realizations of (z,x), but observes y only when $z = 1$. One wants to learn some feature of the probability distribution of y conditional on x, denoted $P(y|x)$; that is, one wants to learn some regression of y on x.

The problem is the failure of the censored-sampling process to identify $P(y|x)$ on the support of x. To isolate the difficulty, decompose $P(y|x)$ into the sum

$$P(y|x) = P(y|x,z = 1)P(z = 1|x) + P(y|x,z = 0)P(z = 0|x). \quad (4)$$

The sampling process identifies the selection probability $P(z = 1|x)$, the censoring probability $P(z = 0|x)$, and the distribution of y conditional on selection, $P(y|x,z = 1)$. It is uninformative regarding the distribution of y conditional on censoring, $P(y|x,z = 0)$. Hence the censored-sampling process reveals only that $P(y|x)$ belongs to a set of distributions, namely

$$P(y|x) \in [P(y|x,z = 1)P(z = 1|x) + \gamma P(z = 0|x), \gamma \in \Gamma], \quad (5)$$

where Γ denotes the space of all probability distributions on the real line.

The logical starting point for investigation of the selection problem is to characterize the problem in the absence of prior information–that is, to learn what restrictions on $P(y|x)$ are implied by (5) alone. Section 3.1 summarizes my recent work on this subject; Sections 3.2 and 3.3 explore identification when prior information and/or richer data are available. Section 3.2 considers various types of prior information brought to bear in the econometric and statistical literatures. Section 3.3 explains the additional identification possi-

---

[4]The assumption that y is scalar will be used only in a few places. Most of the analysis extends immediately to situations in which y is a vector.

bilities that arise in the "switching regression" setting, where censoring of y is accompanied by observation of a different outcome s. Section 3.4 applies these findings to the important problem of identifying treatment effects.

3.1. Identification in the Absence of Prior Information

Inspection of (5) reveals that, in the absence of prior information on the distribution of (y, z, x), one cannot reject the conditional independence hypothesis

$$P(y|x) = P(y|x, z = 1) = P(y|x, z = 0). \qquad (6)$$

Simply observe that (6) holds if one sets $\gamma = P(y|x, z = 1)$ in (5). Econometricians usually refer to the conditional independence hypothesis as "exogenous" selection while some statisticians refer to it as "ignorable" selection.

In the absence of prior information, censoring makes it impossible to learn anything about the mean regression of y on x. To see this, decompose $E(y|x)$ into the sum

$$E(y|x) = E(y|x, z = 1)P(z = 1|x) + E(y|x, z = 0)P(z = 0|x). \qquad (7)$$

The censored-sampling process identifies $E(y|x, z = 1)$ and $P(z|x)$ but provides no information on $E(y|x, z = 0)$, which might take any value between minus and plus infinity. Hence, whenever the censoring probability $P(z = 0|x)$ is positive, the sampling process imposes no restrictions on $E(y|x)$.

These negative results do not, however, imply that the selection problem is fatal in the absence of prior information. In fact, censored data imply informative, easily interpretable bounds on many important features of the conditional distribution $P(y|x)$, including quantiles, probabilities, and the means of bounded functions of y. In what follows, I present some of the findings of Manski (1989, 1993a).

3.1.1. Conditional Means of Bounded Functions of y
The central result, from which others may be derived, concerns the mean of a bounded function of y. Let $g(.)$ be a real-valued function mapping y into a known bounded interval $[K_0, K_1]$, which may depend on $g(.)$. Observe that

$E[g(y)|\mathrm{x}] = E[g(y)|x,z = 1]P(z = 1|x) + E[g(y)|x,z = 0]P(z = 0|x)$. (8)

The sampling process identifies $E[g(y)|x,z = 1]$ and $P(z|x)$ but provides no information on $E[g(y)|x,z = 0]$. The last quantity, however, necessarily lies in the interval $[K_0,K_1]$. This simple fact yields the following:

$$E[g(y)|x,z = 1]P(z = 1|x) + K_0P(z = 0|x) \le E[g(y)|x] \le \qquad (9)$$
$$E[g(y)|x,z = 1]P(z = 1|x) + K_1P(z = 0|x).$$

Thus a censored-sampling process bounds the mean regression of any bounded function of y. The lower bound is the value $E[g(y)|x]$ takes if, in the censored subpopulation, $g(y)$ always equals K_0; the upper bound is the value of $E[g(y)|x]$ if all the censored y equal K_1. The bound is a proper subset of $[K_0,K_1]$, hence informative, whenever censoring is less than total. At each regressor value x_0, the bound width $(K_1 - K_0)P(z = 0|x = x_0)$ is proportional to the censoring probability $P(z = 0|x = x_0)$. It is therefore meaningful to say that the degree of underidentification of $E[g(y)|x = x_0]$ is proportional to the censoring probability at x_0.

3.1.2. *Conditional Probabilities*
The bound (9) has numerous applications. Perhaps the most far-reaching is the bound it implies on the probability that y lies in any set $A \subset Y$. Let $g_A(.)$ be the indicator function $g_A(y) \equiv 1[y \in A]$. Then $E[g_A(y)|x] = P(y\epsilon A|x)$, $K_0 = 0$, and $K_1 = 1$. Hence (9) implies that

$$P(y\epsilon A|x,z = 1)P(z = 1|x) \le P(y \in A|x) \qquad (10)$$
$$\le P(y\epsilon A|x,z = 1)P(z = 1|x) + P(z = 0|x).$$

It is often convenient to characterize a probability distribution by its distribution function $P(y \le t|x)$, where t is any real number. It follows from (10) that

$$P(y \le t|x,z = 1)P(z = 1|x) \le P(y \le t|x) \qquad (11)$$
$$\le P(y \le t|x,z = 1)P(z = 1|x) + P(z = 0|x).$$

It may seem surprising that one should be able to bound the distribution function of a random variable but not its mean. The explanation is a fact that is widely appreciated by researchers in the field of robust statistics: The mean of a random variable is not a continuous function of its distribution function. Hence small perturbations in a distribution function can generate large movements in the mean. See Huber (1981).[5]

3.1.3. Conditional Quantiles

Let $\alpha \in (0,1)$. By definition, the α-quantile of y conditional on x is

$$q(\alpha,x) \equiv \min t: P(y \leq t|x) \geq \alpha. \qquad (12)$$

In particular, the 0.5-quantile is the median. Interest in quantile regression analysis has developed rapidly over the past 15 years, beginning with the work of Koenker and Bassett (1978). For an expository treatment, see Manski (1988a, ch. 4).

The bound (11) on $P(y \leq .|x)$ can be inverted to show that $q(\alpha,x)$ must lie between two quantiles of the identified distribution $P(y|x,z = 1)$. Define

$$r(\alpha,x) \equiv [1-(1 - \alpha)/P(z = 1|x)]\text{-quantile of } P(y|x,z = 1) \quad (13)$$

$$\text{if } P(z = 1|x) > 1 - \alpha$$

$$\equiv -\infty \text{ otherwise.}$$

$$s(\alpha,x) \equiv [\alpha/P(z = 1|x)]\text{-quantile of } P(y|x,z = 1)$$

$$\text{if } P(z=1|x) \geq \alpha$$

$$\equiv \infty \text{ otherwise.}$$

It is proved in Manski (1993a) that

$$r(\alpha,x) \leq q(\alpha,x) \leq s(\alpha,x). \qquad (14)$$

Moreover, in the absence of prior information, this bound on $q(\alpha,x)$ cannot be improved upon.

The lower and upper bounds $r(\alpha,x)$ and $s(\alpha,x)$ are increasing functions of α; hence the bound shifts to the right as α increases. The lower bound is informative if $P(z = 1|x) > 1 - \alpha$; the upper bound if $P(z = 1|x) > \alpha$. So the bound (14) restricts $q(\alpha,x)$ to an interval of finite length if $P(z = 1|x) > \max(\alpha, 1 - \alpha)$ and is uninformative if

[5]To obtain some intuition for this fact, consider the following thought experiment. Let w be a random variable with $\text{Prob}(w \leq t) = 1 - \eta$ and $\text{Prob}(w = s) = \eta$, where $s > t$. Suppose w is perturbed by moving the mass at s to some $s_1 > s$. Then $P(w \leq \tau)$ remains unchanged for $\tau < s$ and falls by at most η for $\tau \geq s$. But $E(w)$ increases by the amount $\eta(s_1 - s)$. Now let s_1 go to infinity. The perturbed distribution function remains within an η-bound of the original one but the mean of the perturbed random variable converges to infinity.

$P(z = 1|x) < \min(\alpha, 1 - \alpha)$. In particular, the bound on the median regression is informative if $P(z = 1|x) > 1/2$.

3.1.4. Sample inference

The selection problem is, first and foremost, a failure of identification. It is only secondarily a difficulty in sample inference. To keep attention focused on the central identification question, it is simplest to suppose that the conditional distributions identified by the sampling process, $P(y|x, z = 1)$ and $P(z|x)$, are known. But it is also important to recognize that the population bounds reported above are easily estimable.

For example, estimation of the bound (9) is a conventional problem in nonparametric regression analysis of the type discussed in section 2.1. Rewrite (9) in the equivalent form

$$E[g(y)z + K_{0g}(1 - z)|x] \leq E[g(y)|x] \leq E[g(y)z + K_{1g}(1 - z)|x]. \quad (9')$$

The random variables $g(y)z + K_{0g}(1 - z)$ and $g(y)z + K_{1g}(1 - z)$ are both bounded; hence their variances exist. It follows that the lower and upper bounds $E[g(y)z + K_{0g}(1 - z)|x]$ and $E[g(y)z + K_{1g}(1 - z)|x]$ can be estimated consistently on the support of x as long as these quantities vary continuously in x. Given additional regularity conditions, asymptotically valid sampling confidence intervals can be placed around estimates of the bounds. An empirical application reporting bootstrapped confidence intervals is presented in Manski, Sandefur, McLanahan, and Powers (1992).

3.1.5. A Historical Note

It is of interest to ask why the simple bound results reported here took so long to appear. I believe that the explanation has at least three parts.

Timing has played a role. The modern literature on selection took shape in the 1970s, when the frontier of social science methodology was nonlinear parametric analysis. At that time, nonparametric regression analysis was just beginning to be developed by statisticians. Social scientists were not yet aware that nonparametric estimation of regressions was possible and did not think in the nonparametric terms needed to derive the bounds.

A second factor is the historical fixation of social scientists on point identification, which has inhibited appreciation of the potential usefulness of bounds. Estimable bounds on quantities that are not point-identified have been reported from time to time; a prominent early example appears in Frisch (1934). But the conventional wisdom has been that bounds are hard to estimate and uninformative. Whatever the validity of this conventional wisdom in other contexts, it does not apply to the bounds (9) and (14).

The preoccupation of researchers with the estimation of mean regressions has been a third factor. It has long been known that, in the absence of prior information, the selection problem is fatal for inference on the mean of an unbounded random variable. Social scientists have, improperly as it turns out, extrapolated that no inference at all is possible in the absence of prior information.

3.2. Varieties of Prior Information

One can improve on the bounds reported in Section 3.1 if one possesses information restricting the distribution of (y,z) conditional on x. A restriction has identifying power if it implies that $P(y|x)$ belongs to a set of distributions smaller than (5). Information restricting $P(y|x)$, $P(y|x,z = 0)$, or $P(z|x,y)$ may have identifying power. Information restricting $P(y|x,z = 1)$ or $P(z|x)$ is superfluous as the latter distributions are identified by the censored-sampling process alone.[6]

Ideally, we would like to learn the identifying power of all types of prior information, so as to characterize the entire spectrum of inferential possibilities. But there does not appear to be any effective way to conduct an exhaustive identification analysis. So researchers have investigated the power of specific bundles of restrictions thought to apply to empirical problems of interest. Section 3.2.1 describes the latent-variable models developed by econometricians. Section 3.2.2 explains the quite different mixture-model approach favored by some statisticians. Section 3.2.3 presents my recent finding characterizing the identifying power of exclusion restrictions.

3.2.1. Econometric Latent Variable Models

Although the selection problem arises in many economic applications, econometricians have analyzed the problem in a sustained way

[6]Although information restricting $P(y|x,z = 1)$ and $P(z|x)$ is superfluous from the perspective of identification, such information may still be useful in practice as it may enable us to obtain more precise sample estimates of $P(y|x,z = 1)$ and $P(z|x)$.

only since the early 1970s. Before then, researchers generally maintained the exogenous-selection hypothesis (6), a notable exception being Tobin (1958).

The empirical plausibility of (6) was eventually questioned sharply. In particular, researchers observed that in many economic settings, the process by which observations on y become censored is related to the value of y (see Gronau 1974). It also became clear that exogenous selection is not necessary to identify $P(y|x)$. An alternative is to specify a latent-variable model jointly explaining (y, z) conditional on x. (for example, see Heckman 1976; Maddala 1983; or Winship and Mare 1992.)

For the past 20 years, econometric thinking on the selection problem has been expressed primarily through latent-variable models of the form

$$y = f_1(x) + u_1 \tag{15a}$$

$$z = 1[f_2(x) + u_2 > 0]. \tag{15b}$$

Here $[f_1(.), f_2(.)]$ are real functions of x and (u_1, u_2) are random variables whose realizations are unobserved by the researcher. The threshold-crossing form of the selection function (15b) is well motivated in empirical analyses where the observability of y is determined by the binary choice behavior of a rational decision maker. In such cases $f_2(x) + u_2$ is the difference between the values of the two alternatives, and (15b) states that the more highly valued alternative is chosen.

Equations (15) alone do not restrict the distribution of (y, z) conditional on x. A model takes on content when restrictions are imposed on $[f_1(.), f_2(.)]$ and on the distribution of (u_1, u_2) conditional on x. The overriding concern of the literature has been to find plausible restrictions that identify the mean regression of y on x, although most of the restrictions studied actually identify the conditional distribution $P(y|x)$ fully. In what follows, I describe the two types of restrictions that have received considerable attention. These restrictions are neither nested nor mutually exclusive. A latent-variable model may impose either or both.

Exogenous Selection. Many authors assume that u_1 and u_2 are statistically independent conditional on x. It follows that

$$P(y|x,z = 1) = P[f_1(x) + u_1|x, f_2(x) + u_2 \geq 0] = P[f_1(x) + u_1|x] \quad (16)$$
$$= P(y|x).$$

Thus independence of u_1 and u_2 conditional on x implies independence of y and z conditional on x, the restriction stated in (6). Given (6), identification of $P(y|x)$ does not require restrictions on $[f_1(.),f_2(.)]$, but empirical researchers typically impose such restrictions anyway. Most make $f_1(.)$ linear in x.

Parametric Models. A second type of restriction became prominent in the mid-1970s. Suppose that $f_1(.)$ is known up to a finite dimensional parameter β_1, $f_2(.)$ up to a finite dimensional parameter β_2, and the distribution of (u_1,u_2) conditional on x up to a finite dimensional parameter γ. Then

$$P(y,z = 1|x) = P[f_1(x,\beta_1) + u_1, f_2(x,\beta_2) + u_2 \geq 0|x,\gamma]. \quad (17)$$

The left side of (17) is identified by the censored-sampling process. The right side is a function of the parameters (β_1,β_2,γ). If there is only one value of (β_1,β_2,γ) solving (17), then $P(y|x)$ is identified.

Parametric latent variable models have usually been studied through analysis of $E(y|x,z = 1)$. Following the practice in the literature, assume that $E(u_1,u_2|x) = 0$. Then

$$E(y|x) = f_1(x,\beta_1) \quad (18a)$$
$$E(y|x,z = 1) = f_1(x,\beta_1) + E[u_1|x, f_2(x,\beta_2) + u_2 \geq 0,\gamma] \quad (18b)$$
$$\equiv f_1(x,\beta_1) + g(x,\beta_2,\gamma).$$

The left side of (18b) is identified by the censored-sampling process. The parameter β_1 is identified, hence $E(y|x)$, if there is only one value of (β_1,β_2,γ) solving (18b).

The most widely applied model makes $f_1(.)$ and $f_2(.)$ linear functions, (u_1,u_2) statistically independent of x, and the distribution of (u_1,u_2) normal with mean zero and unrestricted correlation; the variance of u_1 is unrestricted but that of u_2 is set equal to one as a normalization. In this case,

$$E(y|x) = x'\beta_1 \quad (19a)$$
$$E(y|x,z = 1) = x'\beta_1 + \gamma\phi(x'\beta_2)/\Phi(x'\beta_2), \quad (19b)$$

where $\phi(.)$ and $\Phi(.)$ are the standard normal density and distribution functions and where $\gamma = E(u_1u_2)$. Identification of β_1 hinges on the

fact that the linear function $x'\beta_1$ and the nonlinear function $\gamma\phi(x'\beta_2)/$
$\Phi(x'\beta_2)$ affect $E(y|x,z=1)$ in different ways.

There is a common misconception that the normal-linear
model generalizes the model assuming exogenous selection. In fact,
the two models are not nested. The normal-linear model permits u_1
and u_2 to be dependent but assumes linearity of $[f_1(.),f_2(.)]$, normality
of (u_1,u_2), and independence of the pair (u_1,u_2) from x. The
exogenous-selection model assumes u_1 and u_2 to be independent of
each other conditional on x, but it does not restrict $P(u_1|x)$ or $P(u_2|x)$.
Nor does it restrict the form of $[f_1(.),f_2(.)]$.

3.2.2. Statistical Mixture Models

Statisticians analyzing censored data often assume that selection is
ignorable–that is, hypothesis (6). The term "nonignorable" selection
is used to cover all situations in which y and z are dependent conditional on x (for example, see Rubin 1987).

Some statisticians advocate direct imposition of restrictions on
the censored distribution $P(y|x,z=0)$, an approach called "mixture
modeling." Suppose that $P(y|x,z=0)$ is known to be a member of a
class Γ_{0x} of probability distributions. Then the restriction of $P(y|x)$ to
the set given in (5) can be improved to

$$P(y|x) \in [P(y|x,z=1)P(z=1|x) + \gamma P(z=0|x), \gamma \in \Gamma_{0x}]. \quad (20)$$

Rubin (1987, section 6.2) suggests not only that one express
prior information by limiting the censored distribution to a set Γ_{0x} but
also that one might place a subjective probability distribution on the
elements of Γ_{0x}. This then induces a subjective distribution on the
elements of the set (20) of possible values of $P(y|x)$. Such Bayesian
"sensitivity analysis" is feasible only if the set Γ_{0x} is sufficiently small;
otherwise a subjective distribution cannot be placed on Γ_{0x}. The practice has been to make Γ_{0x} a finite set or at most a finite dimensional
set of distributions. The case of no prior information, in which Γ_{0x} is
the set of all distributions, has not received attention in the statistics
literature.

Two World Views.   Econometric latent-variable models and statistical mixture models express different ideas about the nature of the
selection problem and imply different conclusions about the appropriate way to assert prior information. From the latent-variable-model

perspective, the censored distribution is a derived quantity, not a primitive concept. Hence, a researcher who thinks in latent-variable terms finds it difficult to judge the plausibility of restrictions imposed on $P(y|x,z = 0)$. From the mixture-model perspective, $P(y|x,z = 0)$ is a primitive so it is natural to assert prior information through restrictions on this distribution. Mixture modelers find it difficult to interpret prior information stated as restrictions on latent variable models. The different world views expressed in latent-variable and mixture models have been aired in Wainer (1986, 1989).

The conflict between econometric and statistical perspectives on the selection problem recalls a closely related conflict regarding the analysis of discrete data. Econometricians have typically asserted prior information through latent-variable models of discrete choice. Many statisticians have imposed restrictions through the mixture model, referred to as discriminant analysis in that context. See Manski (1981) or Manski and McFadden (1981) for discussions and references.

3.2.3. Exclusion Restrictions

Empirical analyses often assume that some component of the regressor vector x has no effect on the outcome of y but does affect whether y is observed. To formalize this idea, let $x \equiv (w,v)$ and assume that, holding w fixed, $P(y|w,v)$ does not vary with v but $P(z|w,v)$ does vary with v. The regressor component v is variously said to be an "instrumental variable" or to satisfy an "exclusion restriction."

It has long been recognized that an exclusion restriction may have identifying power when bundled with other assumptions; an example will be given in Section 3.3.1. It is also of interest to determine the identifying power of an exclusion restriction alone, in the absence of other information. This question has been addressed in Manski (1990a, 1993a).

The simple result is that an exclusion restriction allows one to replace the bounds available in the absence of prior information with the intersection of these bounds across all values of v. To see this, let $f(w,v)$ denote the feature of $P(y|w,v)$ that is of interest, perhaps the conditional distribution function or the conditional median. Given an exclusion restriction, $f(w,v)$ must remain constant as w is held fixed and v is varied. Hence, $f(w,v)$ must lie within all of the no-prior-information bounds holding at the different values of v.

For example, the bound (9) on the mean of a bounded function of y is replaced by the tighter bound[7]

$$\sup_v E[g(y)z + K_{0g}(1 - z)|w,v] \tag{21}$$

$$\leq E[g(y)|w] \leq \inf_v E[g(y)z + K_{1g}(1 - z)|w,v]$$

and the bound (14) on the conditional α-quantile is replaced by

$$\sup_v r[\alpha,(w,v)] \leq q(\alpha,w) \leq \inf_v s[\alpha,(w,v)]. \tag{22}$$

These new bounds generally improve on those given in Section 3.1 if the exclusion restriction is nontrivial, in the sense that $P(z|w,v)$ does vary with v. The new bounds do not, however, identify $E[g(y)|w]$ or $q(\alpha,w)$. To achieve point identification generally requires information stronger than an exclusion restriction.

3.3. Switching Regressions

In the selection problem, y is observed when $z = 1$ and no outcome is observed when $z = 0$. The literature on switching regressions considers the somewhat richer sampling process in which y is observed when $z = 1$, and another outcome, say s, is observed when $z = 0$. The quantities identified by the switching regression sampling process are $P(z|x)$, $P(y|x,z = 1)$, and $P(s|x,z = 0)$.

In the absence of prior information, observation of s reveals nothing about y. Hence the selection and switching regression problems are equivalent from the perspective of identification of $P(y|x)$. Given information, observation of s may be informative regarding $P(y|x)$, as is shown below.

3.3.1. Shifted Outcomes
A rather strong form of information that has been applied frequently assumes that there exists a constant v such that for all x

$$P(y = s + v|x) = 1. \tag{23}$$

Thus y and s are assumed to differ by a constant, so that y is a shifted version of s. The implications of (23) have been studied by Heckman

---

[7]The expression "sup" refers to the supremum, or at least upper bound over all values of v, while "inf" is the infimum, or greatest lower bound.

(1978), Heckman and Robb (1985), and Robinson (1989). Their findings are paraphrased here.

It follows from (23) that for all t,

$$P(y \leq t|x,z = 0) = P(s \leq t - \nu|x,z = 0). \tag{24}$$

Hence,

$$P(y \leq t|x) = P(y \leq t|x,z = 1)P(z = 1|x) + P(y \leq t|x,z = 0)P(z = 0|x) \tag{25}$$
$$= P(y \leq t|x,z = 1)P(z = 1|x) + P(s \leq t - \nu|x,z = 0)P(z = 0|x).$$

Thus $P(y|x)$ is known up to a family of distributions indexed by the shift parameter ν.

The parameter ν is identified if $E(y|x)$ satisfies an exclusion restriction. It follows from (23) that

$$E(y|x) = E(y|x,z = 1)P(z = 1|x) + E(s|x,z = 0)\,P(z = 0|x) \tag{26}$$
$$+ \nu P(z = 0|x).$$

Let $x = (w,v)$ and suppose it is known that $E(y|w,v = v_0) = E(y|w,v = v_1)$, where v_0 and v_1 are distinct values of v. Then (26) implies that

$$\nu[P(z = 0|w,v = v_1) - P(z = 0|w,v = v_0)] \tag{27}$$
$$= E(y|w,v = v_0,z = 1)P(z = 1|w,v = v_0) +$$
$$E(s|w,v = v_0,z = 0)P(z = 0|w,v = v_0)$$
$$- E(y|w,v = v_1,z = 1)P(z = 1|w,v = v_1)$$
$$- E(s|w,v = v_1,z = 0)P(z = 0|w,v = v_1).$$

Hence ν is identified provided that $P(z = 0|w,v = v_1) \neq P(z = 0|w,v = v_0)$.

3.3.2. Ordered Outcomes

The combination of shifted outcomes and an exclusion restriction yields great identifying power but requires strong prior information. It is also of interest to learn what can be accomplished with other, perhaps more plausible assumptions. In Manski (1993a), I consider the case in which it is known that

$$P(y \geq s|x) = 1. \tag{28}$$

This "ordered outcomes" assumption may be warranted in some analyses of medical and other treatments. For example, suppose that a cancer patient is treated with chemotherapy ($z = 1$) or with a placebo ($z = 0$). Let the outcomes y and s be life span following each treatment. Then it may be warranted to assume that $y \geq s$ for all patients.

It follows from (28) that for all t,

$$P(y \leq t|x, z = 0) \leq P(s \leq t|x, z = 0). \tag{29}$$

Hence,

$$\begin{aligned} P(y \leq t|x) &= P(y \leq t|x, z = 1)P(z = 1|x) + \\ & \quad P(y \leq t|x, z = 0) \, P(z = 0|x) \\ &\leq P(y \leq t|x, z = 1)P(z = 1|x) + \\ & \quad P(s \leq t|x, z = 0) \, P(z = 0|x). \end{aligned} \tag{30}$$

The upper bound on $P(y \leq .|x)$ given in (30) improves on the bound available if s is not observed when $z = 0$.

3.3.3. Selection by the Ordering of Outcomes

I also consider the class of problems in which one observes either the smaller or the larger of y and s. Suppose first that one observes the smaller of y and s, so that

$$z = 1[y \leq s]. \tag{31}$$

Examples include the short-side model of markets in disequilibrium (see Maddala 1983) and the competing-risks model of survival analysis (see Kalbfleisch and Prentice 1980).

If (31) holds, then $z = 0 \Leftrightarrow y > s$. Hence, for all t,

$$P(y \leq t|x, z = 0) \leq P(s \leq t|x, z = 0). \tag{32}$$

This is the same finding as was reported in (31) under the assumption that outcomes are ordered. So here, as there, (30) is an upper bound on $P(y \leq t|x)$.

Now consider the case in which one observes the larger of y and s, so that

$$z = 1[y \geq s]. \tag{33}$$

Examples of this switching rule include economic models of schooling and occupational choice in which decision makers select the alternative yielding the higher income. Here, $z = 0 \Leftrightarrow y < s$ so

$$P(y \leq t|x, z = 0) \geq P(s \leq t|x, z = 0) \qquad (34)$$

and $P(y \leq t|x) \geq P(y \leq t|x, z = 1)P(z = 1|x) + P(s \leq t|x, z = 0)P(z = 0|x)$. (35)

This lower bound on $P(y \leq .|x)$ improves on that available if s is not observed when $z = 0$.

3.4. Identification of Treatment Effects

In the classical formalization of treatment effects, there are two mutually exclusive treatments, labeled 0 and 1. Each member of the population is characterized by values for the variables (y, s, z, x). Variable y is the outcome that would be observed if a person were to receive treatment 1, and s is the outcome that would be observed if the person were to receive treatment 0. Of these two outcomes, one is realized and the other is latent; y is realized if $z = 1$, and s is realized if $z = 0$.

This sampling process is the same as in the switching regression problem. The analysis of treatment effects differs from that of switching regressions only in that there is a different object of interest. The researcher is not concerned with the conditional distribution $P(y|x)$ per se but rather with the treatment effect

$$T(x) \equiv E(y - s|x) = E(y|x) - E(s|x). \qquad (36)$$

Defined in this way, the treatment effect measures the change in average outcome if one were to replace a hypothetical situation in which a person with attributes x were exogenously assigned to treatment 0 with another hypothetical situation in which a person with attributes x were exogenously assigned to treatment 1.[8]

The identification analysis of Sections 3.1 through 3.3 applies

---

[8]This classical definition of the treatment effect appropriately characterizes randomized experiments and mandated policies, but other definitions may well be more relevant in many social science applications. For example, we might want to compare exogenous assignment to treatment with self-selection of treatment. A variety of treatment effects of potential interest are considered in Maddala (1983, section 9.2) and in Heckman and Robb (1985). Our discussion of identification can easily be extended from the classical treatment effects to these variants.

directly to the treatment effect (36). Section 3.4.1 examines identification in the absence of prior information. Section 3.4.2 shows the identifying power of various forms of prior information and, in a cautionary vein, illustrates the flawed conclusions that can result from the imposition of incorrect assumptions. Section 3.4.3 briefly discusses social experimentation as an approach to securing identifying information.

3.4.1. *In the Absence of Prior Information*

If either y or s is unbounded, then the sampling process alone reveals nothing about the classical treatment effect. On the other hand, the sampling process alone bounds $T(x)$ if y and s are both bounded random variables. In particular, suppose that y and s both lie in the interval $[K_0, K_1]$. Then it follows immediately from (9) that

$$T(x) \, \epsilon \qquad (37)$$

$$[K_0 P(z = 0|x) + E(y|x, z = 1)P(z = 1|x) - E(s|x, z = 0)P(z = 0|x) - K_1 P(z = 1|x),$$

$$K_1 P(z = 0|x) + E(y|x, z = 1)P(z = 1|x) - E(s|x, z = 0)P(z = 0|x) - K_0 P(z = 1|x)].$$

The lower bound on $T(x)$ is the difference between the lower bound on $E(y|x)$ and the upper bound on $E(s|x)$. The upper bound on $T(x)$ is determined similarly.

The width of the bound (37) is $K_1 - K_0$. If no data were available, $T(x)$ could lie anywhere in the interval $[K_0 - K_1, K_1 - K_0]$. Thus the sampling process alone allows one to restrict the treatment effect to one-half of its logically possible range. Observe that the sampling process does not identify the sign of the treatment effect; the bound (37) necessarily covers zero.

The case in which y and s are binary outcomes is of particular practical interest. In many applications the treatment outcome is a logical indicator taking the value one or zero. For example, the outcome of a medical treatment may be (cured = 1, not cured = 0); the outcome of a job training program may be (employed = 1, not employed = 0). In such cases, $E(y|x) = P(y = 1|x)$, $E(s|x) = P(s = 1|x)$, $K_0 = 0$, $K_1 = 1$, and the bound (37) becomes

$$T(x) \, \epsilon \qquad (38)$$

$$[P(y = 1|x, z = 1)P(z = 1|x) - P(s = 1|x, z = 0)P(z = 0|x) - P(z = 1|x),$$

$$P(z = 0|x) + P(y = 1|x, z = 1)P(z = 1|x) - P(s = 1|x, z = 0)P(z = 0|x)].$$

3.4.2. *With Prior Information*
The bound of the preceding section can be improved if prior information is available. For example, an exclusion restriction may be available or it may be known that subjects are always assigned the better
of the two treatments. In these cases, the same argument used to
derive (37) can be used to obtain tighter bounds.

Given enough prior information, the treatment effect is identified. Suppose that assignment to treatment is exogenous as, for example, occurs in a randomized experiment. Then

$$E(y|x) - E(s|x) = E(y|x,z = 1) - E(s|x,z = 0). \tag{39}$$

Or suppose that the shifted-outcomes hypothesis (23) holds. Then
the treatment effect is the contrast v for all values of x. As was shown
in Section 3.3, v is identified if an exclusion restriction is available.
Another route to identification is to invoke a latent-variable model
with enough structure to identify $E(y|x)$ and $E(s|x)$.

The obvious issue arising with the use of prior information to
identify treatment effects is that different assumptions may yield
different conclusions. I shall give two examples of how a researcher
assuming exogenous selection into treatment can reach incorrect conclusions if assignment to treatment is not actually exogenous. These
examples are highly relevant because exogenous selection is commonly assumed in practice (see the discussion of regression contrasts
following the examples). Moreover, as we observed in Section 3.1,
the hypothesis of exogenous selection cannot be refuted empirically
in the absence of prior information. This means that if researchers
believe that selection is exogenous, no data can persuade them that
they are wrong.

Example 1: Suppose that outcomes are shifted, with $y = s + v$
and $v > 0$; hence $T(x)$ is the same positive value v for all x.
Suppose that treatments are assigned based on the magnitude
of y; for some real constant k, $z = 1$ if $y < k$ and $z = 0$ if $y \geq k$.
Then $E(y|x,z = 1) = E(y|x,y < k) < k$ and $E(s|x,z = 0) =
E(s|x,s \geq k - v) \geq k - v$. Hence, $E(y|x,z = 1) - E(s|x,z = 0)
< v$.

Suppose that $\text{Prob}(k - v \leq s < k|x) = 0$. Then $E(s|x,s
\geq k - v) = E(s|x,s \geq k) \geq k$ so $E(y|x,z = 1) - E(s|x,z = 0) <
0$. In this case, a researcher who believes that assignment to

treatment is exogenous would improperly conclude not only that the treatment effect is less than ν but that it is negative.

Example 2: Suppose that $s = 0$ for all members of the population and that y is a binary variable taking the value $-\infty$ or 1 with probabilities $1 - p$ and p for all x; thus, $T(x) = -\infty$ as long as $p < 1$. Suppose that each member of the population selects the better of the two treatments; thus, $z = 1$ if $y = 1$ and $z = 0$ if $y = -\infty$. Then $E(y|x, z = 1) - E(s|x, z = 0) = 1 - 0 = 1$. So a researcher who believes that assignment to treatment is exogenous would improperly conclude that the treatment effect is 1 when it actually is $-\infty$.

Regression Contrasts as Treatment Effects.   The widespread practice of interpreting regression contrasts as treatment effects rests on the assumption that selection into treatment is exogenous. Suppose that, given a random sample of observations of (y,x), one estimates the regression $E(y|x)$, computes a contrast $E(y|x = x_1) - E(y|x = x_0)$ for specified x_0 and x_1, and interprets the contrast as the expected change in y if a person with attributes x_0 were to be given attributes x_1 instead. This interpretation requires an exogenous-selection assumption.

To see why, let us recast the problem in the language of the treatment-effects literature by assuming that each member of the population is characterized by values for the variables $[y(x), z(x), x \in X]$. Here $z(x)$ is an indicator function taking the value 1 at a person's actual regressor value and 0 at all other of the logically possible regressor values X. Variable $y(x)$ is the outcome that would be observed if a person were to be assigned regressor value x. Of these outcomes, $y(x)$ is realized if and only if $z(x) = 1$. Thus the function $y(.)$ is latent at all regressor values except the one that a person actually experiences. The realized outcome is

$$y = \sum_{x \in X} y(x)z(x). \tag{40}$$

This setup is the same as that of the classical treatment effect problem except that now there are more than two treatments; each value of x defines a different treatment.

With this background, we may define the treatment effect $E[y(x_1)] - E[y(x_0)]$ to be the change in average outcome that would be observed if we were to replace a hypothetical situation in which a person were exogenously assigned regressor values x_0 with another hypothetical situation in which that person were exogenously assigned regressor value x_1. In general,

$$E(y|x = x_1) - E(y|x = x_0) = E[y(x_1)|z(x_1) = 1] - E[y(x_0)|z(x_0) = 1](41)$$
$$\neq E[y(x_1)] - E[y(x_0)].$$

But the second inequality becomes an equality if the random outcome function $y(.)$ is statistically independent of the random treatment-selection function $z(.)$.

3.4.3. Social Experimentation
Recognizing that flawed assumptions may yield flawed conclusions, some social scientists advocate that researchers take control of the sampling process by performing social experiments, with subjects randomly assigned to different treatments. In principle, randomization yields exogenous selection of treatments, so a researcher analyzing experimental data can feel confident that the assumption of exogenous selection is valid.

Discussion of social experimentation has at times been highly contentious. In the mid-1980s, various advocates of experimentation asserted that, as a consequence of the selection problem, no reliable inferences can be made from empirical analysis of actual population outcomes. They recommended that efforts to analyze naturally occurring outcomes be abandoned (see Bassi and Ashenfelter 1986; LaLonde 1986; and Coyle et al. 1989). This position has since been embraced by some policymakers. For example, in a recently published letter to the General Accounting Office of the U.S. Congress, an assistant secretary of the Department of Health and Human Services wrote this about the evaluation of training programs for welfare recipients:

> In fact, nonexperimental research of training programs has shown such methods to be so unreliable, that Congress and the Administration have both insisted on experimental designs for the Job Training Partnership Act (JTPA) and the Job Opportunities and Basic Skill (JOBS) programs. (Barnhart 1992)

Calls for exclusive reliance on experimentation are unwarranted. Focusing on the identification problems that arise in the analysis of actual population outcomes, recent proponents of social experiments have tended to ignore the substantial difficulties that arise in executing experiments of interest and in extrapolating from experiments to settings of practical concern. For a discussion of these problems, see Manski and Garfinkel (1992).

4. IDENTIFICATION OF ENDOGENOUS SOCIAL EFFECTS

The broad idea that individuals are influenced by their social environments covers a wide variety of distinct phenomena, from the anonymous process by which markets determine prices to the intensely personal interactions occurring within families. An important objective of social science research is to learn the channels through which society affects the individual. But progress has been limited. Competing hypotheses abound and empirical analysis seems unable to distinguish among them.

Perhaps most notorious is the longstanding interdisciplinary split between economists and other social scientists. Whereas sociologists and social psychologists hypothesize that society affects individuals in myriad ways, economists often assume that society acts on individuals only by constraining their opportunities. Many economists regard such central sociological concepts as norms and reference groups as spurious phenomena explainable by processes operating entirely at the level of the individual. For example, see the Friedman (1957) criticism of Duesenberry (1949).[9]

[9]Although it is valid to distinguish mainstream economic thinking on social effects from the perspectives of the other social sciences, we should not think that economists are concerned only with the operation of markets. The field of public economics has long been concerned with "external effects"— social effects on opportunities that operate outside markets. Moreover, some economists have sought to interpret and make use of key sociological ideas. Duesenberry (1949) is one example. More recently, Schelling (1971) analyzed the residential patterns that emerge when individuals choose not to live in neighborhoods where the percentage of residents of their own race is below some threshold. Conlisk (1980) showed that, if decision making is costly, it may be optimal for individuals to imitate the behavior of other persons who are better informed. Akerlof (1980) and Jones (1984) studied the equilibria of noncooperative games in which individuals are punished for deviation from group norms. Gaertner (1974), Pollak (1976), Alessie and Kapteyn (1991), and Case (1991) analyzed consumer demand models in which, holding price fixed, individual demand increases with the mean demand of a reference group.

Leaving economists aside and restricting attention to sociologists, one still does not find consensus on the nature of social
effects. Consider the ongoing debate about the meaningfulness
of the concept of the underclass and the related controversy about
the existence and nature of neighborhood effects. Or consider the
split between those sociologists who take class, ethnic group, or
gender as the fundamental unit of analysis, and those who view
society as a collection of heterogeneous individuals, families, and
households.

Why do such different perspectives on the nature of social
effects persist? Why do we not converge to common conclusions?
The core problem is that outcome data, which have been our main
source of empirical evidence, can reveal the structure of social effects
only if combined with substantial prior information.

Social scientists have long been aware of some aspects of the
problem. For over 50 years, economists have studied the conditions
under which observations of market-determined prices and quantities reveal the demand behavior of consumers and the supply behavior of firms (for example, see Fisher 1966). Over 20 years ago, sociologists were sensitized to the problem of distinguishing contextual
effects from correlated individual effects; Hauser (1970) offers an
informative and entertaining case study.

Nevertheless, the problem of identifying social effects from
outcome data has many poorly understood aspects. In recent work, I
have sought to add to our knowledge by analyzing the identifiability
of a class of endogenous social effects (Manski 1993d). I summarize
and elaborate on this work here.

Section 4.1 introduces the question of interest informally. Section 4.2 uses a simple linear model to examine the identification of
endogenous effects relative to contextual effects and nonsocial phenomena. Section 4.3 briefly considers some related models. Section
4.4 calls attention to the critical need for reference-group information to identify social effects.

4.1. Endogenous, Contextual, Ecological, and Correlated Effects

Consider the following four distinct phenomena, the first two of
which are social in nature and the second two nonsocial:

Endogenous effects, wherein the propensity of an individual to behave in some way varies with the prevalence of that behavior in some reference group.[10]

Contextual effects, wherein the propensity of an individual to behave in some way varies with the distribution of background characteristics in the reference group.[11]

Ecological effects, wherein individuals in the same reference group tend to behave similarly because they face similar institutional environments.

Correlated individual effects, wherein individuals in the same reference group tend to behave similarly because they have similar individual characteristics.

An example may help to clarify the distinction. Consider the high school achievement of a teenage youth. There is an endogenous effect if, all else being equal, individual achievement tends to vary with the average achievement of the students in the youth's high school or ethnic group, or in another reference group. There is a contextual effect if achievement tends to vary with, say, the socioeconomic composition of the reference group. There is an ecological effect if students in the same school tend to achieve similarly because they are taught by the same teachers. There are correlated individual

[10]I use the term "endogenous effects" to describe a broad class of ideas recurring throughout the social sciences; Erbring and Young (1979) have referred to these phenomena as "endogenous feedback." Sociologists, social psychologists, and some economists have long been concerned with *reinforcing* endogenous effects, wherein the propensity of an individual to behave in some way increases with the prevalence of that behavior in the reference group. A host of terms are commonly used to describe reinforcing endogenous effects: "conformity," "imitation," "contagion," "bandwagons," "herd behavior," "norm effects," "keeping up with the Joneses," and, in economics, "interdependent preferences." Economists have always been fundamentally concerned with a particular nonreinforcing endogenous effect: an individual's demand for a product varies with price, which is partly determined by aggregate demand in the relevant market.

[11]Inference on contextual effects became an important concern of sociologists in the 1960s, when substantial efforts were made to learn the effects on youth of school and neighborhood environment (e.g., see Coleman et al. 1966; Sewell and Armer, 1966). The recent resurgence of interest in spatial concepts of the underclass has spawned many new empirical studies (e.g., Crane 1991; Jencks and Mayer 1989; and Mayer 1991). In Manski (1993*d*), I use the term "exogenous effect" as a synonym for contextual effect, to distinguish the idea from endogenous effects.

effects if students in the same school tend to have similar family backgrounds and these background characteristics tend to affect achievement.

The question of interest is whether the two types of social effects can be distinguished from one another and from the nonsocial effects. This question is of practical importance because the different effects have distinct policy implications. Consider, for example, an educational intervention providing tutoring to some but not all of the students in a school. If individual achievement increases with the average achievement of the students in the school, then an effective tutoring program not only directly helps the tutored students but, as their achievement rises, indirectly helps all students in the school, with a feedback to further achievement gains by the tutored students. Contextual effects do not generate this "social multiplier."

Although endogenous and contextual effects differ conceptually and in their policy implications, these two types of social effect have often been confused. For example, studies of school integration, typified by Coleman et al. (1966), seem to have in mind an endogenous social effect, wherein the achievement of each student is affected by the mean achievement of the students in the same school. But these studies generally estimate contextual-effects models, wherein the achievement of all students is affected by the racial composition of their school.

The same tension appears in recent analyses of neighborhood effects. The theoretical section of Crane (1991) poses an "epidemic" model of endogenous neighborhood effects, wherein a teenager's school dropout and childbearing behavior is influenced by the neighborhood frequency of dropout and childbearing. But Crane estimates a contextual-effects model, wherein the behavior of teenagers depends on the occupational composition of their neighborhood. This juxtaposition of endogenous-effect theorizing and contextual-effect empirical analysis also appears in Jencks and Mayer (1989).

4.2. Identification of a Linear Model: The Reflection Problem

4.2.1. Model Specification
Consideration of a relatively simple linear model suffices to explain the problems that arise in identifying social effects.

Let each member of the population be characterized by a

value for (y,x,z,u). Here y is a scalar outcome (e.g., a youth's achievement in high school), x represents attributes characterizing an individual's reference group (e.g., a set of dummy variables indicating a youth's school), and (z,u) are attributes that directly affect y (e.g., socioeconomic status and ability variables). A researcher observes a random sample of realizations of (y,x,z). Realizations of u are not observed.

I shall assume that

$$y = \alpha + \beta E(y|x) + E(z|x)'\gamma + x'\delta_1 + z'\eta + u, \quad (42)$$

$$E(u|x,z) = x'\delta_2,$$

where $(\alpha,\beta,\gamma,\delta_1,\delta_2,\eta)$ is a parameter vector. Model (42) implies that the mean regression of y on (x,z) has the linear form

$$E(y|x,z) = \alpha + \beta E(y|x) + E(z|x)'\gamma + x'(\delta_1 + \delta_2) + z'\eta. \quad (43)$$

Empirical studies of social effects have generally assumed that values of the regressors $[E(y|x),E(z|x),x,z]$ are assigned exogenously to individuals. Hence the parameters $(\alpha,\beta,\gamma,\delta_1,\delta_2,\eta)$ are the treatment effects associated with a unit change in each regressor, holding the others fixed (see section 3.4.2).[12]

If $\beta \neq 0$, the linear regression (43) expresses an endogenous social effect: A person's response y varies with $E(y|x)$, the mean of the endogenous variable y among those persons in the reference group described by x.[13] If $\gamma \neq 0$, the model expresses a contextual effect: y varies with $E(z|x)$, the mean of the exogenous variables z among those persons in the reference group. If $\delta_1 \neq 0$, the model expresses an ecological effect: y varies directly with x. If $\delta_2 \neq 0$, the model expresses correlated individual effects: Persons in the reference group x tend to have similar unobserved attributes u. The parameter η expresses the direct effect of z on y.

[12]The three regressors $E(y|x)$, $E(z|x)$, and x are functionally dependent in the population and so do not vary separately empirically. Nevertheless, we can contemplate the logical experiment in which one of these regressors is changed and the others held fixed. See the discussion at the end of Section 2.3.

[13]Beginning with Hyman (1942), reference-group theory has sought to express the idea that individuals learn from or are otherwise influenced by the behavior and attitudes of some reference group. Bank, Slavings, and Biddle (1990) give a historical account. Sociological writing has remained predominantly verbal, but economists have interpreted reference groups as conditioning variables, in the manner of (4.2). See Alessie and Kapteyn (1991) or Manski (1993b).

4.2.2. Identification of the Parameters

We are interested in identification of the parameter vector $(\alpha,\beta,\gamma,\delta_1,\delta_2,\eta)$. To focus attention on this question, I shall assume that either (i) x has discrete support or (ii) y and z have finite variances and the two regressions $E(y|x)$ and $E(z|x)$ appearing as regressors in (43) are continuous on the support of x. As indicated in Section 2.1, either of these assumptions implies that the random sampling process identifies $E(y|x)$ and $E(z|x)$ on the support of x. So we can treat the two regressions as known and focus attention on the parameters.[14]

One aspect of the identification problem can be seen immediately by inspection of (43). That is, ecological effects cannot be identified relative to correlated individual effects. The sum $(\delta_1 + \delta_2)$ may be identified but not δ_1 and δ_2 separately.

Less obvious is the "reflection" problem that arises out of the presence of $E(y|x)$ as a regressor in (43). Integrating both sides of (43) with respect to z reveals that $E(y|x)$ solves the "social equilibrium" equation.

$$E(y|x) = \alpha + \beta E(y|x) + E(z|x)'\gamma + x'(\delta_1 + \delta_2) + E(z|x)'\eta. \qquad (44)$$

Provided that $\beta \neq 1$, equation (44) has a unique solution, namely

$$E(y|x) = [\alpha + E(z|x)'(\gamma + \eta) + x'(\delta_1 + \delta_2)]/(1 - \beta). \qquad (45)$$

Thus model (43) implies that $E(y|x)$ is a linear function of $[1,E(z|x),x]$, where "1" denotes the constant. It follows that the parameters α, β, γ, $(\delta_1 + \delta_2)$ are all unidentified. In particular, endogenous effects cannot be distinguished from contextual effects.

---

[14]Assumptions (i) and (ii) cover many but not all cases of empirical interest. They are not appropriate in studies of small-group social interactions, such as family interactions. In analyses of family interactions, each reference group (i.e., family) has negligible size relative to the population, and random sampling of individuals only rarely yields multiple members of the same family. Hence, it is not a good empirical approximation to assume that x has finite support. Moreover, unless one can characterize groups of families as being similar in composition, it is not plausible to assume that $E(y|x)$ and $E(z|x)$ are continuous functions of x. The conclusion to be drawn, not surprisingly, is that random sampling of individuals is not an effective data gathering process for the study of family interactions. It is preferable to use families as the sampling unit. The properties of alternative sample designs for the study of small-group interactions are analyzed in the literature on network sampling. See Marsden (1990) for a recent review article.

What is identified? Inserting (45) into (43) we obtain the linear reduced form model

$$E(y|x,z) = \alpha/(1 - \beta) + E(z|x)'[\gamma/(1 - \beta) + \eta\beta/(1 - \beta)] \quad (46)$$
$$+ x'[(\delta_1 + \delta_2)/(1 - \beta)] + z'\eta.$$

The composite parameters $\alpha/(1 - \beta)$, $\gamma/(1 - \beta) + \eta\beta/(1 - \beta)$, $(\delta_1 + \delta_2)/(1 - \beta)$, and η are identified if the regressors $[1,E(z|x),x,z]$ are linearly independent. Identification of the composite parameters does not enable one to distinguish among the various social and nonsocial effects but does permit one to test the hypothesis that some social or nonsocial effect is present. If $\gamma/(1 - \beta) + \eta\beta/(1 - \beta)$ is nonzero, then either β or γ must be nonzero; so some social effect is present. If $[(\delta_1 + \delta_2)/(1 - \beta)]$ is nonzero, then either δ_1 or δ_2 must be nonzero; so some nonsocial effect is present.

Even these positive identification findings are tenuous. The required linear independence of $[1,E(z|x),x,z]$ is a nontrivial condition that can fail in various ways, including the following:

(a) The attributes x defining reference groups may be a subset of the attributes z directly affecting outcomes. Suppose that $z = (x,w)$ for some vector w. Then $[1,E(z|x),x,z] = [1,\{x,E(w|x)\}, x,\{x,w\}]$ is linearly dependent through the appearance of x in three locations.

(b) The attributes z directly affecting outcomes may be a subset of the attributes x defining reference groups. Suppose that $x = (z,w)$ for some vector w. Then $[1,E(z|x),x,z] = [1,z,\{z,w\},z]$ is linearly dependent through the appearance of z in three locations.

(c) The attributes z directly affecting outcomes may be mean-independent of the attributes x defining reference groups. Suppose that $E(z|x) = z_0$, for some constant vector z_0. Then $[1,E(z|x),x,z] = [1,z_0,x,z]$ is linearly dependent through the appearance of the two constants 1 and z_0.

(d) The regression $E(z|x)$ may be a linear function of x as, for example, occurs if (z,x) are distributed multivariate normal. Suppose that $E(z|x) = Ax$ for some parameter matrix A. Then $[1,E(z|x),x,z] = [1,Ax,x,z]$ is linearly dependent through the appearance of Ax and x.

For example, in a study of school achievement, condition (a) holds if x is (family income) and z is (ability, family income); condition (b) holds if x is (ability, family income) and z is (ability); condition (c) holds if x is (family income), z is (ability), and average ability is the same in all income groups; condition (d) holds if x is (family income), z is (ability), and average ability varies linearly with income.

Taken together, these conditions say that identification fails unless the attributes z and x are "moderately" related in a nonlinear manner. They must be neither functionally dependent (conditions a and b), mean independent (condition c), nor linearly mean-dependent (condition d).

4.2.3. Parameter Restrictions

The possibilities for identification improve if one has prior information restricting some of the parameters. The most common restrictions are assumptions that some parameter values are zero, so that the corresponding effect is null. Suppose it is known that $\beta = 0$, so that there is no endogenous effect. Then the contextual-effect parameter γ is identified if $[1, E(z|x), x, z]$ are linearly independent. Or suppose it is known that $\gamma = 0$, so that there is no contextual effect. Then the endogenous-effect parameter β is identified if $[1, E(z|x), x, z]$ are linearly independent and $\eta \neq 0$.

The only way to relax the linear independence condition is to impose further parameter restrictions. Empirical studies of contextual effects often assume that $\beta = \delta_1 = \delta_2 = 0$; then γ is identified if $[1, E(z|x), z]$ are linearly independent. Empirical studies of endogenous effects often assume that $\gamma = \delta_1 = \delta_2 = 0$; then β is identified if $[1, E(z|x), z]$ are linearly independent and $\eta \neq 0$.

4.2.4. Sample Inference

Our primary concern is with identification of the model (43), but a discussion of sample inference is warranted.

Empirical studies of contextual effects have typically applied a two-stage method to estimate (γ, η). In the first stage, the sample data on (z, x) are used to estimate $E(z|x)$ nonparametrically; generally x is discrete and the estimate of $E(z|x)$ is a cell-average of the form given in equation (1). In the second stage, (γ, η) are estimated by finding the least squares fit of y to $[1, E_N(z|x), z]$, where $E_N(z|x)$ is the first-stage estimate of $E(z|x)$.

Empirical studies of endogenous effects have also applied a two-stage method to estimate (β,η), but in the guise of a "spatial correlation" model of the form

$$y_i = \beta W_{iN} Y + z_i' \eta + u_i, \qquad i = 1, \ldots, N. \qquad (47)$$

Here $Y = (y_i, i = 1, \ldots, N)$ is the $N \times 1$ vector of sample realizations of y, and W_{iN} is a specified $1 \times N$ weighting vector; that is, the components of W_{iN} are nonnegative and sum to one. The disturbances u are assumed to be normally distributed, independent of x, and the model is estimated by maximum likelihood. See, for example, Cliff and Ord (1981), Doreian (1981), Friedkin (1990), or Case (1991).

Equation (47) states that the behavior of each person in the sample varies with a weighted average of the behaviors of the other sample members. Thus the spatial correlation model assumes that a social effect is generated within the researcher's sample rather than within the population from which the sample was drawn. This makes sense in studies of small-group interactions, where the sample is composed of clusters of friends, coworkers, or household members; see, for example, Duncan, Haller, and Portes (1968) or Erbring and Young (1979). But it does not make sense in studies of neighborhood and other large-group social effects, where the sample members are randomly chosen individuals. Taken at face value, equation (47) implies that the sample members know each other and choose their outcomes only after having been selected into the sample.

The spatial correlation model does make sense in studies of large-group interactions if interpreted as a two-stage method for estimating model (43). In the first stage, we use the sample data on (y,x) to estimate $E(y|x)$ nonparametrically, and in the second stage, we estimate (β,η) by finding the least squares fit of y to $[1, E_N(y|x), z]$, where $E_N(y|x)$ is the first-stage estimate of $E(y|x)$. Many nonparametric estimates of $E(y|x_i)$, including the local average (2), are weighted averages of the form $E_N(y|x_i) = W_{iN} Y$, with W_{iN} determining the specific estimate. Hence, estimates of (β,η) reported in the spatial correlation literature can be interpreted as estimates of (43).

The Sampling Distribution of Two-Stage Estimates. It is necessary to point out that empirical studies reporting two-stage estimates of social-effects models have routinely misreported the sampling distribution of their estimates. The practice in two-stage estimation of contextual-effects models has been to treat the first-stage estimate $E_N(z|x)$ as if it were $E(z|x)$ rather than an estimate thereof. The literature on spatial correlation models has presumed that equation (47) holds as stated and has not specified how the weights W_{iN} should change with N.

Two-stage estimation of social-effects models is similar to other semiparametric two-stage estimation problems whose asymptotic properties have been studied recently. Ahn and Manski (1993), Ichimura and Lee (1991), and others have analyzed the asymptotic behavior of various estimators whose first stage is nonparametric regression and whose second stage is parametric estimation conditional on the first-stage estimate. It is typically found that the second-stage estimate is $\sqrt{N}$-consistent with a limiting normal distribution if the first-stage estimator is chosen appropriately. The variance of the limiting distribution is typically larger than that which would prevail if the first-stage regression were known rather than estimated. It seems likely that this result holds here as well.

4.3. Related Models

4.3.1. More General Models
The analysis of the preceding section sends a strong warning about the difficulty of inferring social effects from outcome data. Richer models that include the linear model as a special case bring to bear less prior information and so must be even more difficult to identify. There are many empirically relevant directions for generalization of the linear model. I mention four here.

Nonlinear Models. There is often no good reason to assume that social and nonsocial effects behave linearly. The basic themes of (43) are captured by the class of models of the form

$$E(y|x,z) = f[E(y|x),E(z|x),x,z], \qquad (48)$$

$f(.,.)$ being a member of some family F of functions on $Y \times Z \times X \times Z$. Whereas (43) implies that $E(y|x)$ solves the linear social equilibrium equation (44), (48) implies that $E(y|x)$ solves the possibly nonlinear social equilibrium equation

$$E(y|x) = \int f[E(y|x),E(z|x),x,z]dP(z|x), \qquad (49)$$

where $P(z|x)$ is the probability distribution of z conditional on x. The model (48) is coherent if equation (49) has a solution and is internally inconsistent otherwise.

Heterogeneity and the Strength of Norms. So far, we have assumed that social effects are transmitted only through $E(y|x)$ and $E(z|x)$, and that they operate only on $E(y|x,z)$. It may be, however, that social forces are transmitted through the entire conditional distributions $P(y|x)$ and $P(z|x)$ and that they operate on the entire conditional distribution $P(y|x,z)$. If so, we then have the following abstract generalization of (48):

$$P(y|x,z) = f[P(y|x),P(z|x),x,z].$$ (50)

In particular, it is sometimes said that the strength of the effect of social norms on individual behavior depends on the dispersion of behavior in the population. The more homogeneous the reference-group behavior, the stronger the norm. This idea can be expressed by models in which individual outcomes tend to vary not only with the mean outcome of the reference group but also with the variance of the reference-group outcomes.

Multiple Reference Groups. Another direction for generalizing the linear model is to allow individuals to be influenced by multiple reference groups, giving more weight to the behavior of some groups than to others. Then (50) might be generalized even further to

$$P(y|\{x_m,m = 1, \ldots M\},z) = \\ f[\{P(y|x_m),P(z|x_m),x_m,i = 1, \ldots M\},z].$$ (51)

Here x_m characterizes the mth reference group.

Vector Outcomes. Yet another direction for generalization is to let the outcome y be a vector rather than a scalar. With this done, we can imagine a simultaneous system of endogenous effects, with reference-group outcomes along each dimension affecting individual outcomes along other dimensions.

4.3.2. Binary Response Models
Some interesting social effects models are similar in spirit to the linear model but formally distinct. In particular, let y be a binary random variable and consider the binary response model

$$P(y = 1|x,z) = H[\alpha + \beta P(y = 1|x) + E(z|x)'\gamma + x'\delta + z'\eta], \quad (52)$$

where $H(.)$ is a specified continuous, strictly increasing distribution function. For example, if $H(.)$ is the logistic distribution, we have a logit model with social effects.

Models of form (52) have been estimated by two-stage methods. The usual approach is to estimate $P(y = 1|x)$ nonparametrically and then estimate (β,γ) by maximizing the quasi-likelihood in which $P_N(y = 1|x)$ takes the place of $P(y = 1|x)$. Examples include Case and Katz (1991) and Gamoran and Mare (1989). A multinomial response model estimated in this manner appears in Manski and Wise (1983, ch. 6).

The literature has not addressed the coherency and identification of model (52). The model is coherent if there is a solution to the social equilibrium equation

$$P(y = 1|x) = \int H[\alpha + \beta P(y = 1|x) + E(z|x)'\gamma + x'\delta + z'\eta]dP(z|x). \quad (53)$$

In Manski (1993d), I have shown that this equation does always have at least one solution. The solution is unique if $\beta \leq 0$, but I have not been able to rule out the possibility of multiple solutions (that is, multiple social equilibria) if $\beta > 0$. The conditions under which the parameters $(\alpha,\beta,\gamma,\delta,\eta)$ are identified have not yet been established.

4.3.3. Dynamic Models
Some authors, including Alessie and Kapteyn (1991) and Borjas (1992), have estimated the following dynamic version of the linear model (43):

$$E_t(y|x,z) = \alpha + \beta E_{t-1}(y|x) + E_{t-1}(z|x)'\gamma + x_t'(\delta_1 + \delta_2) + z_t'\eta, \quad (54)$$

where E_t and E_{t-1} denote expectations taken at periods t and $t - 1$. The idea is that nonsocial forces act contemporaneously, but social forces act on the individual with a lag.

If $[E(z|x),x,z]$ are time-invariant and $-1 < \beta < 1$, the dynamic process (54) has a unique stable temporal equilibrium of the form (44). If we observe the process in temporal equilibrium, the identification analysis in Section 4.2 holds without modification. On the other hand, if we observe the process out of equilibrium, the recursive structure of (54) opens new possibilities for identification. In particular, $E_{t-1}(y|x)$ is not necessarily a linear function of $[1,E_{t-1}(z|x),x_t]$.

We should not, however, conclude that dynamic models solve the problem of identifying social effects. To exploit the recursive structure of (54), we must maintain the hypothesis that the transmission of social effects really follows the assumed temporal pattern. But empirical studies typically provide no evidence for any particular timing. Some authors assume that individuals are influenced by the behavior of their contemporaries, some assume a time lag of a few years, while others assume that social effects operate across generations.

4.4. Identification of Reference Groups

So far, we have assumed that researchers know how individuals form reference groups and that individuals correctly perceive the outcomes experienced by their supposed reference groups. There is substantial reason to question these assumptions. Researchers studying social effects rarely offer empirical evidence to support their reference-group specifications. The prevailing practice is simply to assume that individuals are influenced by $E(y|x)$ and $E(z|x)$, for some specified x.[15] One of the few studies of social effects that does attempt to justify its specification of reference groups is Woittiez and Kapteyn (1991). They use individuals' responses to questions about their "social environments" as evidence regarding their reference groups.

It would seem that the research approaches developed by sociological network analysts should be useful in specifying reference groups for studies of social effects. It is difficult for me to speculate on why this has not occurred, but Blalock (1989) and Friedkin (1990) argue that at least part of the reason is the discomfort most sociologists feel when confronted with the mathematics of network analysis.

4.4.1. Tautological Linear Models

If researchers do not know how individuals form reference groups and perceive reference-group outcomes, then it is reasonable to ask

---

[15]The same practice is found in empirical studies of decision making under uncertainty. Researchers assume they know how individuals form their expectations but offer no evidence justifying their assumptions. I have recently criticized this practice in the context of studies of schooling choice. See Manski (1993c).

whether outcome data can be used to infer these unknowns. The answer is negative.

Consider the hypothesis that the linear model (43) holds, with a specified vector z directly affecting individual outcomes and a longer vector $x = (z, w)$ defining reference groups. This hypothesis is not testable. In particular, we cannot reject the hypothesis that mean reference-group behavior dictates individual behavior.

Letting $x = (z, w)$ implies that

$$E(y|x, z) = E(y|x). \tag{55}$$

The reason is that conditioning on z is superfluous once we condition on x. It follows that (43) holds tautologically with $\beta = 1$ and $\alpha = \gamma = \delta_1 = \delta_2 = \eta = 0$. Thus the observed pattern of behavior is necessarily consistent with the hypothesis that the linear model holds and that mean reference-group behavior dictates individual behavior.

For example, consider researchers studying student achievement. Suppose that they observe each student's ability and family income. If the researchers specify x to be (ability, family income) and z to be (ability), they will find that the data are consistent with the hypothesis that individuals do condition on (ability, family income) to form their reference groups, that individual achievement reflects reference-group achievement, and that ability has no direct effect on achievement.

4.4.2. Experimental and Subjective Data

It clearly is very difficult to draw conclusions about social effects from outcome data alone. If the identification of social effects is so tenuous, then why is there such a widespread perception that society influences individual behavior in many ways?

It may be that this common perception is poorly grounded, fed by flawed interpretations of outcome data. But outcome data are not our only source of evidence on social effects. Prevailing views also rest on evidence from controlled experiments and on subjective data, the statements people make about why they behave as they do. (See Jones 1984, for a survey of the experimental literature.) Our analysis of identification from outcome data suggests that experimental and subjective data will have to play an important role in future efforts to learn about social effects.

5. IDENTIFICATION OF SUBJECTIVE PHENOMENA

5.1. *Research Practices in Economics and Sociology*

Policy disputes often reflect disagreement about the roles of objective and subjective forces in determining behavior. Suppose, as do many social scientists, that behavior is determined by objective opportunities and by subjective preferences and expectations. Then we may ask politically sensitive questions such as the following:

> Do young black males have low labor force participation because (a) jobs are unavailable (opportunities), (b) they believe that jobs are unavailable (expectations), or (c) they don't want to work (preferences)?

Social scientists and concerned citizens agree that this question is meaningful and relevant to social policy. They have not, however, been able to reach consensus on the answer.

Distinguishing the objective and subjective determinants of human behavior may be the most challenging identification problem facing social scientists. It is certainly the problem that most clearly separates the social from the natural sciences, where the units of analysis are not thought of as possessing free will. Yet the inherent difficulty of inference on subjective phenomena does not fully explain our lack of knowledge. Research practices in the various social science disciplines also inhibit progress.

For many years, economists have exercised a self-imposed prohibition on the use of subjective data in empirical analysis.[16] In-

---

[16]Economists typically assert that respondents to surveys have no incentive to answer questions carefully or honestly; hence, they conclude, there is no reason to think that subjective responses reliably reflect respondents' thinking. Economists' views on the use of subjective data have not, however, always been so negative. In the 1940s, it was common to interview businessmen about their expectations and decision rules. In an influential article, Machlup (1946) sharply attacked existing survey practices as not yielding credible information. This article apparently played an important role in eventually dampening the enthusiasm of economists for subjective data. It is revealing that a recent National Academy of Sciences panel on survey measurement of subjective phenomena had no economist as a member of the panel and cited almost no economics literature in its report. See Turner and Martin (1984).

stead, they have sought to infer subjective phenomena from data on opportunities and choices. This research approach, referred to as "revealed preference analysis," cannot be used to jointly infer expectations and preferences. So economists have typically imposed assumptions on expectations and attempted to infer preferences from observed choices.[17]

In contrast to economists, social psychologists and sociologists routinely collect and analyze subjective data of many kinds. Unfortunately, the prevailing practice has been to pose loosely worded questions incapable of revealing much about either expectations or preferences. Moreover, researchers typically theorize verbally rather than mathematically. Hence, it can be difficult to determine whether different researchers interpret the terms "preferences" and "expectations" in a common manner.

As I see it, progress in understanding the objective and subjective determinants of behavior requires that the various social sciences break with their conventions. As long as economists continue to rely exclusively on revealed-preference analysis, they have no hope of determining whether they are making empirically valid inferences on preferences or wrong inferences based on incorrect expectations assumptions. As long as sociologists continue to reason verbally rather than mathematically, their empirical analysis will suffer from conceptual ambiguity.

Some of my recent and ongoing work seeks to fuse what I see as the positive aspects of present economic and sociological research practices: the use of formal decision theory by economists and the exploitation of subjective data by sociologists. One completed article examines the conditions under which rational decision makers can learn from the experiences of role models (Manski 1993b). Another, focusing on the analysis of schooling behavior, critiques the conven-

---

[17]The impossibility of jointly inferring expectations and preferences from data on opportunities and choices can easily be seen with a few symbols. The standard economic model assumes that an individual's choice c among specified alternatives C is a function $f(.)$ of the expected outcomes $(r_i, i \in C)$ associated with the various options; that is, $c = f(r_i, i \in C)$. Suppose that we wish to learn the decision rule $f(.)$ embodying preferences and mapping expectations into choices. If we observe $\{c, C, (r_i, i \in C)\}$ for a sample of individuals, then we may be able to infer the decision rule. But if we observe only (c, C), then clearly we cannot infer $f(.)$. The most we can do is infer the decision rule conditional on maintained assumptions on expectations.

tional economic practice of assuming that youth have specific expectations of the returns to schooling (Manski 1993c). In ongoing work, I am attempting to elicit from youth their actual expectations of the returns to schooling.

In this section, I describe my recent work offering a "best-case" decision theoretic treatment of stated intentions, a familiar type of subjective data. The analysis, drawn from Manski (1990b), shows that intentions data have often been misinterpreted. In doing so, it illustrates the importance of interpreting subjective data in a logically coherent manner.

5.2. The Use of Intentions Data to Predict Behavior

In surveys individuals are routinely asked to predict their future behavior—that is, to state their intentions. The fertility question asked female respondents in the June 1987 supplement to the Current Population Survey (CPS) is an example (U.S. Bureau of the Census 1988):

> Looking ahead, do you expect to have any (more) children?
>
> Yes _____   No _____   Uncertain _____

Responses to such fertility-intentions questions have been used to predict fertility for over 50 years; Hendershot and Placek (1981) review the extensive literature. Data on voting intentions have been used to predict election outcomes in the United States since the early 1900s (see Turner and Martin 1984). Surveys of buying intentions have been used to predict consumer purchase behavior since at least the mid-1940s (see Juster 1966). Perhaps the most extensive use of intentions data has been made by social psychologists, some of whom view intentions as a well-defined mental state that causally precedes behavior (see Fishbein and Ajzen 1975).

A Best-Case Analysis.   What information do intentions data convey about future behavior? The answer depends on how people respond to intentions questions and on how they actually behave. In Manski (1990b), I studied the relationship between stated intentions and subsequent behavior under the "best-case" hypothesis that individuals have rational expectations and that their responses to intentions questions are the best predictors of their behavior. My objective was to place an upper bound on the behavioral information contained in intentions data and to determine whether prevailing approaches to the analysis of intentions data respect the bound.

I found that much of the literature interprets intentions data in ways that are inconsistent with the best-case analysis. Authors have expected too much correspondence between intentions and behavior. Not finding the expected correspondence, they have improperly concluded that individuals are poor predictors of their future behavior.

5.2.1. *The Survey Question and the Best-Case Response*

My analysis focuses on the simplest intentions questions, those that call for yes/no predictions of binary outcomes. Suppose that a person is asked to make a point prediction of some binary choice; that is, a yes/no answer is requested. Let i and y be zero-one indicator variables denoting the survey response and future behavior respectively. Thus $i = 1$ if the person responds "yes" to the intentions question, and $y = 1$ if his behavior turns out to satisfy the property of interest.

To form his response, a person with rational expectations would begin by recognizing that his future behavior will depend in part on conditions known to him at the time of the survey and in part on events that have not yet occurred. Let s denote the information available to the respondent at the time of the survey. Let z denote the events that have not yet occurred but will affect his future behavior. Thus z represents uncertainty that will be resolved between the time of the survey and the time at which the behavior is determined. The behavior y is a function of the pair (s,z) and so may be written $y(s,z)$.

Let $P_z|s$ denote the objective probability distribution of z conditional on s. Let $P(y|s)$ denote the objective distribution of y conditional on s. The event $y = 1$ occurs if and only if the realization of z is such that $y(s,z) = 1$. Hence

$$P(y = 1|s) = P_z[y(s,z) = 1|s]. \tag{56}$$

The content of the rational-expectations hypothesis is that, at the time of the survey, respondents know $y(s,.)$ and $P_z|s$; hence they know $P(y = 1|s)$. It does not suffice for respondents to have subjective distributions for z, from which they derive subjective distributions for y. If there are rational expectations, we can assume there is knowledge of the actual random process generating z.

The second part of the best-case hypothesis is that respondents state their best point predictions of their behavior. The best prediction necessarily depends on the losses respondents associate with the two possible prediction errors ($i = 0$, $y = 1$) and ($i = 1$, $y = 0$). These losses may be influenced by the wording of the intentions question; for example, respondents may interpret differently questions that ask what they "expect," "intend," or "are likely" to do. Whatever the loss function, however, the intentions response should satisfy the condition

$$i = 1 \Rightarrow P(y = 1|s) \geq \pi \qquad (57)$$
$$i = 0 \Rightarrow P(y = 1|s) \leq \pi,$$

where the threshold probability π depends on the loss function. Note that $\pi = 0.5$ if the loss function is symmetric.

5.2.2. Prediction of Behavior Conditional on Intentions
Now consider a researcher who wishes to use intentions data to predict the behavior of some respondent. The researcher observes the intentions response i. Continuing the theme of a best-case analysis, assume that the researcher knows that i satisfies (57). Moreover, assume that π is the same for all respondents and that the researcher knows what π is.

The researcher may observe only a subset of the information s available to the respondent. Let x denote the observed component of s. Suppose that the researcher wishes to predict the behavior y conditional on the observed variables x and i. Then he or she would like to learn the probability $P(y = 1|x,i)$. Intentions data do not identify $P(y = 1|x,i)$. They do, however, imply a bound.

Let $P_s|xi$ denote the probability distribution of s conditional on the observed pair (x,i). It is the case that

$$P(y=1|x,i) = \int P(y=1|s)dP_s|xi. \qquad (58)$$

It follows directly from this and from (57) that

$$P(y = 1|x,i = 0) \leq \pi \leq P(y = 1|x,i = 1). \qquad (59)$$

This bound expresses all the information about behavior contained in the intentions data. Note that the bound varies with i but not with x.

The foregoing implies that familiar path models attempting to explain behavior as a function of intentions are not consistent with the best-case hypothesis. Consider a logit model

$$P(y = 1|x,i) = \frac{exp(x\beta + \gamma i)}{1 + exp(x\beta + \gamma i),} \qquad (60)$$

where (β,γ) are parameters. This model has the property

$$x\beta + \gamma i < 0 \Rightarrow P(y = 1|x,i) < 1/2 \qquad (61)$$

$$x\beta + \gamma i = 0 \Rightarrow P(y = 1|x,i) = 1/2$$

$$x\beta + \gamma i > 0 \Rightarrow P(y = 1|x,i) > 1/2.$$

Suppose that $\pi = 1/2$. Then (61) is consistent with (59) only if (x,β,γ) satisfies the special property $x\beta \le 0 \le x\beta + \gamma$.

The problem is, of course, not specific to the logit model and the case $\pi = 1/2$. It is characteristic of any path model which attempts to explain y as a function of a linear index $x\beta + \gamma i$.

5.2.3. Prediction Not Conditional on Intentions

Often a researcher wants to predict the behavior of a nonsampled member of the population from which the survey respondents were drawn. Intentions data are available only for the sampled individuals. But some background variables x may be observed for the entire population. In this setting, we may want to predict behavior conditional on these x. Then the quantity of interest is $P(y = 1|x)$.

Bound (59) implies a bound on $P(y = 1|x)$. Observe that

$$P(y = 1|x) \equiv P(y = 1|x,i = 0)P(i = 0|x) + P(y = 1|x,i = 1)P(i = 1|x). \qquad (62)$$

It follows from (59) and (62) that

$$\pi P(i = 1|x) \le P(y = 1|x) \le \pi P(i = 0|x) + P(i = 1|x). \qquad (63)$$

This bound is useful in practice because $P(i = 1|x)$ can be estimated nonparametrically from the sample data.

Observe that the bound (63), unlike (59), varies with x. The bound width, which is $\pi P(i = 0|x) + (1 - \pi)P(i = 1|x)$, may take any value between zero and one, depending on the magnitudes of π and $P(i|x)$. Thus, depending on the application, intentions data may yield a tight or weak bound on $P(y|x)$. If $\pi = 1/2$, the bound width is 1/2, whatever $P(i|x)$ might be.

It has been known for at least 25 years that the sharp relationship

$$P(i = 1|x) = P(y = 1|x) \tag{64}$$

need not hold (see Juster 1966, p. 665). Nevertheless, some of the literature continues to consider deviations from this equality as "inconsistencies" in need of explanation. For example, Westoff and Ryder (1977) state:

> The question with which we began this work was whether reproductive intentions are useful for prediction. The basic finding was that 40.5 percent intended more, as of the end of 1970, and 34.0 percent had more in the subsequent five years. . . . In other words, acceptance of 1970 intentions at face value would have led to a substantial overshooting of the ultimate outcome. (p. 449)

Seeking to explain the observed "overshooting" of births, the authors state:

> One interpretation of our finding would be that the respondents failed to anticipate the extent to which the times would be unpropitious for childbearing, that they made the understandable but frequently invalid assumption that the future would resemble the present—the same kind of forecasting error that demographers have often made. (p. 449)

More recent demographic work maintains the presumption that deviations from (64) require explanation. See, for example, Davidson and Beach (1981) and O'Connell and Rogers (1983).

The best-case hypothesis implies that (64) should hold in one very special case—that in which future behavior depends only on the information s available at the time of the survey. In this case, respondents can forecast future behavior with certainty. So i always equals y.

In the nondegenerate case where future events z partially determine behavior, the best-case hypothesis does not imply (64). A simple example makes the point forcefully. Let $\pi = 1/2$ and let $P(y =$

$1|s) = 0.51$ for all values of s. Then $P(y = 1|x) = 0.51$ but $P(i = 1|x)$ $= 1$ for all values of x. This demonstrates that individual-level differences between intentions and behavior do not, in general, average out in the aggregate.

5.2.4. *Lessons*

The use of intentions data to predict behavior has been controversial. At least some of the controversy is rooted in the flawed premise that divergences between intentions and behavior show individuals to be poor predictors of their futures. Divergences may simply reflect the dependence of behavior on events not yet realized at the time of the survey. Divergences will occur even if responses to intentions questions are the best predictions possible given the available information. The lesson is that researchers should not expect too much from yes/no intentions data.

In principle, the yes/no form of intentions question can be improved upon by asking the respondent to give his probability for the behavior in question. Whereas a yes/no question reveals at most the bounds (59) and (63) on $P(y|x,i)$ and $P(y|x)$, probability elicitation may reveal $P(y|s)$. See Juster (1966) for an interesting empirical study eliciting probabilistic intentions.

6. CONCLUSION

This chapter has analyzed aspects of four identification problems that arise regularly in social science research. Some findings were positive and others negative. Section 2 pointed out that any continuous regression is identified on the support of the regressors, but identification off the support requires information that restricts the regression globally. Section 3 showed that in the absence of prior information, we can always bound the distribution function of a censored random variable, we can bound a specified quantile if the censoring probability is not too high, but we cannot bound the mean. Section 4 sent the largely negative message that outcome data alone reveal little about the channels through which society influences the individual. Section 5 placed an upper bound on the degree of correspondence between stated intentions and subsequent behavior.

Beyond its specific findings, the chapter illustrates several general themes that will, I hope, influence future studies:

Begin with the data alone: A fruitful approach to the study of inference is to first ask what can be learned from the data alone, in the absence of prior information. Having determined this, we then ask what more can be learned given successively stronger forms of prior information. It has been usual to proceed in the opposite manner—that is, to first assert enough prior information to identify the object of interest and then to ask what happens when assumptions are weakened.

Proceeding from weak assumptions to strong yields valuable new findings, as in sections 2 and 3. Moreover, this research approach has a social benefit. Establishing the set of conclusions that hold up under weak assumptions builds a domain of consensus among researchers and confines disagreements to those questions whose resolution really does require controversial maintained assumptions.

Points and bounds: Identification is not an all-or-nothing proposition. Although we may not have rich enough prior information and data to infer the exact value of a parameter, we may nevertheless be able to bound the parameter, as in sections 3 and 5. The fixation of social scientists on point identification has inhibited appreciation of the usefulness of bounds.

Coping with ambiguity: We need to develop a greater tolerance for ambiguity. Social scientists, policymakers, and the public often seem driven to draw sharp conclusions, even when these can be generated only by imposing much stronger assumptions than can be plausibly defended. Scientific reporting and policy analysis would be improved if we would face up to the fact that we cannot answer all of the questions that we ask.

REFERENCES

Ahn, Hyungtaik, and Charles F. Manski. 1993. "Distribution Theory for the Analysis of Binary Choice Under Uncertainty with Nonparametric Estimation of Expectations." *Journal of Econometrics* 56: Forthcoming.

Akerlof, George. 1980. "A Theory of Social Custom, of Which Unemployment May Be One Consequence." *Quarterly Journal of Economics* 94:749–75.

Alessie, Rob, and Arie Kapteyn. 1991. "Habit Formation, Interdependent Preferences and Demographic Effects in the Almost Ideal Demand System." *The Economic Journal* 101:404–19.

Bank, Barbara J., Ricky L. Slavings, and Bruce J. Biddle. 1990. "Effects of Peer, Faculty, and Parental Influences on Students' Persistence." *Sociology of Education* 63:208–25.

Barnhart, Joan. 1992. Letter to Eleanor Chelimsky, in U.S. General Accounting Office. "Unemployed Parents." GAO/PEMD-92-19BR. Gaithersburg, Md.: General Accounting Office.

Bassi, Laurie, and Oreley Ashenfelter, 1986. "The Effect of Direct Job Creation and Training Programs on Low-Skilled Workers." In *Fighting Poverty,* edited by S. Danziger and D. Weinberg. Cambridge: Harvard University Press.

Blalock, Herbert M., Jr. 1989. "The Real and Unrealized Contributions of Quantitative Sociology." *American Sociological Review* 54:447–60.

Blumstein, Alfred, Jacqueline Cohen, and Daniel Nagin, eds. 1978. *Deterrence and Incapacitation: Estimating the Effects of Criminal Sanctions on Crime Rates.* Washington, D.C.: National Academy Press.

Borjas, George. 1992. "Ethnic Capital and Intergenerational Mobility." *Quarterly Journal of Economics* 107:123–50.

Case, Ann. 1991. "Spatial Patterns in Household Demand." *Econometrica* 59:953–65.

Case, Ann, and Larry Katz. 1991. "The Company You Keep: The Effects of Family and Neighborhood on Disadvantaged Youth." Working Paper No. 3705, National Bureau of Economic Research, Cambridge, Mass.

Cliff, A. D., and J. K. Ord. 1981. *Spatial Processes.* London: Pion.

Clogg, Clifford C. 1992. "The Impact of Sociological Methodology on Statistical Methodology." *Statistical Science* 7:183–96.

Coleman, James S., E. Campbell, C. Hobson, J. McPartland, A. Mood, F. Weinfeld, and R. York. 1966. *Equality of Educational Opportunity.* Washington, D.C.: Government Printing Office.

Conlisk, John. 1980. "Costly Optimizers Versus Cheap Imitators." *Journal of Economic Behavior and Organization* 1:275–93.

Coyle, Susan, Robert Boruch, and Charles Turner, eds. 1989. *Evaluating AIDS Prevention Programs.* Washington, D.C.: National Academy Press.

Crane, Jonathan. 1991. "The Epidemic Theory of Ghettos and Neighborhood Effects on Dropping Out and Teenage Childbearing." *American Journal of Sociology* 96:1226–59.

Davidson, A., and L. Beach. 1981. "Error Patterns in the Prediction of Fertility Behavior." *Journal of Applied Social Psychology* 11:475–88.

Doreian, Patric, K. 1981. "Estimating Linear Models with Spatially Distributed Data." In *Sociological Methodology 1981,* edited by S. Leinhardt, 359–88. San Francisco: Jossey-Bass.

Duesenberry, James. 1949. *Income, Savings, and the Theory of Consumption.* Cambridge: Harvard University Press.

Duncan, Otis D., Archibald Haller, and Alejandro Portes. 1968. "Peer Influences on Aspirations: A Reinterpretation." *American Journal of Sociology* 74:119–37.

Erbring, Lutz, and Alice A. Young. 1979. "Individuals and Social Structure:

Contextual Effects as Endogenous Feedback." *Sociological Methods and Research* 7:396–430.

Fishbein, Martin, and Icek Ajzen. 1975. *Belief, Attitude, Intention, and Behavior: An Introduction to Theory and Research.* Reading, Mass.: Addison-Wesley.

Fisher, Franklin, M. 1966. *The Identification Problem in Econometrics.* New York: McGraw-Hill.

Friedkin, Noah E. 1990. "Social Networks in Structural Equation Models." *Social Psychology Quarterly* 53:316–28.

Friedman, Milton. 1957. *A Theory of the Consumption Function.* Princeton: Princeton University Press.

Frisch, Ragnar. 1934. "Statistical Confluence Analysis by Means of Complete Regression Systems." Oslo, Norway: University Institute of Economics.

Gaertner, W. 1974. "A Dynamic Model of Interdependent Consumer Behavior." *Zeitschrift fur Nationalokonomie* 70:312–26.

Gamoran, Adam. 1992. "Social Factors in Education." In *Encyclopedia of Educational Research,* 6th ed., edited by M. Alkin. New York: Macmillan.

Gamoran, Adam, and Robert Mare. 1989. "Secondary School Tracking and Educational Inequality: Compensation, Reinforcement, or Neutrality?" *American Journal of Sociology* 94:1146–83.

Gronau, Reuben. 1974. "Wage Comparisons—A Selectivity Bias." *Journal of Political Economy* 82:1119–43.

Hanushek, Eric. 1986. "The Economics of Schooling." *Journal of Economic Literature* 24:1141–77.

Hardle, Wolfgang. 1990. *Applied Nonparametric Regression.* Cambridge: Cambridge University Press.

Hauser, Robert M. 1970. "Context and Consex: A Cautionary Tale." *American Journal of Sociology* 75:645–64.

Hayes, Cheryl, and Sandra Hofferth, eds. 1987. *Risking the Future: Adolescent Sexuality, Pregnancy, and Childbearing.* Washington, D.C.: National Academy Press.

Heckman, James J. 1976. "The Common Structure of Statistical Models of Truncation, Sample Selection, and Limited Dependent Variables and a Simple Estimator for Such Models." *Annals of Economic and Social Measurement* 5:479–92.

———. 1978. "Dummy Endogenous Variables in a Simultaneous Equation System." *Econometrica* 46:931–59.

Heckman, James J., and Bo Honore. 1990. "The Empirical Content of the Roy Model." *Econometrica* 58:1121–49.

Heckman, James J., and Richard Robb. 1985. "Alternative Methods for Evaluating the Impact of Interventions." In *Longitudinal Analysis of Labor Market Data,* edited by J. Heckman and B. Singer, Cambridge: Cambridge University Press.

Hendershot, G., and P. Placek, eds. 1981. *Predicting Fertility.* Lexington, Mass.: D. C. Heath.

Huber, Peter. 1981. *Robust Statistics.* New York: Wiley.

Hyman, H. 1942. "The Psychology of Status." *Archives of Psychology,* no. 269.

Ichimura, Hidehiko, and Lung-Fei Lee. 1991. "Semiparametric Estimation of Multiple Indices Models: Single Equation Estimation." In *Nonparametric and Semiparametric Methods in Econometrics and Statistics,* edited by W. Barnett, J. Powell, and G. Tauchen, Cambridge: Cambridge University Press.

Jencks, Christopher, and Susan Mayer. 1989. "Growing Up in Poor Neighborhoods: How Much Does it Matter?" *Science* 243:1441–45.

Jones, Steven. 1984. *The Economics of Conformism.* Oxford: Basil Blackwell.

Juster, Thomas. 1966. "Consumer Buying Intentions and Purchase Probability: An Experiment in Survey Design." *Journal of the American Statistical Association* 61:658–96.

Kalbfleisch, James, and Ross Prentice. 1980. *The Statistical Analysis of Failure Time Data.* New York: Wiley.

Koenker, Roger, and Gilbert Bassett. 1978. "Regression Quantiles." *Econometrica* 46:33–50.

LaLonde, Robert. 1986. "Evaluating the Econometric Evaluations of Training Programs with Experimental Data." *American Economic Review* 76:604–20.

Machlup, Fritz. 1946. "Marginal Analysis and Empirical Research." *American Economic Review* 36:519–54.

Maddala, G. S. 1983. *Qualitative and Limited Dependent Variable Models in Econometrics.* New York: Cambridge University Press.

Manski, Charles F. 1981. "Structural Models for Discrete Data: The Analysis of Discrete Choice." In *Sociological Methodology 1981,* edited by S. Leinhardt, 58–109. San Francisco: Jossey-Bass.

———. 1988*a*. *Analog Estimation Methods in Econometrics.* London: Chapman and Hall.

———. 1988*b*. "Identification of Binary Response Models." *Journal of the American Statistical Association* 83:729–38.

———. 1989. "Anatomy of the Selection Problem." *Journal of Human Resources* 24:343–60.

———. 1990*a*. "Nonparametric Bounds on Treatment Effects." *American Economic Review Papers and Proceedings* 80:319–23.

———. 1990*b*. "The Use of Intentions Data to Predict Behavior: A Best-Case Analysis." *Journal of the American Statistical Association* 85:934–40.

———. 1991. "Regression." *Journal of Economic Literature* 29:34–50.

———. 1993*a*. "The Selection Problem." In *Advances in Econometrics: Sixth World Congress of the Econometric Society,* edited by C. Sims. New York: Cambridge University Press.

———. 1993*b*. "Dynamic Choice in a Social Setting: Learning from the Experiences of Others." *Journal of Econometrics.* 58, 121–36.

———. 1993*c*. "Adolescent Econometricians: How Do Youth Infer the Returns to Schooling?" In *Studies in the Demand and Supply of Higher Education,* edited by C. Clotfelter and M. Rothschild. Chicago: University of Chicago Press.

————. 1993d. "Identification of Endogenous Social Effects: The Reflection Problem." *Review of Economic Studies* 60: Forthcoming.

Manski, Charles F., and Irwin Garfinkel, eds. 1992. *Evaluating Welfare and Training Programs.* Cambridge: Harvard University Press.

Manski, Charles F., and Daniel McFadden. 1981. "Alternative Estimators and Sample Designs for Discrete Choice Analysis." In *Structural Analysis of Discrete Data with Econometric Applications,* edited by C. Manski and D. McFadden, 2–50. Cambridge: MIT Press.

Manski, Charles F., Gary Sandefur, Sara McLanahan, and Daniel Powers. 1992. "Alternative Estimates of the Effect of Family Structure During Adolescence on High School Graduation." *Journal of the American Statistical Association* 87:25–37.

Manski, Charles F., and David A. Wise. 1983. *College Choice in America.* Cambridge: Harvard University Press.

Marsden, Peter V. 1990. "Network Data and Measurement." *Annual Review of Sociology* 16:435–63.

Mayer, Susan. 1991. "How Much Does a High School's Racial and Socioeconomic Mix Affect Graduation and Teenage Fertility Rates?" In *The Urban Underclass,* edited by C. Jencks and P. Peterson. Washington, D.C.: Brookings Institution.

Moffitt, Robert. 1992. "Incentive Effects of the U.S. Welfare System: A Review." *Journal of Economic Literature* 30:1–61.

O'Connell, M., and C. Rogers. 1983. "Assessing Cohort Birth Expectations Data from the Current Population Survey, 1971–1981." *Demography* 20:369–83.

Pollak, Robert. 1976. "Interdependent Preferences." *American Economic Review* 78:745–63.

Robinson, Christopher. 1989. "The Joint Determination of Union Status and Union Wage Effects: Some Tests of Alternative Models." *Journal of Political Economy* 97:639–67.

Rubin, Donald. 1987. *Multiple Imputation for Nonresponse in Surveys.* New York: Wiley.

Schelling, Thomas. 1971. "Dynamic Models of Segregation." *Journal of Mathematical Sociology* 1:143–86.

Sewell, William, and J. Armer. 1966. "Neighborhood Context and College Plans." *American Sociological Review* 31:159–68.

Stigler, Steven. 1986. *The History of Statistics.* Cambridge, Mass: Belknap Press.

Tobin, James. 1958. "Estimation of Relationships for Limited Dependent Variables." *Econometrica* 26:24–36.

Turner, Charles, and E. Martin, eds. 1984. *Surveying Subjective Phenomena,* vol. 1. New York: Russell Sage Foundation.

U.S. Bureau of the Census. 1988. *Fertility of American Women: June, 1987,* Current Population Reports, Series P-20, No. 427. Washington, D.C.: Government Printing Office.

Wainer, Howard, ed. 1986. *Drawing Inferences from Self-Selected Samples.* New York: Springer.

———. 1989. *Journal of Educational Statistics* 14(2).
Westoff, Charles, and Norman Ryder. 1977. "The Predictive Validity of Reproductive Intentions." *Demography* 14:431–53.
Winship, Christopher, and Robert Mare, 1992. "Models for Sample Selection Bias." *Annual Review of Sociology* 18:327–50.
Woittiez, I., and Arie Kapteyn. 1991. "Social Interactions and Habit Formation in a Labor Supply Model." Department of Economics, University of Leiden.

𝓧 2 𝓧

ON STRATEGY FOR
METHODOLOGICAL ANALYSIS

Clifford C. Clogg*
Gerhard Arminger†

Manski (1993) recommends a strategy for methodological analysis built on the notion that the "top-down" mathematical study of identification, not the more conventional "bottom-up" study of statistical models and inference, is the fundamental problem in the social sciences. He illustrates with identification analyses of four key methodological issues: (1) extrapolation (or prediction), (2) selection bias (or inference with missing data), (3) modeling relationships with endogenous social factors as predictors (hierarchical models for cross-level inferences), and (4) modeling the link between attitudes (or intentions) and behavior. His approach relies on nonparametric methods that give bounds on the expectations, probabilities, quantiles, or contrasts that would be estimated from sample data. We recommend Manski's article to all social researchers and methodologists. But we believe that statistical issues broadly conceived are just as pressing as the identification problem and cannot be separated from it.

One of the most important tasks of methodology is determining the limits, or probable limits, on what we can learn from available data.

*Pennsylvania State University
†Bergische Universität Wuppertal, Germany
Clogg's research was supported in part by the Population Research Institute, Pennsylvania State University, which has core support from the National Institute of Child Health and Human Development (Grant 1-HD28263-01). For helpful comments, the writers are indebted to Charles F. Manski and Peter V. Marsden.

Almost always this involves the translation of substantive ideas into mathematical and statistical formulations (or models) that tell us how we can know those limits. A mature methodology also tells us how to collect better data, how to measure the variables of interest, how to combine the measurements, and how to summarize or smooth the data to obtain valid inferences. Manski (1993) is one of the most stimulating papers on the general problem of methodological analysis in social research to have appeared in recent years. The work deals broadly with setting limits on what can be known without imposing strong theoretical or statistical assumptions.

We commend Manski for providing *constructive* criticisms of contemporary research practice in sociology and related areas. Many destructive criticisms have appeared lately. A case in point is Freedman's (1991a) complete rejection of virtually all social science modeling efforts. Freedman (1991b, p. 358), for example, concluded that we "need to take more seriously the job of comparing theory to reality," that "most interesting questions will not have empirical answers," that sometimes "only anecdotal evidence is the best that can be brought to bear [on particular questions]," and "at times" a 2 × 2 contingency table "or even a regression equation" might be useful. Like Freedman, Manski recognizes that the social science enterprise is intrinsically difficult, that the social sciences suffer from immaturity, that debates of all kinds are often colored by ideology, that cumulation of knowledge appears to be painfully slow, and that all too often the answers to hard empirical questions are covered over with a thick veneer of *statisticism*. By statisticism (a term first used by Dudley Duncan—see Duncan and Stenbeck 1989) we refer to the almost ritualistic appeal to sampling error and significance tests when sampling error is not the main problem, the preference for complex "structural" models with complex assumptions in cases where simple models might be more illuminating, and the fixation on computational mechanics rather than substantive concerns. It appears to us that Manski is also dissatisfied with statisticism in social research, but he nevertheless assigns a prominent role to statistical concepts, including inference and modeling. Manski's constructive survey of identification problems in social research shows that progress has been made and that further progress is possible.

1. MANSKI'S GENERAL APPROACH FOR METHODOLOGICAL ANALYSIS

Manski argues that the mathematical study of identification should play a more prominent role in methodological analysis so that researchers can agree on the limits of or bounds for what can be known from available data. Using the analog estimation principle, he can frame most issues of statistical modeling in terms of nonparametric estimation problems that follow more or less automatically from the population-level algebra used to establish identifiability conditions.

Using this general approach, Manski analyzes four of the most important methodological questions in contemporary social research. Identification problems of many kinds have been central to sociological methodology for a generation. It is useful to contrast Manski's general approach with more conventional approaches for the study of identification in sociology and related areas. In addition to the problems that Manski surveys, we could include traditional problems such as cohort analysis, the estimation of mobility effects, identifying latent distributions in covariance structure models, estimating reciprocal effects in panel analysis, intrinsic identification problems in factor analysis or latent structure analysis, and separating biological from environmental influences in models of heterogeneous frailty. Each of these areas, like the areas that Manski analyzes, has spawned a large literature that deals mostly with what can be identified and/or estimated in the particular context. But general guidelines for identification analysis as such have not been attained, to our knowledge, in these other areas taken separately or as a whole. Manski's general approach provides a common framework through which almost all of these other identification problems can be studied.

Manski's strategy for methodological analysis is based primarily on the "analog estimation" principle given, for example, in Manski (1988a^*). This principle guides us to identify population-level relationships using available side conditions provided by the theory of the subject, assuming that this theory actually provides something more than a basketful of variables that are supposed to be "related." Then the quantities of interest—not always parameters in the ordinary sense—are estimated from the available samples by substituting the sample analogs of the population quantities that appear in the population-level algebra. A simple example might be a situation where, in the population, a relationship is defined in terms of (some of) the moments of the distributions involved. In the sample, the "method of moments" that equates sample moments to population moments and "solves" for the parameters of interest might be the appropriate analog method of estimation. The method of moments as a general estimating principle has advantages and disadvantages. The chief advantage is conceptual simplicity: Procedures for combining or smoothing data in the sample follow from the population-level algebra. Disadvantages include, sometimes at least, nonuniqueness of estimates, inefficiency, and lack of smoothness (when judged at least against most standard competitors such as maximum likelihood, robust versions of maximum likelihood, and Bayesian estimation). (Manski (1988a*, chs. 4, 5) shows how many other standard estimators, such as maximum likelihood and least squares, can be derived from the analog principle. Then the problem would reduce in part to picking the most efficient estimator.) We believe that it is difficult if not impossible to make a logical separation between identification algebra and the statistical problem of smoothing data for inferential or descriptive purposes, and we illustrate this theme below.

2. PREDICTION AND EXTRAPOLATION

Much of Manski's strategy can be illustrated with the first case he considers, the problem of prediction. The question we raise is whether mathematical identification, as considered by Manski, is really the single core issue or just one of many issues. Stated another way, can we address the prediction problem without using statistical tools geared for the bottom-up analysis of inference from small or moderately large samples?

Suppose that a specified response variable Y is to be linked to a predictor X, and the goal is to find the "best" predictor of Y at one or more settings of X. To illustrate, suppose that X is discrete having J levels. Let $X_j, j = 1, \ldots, J$, denote the levels of X; this variable can be a nominal-level "group" variable or a quantitative variable with scores (in the sample) equal to x_j. To predict Y for values of X observed (in the sample), we can take sample means of Y for each

*References to work cited in Manski (1993) are marked with an asterisk.

setting of X, which is equivalent to maximum likelihood. That is, we can assume that $Y|X$ is normal; if Y is binary, the same result follows if $Y|X$ is assumed to be binomial. The nonparametric point estimates, in this case, are equivalent to very parametric estimators for an "unrestricted model." Note that a *statistical* criterion of optimality of point estimates has been used: minimize mean squared error. (Nonparametric estimators need not be robust estimators.) The analog estimation principle in this case leads to the standard result that says that group means (or proportions) can be estimated with sample means (or proportions).

The nonparametric method sketched above is not very good even if the sample is moderately large. But we cannot learn about this by working top-down from the population to the sample, using the analog estimation principle that suggests the above estimators. The observed values of $\hat{E}(Y|X)$ that are small will be too small, and the observed values of $\hat{E}(Y|X)$ that are large will be too large, if the number of groups or groupings exceeds three; for example, see James and Stein (1961). (Criteria of unbiasedness and/or minimum mean squared error are not the only criteria useful for analyzing prediction.) Ordinarily some sort of *smoothing* will be required that brings sample means closer to the overall mean. Empirical Bayes methods, among others, having been recommended for this case; for example, see Morris (1983). This simplest of cases indicates that population-level algebra does not always lead to sensible ways of combining information in a sample for the purpose of prediction.

When X is continuous, the "nonparametric" smoothing described in Manski's equation (2) has to be understood as a set of rules or assumptions on how to choose the bandwidth to perform local averaging. The procedures suggested by Manski can be viewed as regression counterparts of histogram construction or density estimation. At least some of the nonparametric methods surveyed in Härdle (1990*) use weighted averages, and various forms of trimmed means have also been used, for purposes of robustness. The smoothing method that should be used is not obvious in the context of a given sample of data, which is an important point.

Now suppose that X is (highly) multivariate, say a composite of K component variables (for example $K > 5$). If each component is discrete, with J levels each, say, then the possible number of response patterns is J^K, which can be quite large. Analog estimation principles here lead to the estimation of J^K cell means (Y quantitative) or cell proportions (Y binary), but this approach will often be useless if the sample size N is not very large compared to the number of potentially observable response patterns. Moreover, even if the sample size is large enough to support maximum likelihood estimation under the completely unrestricted model (placing no constraints on the structure of the cell means), it is usually the case that results will be difficult to interpret. Imagine a case with five predictors, each with five levels, giving 3125 cell means or proportions that must be repackaged, interpreted graphically, or smoothed ("modeled") somehow. This problem has led to many developments that have come to be regarded as standard methodology for statistical modeling. The most obvious case is the estimation, testing, and diagnosis of a restricted model setting many of the possible interactions to their null values. Some of the statistical benefits of smoothing with a model, including sharpening the inferences about prediction, are taken up in Altham (1984). Bayesian-type remedies that incorporate additional smoothing besides model smoothing are taken up in Clogg et al. (1991) for the case where Y is binary. Another extremely important aspect of the problem is assessing precision of estimates ("sampling variance"). The quality of point estimates cannot be assessed without a study of precision and/or the adequacy of approximate formulas that would be used to assess precision. It is often the case that nonparametric regression amounts to maximum likelihood estimation, assuming either normal or binomial or multinomial distributions for Y given discretized versions of the predictors, but we would usually want to assess variation, dispersion, or sampling error under alternative assumptions that are more realistic.

If X is multivariate but composed of all scalar variables, most methods of estimation, whether model-based or nonparametric, must impose some smoothing in order to work well in a sample. (We do not refer here to the type of smoothing that occurs when assumed population-level restrictions are imposed in the sample.) Note that the kind of nonparametric smoothing advocated by Härdle (1990*; see part III, "Smoothing in High Dimensions") requires really large samples, and most of our social science data bases are not large enough for that as yet. Perhaps researchers who want to employ the nonparametric strategy would do so by first reducing the dimension of the problem substantially—for example, by discarding many covariates or by forcing a statistical model on the data before estimating the parameters of the model nonparametrically. We do not doubt that in the future sensible algorithms and smoothing methods analogous to Manski's equation (2) will be developed for truly multivariate settings. To us, the issue is whether these methods will be superior to modern counterparts of parametric regression coupled with *serious* diagnostic methods.

We believe that the analog estimation principle leads to nonparametric methods of estimating that are impractical in common settings, to estimates that do not smooth or shrink the data enough in many settings. But the nonparametric method incorporates smoothing of data, just a different kind of smoothing (in multivariate situations at least) than would be done by fitting a regular parametric model. The term "nonparametric" has to be interpreted cautiously in the 1990s. Nonparametric does not mean assumption-free. *Something* is assumed in developing the smoothing methods. Manski's main point, however, is that it is impossible to say that estimates obtained from a sample of $(Y \times X)$ can be used to extrapolate to a hypothetical sample of $(Y \times X_0)$, where X_0 is not observed in the original sample. On this issue, there should be no disagreement between statistical modelers and nonparametric smoothers. We should either try to obtain the necessary data (not always possible) or examine the smoothness assumptions (model-based or otherwise) that give us inferences in the observed sample for values of X "close to" X_0. Better yet, we should consider a family of estimators from "reasonable" models and somehow take account of the inter-model uncertainty. It is also important to note that to obtain the necessary data covering the whole range of values or categories in X it might be necessary to appeal to other types of sampling besides random sampling or "representative" equivalents. Exploratory surveys might be useful to determine the range of X; stratified sampling with over-sampling in particular regions of X might also be necessary.

3. THE SELECTION PROBLEM

Manski's formal analysis of the selection problem is very instructive and ought to be required reading for both methodologists and researchers who routinely encounter censoring, truncation, or other missing data problems in their work. Most social researchers have been introduced to selection problems either through Heckman (1976*) or Little and Rubin (1987), or works derivative from these. As Manski notes, the literature derived from the Heckman approach focuses attention almost entirely on point estimates of means or point estimates of contrasts of means given by the parameters in particular "structural" models.

In contrast, the literature stemming from the Little-Rubin approach focuses attention on proper inferences. The main goal with this approach is to develop confidence intervals, standard errors or other measures of precision, and hypothesis-testing procedures that are valid given the uncertainty created by missing values. This approach can be applied either to the case where the missing data are missing at random (the selection is "ignorable") or to the case where the mechanisms generating missing values produce selection bias ("nonignorable" selection). Multiple imputation of "plausible values" for the missing values is just one of the statistical approaches recommended in this approach to measure the uncertainty produced by missing values (see also Rubin 1987*).

The bounds given in Manski's equations (9) through (11) and (13) can be used immediately to examine so-called selection biases for the nonignorable case. Note that the implicit strategy put forth here leads us to examine discretized versions of the response variable Y, and it can be used directly if Y is qualitative. That is, we do not have to assume that $Y|X$ is normally distributed, which is implicit in most of the applications of Heckman's approach, in sociology at least.

Consider first a simple case where variable Y is bounded in the interval $[K_0, K_1]$. This covers most interesting cases in social research: Occupational status measures are defined on the interval $[0,100]$, summated scales can be normed to the $[0,1]$ interval, binary variables are coded as 0, 1, etc. (The case where Y is earnings would be a major exception, but in the sample even the upper bound is essentially fixed, and if earnings are measured in a survey format by checking one of 10 to 20 possible income categories, then even this variable is strictly bounded.) Manski's method of deriving nonparametric bounds can be easily illustrated with the bounded-Y case. It is also easy to see the relationship between Manski's method of estimating bounds and more statistical approaches such as multiple imputation.

Suppose the data have been arranged so that Y is observed for the first n_1 observations but is not observed for the remaining n_2

observations; the total sample size is $N = n_1 + n_2$. A "nonparametric" bound on practically *anything* that would be estimated can in this case be obtained by replacing all missing Y values by either K_0 (to obtain the lower bound) or K_1 (to obtain the upper bound). (The terms "upper" and "lower" could be defined differently depending on which parameter or quantity is examined.) If Y is binary, for example, first replace all missing Ys by zero ($= K_0$); then replace all missing Y's by one ($= K_1$). Next calculate the quantities of interest for both augmented samples.

The potential value of bounds derived in this way–whether the bounds are "informative" or not to use Manski's terminology–can be illustrated in a simple case where no predictor is used. Let $\bar{Y} = \Sigma_{i=1}^{n_1} Y_i / n_1$ denote the sample mean for nonmissing cases. The lower bound would be

$$\bar{Y}_L = (\sum_{i=1}^{n_1} Y_i + n_2 K_0)/N = (n_1/N)\bar{Y} + (n_2/N)K_0,$$

and the upper bound would be

$$\bar{Y}_U = (\sum_{i=1}^{n_2} Y_i + n_2 K_1)/N = (n_1/N)\bar{Y} + (n_2/N)K_1.$$

This gives $\bar{Y}_U - \bar{Y}_L = (n_2/N)(K_1 - K_0)$ as the bound width, which is a measure of the information in the bound or the degree of uncertainty. If Y were occupational status as typically scored ($Y \in [0,100]$) and the fraction missing is $n_2/N = .3$, then the bound has width 30, which is probably not very informative. No one should quarrel with the definition or calculation of the bound in this simple case. Our point is that neither bound is credible because no one would assume that all missing values are either all K_0 or all K_1.

A more statistical approach is to randomly impute values for the missing Ys by drawing from an assumed distribution defined on the interval $[K_0, K_1]$. Drawing multiple values for each case (say five or more) makes it possible to quantify the uncertainty due to imputation. Clearly, assumptions have to be made; see Rubin (1987*). But the Manski approach sketched out above for an interesting special case is essentially the same as drawing *deterministically* once from one extreme and once from the other extreme. The bound width in this case is a very extreme bound on the uncertainty created by missing data. We think that this bound (a) may not be informative in interesting cases and (b) might be misleading because it is both deterministic and based on extreme assumptions.

It might be supposed that nothing else can be done without making assumptions. But this is not the case if the bounds are to be calculated in a sample. Even for unbounded Ys where the substitution method outlined above cannot be used directly, there are still several *statistical* issues that have to be resolved. These statistical issues should not be divorced from the mathematical manipulation of the basic identity in Manski's equation (4). Using Manski's notation, let $g(y)$ denote a *reasonable* function of the response variable Y, such as $Pr(Y < 10,000)$ if Y is earnings, giving $K_0 = 0$, $K_1 = 1$. (Essentially, the strategy is to form binary splits on the continuous variable that summarize the cumulative distribution function.) The bounds are not useful unless we can estimate them. For truly multivariate X, the sample analogs to the bounds in Manski's equation (10) are not obvious. We must specify how to *estimate* the two kinds of conditional probabilities given in these expressions. The "selection" probabilities $Pr(Z = 1|X)$ might be estimated with a logit or probit model for the "selection equation," and we must have a good model for this, which cannot be judged without statistical criteria. The probabilities $Pr(g(Y)|X,Z = 1)$ must also be modeled. These are nonparametric transformations of what is usually called the structural equation; the model for these quantities should be a good-fitting model, which cannot be judged without statistical criteria. Finally, the two sets of probabilities must be combined to form the lower and upper bounds, for each setting of X. There are many statistical issues in estimating the bounds, and, of course, the bounds will not be known in the sample (i.e., will have stadard errors). Finally, there are bounds for every setting of X, which may or may not translate into simple inferences or descriptions of the "nonparametric" bounds on the selection effect. It seems to us that these concerns apply also to each of the special cases of the selection problem that Manski analyzes (causal effects of treatments, switching regressions, etc.).

Besides the statistical problem of estimating the bounds and summarizing what they mean in a realistic situation with several (scalar-valued) predictors, it should be noted that the bounds are extreme bounds, derived from the extreme assumption that the missing Y values are either all equal to $K_0(= 0$ in the case of $g(y) = Pr(Y <$

10,000)) or all equal to $K_1(= 1$ for this particular $g(y)$). Most of us would surely not believe that the selection effect is uniformly distributed over the range given by the bounds, even if one could estimate them precisely. Choosing the functional $g(y)$, modeling the two conditional probabilities, evaluating precision of the relevant products of the estimates, and summarizing effects of selection in a truly multivariate setting are all statistical issues of one kind or another. This may be contrasted with the more traditional approach due to Heckman and others, which amounts to specifying a special form, given in Manski's equation (19), based on a strong type of prior information. It is possible that model-based approaches would be as practically informative in the *sample* as the bound-generation method put forth by Manski.

4. ENDOGENOUS SOCIAL EFFECTS

Manski's analysis of the problem of estimating social effects, such as group-level effects, is very important in our judgment. Because our purpose is to be critical, we will not say much about his treatment of this problem. In this case, we concede the point that serious work on the top-down analysis of identification is required before we can determine what our best multilevel or contextual-effects models are really estimating. Apparent identification *in a sample* for models that include endogenous, contextual, and individual effects is not a sufficient condition for logical inferences, which is one of the implications of Manski's argument here. The methodological literature on these topics, in sociology and education at least, has probably focused too much on sampling issues, the complications in error structure created by the sampling process, the correlation between parts and the whole, and the associated problems of smoothing random effects. (Coefficients in many hierarchical models of interest are random coefficients.) See Bryk and Raudenbush (1992) for the bottom-up analyses that have figured so prominently in this area of methodology.

5. ANALYZING "EFFECTS" OF ATTITUDES OR INTENTIONS

The difference between economics and sociology is most apparent in Manski's section 5, which draws heavily from Manski (1990*b**).

Manski refers to this section as the "identification of subjective phe-nomena," which might seem to imply that he is dealing with measure-ment of attitudes. But Manski is here concerned with the somewhat different problem of modeling the possible effect of a measure of a subjective state on an objective outcome or behavior. The case he considers is useful because it illustrates methodological strategy de-rived from a viewpoint quite different from that associated with the conventional social psychology of attitudes and behavior.

A host of methodological and theoretical issues arises in study-ing the link between attitudes and behavior. Not all of the issues reduce to identification analysis of the predictive value of an inten-tions indicator assuming rational expectations. Is voting a behavior subject to economic assumptions or just a crude binary measure of an attitude or intention? (Some so-called intentions are very much like behaviors, so a symmetric treatment of the two things is at least plausi-ble.) How can we measure an intention or an attitude? Most attempts to do this produce multiple measures, each grounded in a situation or condition—for example, measuring the attitude toward approval of abortion *if the woman is poor* compared to other (hypothetical or real) conditions. For intentions loosely tied to future behavior, specifying the time horizon can be useful, perhaps necessary. For the average (economic or sociological) man or woman, an intention to behave one way or another tomorrow is more reliable than an intention to behave one way or another ten years from now. What is called an intention is probably an attitude in the latter case. For example, asking a woman whether she intends to have a child would elicit different kinds of responses and have different reliabilities if the time frame were "five months from now" compared to "five years from now." It seems to us that most sociologists concentrate on measuring the attitude (multiple measures, ordinal intentions or attitude items, "filter" questions) and on specifying time lags or temporal dynamics, not all of which can be illustrated with the fertility-intentions item on the June Current Popu-lation Survey. Also, intentions or attitudes are important in their own right, not just as predictors of behavior: attitudes toward abortion and voting are two important examples.

Other differences in methodological strategy (or research ob-jectives) are also evident in this case. We illustrate by reframing the problem posed by Manski in what we believe is a more conven-tional (sociological) manner. Suppose the problem is to predict behavior (vote, have a child) at time T; call the binary measure of behavior Y_T. At the beginning, say time $t = 0$, a set of covariates is available, say X_0. Also at time $t = 0$ we have a binary variable A_0, which for now can be regarded as the attitude or intention indicator. Covariates ("new information") become available after the start, say $X_1, \ldots, X_{T-1}$ for a discrete-time or panel version. Some covariates (race or gender) might not change, but at least some are allowed to be time-varying (really new information). The problem can be illustrated by assuming that all of the data are available. (The setup is not unlike that used to study voting behavior. If Y_T is the vote on November 3 in the recent U.S. election, then we handle Ross Perot as a time-varying dummy variable.)

Most readers would automatically consider a model something like the following:

$$logit(Pr(Y_T)) = \alpha + \beta X_0 + \sum_{t=1}^{T-1} \gamma_t X_t + \delta A_0.$$

If repeated measures of A are available, they could be used as well, and, of course, A_t measures closest to T will be better predictors than the measures further back in time. The choice of the logit model is not particularly relevant. Other models (or "link functions") could be used, but the logit model is hard to improve upon for purposes of prediction in the usual statistical sense. We would analyze the value of A_0 as a predictor by estimating the above model (estimate δ as well as the other coefficients) and by considering restricted versions of the model (delete the X_t, for example). If there is a big gap between the start-up (time 0) and the end point (time T), it is not surprising to learn that A_0 has little or no effect. Nor would it be surprising to learn that A_0 had little or no effect once the extra information in the $X_t, t = 1, \ldots, T - 1$ is included. Surely most social psychologists would not be surprised to learn that A_0 is not a good predictor in these cases.

Manski's arguments almost reduce to the above set of findings, but not quite. Manski's person with rational expectations responds to A_0 in the following way. First, this person records $A_0 = 1$ (expects to have a child, or to vote for Clinton, at time T or thereabouts) if $P(Y_T|X_0) > \pi$ and records $A_0 = 0$ (does not expect to have a child, or to vote for Clinton) if $P(Y_T|X_0) \leq \pi$, for some constant π assumed to be the same for each individual. (Manski appears to assume *homogeneity* in probabilities or expectations throughout; relaxing this assumption for more realism appears to make the identification analysis quite complicated.) For simplicity, we have assumed that the information available to the rational person is the same information that is available to the analyst.

Suppose there are no background or other kinds of covariates at all. Then Manski would say that the logistic regression model is inappropriate because it would lead to the condition that $\alpha \le 0 \le \alpha + \delta$, if $\pi = 0.5$. Here δ is merely the logarithm of the odds-ratio between Y_T and A_0, and α is merely the log-odds that $(Y_T = 1|Z_A = 0)$, which would most likely be negative. If α is not negative, then perhaps we should question whether $\pi = 0.5$, or whether the π values are the same for each person, or whether the logit link function is appropriate.

Our unease with this formalization stems from the asymmetric handling of a subjective intention as compared to an "objective" factor. Suppose that A_0 is not intention or attitude but race, scored dichotomously, perhaps one of the background variables in X_0. Then we can go through the above algebra of threshold crossing as related to the same probabilities to deduce the same allegedly harmful restrictions on the logit model, the same difficulties in bounding the "effect" of race. Intentions, attitudes, or any other predictor variable such as race might be poor predictors of actual behavior, depending on the other predictors used and the time lag.

6. CONCLUSION

Our assessment has touched on only about 20 percent of the content of Manski's paper. We have good intentions (or good attitudes) about the other 80 percent; readers should assume that our subjective impressions are reliable predictors of our future methodological behavior in this case. We have for the most part concentrated on the logical necessity of both top-down analysis of identification and bottom-up study of statistical modeling or inference, using what to us are the best-case examples where this can be demonstrated. There are other methodological strategies that deserve comment in this context. We conclude with some of the ones that are also hinted at in Manski's paper or in our attempts to come to grips with it.

(1) Results from field experiments or quasi-experiments have

to be taken more seriously, at least as a strategy for evaluating assumptions that might be made with other types of data. Berk et al. (1992) is an interesting case in point. At the same time, we agree with Manski that "exclusive reliance on experimentation" is unwarranted, at least in many interesting cases. See Heckman and Hotz (1989) for one appraisal of the evidence in manpower training where modeling strategies of various kinds are used. But also see Efron and Feldman (1991) for a detailed analysis of how compliance in clinical trials—a best-case scenario for causal inference if there ever was one—creates both identification problems and statistical inference problems.

(2) The type of data available plays a major role in either identification analysis or statistical modeling. Most of us think in terms of large-scale data collection strategies that lead to the cross-sectional survey, the panel study, or event-history data. In sociology at least, what can be identified (or estimated) appears to depend critically on the type of data, particularly the degree to which the data allow for specifying dynamic processes. We think that the effort to identify and model temporal change has been productive. But there are many other types of data collection that can be used. Kish (1987) is the best source we know of on this subject. He shows that statistical issues in design for data collection have to be tied realistically to research objectives (what can be identified or what one wants to identify), which is a good lesson for all of us. There are more ways to "control" for confounders besides experimental manipulation and covariate adjustment (Kish 1987, ch. 4).

(3) Measurement must continue to be taken seriously. Measurement means first of all recording the right values for predictors or estimands; it often involves knowing how to ask the right questions in the right format, for whatever unit is analyzed. Developments in the art of asking questions in survey research show that progress has been made; for example, see Turner and Martin (1984*). But measurements often have to be modeled if for no other reason than to reduce the effective dimension of the data. A large literature on measurement models has developed because of this; for example, see Bollen (1989). The most questionable assumption in measurement models used widely in social research is the assumption of random measurement error. A Manski-style treatise on identification in standard measurement error models (factor analysis, latent structure analysis, etc.) would be most welcome. What can actually

be identified or estimated is surely important and determining plausible "bounds" ought to have priority. An example is Lindsay, Clogg, and Grego (1991) who show, in a special case, that we cannot identify more than $(J + 1)/2$ scaled latent classes with J dichotomous items. An assumption of a continuous latent variable is superfluous in this particular setting. This is a "nonparametric" finding much in the spirit of Manski. (This result derived more from analysis of likelihoods and conditional likelihoods than from purely mathematical analysis of the models as such.)

We ought to have a healthy skepticism about inferences based on assumptions of random measurement error. But when no prior information casting doubt on the assumption of random measurement error is available (or detectable in principle without extra data), we do not think that measuring methods that make this assumption are wrongheaded. Most so-called latent variable models with these assumptions built in can be viewed simply as methods for combining the information in multiple measurements (cf. Clogg 1992*).

(4) Greater attention should be given to modifying the *language* used to summarize statistical analysis. We think one of Manski's main contributions is a slang-purged dialect of what might be a clearer language for methodological discourse. But the language problem is severe and changes have to be made in many areas. An example illustrates what we mean. Suppose that one compares two models, the "full" model $Y = X\beta_1 + Z\gamma + u$, and a "reduced" model $Y = X\beta_2 + v$, which is often a good thing to do. In Clogg et al. (1992), the estimates of the two β's are compared, conditional on the full model; the null case where $\beta_1 = \beta_2$ is described as the situation where Z can be "collapsed." The language is important because it is "statistically correct" (a methodological equivalent to "politically correct" perhaps); the assumption-laden language of specification error or "omitted-variables bias" is not used. We think that many adjustments in the language used to convey findings from complex models have been made in recent years. For example, we do not hear so much now about "causal modeling" as a catchall term for covariance structure analysis. Perhaps more emphasis should be given to statistical models as descriptive summaries of data, as in the recent development of association

models and correspondence analysis (see Goodman 1991). This, too, represents a changing language of methodological discourse. Despite a few qualms here and there, mostly about matters of emphasis, we want to encourage readers to study Manski (1993) and his other work seriously. As he shows, there is much work to be done. With a combination of top-down, bottom-up, and through-the-sides methodological strategies, much more can be done.

REFERENCES

Altham, P. M. E. 1984. "Improving the Precision of Estimation by Fitting a Model." *Journal of the Royal Statistical Society, Ser. B* 46:118–19.

Berk, R. A., A. Campbell, R. Klap, and B. Western. 1992. "The Deterrent Effect of Arrest in Incidents of Domestic Violence: A Bayesian Analysis of Four Field Experiments." *American Sociological Review* 57:698–708.

Bollen, K. A. 1989. *Structural Equations with Latent Variables.* New York: Wiley.

Bryk, A. S., and S. W. Raudenbush. 1992. *Hierarchical Linear Models: Applications and Data Analysis Methods.* Newbury Park, Calif.: Sage.

Clogg, C. C., D. B. Rubin, N. Schenker, B. Schultz, and L. Weidman. 1991. "Multiple Imputation of Industry and Occupation Codes in Census Public-Use Samples Using Bayesian Logistic Regression." *Journal of the American Statistical Association* 86:68–78.

Clogg, C. C., E. Petkova, and E. S. Shihadeh. 1992. "Statistical Methods for Analyzing Collapsibility in Regression Models." *Journal of Educational Statistics* 17:51–74.

Duncan, O. D., and M. Stenbeck. 1989. "Panels and Cohorts: Design and Model in the Study of Voting Turnout." In *Sociological Methodology 1989*, vol. 18, edited by C. C. Clogg, pp. 1–36. Washington: American Sociological Association.

Efron, B., and D. Feldman. 1991. "Compliance as an Explanatory Variable in Clinical Trials" (with discussion). *Journal of the American Statistical Association* 86:9–26.

Freedman, D. A. 1991a. "Statistical Models and Shoe Leather." In *Sociological Methodology 1991*, vol. 21, edited by P. V. Marsden, pp. 291–313. Oxford: Blackwell Publishers.

Freedman, D. A. 1991b. "Rejoinder to Berk, Blalock, and Mason." In *Sociological Methodology 1991*, vol. 21, edited by P. V. Marsden, pp. 353–58. Oxford: Blackwell Publishers.

Goodman, L. A. 1991. "Models, Measures, and Graphical Displays in the Analysis of Contingency Tables" (with discussion). *Journal of the American Statistical Association* 86:1085–138.

Heckman, J. J., and V. J. Hotz. 1989. "Choosing Among Alternative Nonexperimental Methods for Evaluating the Impact of Social Programs: The Case of Manpower Training Programs" (with discussion). *Journal of the American Statistical Association* 84:862–80.

James, W., and C. Stein. 1961. "Estimation with Quadratic Loss." In *Proceedings of the Fourth Berkeley Symposium on Mathematical Statistics and Probability*, pp. 361–79. Berkeley: University of California Press.

Kish, L. 1987. *Statistical Design for Research.* New York: Wiley.

Lindsay, B., C. C. Clogg, and J. M. Grego. 1991. "Semi-Parametric Estimation in the Rasch Model and Related Exponential Response Models, Including a Simple Latent Class Model for Item Analysis." *Journal of the American Statistical Association* 86:96–107.

Little, R. J. A., and D. B. Rubin. 1987. *Statistical Analysis with Missing Data.* New York: Wiley.

Manski, C. F. 1993. "Identification Problems in the Social Sciences." *Sociological Methodology 1993*, vol. 23, edited by P. V. Marsden, pp. 1–56. Oxford: Blackwell Publishers.

Morris, C. N. 1983. "Parametric Empirical Bayes Inference: Theory and Applications." *Journal of the American Statistical Association* 78:47–55.

🌿 3 🌿

CODING CHOICES FOR TEXTUAL ANALYSIS: A COMPARISON OF CONTENT ANALYSIS AND MAP ANALYSIS

Kathleen Carley*

Content and map analysis, procedures for coding and understanding texts, are described and contrasted. Where content analysis focuses on the extraction of concepts from texts, map analysis focuses on the extraction of both concepts and the relationships among them. Map analysis thus subsumes content analysis. Coding choices that must be made prior to employing content-analytic procedures are enumerated, as are additional coding choices necessary for employing map-analytic procedures. The discussion focuses on general issues that transcend specific software procedures for coding texts from either a content-analytic or map-analytic perspective.

INTRODUCTION

Are female role models for children changing? Are concepts like freedom and love universal invariants across humans or are there cultural differences in what is meant when such concepts are used? Does the language of a group change as it becomes a profession? When do the advertisements of companies or the speeches of politicians signal real shifts in intent or focus and when do they reflect just shifts in the rhetoric? Questions such as these can be addressed by analyzing texts. Indeed, much social information is in the form of

*Carnegie Mellon University

texts such as answers to interview questions, books, articles, newspaper clippings, and essays. Such texts are a rich and valuable resource for understanding social behavior, but they are very difficult to analyze. Still, many questions are best addressed by examining texts, and in many cases an extremely large number of texts.

Textual analysis is vital to social science research, and a wide range of techniques have emerged. These include computational hermeneutics (Mallery 1985; Mallery and Duffy 1986), concordance analysis (for example, see Young, Stevenson, Nicol, and Gilmore's concordance of the Bible (1936) or Ellis's concordance of the works of Shelley [1968]); content analysis (see Weber 1984 for an overview; for a slightly different approach, see also Neuman 1989); conversational analysis (Sacks 1972); data-base techniques for conducting ethnographic and qualitative studies (vol. 7 of *Qualitative Sociology* 1984 was devoted to this issue; see also Blank, McCartney, and Brent 1989; Sproull and Sproull 1982; Qualis 1989); discourse analysis (Stubbs 1983; Polanyi 1985; Sozer 1985); linquistic content analysis (Lindkvist 1981; Hutchins 1982; Roberts 1989); semantic grammars (Franzosi 1990*a*, 1990*b*); protocol analysis (Ericsson and Simon 1984); procedural task analysis (VanLehn and Garlick 1987); proximity analysis (Danowski 1980, 1982, 1988; Van Meter and Mounier 1989); and story processing (for example, see Lehnert and Vine 1987; Mandler 1984; Dyer 1983). Each of these techniques has advantages that enable the researcher to consider the text in a certain fashion. While it is not the purpose of this paper to describe and contrast this plethora of approaches in detail, a few covering comments are appropriate.

Textual analysis techniques tend to be extremely time-consuming to apply. Many of the techniques are not automated. As a consequence, many researchers resort to handling only a few texts in a highly qualitative fashion. Despite their richness, such analyses typically lack precision and inferential strength. Alternatively, researchers engaged in more empirical investigations often "reinvent the wheel"—for example, developing yet another word counting program. Of the automated and semiautomated techniques, most are ad hoc, developed for a specific research group or applied to a specific problem, and they are not generalizable to different groups with different problems. Still other automated techniques, particularly those that focus on generating concordances or retaining the original text, often have substantial associated processing and storage costs. Many of the techniques developed have been applied only to a single text. Consequently, issues centering around the comparison of multiple texts have not been addressed. Finally, even those techniques that are automated and robust have rarely been designed to be used in conjunction with other methodological tools such as statistical packages.

In response to this morass of problems, attention has often been directed to the characteristics of a particular analysis technology rather than to the underlying choices that a researcher must make in order to use that technology. Such choices, however, are critical. They can dictate what technology is appropriate and affect the types of findings possible.

Within the social sciences, the dominant solution to textual analysis problems has historically been content analysis (Fan 1988; Namenwirth and Weber 1987; Garson 1985; Stone et al. 1968). Content analysis enables quantitative analysis of large numbers of texts in terms of what words or concepts are actually used or implied in the texts. Although extensively used, this approach has met with only limited success for a variety of reasons, including lack of simple routines, time-consuming data preparation, difficulties in relating textual data to other data, and a lack of a strong theoretical basis.[1] By taking a content-analytic approach, the researcher has chosen to focus on largely isolated concepts. This choice vastly simplifies coding, and it allows the researcher to address a variety of questions: How does the distribution of word usage change over time? Is the style of two texts similar in terms of the proportions of types of words? However, as will be demonstrated, the focus on concepts implicit to traditional content analysis often results in an overestimation of the similarity of texts because meaning is neglected.

An important class of methods that allows the researcher to address textual meaning is map analysis. Where content analysis typically focuses exclusively on concepts, map analysis focuses on concepts and the relationships between them and hence on the web

[1]For a more extensive discussion of the difficulties and advantages of this approach, see Weber 1984; Roberts 1989; Namenwirth and Weber 1987; and Neuman 1989.

of meaning contained within the text.[2] While no term has yet to emerge as canonical, within this paper the term *map analysis* will be used to refer to a broad class of procedures in which the focus is on networks consisting of connected concepts rather than counts of concepts. Alternate terms that have been suggested include cognitive mapping, mental model analysis, frame analysis, cognitive network analysis, scheme analysis, relational analysis, meaning analysis, and relational meaning analysis. Map analysis is a family of techniques, all of them emphasizing situated concepts and the relationships between them but varying in whether they look at relationships from a simple semantic (Carley 1986; forthcoming), proximal (Danowski 1982), or linguistic (Roberts 1989; Dyer 1983) perspective.[3] Like content analysis, map analysis enables quantitative analysis of large numbers of texts.[4] But unlike content analysis, map analysis has a strong theoretical base stemming from a variety of research: the construction of meaning (Fauconnier 1985); mental models (Johnson-Laird 1983; Gentner and Stevens 1983); knowledge representation (for overviews see Bobrow and Collins 1976 and Brachmand and Levesque, 1985); conceptual structures (Sowa

[2]Several researchers have employed techniques based on content analysis to extract "maps" limited in form to a particular type of relationship. For example, particular models of communication, sentence structure, or story format are predefined by the researcher and then texts are analyzed by coding the content into these predefined categories with predefined relations. The results of these analyses are typically treated in terms of "counts" of the predefined patterns that occur, not in terms of the web of meaning within the text. The map procedure described herein enables the researcher to extract these specialized "maps," but also to extract more generalized webs. A second example is "contingency analysis," where the researcher looks for the co-occurence of two concepts in some unit of text (such as 120 words) (Holsti 1954; Osgood 1959). This technique is similar to Danowski's (1980, 1982) proximity analysis. Unlike map analysis, these techniques focus on counts (in this case, of paired concepts) and not on the overall pattern of concepts.
    [3]Linguistic approaches are not typically viewed from this perspective because of their emphasis on story lines, the temporality of events, and/or procedures. Nevertheless, texts coded from a linguistics perspective can be represented and analyzed as maps, although this is rarely done. Rather, the focus is often on translation, abstraction, and story regeneration. This difference in emphasis, as well as the additional syntactic difficulties in coding texts from this perspective, often lead researchers to consider this approach as fundamentally different from the simpler semantic and proximity approaches.
    [4]Linguistic approaches, unlike either simpler semantic or proximity approaches, have rarely been used on large numbers of texts.

1984); schemas (Mandler 1984); social language usage (Dietrich and Graumann 1989; Kaufer and Carley 1993); personal knowledge (Polanyi 1962); social knowledge (Cicourel 1974); and cultural truth (Romney, Weller, and Batchelder 1986). Carley and Palmquist (1992) or Carley (1988) provide additional details on the theoretical base for the map analysis and procedures followed to code data that employ a simple semantic approach using one possible software package.

By taking a map-analytic approach, the researcher has chosen to focus on situated concepts. This choice increases the complexity of the coding and analysis process, and places the researcher in the position where a number of additional choices must be made regarding how to code the relationship between concepts. As I will demonstrate, these additional choices can also affect the degree of similarity found between texts. Because they focus on situated concepts, map-analytic techniques produce networks of concepts that can be examined at both a graphical and a statistical level. Given a set of maps and using either graphical or statistical techniques, we can ask a variety of questions: Do individuals' mental models become more complex over time (i.e., do they come to contain more concepts, more relationships, or a higher ratio of relationships to concepts)? Do concepts denoting emotions have different structural properties than do other concepts (i.e., do they have more relationships, different types of relationships)? Because map analysis makes it possible to examine the data graphically and statistically, the researcher can stay close to the text and so augment qualitative techniques and capture the precision and inferential ability of quantitative techniques.

Choices, such as whether to focus on isolated or situated concepts, with all the attendant options, transcend specific software procedures for coding texts and, in general, should be made prior to choosing a software package so as to ensure that the chosen software does not constrain the choices for the researcher. This paper discusses the coding choices that the researcher must make when taking either a content-analytic or map-analytic approach. This will lead to a discussion of the relative advantages of these highly useful techniques. In addition, the discussion will briefly touch on how to compare texts given the way in which they were coded using either content-analytic or map-analytic techniques. Comparison of coded texts, however, is a major issue and, for the most part, is well beyond the scope of this paper. Rather, this paper centers on those choices and issues that the researcher should be aware of prior to engaging in the coding and analysis of texts.

Clearly, all of the other approaches for textual analysis previously alluded to require the researcher to make choices that affect how the texts are interpreted and the potential results. As a consequence, each approach has its advantages and disadvantages. In this paper, however, the primary emphasis will be on content analysis and map analysis as they both share certain characteristics: They require the researcher to address many of the same coding and theoretical questions; they are automated or semiautomated; they facilitate automated comparisons of large numbers of texts; and they have a wide range of usage and applicability across the social sciences and humanities. Moreover, in terms of coding choices, the contrast of content and map analysis is particularly interesting as map analysis subsumes content analysis. I will explicitly discuss the additional analytical power of map analysis over content analysis and the associated additional analysis requirements.

Discussions of the coding and analysis of texts often include information on the procedures and tools available. In this paper, all coding and analyses are done using various procedures from the MECA toolkit (Carley 1990).[5] By analogy with statistical packages, MECA is a general "package" or "toolkit" for analyzing texts that contain a set of techniques—some of which retain the richness of more qualitative approaches, automate or semiautomate coding procedures, and enable quantitative analysis; many of which generate data in a form that can be used with standard statistical packages; and all of which can be used in conjunction with a qualitative or quantitative approach. Nevertheless, this paper is not about MECA, nor is its purpose to describe the tools.[6] Rather, it centers on questions that transcend particular tools: What is the difference between content and map analysis? What are the relative advantages of the two approaches? What are the issues underlying their usage? Be-

[5]The MECA tools are written in C and are available for many PC, Macintosh, and UNIX platforms. Additional information on MECA is available from the author. Many tools other than MECA are available for content analysis and map analysis.

[6]Additional details on MECA are available in Carley 1990a.

cause of this emphasis, details on what procedures were used are, when necessary, relegated to footnotes and the appendix. As noted, the ensuing discussion presents a series of coding choices that the researcher must make when analyzing texts. The MECA tools do not make these choices but allow the researcher to make any set of choices for either content or map analysis.

1. CONTENT ANALYSIS

Content analysis focuses on the frequency with which words or concepts occur in texts or across texts. This approach has been used to examine a variety of topics such as conceptual shifts in presidential addresses (Sullivan 1973) and cultural changes (Namenwirth and Weber 1987). The basic idea is to take a list of concepts and a set of texts and then simply count the number of times each concept occurs in each text. Differences in the distribution of counts across texts provide insight into the similarities and differences in the content of the texts.

Before continuing, it will be useful to define the term *concept*. A concept is a single idea, or ideational kernel (Carley 1986), regardless of whether it is represented by a single word or a phrase. Examples of concepts are "friends," "textual analysis," and "likes to play golf."

1.1. *Coding Choices*

There are a large number of choices that must be made by the researcher when doing content analysis—e.g., level of analysis and generalization. These choices—those discussed below as well as many others—affect what results are achieved, the interpretation of the results, and whether it is easy to automate the coding process. Further, it is important that the researcher be aware that not only are these choices being made because of potential methodological bias but also because such choices require semantic and cultural interpretations of the data (Cicourel and Carley 1990). Moreover, the researcher should be aware when choosing an automated or semi-automated procedure for conducting content analysis that many of these choices already may have been made.

1.1.1. *Level of Analysis—What Constitutes a Concept*

Different results will emerge if single words, as opposed to phrases, are used in the coding. Using single words is particularly useful if the researcher wants to contrast the results in a specific text or type of text with general usage. In contrast, phrases are useful when the researcher is interested in capturing broad-based concepts or terms of art in a particular sociolinguistic community (e.g., the phrase "Standard Operating Procedure" or "SOP" in the military).

1.1.2. *Irrelevant Information*

Should irrelevant information be deleted, skipped over, or used to dynamically reassess and alter the coding scheme (thus effectively treating no information as irrelevant)? Some methods for dealing with irrelevant information—such as deleting it from the text—can facilitate a more automated approach to content analysis by (1) minimizing storage and processing costs; (2) facilitating automatic coding of texts, and (3) generating a simplified text that can be visually inspected. Procedures for deleting concepts are particularly useful when the researcher wants to eliminate special notation, proper names, articles, and so forth. When there are large sections of text, such as paragraphs, that are simply irrelevant, it is more efficient to simply delete them with a text editor. There are two main difficulties associated with deleting concepts: embedding and interpretation. If the concept to be deleted is embedded in another concept (e.g., the concept "in" is embedded in "fits in with the hall"), then deletion of the embedded concept may interfere with locating those concepts that are to be coded. Thus deleting all occurrences of "of" may make it difficult to locate the concept "fortress of solitude." Deleting unwanted concepts also may make the resultant text difficult to read. Consider the following text:

> Killishandra and Ezra tailed the merchant through many corridors in order to find the robbers' lair. Unfortunately, he managed to elude them.

Now, let us delete all proper names, pronouns, conjunctions, articles, prepositions, and notation.[7] The resultant text is:

---

[7]This can be done, for example, by applying the MECA program DELCON to a file containing the text.

> tailed merchant through many corridors find
> robbers lair Unfortunately managed elude

Thus in many cases researchers may want to keep copies of both the processed and unprocessed text.

Determining what information is irrelevant is in itself a choice that must be made by the researcher. There are no set standards for defining information as irrelevant. Common standards are deletion of text not central to the research question and deletion of articles. A focus on "action" may lead to the deletion of proper names, pronouns, etc., as in the foregoing example.

1.1.3. *Predefined or Interactive Concept Choice*

When coding a text the researcher must choose between using a predefined set of concepts or developing a list of concepts incrementally during the process of coding. Unless the researcher is interested in coding all of the concepts that occur in the text, having a predefined list is a prerequisite for automated coding. Having a predefined list of acceptable concepts can be done by specifying either which concepts are to be coded or which are to be deleted.

1.1.4. *Level of Generalization*

Are all explicit concepts to be coded exactly as they occur in the text or are they to be recoded in some altered or collapsed form? Coding concepts as they occur in the text facilitates automation but at the cost of cross text comparability. Generalization—for example, when tense is ignored or all pronouns are converted to proper nouns— admits greater comparability across texts but at the cost of lost information. Choosing the right level of generalization is in many ways an art form dictated both by theoretical concerns and by the type of analysis in which the researcher wishes to engage. Some of the concerns in deciding the appropriate level of generalization can be illustrated using the following two texts:

> *Text A:* Killishandra and Ezra tailed the merchant through many corridors in order to find the robbers' lair. Unfortunately, he managed to elude them.

Text B: Blair and Tony followed the store-
owner across town to find the thiefs. Unfortunately,
he managed to lose them.

Both passages might represent to the researcher the idea of
"failed search." A content analysis using only explicit concepts and
no generalization reveals that the only concepts the two passages
have in common are "and," "the," "to," "find," "the," "unfortunately," "he," "managed," and "them." None of these shared concepts reveal the idea of "failed search." Now, let us allow generalization. The first thing to note is that there exists no single word or
phrase in these passages that corresponds to the idea "failed search."
Rather, this is a gestalt impression achieved by reading both sentences in each passage. Thus direct translation of words or phrases
into "failed search" will not reveal any similarity in the texts. The
general principle is that the more complex the concept that one is
trying to generalize to the less likely it is that specific synonyms will
appear in the text. Thus to extract more complex concepts, the appropriate approaches are those that involve locating the co-occurrence
of simple concepts or those that use rules to translate co-occurring
concepts into new concepts. (An example of this latter approach can
be seen in Fan 1988.)

A more bottom-up approach that separately locates the concept "failed" and "search" may be more successful. Make the following translations: the concepts "tailed," "find," "followed" into the
concept "search"; the concepts "elude" and "lose" into "failed"; the
concepts "merchant" and "store-owner" into "businessman"; and
the concepts "robbers" and "thiefs" into "crooks." The resultant
texts would appear as:[8]

Modified Text A: Killishandra and Ezra search
the businessman through many corridors in order to
search the crooks' lair. Unfortunately, he managed to
failed them.

Modified Text B: Blair and Tony search the
businessman across town to search the crooks. Unfortunately, he managed to failed them.

[8]This translation was accomplished by employing the MECA program
TRANSLATE. See appendix for additional information.

A content analysis of these modified texts reveals that these passages share not only the concepts described above but also the concepts "search," "businessman," "crooks," and "failed." The main problem is overgeneralization—that is, using categories of concepts that are so vague that important semantic distinctions are lost. For the above example, this might occur if all proper-person-names, pronouns, and types of people were converted to the concept "person," and all location names were translated to the concept "place." Applying this translation to the modified Text A results in:

> *Remodified Text A:* Person and person search the person through many place in order to search the persons' place. Unfortunately, person managed to failed person.

Such overgeneralization not only produces ludicrous sounding texts but can also make texts that are different appear identical.

1.1.5. *Creation of Translation Rules*
In order to systematically generalize concepts in the texts, it is necessary to create a series of "rules" or a thesaurus that translates less general concepts into more general ones. How these rules are created depends on the researcher's goals. There are two generic approaches: using an actual thesaurus and using a specially constructed thesaurus. Using an actual thesaurus has the advantage that the information is predefined. Such thesauruses are now available on line and their data bases can be easily converted to the form required for textual analysis. The disadvantage of this approach is that special slang or meanings within a particular sociolinguistic environment are likely to be missed. An alternative is to construct a special purpose thesaurus for the texts that will be analyzed based on detailed analysis of a sample of the texts. This guarantees that the thesaurus contains information to deal with the peculiarities of the particular sociolinguistic environment. Since only a sample of the texts is used, however, some possible synonyms may be missed.

1.1.6. *Level of Implication for Concepts*
Are the texts to be coded in terms of which concepts are explicitly present or in terms of which concepts are implied? Locating implicit

knowledge goes beyond generalization as it involves not just mapping one concept onto another, as in the case of generalization, but determining from a set of concepts what other concepts are missing. The ability to extract implicit concepts is vital to much research as meaning is lost when only explicit concepts are used (Ogilvie, Stone, and Kelly 1982; Woodrum 1984), or as Merleau-Ponty (1964, p. 29) contends: "The totality of meaning is never fully rendered: There is an immense mass of implications, even in the most explicit of languages." The level of implication affects the type of results, their interpretation, and the possible level of automation. For example, if only explicit concepts are used, then texts can be compared in terms of differences in style (i.e., word usage), and a completely automated procedure can be followed. In contrast, the use of implied concepts may allow the researcher to compare texts in terms of underlying shared meanings and social knowledge, but it may make it more difficult to completely automate the process. Locating implicit knowledge in the text is quite difficult, and limited success has been achieved using knowledge of the sociocultural environment that generated the text (Carley 1988) and the requirements of the story line (Schank and Riesbeck 1981).

1.1.7. *Existence or Frequency*
Should texts be compared in terms of simply whether or not a concept occurs or in terms of how frequently the concept occurs? While simple occurrence-based comparisons simplify discussions of co-occurrence and eliminate frequency biases due to syntactic requirements, frequency-based comparisons make possible discussions of saliency and emphasis. This decision can be put off to the analysis stage. That is, the researcher can code the data in terms of frequencies and then later collapse to existence.

1.1.8. *Number of Concepts*
How many concepts should be used in the analysis? This choice is not independent of the previous set of choices. In general, a total of approximately 100 to 500 concepts seems sufficient to code the knowledge on a specific topic in any sociolinguistic environment. For example, Carley (1984) used 217 concepts for describing talk about tutors among students engaged in a decision-making context; Palmquist (1990) used 212 concepts for describing talk in the conventional class-

room and 244 concepts in the nonconventional classroom; Cicourel and Carley (1990) used 174 concepts for describing the content of a story and its recall by children; Carley and Kaufer (forthcoming) used 310 concepts for describing information on drama and comedy; and Thomas (1991) used 395 concepts for describing the portrayal of robots in science fiction books. A set of 100 to 500 concepts generally represents a slight level of generalization, which means a decrease from the absolute number of concepts in the texts. Concordances, for example, which can contain every word in the text, may list thousands and even tens of thousands of words. Coding texts with many fewer concepts, such as less than 25, tends to obfuscate meaning. Coding texts with many more concepts, such as more than 1000, tends to prevent text comparison (unless one is interested in separating exact word usage). That is, while a total of 100 to 500 concepts seems sufficient to capture many of the nuances and individual differences within texts, it is still a small enough number that some generalization and some comparison in terms of shared meanings is possible.

These eight coding choices serve to illustrate the types of questions that the researcher must address when coding texts using a content-analytic technique. The choices that are made affect what tools are needed by the researcher and even the likelihood that there will be a tool available.

1.2. Advantages and Limitations

Content analysis is a fairly versatile technique that can be applied to a wide range of texts. It lends itself to automation, and, as I mentioned above, it is easy to create automated tools for locating those concepts that are explicit in the text. As a result, there are a large number of programs for doing this, including basic UNIX utilities like *grep,* large general systems such as the General Inquirer (Stone and Cambridge Computer, 1968; Stone et al. 1968), and assorted smaller or special purpose programs developed by individual researchers, such as those by Garson (1985) or Carley (1990). Such tools differ from each other primarily in the length of text that they can analyze, the complexity of the concepts they can locate, the number of texts they can process at once, and the hardware on which they run.

When the research question requires the extraction of information that is implicit only in the text, content analysis fares less well. Furthermore, it is doubtful that a simple solution within the scope of content analysis will be found. Indeed, the search procedures to explicate implicit information has been one of the central problems faced by researchers in artificial intelligence who are interested in locating the deep structure or complete understanding of texts (and in particular stories) (Schank and Riesbeck 1981; Bruce and New-man 1978; Lehnert 1981; Dyer 1983). When implicit as well as ex-plicit concepts are coded, it is possible to extract from the text a richer definition of meaning but at the cost of ease of automation (at least with current technology). One reason for this is that the extrac-tion of implicit concepts often requires impressionistic judgments (Holsti 1969; Krippendorf 1980), which when made by humans fre-quently result in coding mistakes such as errors of omission (see Carley 1988).[9]

Techniques developed by researchers in artificial intelligence for locating implicit meaning—such as conceptual dependency-based scripts (Schank and Abelson 1977), plot units (Lehnert 1981), and techniques for coding affect (Dyer 1983)—provide wonderfully de-tailed representations of the text's implicit content. These tech-niques, however, require such vast amounts of preanalysis of the texts by the researchers that they have been applied to only a few sample texts (i.e., to two or three) and thus, though they illustrate the power of the approach, are not practical tools for the researcher interested in coding and comparing vast numbers of texts. The need to analyze vast numbers of texts is the problem more commonly faced by social scientists. Thus, within the social sciences, it has become more common to use dictionaries to locate implicit knowl-edge. The compilation of such dictionaries or thesauruses is fraught with difficulties. (For additional details see Namenwirth and Weber 1987, ch. 8, and Carley, forthcoming *a*.) Even so, they tend to in-crease reliability (Grey, Kaplan, and Lasswell 1965; Saris-Gallhofer, Saris, and Morton 1978). One such difficulty is trying to distinguish between homographs—words that have the same written form but a different origin and meaning, as in record (transcribe), record (vinyl disk), and record (best past achievement). Rule-based approaches

---

[9]For a more detailed discussion of errors and the procedures for prevent-ing or detecting them via a grammatical approach, see Franzosi 1990*c*.

often are used (Dunphy, Bullard, and Crossing 1974; Namenwirth and Weber 1987; Fan 1988; Carley 1988) to overcome this and other difficulties. Another difficulty is that construction of dictionaries, thesauruses, and rule sets is a time-consuming process.

Even when implicit concepts are used, the main strength of content analysis is that it can be (although it is not always) totally automated and so applied to vast numbers of texts, thus making possible empirical cross-subject and cross-time comparisons. There is, however, a fundamental theoretical problem with simply extracting concepts. That is, the presence of concepts may not be sufficient to denote meaning as people can use the exact same words, even when they are not homographs, and yet mean very different things. In part, this is because the same words used in different contexts have very different implications. This difficulty can be addressed using procedures such as contextual content analysis (McTavish and Pirro 1990). However, even given functionally identical contexts, the problem still may arise. Consider the following texts, representing the views of two students about scientists:

> *Student A:* I found that scientists engage in research in order to make discoveries and generate new ideas. Such research by scientists is hard work and often involves collaboration with other scientists which leads to discoveries which make the scientists famous. Such collaboration may be informal, such as when they share new ideas over lunch, or formal, such as when they are co-authors of a paper.

> *Student B:* It was hard work to research famous scientists engaged in collaboration and I made many informal discoveries. My research showed that scientists engaged in collaboration with other scientists are co-authors of at least one paper containing their new ideas. Some scientists make formal discoveries and have new ideas.

Clearly the meanings of the texts are different. Yet this difference may not be revealed by content analysis. These two texts were

TABLE 1
Content Analysis Comparison of Two Texts

Concept	Student A	Student B
I	1	1
scientists	4	4
research	2	2
hard work	1	1
collaboration	2	2
discoveries	2	2
new ideas	2	2
formal	1	1
informal	1	1
coauthors	1	1
paper	1	1

coded using only the explicit concepts: I, scientists, research, hard work, collaboration, discoveries, new ideas, formal, informal, coauthors, and paper.[10] Table 1 contains the result. As this table illustrates, each concept is used exactly the same number of times. Not only is there no difference in which concepts are used, there is also no difference in emphasis (frequency with which the concepts are used). This is not to imply that content analysis can never locate differences in meaning. In fact, content analysts typically try to locate meaning shifts over time or across people by analyzing differences in the frequency with which different concepts are used across texts using factor and/or cluster analysis (Namenwirth and Weber 1987; Gallhofer and Saris 1988), analysis of variance (Potter 1982), or other statistical techniques. As noted by Namenwirth and Weber (1987, p. 195), content-analytic procedures are appropriate and work well at macro levels where the interest is in broad cultural concepts but seem less effective at the micro level where psychological or cognitive phenomena need to be examined. The comparison of the texts by Students A and B is at this micro level, and as Table 1 illustrates content analysis reveals no difference.

Why is the difference in meaning not revealed by this analysis? One reason is that individuals may differ in their definition of

---

[10]The MECA program CMATRIX2 for doing content analysis was used. See the appendix for additional information.

words. For example, Student A seems to have a more elaborate definition of "collaboration," involving both formal and informal interactions; Student B seems to define "collaboration" exclusively in terms of coauthoring. Or to draw on another rhetorical context, one political analyst's definition of a military crisis might require the presence of nuclear weapons, while another's might require only projected differences in available forces. A second reason is that the same word may be employed in different syntactic locations. For example, Student B uses the concept "scientists" in the first sentence as an object-noun in the prepositional phrase "to research famous scientists," whereas later, in the third sentence, Student B uses the concept "scientists" as the subject of the sentence "scientists make formal discoveries." A third reason is that the same word may be used in multiple semantic contexts. For example, these students are discussing scientists relative to the context of a class assignment and are focusing on generalities. Within the context of an NSF panel review, the discussion of scientists would assuredly be quite different.

Under each of these conditions, the difference in meaning is revealed not by differences in which concepts are used but by differences in the relationships between concepts. In terms of definitions, Student A links "collaboration" to "formal" and "informal" and links "formal" to "coauthors" and "paper," whereas Student B directly links "collaboration" to "coauthors" and "paper." In terms of syntax, Student A has a link from "research" to "discoveries" to "scientists," whereas Student B has a link from "research" to "scientists" to "discoveries." In terms of semantic context, Student A links "scientist" to "research" and Student B links "I" to "research." Thus at the micro level, particularly when the researcher is interested in differences in meaning, it is necessary to examine how people actually interrelate concepts, rather than just how concepts covary across texts, in order to preserve the semantic and syntactic structure of the text (Carley 1986; Carley and Palmquist 1992; Roberts 1989).

2. MAP ANALYSIS

Map analysis compares texts in terms of both concepts and the relationships between them. This approach has been used to examine a variety of topics, including voting behavior (Carley 1986), shifts in views toward research writing (Palmquist 1990), children's memory of stories (Cicourel and Carley 1990), across country and time differences in the World Bank's strategy (Saburi-Haghighi 1991), and shifts in the cultural perception of robots as evinced by science fiction writers (Thomas 1991). The basic idea is to take a list of concepts and a set of texts and then to determine for each text whether these concepts occur in the text as well as the interrelationships between those concepts that do occur. Frequency information also may be gathered. Differences in the distribution of concepts and the relationships among them across texts provide insight into the similarities and differences in the content and structure of the texts.

Before continuing, the terms *concept type, relationship,* and *statement* need to be defined. Concepts can be organized into categories or types such that one specific concept is an instance of another more general type; for example, "Corwin" and "Cassandra" are instances of people. A relationship is a connection between concepts, whereas a statement is two concepts and the relationship between them. Different relationships have different *strength, sign, direction,* and *meaning.* These characteristics are defined in detail in Carley and Palmquist (1992) and Carley (1988). It will suffice here to simply provide illustrations of each of these characteristics. Consider the following statements:

1. Cassandra loves Corwin.
2. Corwin loves Cassandra.
3. Peter likes Cassandra.
4. Corwin does not like Peter.
5. A table has 4 legs.

Statements 2 and 3 differ in the strength of the relationship—"loves" being stronger than "likes." Statements 3 and 4 differ in the sign of the relationship—"likes" indicates a positive relationship whereas "does not like" indicates a negative relationship. Statements 1 and 2 differ in the directionality of the relationship—in statement 1 the relation goes from Cassandra to Corwin and in statement 2 the relation goes from Corwin to Cassandra. Finally, statement 5 contains a different type of relationship than do all other statements—the relationship in statement 5 is one of possession, whereas the relationship in the other statements has to do with friendship.

2.1. *Additional Coding Choices for Map Analysis*

There are a large number of choices that must be made by the researcher when doing map analysis. As map analysis subsumes content analysis, all of the issues previously raised still apply and the same set of choices must be made. In addition, choices also arise concerning the possible concept types, the relationships between concepts, and the use of social knowledge. As with content analysis, different tools for doing map analysis may place different restrictions on the researcher as to which of these choices are available. For example, some procedures predefine a set of concept types or the meaning of relationships. Others, such as MECA, do not.[11]

2.1.1. *Concept Types*

The basic issue here is how many categories or types of concepts should be used. The researcher needs to choose how many types of concepts are to be used. In addition, if more than one type is needed, the researcher must develop a set of concept types that span the set of categories of interest in that research. Despite the work by numerous researchers in multiple fields, no single overarching set of concept types has emerged that is valuable across all research questions. In many studies, one category of concepts is sufficient. The only justification for multiple categories of concepts occurs if there are predefined classes of concepts, each of which the researcher wants to examine separately. If there are no predefined categories then only one category of concepts should be used and concepts should be classified into categories after the coding.

The advantage of a single concept type is that it facilitates rapid and more automated coding. This is particularly important for exploratory research or when the researcher wants the data to dictate what is coded. Palmquist (1990) examined the difference in learning in two classrooms in which "research writing" was taught. Because the study was highly exploratory, all concepts were treated as though they were in a single category. Using multiple concept types, however, can facilitate analysis as it allows the researcher to examine

[11]In order to use the MECA procedures for coding maps, the researcher must first use STARTUP, the MECA routine for storing the set of coding choices being made. See appendix for additional details. See also Carley and Palmquist (1992) for an extended example.

differences between categories of knowledge. This is usually more appropriate when the researcher has either predetermined concepts, or has a theoretical interest that specifies different claims for different types of knowledge. For example, Carley (1984, 1986) used map-analytic techniques to examine differences in students' views of what they wanted in a tutor. In this study, four categories of concepts were used because of the different roles that the types of knowledge were thought to play in decision making: aspects of the tutoring job, requirements of the tutoring job, facts about candidates, and qualities of candidates. As another example, Cicourel and Carley (1990) used map-analytic tools to examine the role of social knowledge in children's memory of stories. They utilized six concept types corresponding to story components: people, places, actions, objects, adjectives, and statements. They note that categorizing concepts into these types is a de facto recognition by the researcher of knowledge that is social—that is, shared by the researcher, the story author, and the readers of the story.

2.1.2. Level of Analysis—What Constitutes a Relationship
When a map-analytic approach is taken, the researcher can choose how much information to preserve about the relationship. The researcher may choose to simply note that two concepts are related. This choice implies a specific series of secondary choices—all relationships are of the same strength, all have the same sign, all are bidirectional, and all have the same meaning (i.e., differences in meaning are not preserved). This choice is appropriate when the researcher is engaged in exploratory research or when there are no theoretical reasons to distinguish between types of relationships. For example, Thomas (1991) examined shifts in Americans' perception of "robots" as portrayed in American science fiction literature in the past 50 years. Because this study was highly exploratory and because only a few texts were being analyzed, Thomas used relationships to simply denote the existence of a link between two concepts. Similarly, Palmquist (1990) also used existence relationships. Alternatively, the researcher may choose to preserve a large amount of information about each relationship, including its strength, sign, direction, and meaning. Each of these secondary choices will now be discussed.

1. *Strength.* The issue is whether relationships should vary in strength. When all relationships are the same strength, then maps are easier to compare, and many graph comparison techniques are applicable. Having multiple strengths, however, lets the researcher retain more information and makes the resultant maps a closer replica of the underlying text. Such an approach is especially useful when the researcher wants to use the coded maps to augment more qualitative discussions. Having strengths is also useful when the researcher is interested in the emphasis that is placed on the relationship between concepts. For example, Carley (1986) used a range of 1 to 3 to denote whether the relationship was implied in the text (1), stated explicitly (2), or emphasized (3). Strength can also be used to denote frequency. For example, Danowski (1982) conducts map analyses using proximity and defines the strength of the relationship as simply a count of the number of times the two concepts are proximal within the text.

2. *Sign.* Sign is related to whether the researcher can identify a positive or negative relationship between the two concepts. Consider the statements "Jess fits in" and "Frank does not fit in." The first statement could be coded as a positive link between "Jess" and "fits in." The second statement could be coded as a negative link between "Frank" and "fits in." Or, the second statement could be coded as a positive link between the concept "Frank" and the concept "does not fit in." The difference here is in the location of the negation. In the first example, the negation is placed on the relationship, thus implying that "fits in" and "does not fit in" are conceptual opposites. In the second case, negation is directly attached to the concept implying that the concepts "fits in" and "does not fit in" are simply different concepts. Which is the more appropriate coding scheme for texts is a point for future research. Placing negation on the concepts facilitates map comparison, however. For example, Carley (1984; 1986) used both positive and negative relationships and so had to define procedures for comparing statements with the same concepts but relationships of different signs. In contrast, Palmquist (1990), Cicourel and Carley (1990), and Thomas (1991) used only positive relationships and, where necessary, used "negative"

concepts. As a result, it was easy to combine and compare maps to examine differences across texts. As a final note, in some cases sign is not an issue. For example, Carley and Kaufer (forthcoming) coded general social knowledge about "Comedy" and "Drama" as available in a thesaurus. Since only synonyms were coded, negation was not an issue; that is, in this case all relationships can be thought to denote the positive sentiment "is a synonym of," and since only synonyms were used there was no need to denote the negative "is not a synonym of."

3. *Direction.* Direction has to do with whether the first concept is seen to have some type of "prior" relationship to the second concept. Various types of prior relationship can be thought of— for example, "*a* implies *b*," "*a* comes before *b*," "if *a* is true, then *b* is true," and "*a* qualifies *b*." Choosing to ignore directionality (or equivalently to treat all relationships as bidirectional) is appropriate when the research is exploratory and facilitates automatic coding. When a proximity approach is taken directionality is often ignored. For example, Palmquist (1990) treated all relationships as bidirectional. In contrast, coding directionality can provide information about the way in which the impact of new information propagates through the network and affects decisions (Carley 1984), and the structure of meaning. If a researcher is interested in separating procedural or temporal knowledge from declarative or definitional knowledge, eliminating directionality can make it impossible to locate these differences.

4. *Meaning.* Relationships can also vary in meaning. In many studies, one type of relationship (one category of "meaning") is sufficient as the dominant interest of the researcher is simply to determine which concepts are related. For example, when a proximity approach is taken, all relationships are of the type "is proximal to." In fact, in many of the studies previously mentioned (Thomas 1991; Palmquist 1990; Saburi-Haghighi 1991; Carley and Kaufer, forthcoming), there was no need for preserving any aspect of the relationship other than its strength, direction, and sign. Nevertheless, preservation of meaning may be especially useful in story understanding and in examining semantic structures where it is important to distinguish among temporal, logical, and definitional linkages. In these cases the researcher must develop a set of relationship types that span the set of "meanings" of interest in that

research. This is analogous to the selection of concept types by the researcher. And, as with concept types, despite the work by numerous researchers in multiple fields, no single overarching set of relationship types or meanings has emerged that is valuable across all research questions. For example, Carley (1988) defined three types of relationships—definitives, logicals, and simples—in order to use the expert's knowledge of the sociolinguistic environment to automatically explicate information implicit in the text. As another example, Cicourel and Carley (1990) were interested in distinguishing those statements that were spontaneously provided by the subjects and those that occurred only after prompting. They thus employed two types of relationships: "normal" and "after prompting" (Cicourel and Carley 1990).

2.1.3. *Level of Implication for Relationships*
The researcher also needs to determine the desired level of implication for relationships. For example, are relationships to be coded only when explicit words occur in the text linking two concepts (as "is" links "Liesel" and "boy's mother" in the statement "Liesel is the boy's mother")? Or are relationships to be coded even when the link is implied (as in the statement "Liesel, the boy's mother")? Coding only explicit relationships facilitates automatic coding and may minimize errors due to the coder "reading in" information into the text. In contrast, coding implicit relationships provides a richer, more detailed map and facilitates cross text comparison.

2.1.4. *Social Knowledge*
The researcher needs to determine whether social knowledge is to be included in the coded texts. Social knowledge can be defined as knowledge that one can reasonably expect all members of the sociolinguistic environment to share—for example, that parents are older than their children.[12] Clearly, the determination of what knowledge is social knowledge varies across cultures and time. Vast quantities of social information are implicit within any text, regardless of the source—interviews, children's stories, or newspaper articles. Different members of the same sociolinguistic environment may have different proclivities for explicating such knowledge in the texts they

---

[12]For more extensive discussions of social knowledge, see Carley (forthcoming b).

generate. Thus adding social knowledge can actually bring out the hidden similarities in texts. Consider the following two passages:

Joe's a gnerd who always studies in the library.

Joe's a gnerd who always studies in the library and doesn't fit in. His door is never open, he works too hard.

Coding only the explicit knowledge leads to maps that appear very different, as illustrated in Figure 1.[13]

For ease of illustration, this coding was done using the following choices: only one type of concept used; relationships can differ in direction and sign; and all relationships are of the same type and same strength. Furthermore, relationships are coded based on whether there is an implicit semantic connection between the concepts. When a semantic approach is taken, each statement forms a simple sentential unit—such as "if a then b" or "a is an example of b" or "a ‹verb› b."[14] Since all relationships are treated as being of the same type, the specific semantic connection between the two concepts is not preserved. These particular coding choices tend to generalize relationships and emphasize the degree of similarity between the texts. Because these particular coding choices will be used in later illustrations in this paper, this set of choices will be referred to as the "simple semantic method."

As Carley argued (1984, 1988), within the sociolinguistic environment that produced these texts there is a set of common understandings or social knowledge that the students tend to take for granted. These include (but are not limited to) the following:[15]

[13]These texts were first coded using CODEMAP, which produced a data base for each text. The actual drawings were produced using a two-step process. First, the data bases for the maps were run through the MECA program DRAWMAP, which generates a MacDraw data base file. These files were then ported to MacDraw, where they were annotated to produce the figures seen here. See appendix for additional details.

[14]For additional information on two different procedures for coding relationships from a semantic perspective, see Cicourel and Carley (1990).

[15]Each of these statements is, in Carley's (1988) terms, a definitive and so indicates an implication that is agreed upon by all individuals in the group. They have been written here as English statements for ease of understanding, rather than in the format used by Carley.

MAP 1: Joe's a gnerd who always studies in the library.

Joe ——➤ gnerd ——➤ studies in the library

MAP 2: Joe's a gnerd who always studies in the library and doesn't fit in. His door is never open, he works too hard.

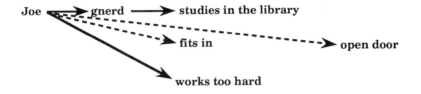

Shared Concepts 3
Shared Statements ... . (1 bidirectional= 2 relations) 2
Shared Concepts given Shared Relationships 2
Concepts Map-1 Only.................................. 0
Concepts Map-2 Only.................................. 3
Statements Map-1 Only............................... 0
Statements Map-2 Only............................... 3

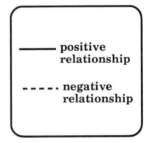

FIGURE 1. Maps coded using only explicit information.

- If someone studies in the library, then his/her door is never open.
- If someone studies in the library, then he/she is not accessible.
- If someone has an open door, he/she interacts with students.
- If someone is a gnerd, then he/she works too hard.
- If someone is a gnerd, he/she is not friendly.
- If someone is a gnerd, he/she interacts with students.

• If someone interacts with students, he/she fits in.
• If someone interacts with students, he/she is friendly.
• If someone is friendly, he/she interacts with students.
• If door is open, then he/she is accessible.
• If he/she is accessible, then door is open.

This social knowledge lies behind the texts. Making this implicit information explicit demonstrates that there is a great deal of shared meaning between the two texts (Figure 2).[16] As with Figure 1, a simple semantic method was used to code the maps in Figure 2. For further discussion of a procedure for making such implicit knowledge explicit, see Carley 1988.

Explicating maps using social knowledge can, to an extent, overcome underestimations of similarity in texts. Furthermore, such explication can minimize the need to extensively train coders, thus allowing the researcher to utilize more "novice" labor, and it can increase the reliability and validity of the coded maps (Carley 1988). Nevertheless, such a procedure is not a panacea. Misestimation of social knowledge can make texts appear more similar than they truly are. In addition, the researcher must be careful not to be overly normative in making judgments about social knowledge. Comparison of verbal discourse strategies with written texts from the same speech community can be helpful here. In addition, there are many research questions where utilization of such a procedure would be inappropriate. Such a case may occur if the researcher is interested in comparing a "naive" respondent's viewpoint and that of an expert, which means that the utilization of expert knowledge to explicate maps is incorrect. For example, when Palmquist (1990) compared students' conceptions of research writing with the teacher's conception, explication of the students' maps with the expert's (in this case the teacher's) knowledge would have been inappropriate. A second such case occurs if the researcher is interested in comparing how different individuals portray their information. In this case the correct analysis uses information explicit in the text and not the underlying social knowledge.

---

[16]These modified or explicated maps were produced using the MECA program SKI. See the appendix for additional details.

MAP 1: Joe's a gnerd who always studies in the library.

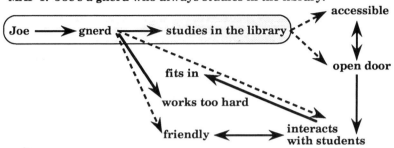

MAP 2: Joe's a gnerd who always studies in the library and doesn't fit in. His door is never open, he works too hard.

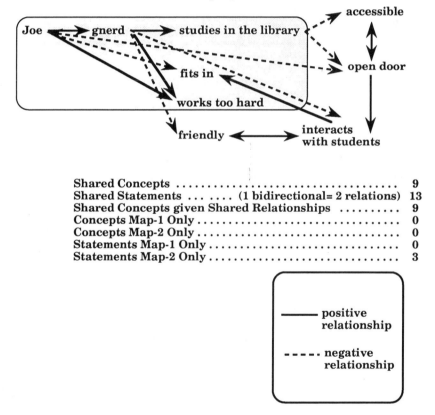

```
Shared Concepts ....................................  9
Shared Statements ... ....  (1 bidirectional= 2 relations)  13
Shared Concepts given Shared Relationships ..........  9
Concepts Map-1 Only.................................  0
Concepts Map-2 Only.................................  0
Statements Map-1 Only...............................  0
Statements Map-2 Only...............................  3
```

——— positive relationship

- - - - - negative relationship

FIGURE 2. Maps recoded using implicit social knowledge.

2.2. *Advantages and Limitations*

There are several advantages to map-analytic techniques: (1) They allow the researcher to examine the micro-level differences in individuals' maps and to get at differences in meaning. (2) They subsume content-analytic techniques; thus, if the researcher starts by coding maps, it is always possible to backtrack and do a more traditional content analysis. (3) They facilitate examining hierarchies of meaning, as happens when categorizing concepts or types or relationships. (4) They typically provide researchers with the ability to stay close to the text but also to move beyond it as they are given the luxury of alternating between actually examining what specific concepts and relationships occur in a text and statistically analyzing the coded form of the texts. In addition, since all knowledge is coded in terms of statements, it is in many cases possible to interpret these statements (if the relationships are unidirectional) as rules, and thus as the knowledge base for an expert system. This in turn facilitates examining the decision-making process implicit within the map. A final advantage is that by focusing on the structure of relations between concepts and relations, and the relationships between concepts, the attention of the researcher is directed toward thinking about "what am I really assuming in choosing this coding scheme?" Consequently, researchers may be more aware of the role that their assumptions are playing in the analysis and the extent to which they want to, and do, rely on social knowledge.

A disadvantage to map-analytic techniques is that they are harder to automate. In particular, it is harder to automate the coding of relationships than it is to automate the coding of concepts. Coding relationships appears to require a higher level of interpretation than the coding of concepts. If this is the case, then analyses based on maps rather than just concepts may be more prone to error. Whether this is true, however, is a point for future research.

3. COMPARISON OF ANALYSIS TECHNIQUES

In this section various additional comparisons are made in order to further illustrate how different coding choices affect the results of textual analyses. First, content analysis and map analysis are contrasted, thus illustrating the effect of choosing to examine only concepts or concepts and relations. Second, multiple map-analytic approaches, each of which uses a different procedure for defining the relationship between concepts—semantic-based, proximity-based, and story-line–based—are contrasted. Finally, concordance analysis is examined in order to illustrate the effect of using a reduced form of the text for doing either content analysis or map analysis.

3.1. *Content Analysis and Map Analysis*

Both content-analytic and map-analytic techniques can be used on the same texts. In such cases, as was suggested earlier, each technique may lead to a different interpretation of the texts. The extent and nature of these differences are going to depend on the coding decisions made by the researcher, as in the example cited earlier, where the texts of Students A and B, which discuss scientists, were coded from a content-analytic perspective using only explicit concepts. This demonstrated that two texts, though differing in meaning, could appear identical when only concepts were coded. These two texts were recoded as maps, using the simple semantic method previously described.[17] The resultant maps appear at the top of Figure 3 and statistical information on the two maps appears at the bottom of this figure.[18] Note that when relationships are ignored, the information for shared concepts is identical to the information garnered via traditional content analysis (refer back to Table 1).

In contrast to the content-analytic case, when a map-analytic approach is taken, the two texts appear quite different. In fact, although they still share all the same concepts, they share only five of the statements. When we consider only these five shared statements, we find that the two students have only five concepts in common. In other words, although they use the same words, they use only five of the concepts in anything approaching the same way. Specifically, Student A reports on what "I" found about "scientists" and has an elaborated notion of "scientists" as doing "research." Thus "research" is needed to make "discoveries." In contrast, Student B focuses on the "research" conducted by "I" and does not see "scientists" as doing "re-

---

[17]The MECA procedure CODEMAP was used to code the text as a data base from which the figure was produced using DRAWMAP.

[18]Statistical information was collected using the MECA program COMPRA. See appendix for details.

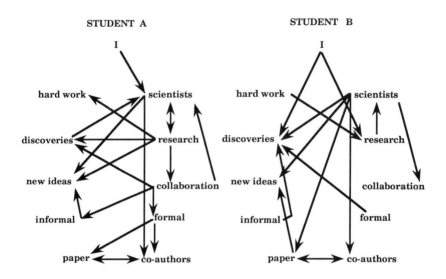

STUDENT A   STUDENT B

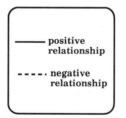

Shared Concepts 11
Shared Statements .... (1 bidirectional= 2 relations) 5
Shared Concepts given Shared Relationships 5
Concepts Student A Only 0
Concepts Student B Only 0
Statements Student A Only 13
Statements Student B Only 9

FIGURE 3. Coded maps for comparison with content analysis.

search" but as simply making "discoveries." For Student A, the key theoretical constructs (most lines in and out of the concept node) are "scientists," "research," and "collaboration"; whereas for Student B, the key constructs are "scientists" and "discoveries."

3.2. *Proximity Analysis*

When a map-analytic perspective is taken, relationships can be coded from a variety of approaches other than the semantic approach described above. For example, the researcher might employ a proximal (Danowski 1982) or temporal (Roberts 1989; Dyer 1983, for example) approach. When a proximity approach is taken, a relationship is placed between two concepts in the event that they occur within some prespecified window (for example, within the same sentence). While using proximity to define relationships greatly facilitates automatic coding, it can obscure meaning. Consider the following two passages:

The president fired James and promoted Karin.

The president fired Karin and promoted James.

Now assume that a preparser is being used such that all articles and conjunctions are deleted.[19] Then, using the sentence as the "window" length, a proximity approach would locate maps like those in Figure 4. Here, since all the same words occur within each sentence, the maps for both sentences are identical. Moreover, the proximity approach cannot automatically distinguish the sign of a relationship, nor the direction (other than by word order), nor the meaning. The strength of the relationship can be, but need not be, measured by the number of times the two concepts are proximal. When a less automated approach like that proposed by Carley (1986; 1988; 1990*a*) is used, distinctions between relationships can be drawn. For example, these two texts were coded using the simple semantic method and the resultant maps are displayed in Figure 5. Under this coding procedure, the maps for both sentences are different, with directionality indicating who did the firing/promoting and who was fired/promoted and with the sign showing that firing and promoting are in some sense "opposite" relationships.

[19]Within the MECA package, DELCON could be used for this purpose.

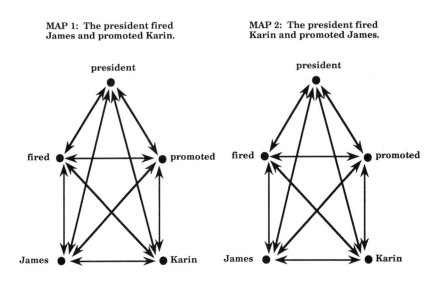

MAP 1: The president fired
James and promoted Karin.

MAP 2: The president fired
Karin and promoted James.

Shared Concepts	5
Shared Statements ... . (1 bidirectional= 2 relations)	20
Shared Concepts given Shared Relationships	5
Concepts Map 1 Only...............................	0
Concepts Map 2 Only...............................	0
Statements Map 1 Only.............................	0
Statements Map 2 Only.............................	0

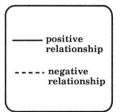

—— positive
relationship

- - - - negative
relationship

FIGURE 4. Maps produced by proximity analysis.

3.3. *Linguistic Approaches*

Now let us contrast map-analytic techniques that take a semantic
approach with more linguistic, story-line, approaches that, though
concerned with semantics, emphasize syntax—linguistic content
analysis (Lindkvist 1981; Hutchins 1982; Roberts 1989), semantic

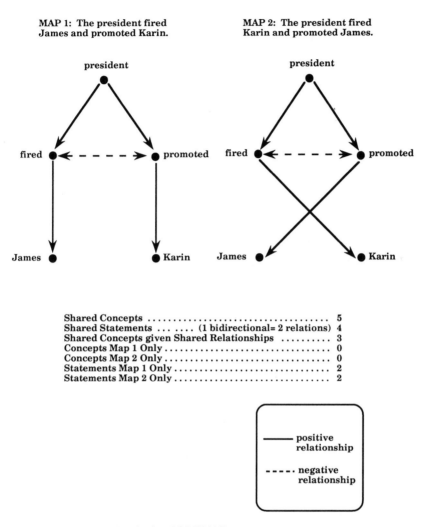

FIGURE 5. Maps produced using CODEMAP.

grammars (Franzosi 1990*a, b*), and story processing (Lehnert and Vine 1987; Dyer 1983, for example). All such approaches produce networks of concepts or maps and can be thought of as map-analytic approaches. The major difference between these approaches and the purely semantic approach described above is one of emphasis. Map-analyses that take a semantic approach emphasize the conceptual or definitional relationships between concepts, whereas a story-line approach would emphasize the sequential story relationships.

This difference can be seen by contrasting the way these two approaches would code the sentence "Cassi throws a ball to Corwin." A story-line approach always, regardless of the focus of the research, would code this sentence in a form like—‹sending-actor› Cassi ‹action› throws to ‹object› ball ‹object-modifier› a ‹receiving-actor› Corwin. In terms of the map representation, there are in this example five types of concepts: sending-actor, action, object, object-modifier, and receiving-actor. In contrast, the coding resulting from a purely semantic approach depends on the researcher's focus. If the focus is on locating definitions of "ball," then only a single type of concept might be used and only a single statement coded containing the concepts "ball" and "throw" and a relation from ball to throw. Whereas, if the focus is on examining Cassi's actions, then the researcher might use two types of concepts, "actors" and "actions," and code two statements, the first with a relationship from "actor:Cassi" to "action:throw ball" and the second with a relationship from "action:throw ball" to "actor:Corwin."

An advantage of story-line approaches is that the researcher can make use of shared sociocultural knowledge about the appropriate relationship between concept types to minimize coding effort. Such a facility is not, at least currently, a part of the purely semantic-based or proximity-based approaches. A further difference is that semantic-based and proximity-based approaches lend themselves to, and are typically used for, generating graphs and numerical evaluations of the text, while story-line techniques lend themselves to processes for regenerating the story given the coded representation. Semantic and proximity approaches are appropriate when examining decision processes, mental models, definitions, conceptual frameworks, and the role of social knowledge within these. Story-line approaches are appropriate when examining the sequence of actions and the similarity between different sequences of action.

3.4. *Concordance Analysis*

A concordance is an alphabetical list of the words (or concepts) in a text with reference to the passage(s) in which they occur. It is typically used in examining plays, poetry, songs, and religious texts such as the Bible. Analytic concordances match words in one text with the corresponding word in a translated version of the text—for example, words in the English Bible may be matched with their Hebrew original (Young et al. 1936). Lexical concordances try to classify words by their signification, as in Ellis's (1968) concordance of Shelley's poetry. Classification schemes, however, vary across concordances. Advances in automated textual analysis and artificial intelligence are making it possible to, under certain conditions, automatically generate a concordance and associated lexical statistics that enable content analysis and facilitate map analysis (such as the frequency with which words occur). The main advantage of a concordance to qualitative research is that information on where the word occurs in the original text is preserved. Semiautomated procedures such as ASKSAM retain this feature. Although concordances have not typically been used to perform content or map analysis, they can be used in either procedure. For example, researchers can use a concordance to do content analysis if they wish to make use of the exact words or phrases in the text and are willing to either do without implication, translation, and generalization or to develop a thesaurus based on the words in the concordance that automates this process.

To illustrate this type of analysis, the statements of Students A and B will be used and each sentence will be treated as a separate "passage." The resulting concordances are displayed in Table 2. As can be seen, Student A uses 64 words and Student B uses 48 words. And, although Student A and B both use "scientists" four times, A uses it three times in one sentence (sentence 2), whereas B uses it in all three sentences. As noted, a concordance can be used to do either a content analysis or a proximity analysis. Given the set of concepts used in Table 1, one can extract from the concordance the frequency with which each of those concepts was used, thus facilitating content analysis. Alternatively, a concordance can be sorted by location and then, given a set of concepts, a map can be drawn. In this case, the relationship would be based purely on proximity. The strength of the relationship could be characterized as the number of times the two concepts co-occurred. Based on the set of concepts in Table 1, the resultant maps coded from the concordance using proximity are shown in Figure 6. For ease of comparison with other codings of

TABLE 2
Concordances for Two Texts

	Student A			Student B	
Concept	Number	Sentence	Concept	Number	Sentence
I	1	1	I	1	1
a	1	3	It	1	1
and	2	1 2	My	1	2
are	1	3	Some	1	3
as	2	3 3	and	2	1 3
be	1	3	are	1	2
by	1	2	at	1	2
coauthors	1	3	coauthors	1	2
collaboration	2	2 3	collaboration	2	1 2
discoveries	2	1 2	containing	1	2
engage	1	1	discoveries	2	1 3
famous	1	2	engaged	2	1 2
formal	1	3	famous	1	1
found	1	1	formal	1	3
generate	1	1	hard work	1	1
hard work	1	2	have	1	3
in	2	1 1	in	2	1 2
informal	1	3	informal	1	1
involves	1	2	least	1	2
is	1	2	made	1	1
leads	1	2	make	1	3
lunch	1	3	many	1	1
make	2	1 2	new ideas	2	2 3
may	1	3	of	1	2
new ideas	2	1 3	one	1	2
of	1	3	other	1	2
often	1	2	paper	1	2
or	1	3	research	2	1 2
order	1	1	scientists	4	1 2 2 3
other	1	2	showed	1	2
over	1	3	that	1	2
paper	1	3	their	1	2
research	2	1 2	to	1	1
scientists	4	1 2 2 2	was	1	1
share	1	3	with	1	2
such	4	2 3 3 3			
that	1	1			
the	1	2			
they	2	3 3			
to	2	1 2			
when	2	3 3			
which	2	2 2			
with	1	2			

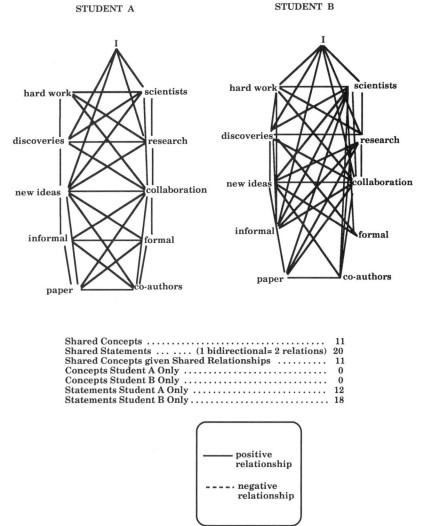

FIGURE 6. Coded maps based on concordance.

these texts, the strength of all relationships is identical; thus strength simply denotes whether there is or is not a relationship between those concepts. As can be seen, this proximity based coding overestimates the similarity of the texts compared with that produced when a more semantic approach is taken, as in Figure 3.

4. THE NEXT STEP

Once frequency counts of concepts and sets of statements have been extracted from the texts, the process of textual comparison begins. A detailed discussion of how to compare texts is well beyond the scope of this paper. Nevertheless, in keeping with the foregoing discussion, it is worth pointing out that there is a series of analysis choices that goes beyond specific coding and analysis procedures. Ideally, the tools that help the researcher to code the texts put the resultant information in a data-base form that facilitates comparison, regardless of the choices made by the researcher. Unfortunately, this is not always the case. Thus knowing what choices need to be made and the types of factors that should be considered should aid the researcher in selecting tools.

When content-analytic techniques are used, text comparison is fairly straightforward and typically focuses on the number of concepts shared and whether there is a pattern to what concepts are shared or not shared. Standard procedures for categorical analysis, clustering, grouping, and scaling are all useful. Map-analytic techniques provide the researcher with a greater number of choices. For example, maps can be compared either in terms of shared concepts, shared statements, or both. Comparison of maps in terms of shared concepts moves the researcher back into the realm of content analysis and facilitates comparison of map-analytic tools with content-analytic tools. Comparison of maps in terms of statements facilitates locating differences in meaning. Using measures of similarity for both concepts and statements is often the most satisfying as it enables the researcher to discuss the extent to which the authors of the texts have the same words but different meanings. For example, when comparing two maps in terms of concepts, the researcher can choose to compare the maps in terms of what concepts are or are not present or to compare maps in terms of what concepts are or are not present given the statements that the two maps have in common. Contrasting these two comparisons provides insight into differences in meaning across the texts. For example, two maps may contain all the same concepts (e.g., as in Figure 3), but when the statements are considered they share only five of the eleven concepts. In other words, although they use many of the same concepts, they use them in different ways.

The ease with which maps can be compared in terms of statements depends on how the statements are coded and on the number of types of concepts. Indeed, what coding choices are made affects the range of tools available for analyzing and comparing the resultant map. For example, if all concepts are the same type, if the relationships are identical in terms of sign, strength, and meaning, and if the relationships are all bidirectional, then standard graph analysis techniques can be used. In contrast, simply making the relationships directional moves the researcher into the realm of digraph analysis. Whereas having multiple types of concepts moves researchers into the realm of colored graphs, and having multiple strengths on the relationships moves them into the realm of network analysis.

A related issue is the level of similarity between statements that is necessary to say that two maps contain the same statement. This issue depends in part on how relationships are coded. For example, assuming that relationships are simply coded as either existing or not existing, that there are no differences in strength, sign, directionality, or meaning, and that the two maps have a relationship between the same two concepts, then the two maps can be said to contain the same statement. This approach was used by Palmquist (1990), Thomas (1991), and Saburi-Haghighi (1991). More complex schemes for coding relationships require that the researcher define schemes for combining statements and making similarity judgments (for example, see Carley 1984). Consider again Figure 3. In this case relationships are allowed to vary in directionality. As a result, the two maps are found to share five statements. If all relationships had been treated as bidirectional, then three additional statements would be shared (hard work—research; discoveries—scientists; and scientists—collaboration). Treating a statement with a bidirectional relationship as two statements would lead to the following statistics in place of the ones at the bottom of Figure 3:

• Shared Concepts 11
• Shared Statements 14
• Shared Concepts Given Shared Relationships 8
• Concepts Student-A Only 0
• Concepts Student-B Only 0
• Statements Student-A Only 20
• Statements Student-B Only 12

Another important consideration is that even when social knowledge is included in the coded maps, it tends to be quite sparse. That is, there are very few relationships per concept. For example, for Carley (1984, 1986) the average number of statements per concept per map was four. Although the distribution of statements across concepts is very nonuniform, with some concepts occurring in only one statement and others in over 20 statements. This sparsity affects what analysis techniques are viable and also the storage cost of various database schemes. One area where this is significant is when one wants to contrast actual statement usage with potential usage. Barring linguistic constraints on what types of concepts can be related to what other types, in general, there are potentially between each pair of concepts as many relationships as four times the number of possible strengths times the number of possible meanings. This assumes that there can be one relationship for each direction and for each sign. Assuming even a highly simple coding scheme in which relationships simply denote existence (which means there is no differentiation in strength, sign, directionality, or meaning), there are $N(N - 1)$ possible statements (assuming concepts cannot be related to themselves). Thus, for even a moderate-sized data base of about 200 concepts, the number of possible statements would be 39,800, but the number of statements in any one map might be more on the order of 100.

A further choice is whether maps are to be compared quantitatively or graphically (or both). One of the advantages of map-analytic techniques is that the researcher can use both modes of analysis in a complementary manner. Quantitatively comparing maps allows for a basic understanding of the degree of similarity and difference. Visual comparison of the graphs helps motivate rich detailed discussions of the factors in the individual and the sociolinguistic environment that led to these differences and enhances qualitative studies. In general, choices about how to compare maps can be made, unlike the other choices discussed, after the researcher has coded the maps.

This brief discussion does not begin to cover the full extent of the range of issues present in analyzing the coded textual data. Furthermore, this discussion should not be taken as evidence that there exists an analysis procedure for any coding scheme, or that all analysis issues have been solved. In particular, the greater the complexity in coding relationships the lower the likelihood that an appropriate analysis tool exists. In general, our ability to code texts and retain vast information on both concept types and relations far exceeds our ability to analyze the resultant data. A great deal of additional research is needed on exactly how to combine and compare maps under more complex coding scenarios.

5. FINAL REMARKS

Both content-analytic and map-analytic techniques help the researcher to code and analyze texts. The two approaches can be carried out manually or with the aid of computer-based tools. For effective use of such tools, the researcher will need to know the specific procedures followed by the coding software, an issue that is beyond the scope of this paper. There are, as was detailed here, a set of coding choices and some general guidelines that transcend particular coding protocols. These choices, the eight that are needed whenever concepts are coded and the additional four that are needed to engage in map analysis, should in general be made prior to selecting a coding procedure (manual, computer-assisted, or completely automated). These coding choices affect the conclusions that the researcher can draw from the data. Associated with these choices are a set of guidelines. The guidelines presented here are garnered from a variety of experiences in coding texts using both content-analytic and map-analytic procedures. These experiences suggest that the researcher should make choices that simplify the coding scheme—e.g., reduce the number of concepts (for both content and map analysis) and the number of concept and relationship types (for map analysis) to a manageable size that admits a meaningful comparison of texts.

Using the simplest possible coding scheme given the research question will increase the ease of coding, the ease with which texts can be compared, the extent to which the comparisons are meaningful, and the likelihood that existing tools can be used for automating the coding and analyzing the resultant coded data. Nevertheless, a simple coding scheme will lock the researcher into a certain way of analyzing the data. Data coded via more complex schemes can always be recoded during analysis to a more simple scheme. The ease with which such recoding is possible, however, depends on the particular coding procedures employed.

Regardless of the procedures employed, textual analysis is very detailed, time-consuming, and tedious work. When coding texts, people are quite prone to making errors. These errors can occur for a variety of reasons, such as inconsistency in generalizing concepts and changing what information is considered relevant part way through and then failing to recode earlier texts. There are several advantages to computer-based tools that either completely automate the coding process or simply assist the researcher. These include, but are not limited to, the following: They decrease the amount of time required to code texts; they eliminate or minimize errors due to inconsistency; they eliminate errors due to miscounting; they often eliminate spelling errors; they encourage systematicity; and they put the data into a form where it is easier to compare analytically. Furthermore, the startup costs of using computer-based tools are substantial enough that they encourage researchers to spend time thinking through coding choices such as those discussed here. Such tools do not, however, make textual analysis trivial. Further advances, particularly in map-analytic techniques, are needed to create tools that more completely automate the coding process and make it easier for the researcher to dynamically change coding choices and then compare the results.

Computer-based tools are most helpful when the researcher is interested in analyzing a large number of texts or texts that are extremely lengthy. Even for as few as ten texts, these approaches are very valuable. This is due in part to the possible reduction in errors. In addition, in the case of the map-analytic techniques, once the maps are coded it is relatively easy to extract vast quantities of empirical information. Such data make feasible analyses that were heretofore extremely difficult if not impossible. Map-analytic techniques focus on the extraction of both concepts and the relationships between them. Since this subsumes content analysis, the results can also be analyzed from a traditional content-analytic perspective. The addition of relational information, however, allows the researcher to examine not just shifts or differences in word usage across time and/ or people but also shifts or differences in meaning.

APPENDIX: EXAMPLE OF CODING, DISPLAYING, AND ANALYZING MAPS

This appendix provides a brief overview of the various MECA routines for coding and analyzing texts. Software routines, other than those in MECA, exist for doing content analysis and map analysis, but they will not be discussed. Additional information on the MECA procedures for coding maps is available in Carley (1988, 1990*a*) and Carley and Palmquist (1992). Many additional details of the programs that are not particularly germane here, such as storage requirements and exact file formats for input and output files, are suppressed. See Carley (1990*a*) for details.

Content Analysis

Three procedures exist within the MECA package that aid the researcher in doing content analyses: DELCON, TRANSLATE, and CMATRIX2.

DELCON: A program for deleting concepts from a text.

Input: 1. A file containing the list of concepts to be deleted. This list might contain the concepts—Killishandra, Ezra, he, she, them, and, or, the, in, order, and to—as well as notation such as ",", "'", and ".".

2. A file containing the list of texts that the researcher wants to delete information from.

3. A set of files, one for each text, from which the researcher wants to delete the irrelevant concepts. One such text, "tailed," might contain the passage described earlier about Killishandra and Ezra tailing the merchant.

Output: A modified version of each of the texts created and stored under the name ‹text›.del—i.e., the extension .del is added to the original text name. For the example just given, the output file would be "tailed.del."

TRANSLATE: A program for deleting concepts from a text.

Input: 1. A file containing a translation thesaurus. This file has the form, one concept per line with the general concept into which the following concepts are translated identified by a leading "$." A possible thesaurus file might contain:

```
$search
tailed
find
followed
$failed
```

```
elude
lose
$businessman
merchant
store-owner
$crooks
robbers
thiefs
```

2. A file containing the list of texts that the researcher wants translated.

3. A set of files, one for each text, on which the researcher wants to perform the translation. For example, one such text might be the text "tailed" previously mentioned.

Output: A modified version of each of the texts created and stored under the name ‹text›.tr—i.e., the extension .tr is added to the original text name. For the example given above, the output file would be "tailed.tr." It would contain the text "Killishandra and Ezra search the businessman through many corridors in order to search the crooks' lair. Unfortunately, he managed to failed them."

CMATRIX2: A program for counting the number of times concepts occur within texts.

Input: 1. A file containing the concepts that the researcher wants to look for in the texts. This file might contain the concepts— I, scientists, research, hard work, collaboration, discoveries, new ideas, formal, informal, co-authors, and paper.

2. A file containing the list of texts that the researcher wants to translate.

3. A set of files, one for each text, on which the researcher wants to perform a content analysis. For example, one such text might be "Student A" and another might be "Student-B." The texts for Student A and Student B would be the passages previously described.

4. Information on whether the researcher wants the program to simply denote that the concept occurs in the text (occurrence mode) or to count the number of times that the concept occurs (frequency mode).

Output: 1. A file *cmatrix2.dat* is created, containing a matrix such that each row represents a text (in the order in which they occur in the list of texts file) and each column a concept (in the order in which the concepts occur in the concepts file). The entries in this matrix depend on the mode in which CMATRIX2 is used—occurrence or frequency. In the occurrence mode, each entry is a "1" if that concept occurs in that text and a "0" otherwise. In the frequency mode, each entry is the number of times that the concept occurs in that text. For the student example, cmatrix2.dat would contain the following information when the occurrence mode was chosen:

1 1 1 1 1 1 1 1 1 1 1
1 1 1 1 1 1 1 1 1 1 1

Alternatively, when the frequency mode is chosen, cmatrix2.dat would appear as:

1 4 2 1 2 2 2 1 1 1 1
1 4 2 1 2 2 2 1 1 1 1

2. The file *cstats2.dat* contains general statistics on concept usage.

Map Analysis

Most of the procedures within the MECA package aid the researcher in doing map analysis. Only those procedures directly relevant to this paper will be described. These are STARTUP, CODEMAP, COMPRA, DRAWMAP, and SKI.

STARTUP: A program for defining a coding template.

Input: The STARTUP program is interactive, asking the researcher a set of questions about what coding choices are being made. The choices are recorded in a setup file, which then affects the operation of most other MECA programs. The researcher should have made the following decisions ahead of time: (1) the name of the file that will contain the coding choices (e.g., student.set); (2) the number of concept categories; (3) whether statement directionality will be imposed; (4) how strength will be used; and (5) the number of relationship types. It is not necessary to know apriori the number of concepts per category or the names of the concepts in those categories.

Output: A text file containing the coding choices. This is a text file with the name identified by the researcher (e.g., student.set).

CODEMAP: A program for assisting the researcher in coding the text.

CODEMAP is a semiautomated tool for coding maps. This tool is a new and improved version of the tool CODEF discussed in Carley (1986, 1988).

Input: The CODEMAP program is interactive, asking the researcher a set of questions that lead the researcher through coding the text one statement at a time. The researcher should have the following material ready: (1) the setup file (e.g., student.set); (2) the name for the file that will contain the coded map (e.g., sa.map); and (3) the text file that is being coded. The text file is not directly analyzed by CODEMAP; rather, the researcher reads the text and decides, sentence by sentence, what statements to code.

Output: The output is a text file with one line per coded statement. After the entire text from Student A is coded, the resultant output file would contain the following information:

```
created by researcher 11-91:
1$concept$I$concept$scientists$1
1$concept$scientists$concept$research$2
1$concept$scientists$concept$new ideas$1
1$concept$scientists$concept$co-authors$1
1$concept$research$concept$scientists$2
1$concept$collaboration$concept$scientists$1
1$concept$collaboration$concept$discoveries$1
1$concept$collaboration$concept$formal$1
1$concept$discoveries$concept$scientists$1
1$concept$research$concept$collaboration$1
1$concept$research$concept$hard work$1
1$concept$research$concept$discovery$1
1$concept$research$concept$new ideas$1
1$concept$informal$concept$new ideas$1
1$concept$formal$concept$co-authors$1
1$concept$formal$concept$paper$1
1$concept$co-authors$concept$paper$2
1$concept$paper$concept$co-authors$2
```

The first number indicates the strength, the second and fourth positions denote the concept categories, the third and fifth positions denote the concepts, and the last number indicates the directionality. For example, line 3, the statement linking scientist to research has a "2" as the last piece of information, thus indicating that there is a bidirectional relation.

COMPRA: A program for comparing two maps.

COMPRA can be used to compare and/or combine two maps. The program generates a comparison in terms of just concepts and in terms of relationships. It does this first across all concept types and relationship types and then by each type separately. It assumes that the number of possible concepts is the number in the setup file.

Input: 1. Two map files that the researcher wishes to compare.

2. A setup file.

Output: As output COMPRA can create any or all of the following output files: (1) a map file containing the symmetric difference map for the first map; (2) a map file containing the symmetric difference map for the second map; (3) a map file containing the intersection map; (4) a map file containing the union map; (5) a map file containing statistics on the comparison of the two maps.

DRAWMAP: A program for converting a map data base into a picture. Generates a graph by placing the concepts around a circle and placing a line between each pair of concepts that occur in a statement. It can, though need not, place arrows on the lines to indicate directionality, and it can label the lines according to their strength or show strength by the boldness of the lines. Sign can be shown through either dotted lines or by labeling the lines. It ignores concept type and relationship type information.

Input: DRAWMAP requires as input a coded map file. Optional input files include a position file that lists the location of each concept around the circle and an abbreviation file that lists alternative names for each concept.

Output: The output is a file in MacDraw format.

SKI: A simple expert system for explicating implicit knowledge in a coded map. This program is described in detail in Carley (1988). This program operates entirely in batch mode.

Input: Four files are required as input, each in the same format as the map. These files are the map to be converted, the set of definitives, the set of logicals, and the set of simples. Definitives are statements that are presumed to embody whatever information is socially shared. Logicals and simples contain information that though social may not have the same level of agreement.

Output: The output is a modified version of the map containing the new social statements.

REFERENCES

Blank, G., J. L. McCartney, and E. Brent, eds. 1989. *New Technology and Sociology: Practical Applications in Research and Work.* New Brunswick, N.J.: Transaction Publishers.

Bobrow, D. G., and A. Collins, eds. 1976. *Representation and Understanding: Studies in Cognitive Science.* New York: Academic Press.

Brachman, R. J., and H. J. Levesque, eds. 1985. *Readings in Knowledge Representation.* Los Altos, Calif.: M. Kaufmann.

Bruce, B., and D. Newman. 1978. *Interacting Plans* (Tech. Rep.). Champaign, Ill.: Center for the Study of Reading.

Carley, K. M. 1984. "Constructing Consensus." Ph.D. diss., Harvard University.

———. 1986. "An Approach for Relating Social Structure to Cognitive Structure." *Journal of Mathematical Sociology* 12(2): 137–89.

———. 1988. "Formalizing the Social Expert's Knowledge." *Sociological Methods and Research* 17:165–232.

———. 1990. "Computer Analysis of Qualitative Data—Copy of Overheads for Didactic Seminar." Paper presented at annual meeting of the American Sociological Association.

———. Forthcoming *b*. "The Social Construction of Knowledge." In *Experiments in Epistemology,* edited by R. Lawler. Norwood, N.J.: Ablex.

———. Forthcoming *a*. "Content Analysis." In *The Encyclopedia of Language and Linguistics,* edited by R. E. Asher et al. Edinburgh: Pergamon Press.

Carley, K., and D. Kaufer. Forthcoming. "Semantic Connectivity: An Approach for Analyzing Semantic Networks." *Communication Theory.*

Carley, K., and M. Palmquist. 1992. "Extracting, Representing, and Analyzing Mental Models." *Social Forces* 70:(3) 601–36.

Cicourel, A. V. 1974. *Cognitive Sociology.* New York: Free Press, Macmillan.

Cicourel, A. V., and K. Carley. 1990. "The Coder of Narrative as Expert: The Ecological Validity of Coding Practices." Paper presented at the annual meeting of the American Anthropological Association.

Conrad, P., and S. Reinharz. 1984. "Computers and Qualitative Data." *Qualitative Sociology* 7:3–15.

Danowski, J. A. 1980. "Computer-Mediated Communication: A Network-based Content Analysis Using a CBBS Conference." In *Communication Yearbook,* edited by M. Burgoon, 905–24. Beverly Hills: Sage.

———. 1982. "A Network-based Content Analysis Methodology for Computer-Mediated Communication: An Illustration with a Computer Bulletin Board." In *Communication Yearbook,* edited by R. Bostrom, 904–25. New Brunswick, N.J.: Transaction Books.

———. 1988. "Organizational Infographics and Automated Auditing: Using Computers to Unobtrusively Gather and Analyze Communication." In *Handbook of Organizational Communication*, edited by G. Goldhaber and G. Barnett, 385–433. Norwood, N.J.: Ablex.

Dietrich, R., and C. F. Graumann. 1989. *Language Processing in Social Context*. New York: Elsevier Science Publishing.

Dunphy, D.C., C.G. Bullard, and E.E.M. Crossing. 1974. "Validation of the General Inquirer Harvard IV Dictionary." Paper presented at 1974 Conference on Content Analysis, Pisa, Italy.

Dyer, M. 1983. "The Role of Affect in Narratives." *Cognitive Science* 7:211–42.

Ellis, F. S. 1968. *A Lexical Concordance to the Poetical Works of Percy Bysshe Shelley*. New York: B. Franklin.

Ericsson, K. A., and H. A. Simon. 1984. *Protocol Analysis: Verbal Reports as Data*. Cambridge: MIT Press.

Fan, D. 1988. *Predictions of Public Opinion From the Mass Media: Computer Content Analysis and Mathematical Modeling*. New York: Greenwood Press.

Fauconnier, G. 1985. *Mental Spaces: Aspects of Meaning Construction in Natural Language*. Cambridge: Bradford Books, MIT Press.

Franzosi, R. 1990a. "From Words to Numbers: A Generalized and Linguistic-based Coding Procedure for Collecting Textual Data." In *Sociological Methodology*, edited by C. Clogg. San Francisco: Jossey-Bass.

———. 1990b. "Computer-Assisted Coding of Textual Data: An Application to Semantic Grammars." *Sociological Methods and Research*, 19:(2)225–57.

———. 1990c. "Strategies for the Prevention, Detection, and Correction of Measurement Error in Data Collected from Textual Sources." *Sociological Methods and Research* 18:(4)442–72.

Gallhofer, I. N., and W. E. Saris. 1988. *Sociometric Research VI: Data Collection and Scaling*. New York: St. Martin's Press.

Garson, D. 1985. "Content analysis machine-readable data file V 1.0." Raleigh, N.C.: National Collegiate Software Clearinghouse.

Gentner, D., and A. L. Stevens, eds. 1983. *Mental Models*. Hillsdale, N.J.: Lawrence Erlbaum Associates.

Grey, A., D. Kaplan, and H. D. Lasswell. 1965. "Recording and Context Units–Four Ways of Coding Editorial Content." In *Language of Politics*, edited by H. D. Laswell and N. Leites, 113–26. Cambridge: MIT Press.

Holsti, O. R. 1954. Content Analysis. In *The Handbook of Social Psychology*, vol. II, edited by G. Lindzey and E. Aronson, 596–692. Reading, Mass.: Addison-Wesley.

———. 1969. *Content Analysis for the Social Sciences and Humanities*. Reading, Mass.: Addison-Wesley.

Hutchins, W. J. 1982. "The Evolution of Machine Translation Systems." In *Practical Experience of Machine Translation: Proceedings of a Conference, London Nov. 1981*, edited by V. Lawson, 21–38. New York: North-Holland.

Johnson-Laird, P. 1983. *Mental Models: Toward a Cognitive Science of Language, Inference, and Consciousness*. Cambridge: Harvard University Press.

Kaufer, D. S., and K. M. Carley. 1993. *Communication at a Distance: The*

Influence of Print on Sociocultural Organization and Change. Hillsdale, N.J.: Lawrence Erlbaum Associates.

Krippendorf, K. 1980. *Content Analysis: An Introduction to its Methodology.* Beverly Hills: Sage.

Lehnert, W. 1981. "Plot Units and Narrative Summarization." *Cognitive Science* 5:293–331.

Lehnert, W., and E. Vine. 1987. "The Role of Affect in Narrative Structure." *Cognition and Emotion* 1:299–322.

Lindkvist, K. 1981. "Approaches to Text Analysis." In *Advances in Content Analysis,* edited by K. E. Rosengren, 23–42. Beverly Hills: Sage.

Mallery, J. 1985. "Universality and Individuality: The Interaction of Noun Phrase Determiners in Copular Clauses." *Twenty-third Annual Meeting of the Association for Computational Linguistics: Proceedings of the Conference.* Chicago.

Mallery, J., and G. Duffy. 1986. *A Computational Model of Semantic Perception* (Tech. Rep. AI memo no. 799). Cambridge: MIT Artificial Intelligence Laboratory.

Mandler, J. M. 1984. *Stories, Scripts, and Scenes: Aspects of Schema Theory.* Hillsdale, N.J.: Lawrence Erlbaum Associates.

McTavish, D. G., and E. B. Pirro. 1990. "Contextual Content Analysis." *Quality and Quantity* 24:245–65.

Merleau-Ponty, M. 1964. *Consciousness and the Acquisition of Language.* Evanston, Ill.: Northwestern University Press.

Namenwirth, J., and R. Weber. 1987. *Dynamics of Culture.* Boston: Allen & Unwin.

Neuman, W.R. 1989. "Parallel Content Analysis: Old Paradigms and New Proposals." *Public Communication and Behavior* 2:205–89.

Ogilvie, D.M., P.J. Stone, and E.F. Kelly. 1982. Computer-Aided Content Analysis." In *A Handbook of Social Science Methods,* vol. 2, edited by R. B. Smith and P. K. Manning, 219–46. New York: Ballinger.

Osgood, C. E. 1959. "The Representational Model and Relevant Research Methods." In *Trends in Content Analysis,* edited by I. S. Pool, 33–88. Urbana: University of Illinois Press.

Palmquist, M. E. 1990. "The Lexicon of the Classroom: Language and Learning in Writing Classrooms." Ph.D. diss. Carnegie Mellon University, Pittsburgh, PA.

Polanyi, L. 1985. *Telling the American Story: A Structural and Cultural Analysis of Conversational Storytelling.* Norwood N.J.: Ablex.

Polanyi, M. P. 1962[1958]. *Personal Knowledge: Towards a Post-Critical Philosophy.* Chicago: University of Chicago Press.

Potter, R. G. 1982. "Reader Responses and Character Syntax." In *Computing in the Humanities,* edited by R. W. Bailey, 65–78. New York: North-Holland.

Qualis Research Associates. 1989. *The Ethnograph.* Littleton, Colo.:

Roberts, C. W. 1989. "Other Than Counting Words: A Linguistic Approach to Content Analysis." *Social Forces* 68:147–77.

Romney, A. K., S. C. Weller, and W. H. Batchelder. 1986. "Culture as Consensus: A Theory of Culture and Informant Accuracy." *American Anthropologist* 88:(2) 313–38.

Saburi-Haghighi, N. 1991. "World Bank's Adjustment Lending Policy 1980–1989: Towards Understanding the Socio-Political Dimensions of Adjustment." Ph.D. diss. American University, Washington, D.C.

Sacks, H. 1972. "On the Analysability of Stories by Children." In *Directions in Socio-linguistics,* edited by J. Gumprez and D. Hymes, 329–45. New York: Holt, Rinehart & Winston.

Saris-Gallhofer, I. N., W. E. Saris, and E. L. Morton. 1978. "A Validation Study of Holsti's Content Analysis Procedure." *Quality and Quantity* 12:131–45.

Schank, R. C., and R. Abelson. 1977. *Scripts Plans and Goals and Understanding.* New York: Wiley.

Schank, R. C., and C. K. Riesbeck, eds. 1981. *Inside Computer Understanding.* Hillsdale, N.J.: Lawrence Erlbaum Associates.

Sowa, J. F. 1984. *Conceptual Structures.* Reading, Mass.: Addison-Wesley.

Sozer, E. 1985. *Text Connexity, Text Coherence: Aspects, Methods, Results.* Hamburg, Germany: Buske.

Splichal, S., and A. Ferligoj. 1988. "Ideology in International Propaganda." In *Sociometric Research V1: Data Collection and Scaling,* edited by W. E. Saris and I. N. Gallhofer, ch. 5. New York: St. Martin's Press.

Sproull, L. S., and R. F. Sproull. 1982. "Managing and Analyzing Behavioral Records: Explorations in Non-Numeric Data Analysis." *Human Organization* 41:283–90.

Stone, P. J., D. C. Dunphy, M. S. Smith, and D. M. Ogilvie. 1968. *The General Inquirer: A Computer Approach to Content Analysis.* Cambridge: MIT Press.

Stone, P. J., and Cambridge Computer Associates. 1968. *User's Manual for the General Inquirer.* Cambridge: MIT Press.

Stubbs, M. 1983. *Discourse Analysis: The Sociolinguistic Analysis of Natural Language.* Chicago: University of Chicago Press.

Sullivan, M. P. 1973. *Perceptions of Symbols in Foreign Policy: Data from the Vietnam Case* (Tech. Rep.). Ann Arbor: Inter-University Consortium for Political Research.

Thomas, D. 1991. "Changing Cultural Perception of Robots As Seen in Science Fiction." Bachelor's thesis, Carnegie Mellon University.

VanLehn, K., and S. Garlick. 1987. "Cirrus: An Automated Protocol Analysis Tool." In *Proceedings of the Fourth International Workshop on Machine Learning,* edited by P. Langley, 205–17. Los Altos, Calif.: Morgan-Kaufman.

Van Meter, K. M., and L. Mounier. 1989. "East Meets West: Official Biographies of Members of the Central Committee of the Communist Party of the Soviet Union Between 1981 and 1987, Analyzed with Western Social Network Analysis Methods." *Connections* 12:32–38.

Weber, R. 1984. "Computer-Aided Content Analysis: A Short Primer." *Qualitative Sociology* 7:126–47.

Woodrum, E. 1984. " 'Mainstreaming' Content Analysis in Social Science: Methodological Advantages, Obstacles, and Solutions." *Social Science Research* 13:1–19.

Young, R., W. B. Stevenson, T. Nicol, and G. W. Gilmore. 1936. *Analytical Concordance to the Bible on an Entirely New Plan Containing About 311,000 References, Subdivided under the Hebrew and Greek Originals, with the Literal Meaning and Pronunciation of Each Designed for the Simplest Reader of the English Bible.* New York: Funk and Wagnalls.

☒ 4 ☒

USING GALOIS LATTICES TO REPRESENT NETWORK DATA

*Linton C. Freeman**
*Douglas R. White**

Galois lattices are introduced as a device to provide a general representation for two mode social network data. It is shown that Galois lattices yield a single visual image of such data in cases where most alternative models produce dual images. The image provided by the Galois lattice produces, moreover, an image that can suggest useful insights about the structural properties of the data.

An example, based on data from Davis, Gardner, and Gardner (1941), is used to spell out in detail the kinds of structural insights that can be gained from this approach. In addition, other potential applications are suggested.

1. INTRODUCTION TO THE PROBLEM

Social network analysis is focused on the patterning of the social relationships that link social actors. Typically, network data take the form of a square—actor by actor—binary *adjacency matrix,* where each row and each column in the matrix represents a social actor. A cell entry is 1 if and only if a pair of actors is linked by some social relationship of interest (Freeman 1989).

The success of social network analysis rests in large part on the fact that network analysts have used graph theory to represent the networks they study. Graph theoretic representations permit the visu-

*University of California, Irvine

alization of networks. As Hage and Harary (1983, p. 9) put it, "graphical models are in some sense iconic; they look like what they represent."

The images provided by graph theory call attention to structural properties of networks that might not be apparent otherwise. Klovdahl (1981) proposed that without graph theory, or some other means of representing social structure visually, social network analysis would not have developed some of its most important ideas (see also Koestler 1964; Arnheim 1970; Taylor 1971; Tukey 1972; and Tufte 1983, all of whom argue the importance of visual metaphors in the development of scientific specialties). Ideas like distance, reachability, density, clique, cluster, centrality, betweenness, flow and bridge—ideas that are crucial in the field—have emerged from insights gained by representing social networks as graphs.

This commitment to adjacency matrices and their corresponding graph theoretic representations, however, has not been without cost. As Seidman (1981), McPherson (1982) and Wilson (1982) have all indicated, by recording only those linkages that connect pairs of actors, we limit our capacity to uncover potentially important structural features of social linkage patterns. We lose the ability to distinguish between patterns of ties that actually link pairs, and those that link larger collections of actors.

Consider, for example, three individuals—Amy, Bess, and Cheryl. Amy and Bess, let us say, were best friends in grammar school. In high school, Bess and Cheryl were always together, and in college, Amy and Cheryl were very close. What we have, then, is three pairs of individuals who—at different times and different places—have been linked together by close friendship ties.

In contrast, suppose there were three other individuals—Dorothy, Edna, and Florence. All three, let us say, were inseparable—they made up a tight little threesome—in high school. Theirs was what Wilson (1982) has called a "multiple" relation. They were not simply linked by a disjoint series of pairwise ties, they were simultaneously bound together at a single time and in a single setting.

Intuitively, the distinction between these two patterns of linkage is, as Breiger (1974) suggested, critical. The kind of "multiple" relation that linked Dorothy, Edna, and Florence is usually taken to be an emergent structural form. Bott (1957), among others, has shown that such emergent forms, that link the members of collectivities larger than pairs, can have important consequences for the behaviors of the individual involved.

To maintain the distinction between these two kinds of structures, we need to record information—not simply about the social relationships that link pairs of actors, but about how actors are linked together into collectivities of any size. We need what Wasserman and Faust (1993) have called *two mode* network data.

Two mode network data define a triple (A,E,I). One mode is a set of n actors $A = \{a_i, a_j, \ldots, a_n\}$ and the other mode is a set containing m *social events* (or collectivities or organizations) $E = \{e_i, e_j, \ldots, e_m\}$. These two sets are linked by an involvement (or membership) relation $I \subseteq A \times E$. When an actor a_i is involved as a participant in an event e_j, then the $\langle a_i, e_j \rangle \in I$. A two mode network is recorded as an $n \times m$ binary matrix P of participation, where $p_{ij} = 1$ if $\langle a_i, e_j \rangle \in I$ and $p_{ij} = 0$ otherwise. By definition, then, a social event in E may link *more than two* of the actors in A.

Given the need to record at least some network data in two mode form, we are faced with a problem. Graph theory is perfectly satisfactory for representing traditional one mode network data. So far, however, network analysts lack a model for representing two mode networks in a manner that facilitates the kind of visualization that graph theory provides in the one mode case.

Various suggestions have been made, but as we will show, none of them is entirely satisfactory. Our aim in the present paper, then, is to introduce a representation that can provide the same kinds of rich structural insights about two mode data that graph theoretic visualization provides for one mode data. We begin, in the next section, by reviewing previous attempts along this line.

2. THE PROBLEM OF REPRESENTING TWO MODE NETWORK DATA

As Breiger (1974) indicated, two mode network data embody an important structural duality. Two mode data are based explicitly on a relation that links social actors to social events. But the form of that relation determines other structural properties in the data. It determines both the patterning of the linkages among the actors and the patterning of the linkages among the events. To be entirely satisfactory, then, a representation should facilitate the visualization of three kinds of patterning: (1) the actor-event structure, (2) the actor-actor structure, and (3) the event-event structure.

Doreian (1980) and Freeman (1980) both drew on earlier work in discrete algebraic topology by Atkin (1974) and proposed representing two mode network data using Atkin's simplicial complexes. In addition, Seidman (1981) showed that the hypergraphs defined by Berge (1973) could be used to provide a similar—and perhaps simpler—representation of two mode data.

Both simplicial complexes and hypergraphs reflect the duality Breiger described. They each provide not one but two images—one revealing the way actors are linked to each other in terms of the patterning of their involvement in events and the other how events are linked to each other in terms of the ways in which they bring actors together. Both images display the relation of actors to events fairly clearly, but, since there are two of them, neither image provides an overall picture of the total, actor-actor, event-event, and actor-event structure.

In 1982 Wilson suggested a way to represent two mode networks with a single model, using bipartite graphs. Such bipartite representations succeed in providing a single image for two mode data, but they do so by displaying only the actor-event structure. They do not provide a clear image of the linkages among actors nor of those among events.

What is needed, then, is a representation that can display all three of these kinds of relations both clearly and in a single model that can facilitate visualization. In the next section we will introduce a representation, based on Galois lattices, that meets these requirements.

3. GALOIS LATTICES

We will begin by defining the properties of lattices generally and then move on to a discussion of lattices that have the Galois property. A lattice is a special kind of ordered set. Consider a finite nonempty set $X = \{x, y, z, \ . \ . \ .\}$ along with a binary relation $\leq$ in $X \times X$. Let $\leq$ be a reflexive, antisymmetric, and transitive relation that imposes a *partial order* on X.

Given a pair of elements x and y in X, a *lower bound* of x and y

is an element m such that $m \leq x$ and $m \leq y$. A lower bound m is the greatest lower bound, or *meet* when there is no other element b such that $b \leq x$ and $b \leq y$ and $m \leq b$. Equivalently, an *upper bound j* is an element such that $x \leq j$, $y \leq j$. If there is no element b such that $x \leq b$, $y \leq b$, and $b \leq j$, j is the least upper bound, or *join*. Any partially ordered set in which every pair of elements has both a meet and a join is a *lattice*.

An example may clarify these ideas. Consider the set $X =$ $\{1,2,3\}$. The *power set P(X)* consists of all the subsets X_i of the set X. $P(X)$, of course, includes X itself and the null set $\varnothing$. In this case, then, its elements are $\{1,2,3\}$, $\{1,2\}$, $\{1,3\}$, $\{2,3\}$, $\{1\}$, $\{2\}$, $\{3\}$, and $\{\varnothing\}$.

The elements of this power set form a partial order, based on inclusion, where $(X_i) \leq (X_j) \Leftrightarrow (X_i \subseteq X_j)$. This order is diagramed in Figure 1. Note that in the figure each pair of elements has both a meet and a join. the elements $\{1,2\}$ and $\{2,3\}$, for example, have $\{2\}$ as their meet and $\{1,2,3\}$ as their join. The elements $\{1\}$ and $\{2,3\}$ have $\{\varnothing\}$ as their meet and $\{1,2,3\}$ as their join. Since this power set is partially ordered and every pair of elements in it has both a meet and a join, it is a lattice.

A Galois lattice embodies a dual ordering. The foundations for Galois lattices were introduced by Birkhoff (1940). He characterized the structure he defined as "Galois" precisely because of its duality. Important generalizations of Birkhoff's original formulation,

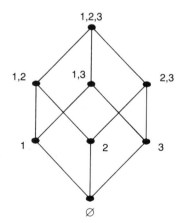

FIGURE 1. Lattice of the power set $P(X)$.

	EVENT			
	A	B	C	D
ACTOR				
1	1	0	1	1
2	1	0	0	1
3	1	0	0	0
4	0	1	1	1
5	0	1	0	0
6	0	1	0	1

FIGURE 2. Hypothetical two mode data.

leading to the modern theory of Galois lattices, were made first by Barbut and Monjardet (1970) and more recently by Wille (1982, 1984) and by Duquenne (1987, 1991).

Galois lattices are based on the kind of triple (A,E,I) defined by two mode social network data. A and E are finite nonempty sets and I is a binary relation in $A \times E$. As an example, consider the hypothetical data matrix shown in Figure 2. There are six actors, labeled 1 through 6. And there are four social events, labeled A through D. An entry of 1 in a cell indicates that the actor designated by the row was involved in the event designated by the column.

Consider $P(A) = \{A_1, A_2, \ldots\}$, the collection of subsets of A, and $P(E) = \{E_1, E_2, \ldots\}$, the collection of subsets of E. The I relation can be used to define a mapping $\uparrow : B \rightarrow B \uparrow$ from $P(A)$ to $P(E)$:

$$B \uparrow = \{e \in E \mid (a,e) \in I \text{ for all } a \in A\}.$$

In Figure 2, for example, we can see that the subset containing actor 1 is associated with the subset of events containing A, C, and D, and the actor subset containing 1 and 2 is associated with events A and D.

In a similar way, I can be used to define another mapping $\downarrow : F \rightarrow F \downarrow$ from $P(E)$ to $P(A)$:

$$F \downarrow = \{a \in A \mid (a,e) \in I \text{ for all } e \in E\}.$$

Thus, in Figure 2, the subset containing events A and C is associated with the actor subset containing 1, and the event subset containing B, C, and D is associated with the actor subset containing actor 4.

Let $S(A) = \{A_1 \uparrow, A_2 \uparrow, \ldots\}$, the collection of images of $\uparrow$, and $S(E) = \{E_1 \downarrow, E_2 \downarrow, \ldots\}$, the collection of images of $\downarrow$. Since these two mappings, $\uparrow$ and $\downarrow$, are both constructed from the same pairs in the relation I, they contain the same number of elements, and subscripts can be assigned in such a way that $A_i \uparrow = E_i$ for some $E_i \subseteq P(E)$ and $E_i \downarrow = A_i$ for some $A_i \subseteq P(A)$. In Figure 2, for example, the subset of actors containing actor 1 is mapped to that subset of events containing events A, C, and D, and the event subset containing events A, C, and D is mapped to the actor subset containing actor 1.

The subsets of $P(A)$ that are the elements of $S(E)$ form a lattice under inclusion, as do the subsets of $P(E)$ that are the elements of $S(A)$. Moreover, these two lattices are dual inverse:

$$(E_i \downarrow \subseteq E_j \downarrow \Leftrightarrow A_i \uparrow \supseteq A_j \uparrow).$$

Thus the order of the elements of $S(A)$ is the inverse of the order of the elements of $S(E)$. A single partial order of *pairs* $(E_i \downarrow, A_i \uparrow)$ can be used to represent both the order of $S(A)$ and the inverse order of $S(E)$:

$$(E_i \downarrow, A_i \uparrow) \leq (E_j \downarrow, A_j \uparrow) \Leftrightarrow E_i \downarrow \subseteq E_j \downarrow \ \& \ A_i \uparrow \supseteq A_j \uparrow.$$

An element $(E_i \downarrow, A_i \uparrow)$ of this dual lattice is a lower bound of another $(E_j \downarrow, A_j \uparrow)$ when $E_i \downarrow$ is contained in $E_j \downarrow$, or equivalently, when $A_j \uparrow$ contains $A_i \uparrow$. In such a case, $(E_j \downarrow, A_j \uparrow)$ is an upper bound of $(E_i \downarrow, A_i \uparrow)$. The universal upper bound of the lattice contains all the elements in A, and its universal lower bound contains all the elements in E. A dual lattice of this sort, where each element is a pair, is called *Galois*.

A Galois lattice may be displayed pictorially as a labeled line diagram. In such a diagram, each element is represented as a point and points are linked by ascending and descending lines to show their partial orderings. Each point is assigned two labels, one indicating the subset of elements in A that it represents and the other indicating the subset of elements in E that it represents.

The diagram of the Galois lattice representing the data of Figure 2 is shown in Figure 3.[1] The inclusion relation I defines ten

---

[1]There is no general theory of lattice drawing, but there are several PC programs for drawing lattices, two of which have been used here. One, written by Vincent Duquenne of the Maison des Science de l'Homme in Paris, France, is called *General Lattice Analysis and Design (GLAD)*. The other, prepared by

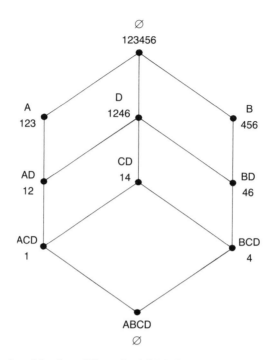

FIGURE 3. Lattice of the data of Figure 2—full labeling.

relevant subsets of both actors and events. At the bottom is the union of all events; the null symbol ∅ indicates that *no* actor was involved in all four events. Above and to the right, we can see that actor 4 attended events B, C, and D. And to the left, we see that actor 1 was present at events A, C, and D.

Each point in the lattice is labeled with both the actors and the events that define it. As we move up, we encounter larger collections of actors and smaller collections of events. Finally, at the top, we see that there were no events at which all six actors were present.

In practice, it is usually easier to make sense of a lattice in which the labeling is reduced. Each point is labeled only with the names of actors for which it is the least element containing those actors. Similarly, each point gets the names of any events for which it

Frank Vogt and Joerg Bliesener at the Technische Hochschule in Darmstadt, Germany, is named *Diagram*.

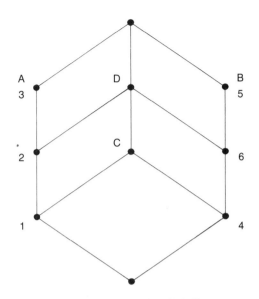

FIGURE 4. Lattice of the data of Figure 2—reduced labeling.

is the greatest element containing those events. Points that are neither the least element containing any actor nor the greatest element containing any event remain unlabeled. The lattice of Figure 3 with reduced labeling is shown in Figure 4.

Figure 4 provides a pictorial image of which actors were present at which events. Any actor falling on a line descending from any event was present at that event, and, of course, any event falling on a line ascending from an actor involved that actor.

In addition, the figure also displays the containment structures for both actors and events. Event D, for example, contains event C in the sense that any actor present at event D was *certainly present at event C*. In the same way, the figure shows that actor 5 was never present at any event unless actors 6 and 4 were both present, and 6's attendance required that 4 be there. Thus from this single pictorial representation we can see all three patterns: (1) the actor-event structure, (2) the event-event structure, and (3) the actor-actor structure. In the next section, we will take up an example using actual two mode data and see what sorts of visual insights a Galois lattice representation can provide.

4. AN EXAMPLE: DAVIS, GARDNER, AND GARDNER'S SOUTHERN WOMEN

Systematic two mode data were collected as part of an ethnographic study conducted in a southern community in the United States over a period of two years (Davis, Gardner, and Gardner 1941). The researchers used interviews, records of observations, guest lists, and newspaper accounts to discover who was involved with whom in a series of social events in the community. Their data on the participation of 18 women in 14 social events is shown in Figure 5 (from Davis, Gardner, and Gardner, p. 148).

The researchers used these data, along with their general ethnographic wisdom, to generate an informal description of social life among these women. They concluded that the women shown in Figure 5 were organized into two main groups and that there were three intuitively determined "levels" of participation in each group. Women 1 through 8 were assigned to group one, with 1, 2, 3, and 4 defined as core members. Women 5, 6, and 7 were seen as second level members and woman 8 was described as a third level member. Women 10

							EVENT							
	A	B	C	D	E	F	G	H	I	J	K	L	M	N
ACTOR														
1	1	1	1	1	1	1	0	1	1	0	0	0	0	0
2	1	1	1	0	1	1	1	1	0	0	0	0	0	0
3	0	1	1	1	1	1	1	1	1	0	0	0	0	0
4	1	0	1	1	1	1	1	1	0	0	0	0	0	0
5	0	0	1	1	1	0	1	0	0	0	0	0	0	0
6	0	0	1	0	1	1	0	1	0	0	0	0	0	0
7	0	0	0	0	1	1	1	1	0	0	0	0	0	0
8	0	0	0	0	0	1	0	1	1	0	0	0	0	0
9	0	0	0	0	1	0	1	1	1	0	0	0	0	0
10	0	0	0	0	0	0	1	1	1	0	0	1	0	0
11	0	0	0	0	0	0	0	1	1	1	0	1	0	0
12	0	0	0	0	0	0	0	1	1	1	0	1	1	1
13	0	0	0	0	0	0	1	1	1	1	0	1	1	1
14	0	0	0	0	0	1	1	0	1	1	1	1	1	1
15	0	0	0	0	0	0	1	1	0	1	1	1	0	0
16	0	0	0	0	0	0	0	1	1	0	0	0	0	0
17	0	0	0	0	0	0	0	0	1	0	1	0	0	0
18	0	0	0	0	0	0	0	0	1	0	1	0	0	0

FIGURE 5. Davis, Gardner, and Gardner's two mode data.

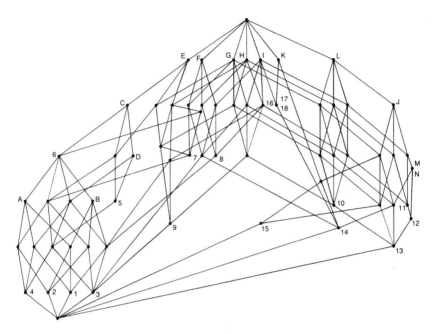

FIGURE 6. Lattice of the Davis, Gardner, and Gardner data.

through 18 were assigned to group two. Women 13, 14, and 15 were defined as core, 11 and 12 as second level and 10, 16, 17, and 18 as third level members. They assigned woman 9 as a third level member of both groups.

A Galois lattice that displays the structure of the data of Figure 5 is shown in Figure 6. All of the paired subset elements in $S(E)$ and $S(A)$ are shown in the figure. The topmost point represents the set of all 18 women and, at the same time, it represents the null set of events—there was no event that all 18 women attended. The bottommost point represents the set of all 14 events and the null set of actors—there was no actor who attended all the events. Labels on intermediate points show where each event and each actor entered the structure.

As students of social networks, what are we to make of this lattice diagram? Five kinds of patterning are immediate:

1. *We can see the pattern of participation of actors in events.* Each actor (or set of actors) participated in those events labeled at or

above her labeled point in the line diagram and each event (or set of events) included all the actors labeled at or below its point. There are lines, for example, ascending from actor 9 to events E, G, H and I, those in which she participated. And event A is connected by descending lines to three actors, 1, 2, and 4. Thus the relation I is displayed, and the original data are completely recoverable from the diagram.

2. *We can see the downward containment structures of events.* The uppermost set of seven labeled events (E, F, G, H, I, K, and L) are the events that involved the largest sets of actors. Other events are contained in the lower intersections (meets) of these events. Event C is a second level event: It is contained in event E, and events A, B, and D are, in turn, third level events; they are contained in C (and therefore in E). Similarly, event J is second level, contained in L, and M and N are third level, contained in J.

3. *We can see the upward containment structures of actors.* The lowest labeled actors (1, 2, 3, 4, 13, 14, and 15) are primary. They are the actors who were active in the largest sets of events. Other actors are contained in the upper intersections (joins) of these seven actors. Actors 5, 6, 7, 8, 9, 10, 11, 12, 17, and 18 are second level; the events they attended are all subsets of the events attended by one or more primary actors. Actor 16 falls at the third level; the two events she attended were also attended by second level actors 8, 9, 10, 11, and 12 as well as by primary actors 1, 3, and 13.

4. *We can distinguish classes of events.* Two sets of events $E_1 = \{A, B, C, D, E\}$ and $E_2 = \{J, K, L, M, N\}$ share no common actor. This is shown by the fact that their lower bound falls at the bottommost point, the point that contains no common actors. Therefore, E_1 and E_2 are *group-defining* events. In contrast, the four events $E_3 = \{F, G, H, I\}$ each share at least one actor with events in E_1 and at least one actor with events in E_2; they might be called *bridging* events.

5. *We can see the segregation of actors by the event classes.* The nonoverlapping event sets E_1 and E_2 segregate all but two of the actors into two sets $A_1 = \{1, 2, 3, 4, 5, 6, 7, 9\}$ and $A_2 = \{10, 11, 12, 13, 14, 15, 17, 18\}$. Actors from these different subsets never interact in the nonoverlapping events. The other two actors $A_3 =$

{8, 16}, attend one or more of the bridging events in E_3 but none of the group-defining events in either E_1 or E_2.

These five patterns capture the same kinds of structural features of the data as those described by Davis, Gardner, and Gardner. Pattern 5 reveals the two groups that were described in their report. And, in most details, it assigns the women to groups in the same way that they did. The lattice analysis was unable to assign actors 8 and 16 to either group, and it did assign the actor that they put in both groups (woman 9) to the first group. Fifteen of the eighteen actors, however, are assigned to groups exactly as they were in the ethnographic report.

In addition, pattern 3 specifies exactly the same core members of the two groups as those listed by Davis, Gardner, and Gardner. Every actor they listed at the second level is also assigned at that level in the present analysis. Here, we did assign more actors to that second level, but the one third level actor uncovered here (woman 16) was also defined as third level in their intuitive description.

Overall, then, it would seem that a Galois lattice can be used to display the form of an actor-event structure in a way that makes it easy to see the kinds of structural features that are important to sociologists.[2] A Galois lattice is constructed in such a way that it immediately reveals more structural information than we could see easily in a bipartite graph. Moreover, the use of Galois lattices solves the problem of duality; unlike hypergraphs or simplicial complexes, Galois lattices permit the simultaneous examination of the structural features of both actor-actor and event-event patterning.

We suggested in section 1 above, that an effective representation should yield new structural insights. In the final section, we will

[2]It should be noted that the actor sets, A1, A2, and A3 and the event sets E1, E2, and E3 uncovered here are almost perfectly regular blocks (White and Reitz 1983), and they are the largest proper set of such blocks in these data. The conditions for regular equivalence can be read directly from the original lattice in Figure 5. Every actor in A1 = {1,2,3,4,5,6,7,9} attended one or more events in E1 = {A,B,C,D,E} and one or more events in E3 = {F,G,H,I}. Every actor in A2 = {10,11,12,13,14,15,17,18} attended one or more events in E2 = {J,K,L,M,N} and one or more in E3. Every actor in A3 = {8,16} attended one or more events in E3. Every event in E1 was attended by one or more actors in A1. Every event in E2 was attended by one or more actors in A2. Finally, every event in E3 (with the sole exception of event G in which no actor from A3 was involved) was attended by one or more actors in A1, A2 and A3.

continue using the Davis, Gardner, and Gardner example to show how Galois lattices can call attention to novel structural features and thereby enrich the analysis of network data.

5. EXTENDING LATTICE REPRESENTATIONS

The lattice representation of the Davis, Gardner, and Gardner data can be extended beyond the description of groups and levels of membership. Pattern 4 above, for example, partitions the events into three classes. The sets E_1 and E_2 are group-defining events: They share no actors in common. In contrast, the set containing events F, G, H, and I includes those that are bridging: events that bring the actors associated with E_1 and E_2 together in common settings. By considering these three classes of events separately, we can learn something about how the actors are linked together into groups and how they are involved in the structure of ties between the groups.

Figure 7 is the lattice of E_1. It is constructed from the first five columns of Figure 5 (events A through E) and includes all the

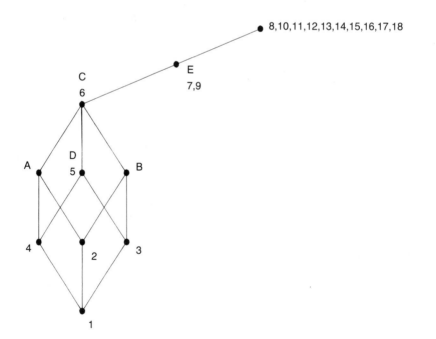

FIGURE 7. Lattice of the events in E_1.

women (1 through 18). The women listed at the topmost point (8, and 10 through 18) are those who were not involved in any of these events. Within this group, event E is the most inclusive, C is next, and A, B, and D are the least inclusive. Woman 1 was the most involved in these group activities, and she was followed by women 2, 3, and 4, then 5, then 6, and finally by 7 and 9.

In this group lattice we see not three but rather five levels of participation. Woman 1 is more involved than 2, 3, and 4, but the latter three are all right there at the next level. These are the women that Davis, Gardner, and Gardner located at the core, and here they are all shown to be more involved than any women that those authors classified at the second level (5, 6, and 7). Furthermore, woman 9, whom they classified at the third level, appears at the top of this lattice. Thus the present analysis suggests that Davis, Gardner, and Gardner's descriptions pretty well capture these women's roles *at the level of group participation.*

The same can be said for the second group. Its lattice structure (based on events J through N) is shown in Figure 8. This time women

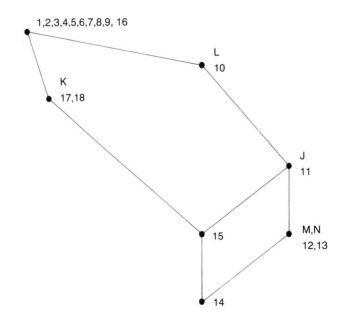

FIGURE 8. Lattice of the events in E_2.

1 through 9 and 16 appear at the top because they were not active in these events. Woman 14 is the most active, and she is followed closely by women 12, 13, and 15. Davis, Gardner, and Gardner defined women 13, 14, and 15 as the core members and put woman 12 at the next level. Their other second level woman (11) falls above women 12, 13, and 15, so the agreement is substantial. Finally, the women they assigned to the periphery (10, 17, and 18) are all located near the top—the most peripheral level here. So again, we see a close corrrespondence between the results of lattice analysis at the group level and those described by Davis, Gardner, and Gardner.

Finally, the lattice for events F through I is shown in Figure 9. This is a Boolean lattice 2^4. The fact that it is Boolean indicates that all of the possible combinations of the four events occur in the data. In the two "group" lattices (Figures 7 and 8) some, but not all, combinations of events were observed. In the case of this "bridging" lattice, however, the women's attendance patterns reflect that every possible combination of the four bridging events occurred.

If we examine the positions of actors in Figure 9, we can see that woman 3 plays the primary bridging role; she was present at all

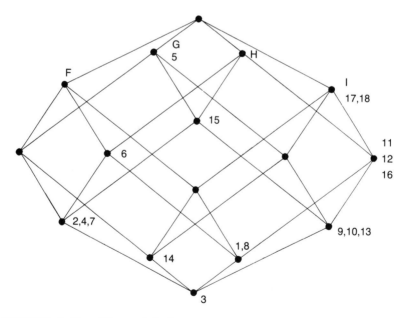

FIGURE 9. Lattice of the events in E_3.

four bridging events. Women 1, 2, 4, 7, 8, 9, 10, 13, and 14 all fall at the next level and played significant bridging roles. Women 6, 11, 12, 15, and 16 had a smaller role, and women 5, 17, and 18 were involved in bridging only in a very peripheral way.

From these comparisons, we can begin to differentiate not only between core and peripheral roles, but between those roles that solidify the groups and those that bridge across group boundaries. Woman 1, for example, played a critical role in tying the first group together. In contrast, woman 3, who was also a rather central member of that same group, had *the* major role in linking the two groups together. Examined in this way, the lattice structure suggests a new and more subtle basis for differentiating among the roles played by individuals.

All in all, most of the structural properties of the Davis, Gardner, and Gardner data that we have uncovered here are quite similar to those described in their ethnography. But while their report was based on impressions, the lattice analysis is systematic. In addition, we have been able to uncover a kind of role differentiation that they did not anticipate. Lattice analysis of structural properties of the data has suggested that some of these women were important to the integration of the groups while others were active primarily as bridges between groups, knitting the whole structure together. This illustrates precisely the kind of structural insight that a powerful representation can provide.

Like graph theory, Galois lattices provide an isomorphic image of binary data. Like graphs, their principal use is to represent, not to reduce, data. Thus, lattices share the limitation of graphs that, due to the inability of observers to untangle extremely complex images, they may not be useful for displaying large data sets.

Some binary data structures embody restrictions on possible orderings that lend visual simplifications to their lattice representation. Lattices of cliques, for example, generate easily interpretable structures (Freeman 1992), as do dual orderings of kinship relations (White and Jorion 1993).

In addition, statistical or algebraic data reductions may be used prior to lattice representations. Duquenne (1992) and White (1992) show how statistical reductions that are quasiordered (with exceptions) yield relationships between sets that can be usefully represented as lattices. Freeman and Duquenne (1993) also show how regular equivalence (White and Reitz 1983) can provide a reduction of person by event data prior to its representation. The visual representation of the dual orderings provided by lattice representations are potentially applicable in a wide range of substantive problems. These include the analysis of group structure illustrated here, but they also may yield important insights in any applications where two mode data appear. A number of potential applications suggest themselves. These include research on voluntary associations (McPherson 1982), the structure of policy domains (Laumann and Knoke 1987; Knoke 1990), upper-class inner circles (Kadushin 1974; Useem 1984), business complexes (Levine 1972; Stokman, Ziegler, and Scott 1985; Mizruchi and Schwartz 1987) and kinship relations (White and Jorion 1993).

REFERENCES

Arnheim, R. 1970. *Visual Thinking*. London: Faber.

Atkin, Ronald H. 1974. *Mathematical Structure in Human Affairs*. New York: Crane, Rusak.

Barbut, Marc, and Bernard Monjardet. 1970. *Ordre et Classification*. Paris: Hachette Université.

Berge, Claude, 1973. *Graphs and Hypergraphs*. Amsterdam: North-Holland.

Birkhoff, Garrett. 1940. *Lattice Theory*. Providence: American Mathematical Society.

Bott, Elizabeth. 1957. *Family and Social Network*. London: Tavistock Publications.

Breiger, Ronald. 1974. "The Duality of Persons and Groups." *Social Forces* 53:181–90.

Davis, Allison, Burleigh B. Gardner, and Mary R. Gardner. 1941. *Deep South*. Chicago: University of Chicago Press.

Doreian, Patrick. 1980. "On the Evolution of Group and Network Structure." *Social Networks* 2:235–52.

Duquenne, Vincent. 1987. "Contextual Implications between Attributes and Some Representation Properties for Finite Lattices." In *Beitraege zur Begriffsanalyse*, edited by Bernard Ganter, Ruldolph Wille, and Karl Erich Wolf, 213–39. Mannheim: Wissenschaftsverlag.

———. 1991. "On the Core of Finite Lattices." *Discrete Mathematics* 88:133–47.

———. 1993. "On Lattice Approximations I: Syntactic Aspects." *Social Networks*, forthcoming.

Freeman, Linton C. 1980. "Q-analysis and the Structure of Friendship Networks." *International Journal of Man-Machine Studies* 12:367–78.

———. 1989. "Network Representations." In *Research Methods in Social Network Analysis,* edited by Linton C. Freeman, Douglas R. White, and A. Kimball Romney, 11–40. Fairfax, Va: George Mason University Press.

———. 1992. "La Resurrection des Cliques: Application du Treillis de Galois." *Bulletin de Méthodologie Sociologique* 37: 3–24.

Freeman, Linton C., and Vincent Duquenne. 1993. "A Note on Regular Colorings of Two Mode Data." *Social Networks,* forthcoming.

Hage, Per, and Frank Harary. 1983. *Structural Models in Anthropology.* Cambridge: Cambridge University Press.

Kadushin, Charles. 1974. *The Americal Intellectual Elite.* Boston: Little Brown.

Klovdahl, Alden S. 1981. "A Note on Images of Networks." *Social Networks* 3:197–214.

Koestler, A. 1964. *The Act of Creation.* New York: Macmillan.

Knoke, David. 1990. *Organization for Collective Action: The Political Economics of Association.* New York: A. de Gruyter.

Laumann, Edward O., and David Knoke. 1987. *The Organizational State: Social Choice in National Policy Domains.* Madison: University of Wisconsin Press.

Levine, Joel. 1972. "The Sphere of Influence." *American Sociological Review* 37:14–27.

McPherson, J. Miller. 1982. "Hypernetwork Sampling: Duality and Differentiation among Voluntary Organizations." *Social Networks* 3:225–49.

Mizruchi, Mark S., and Michael Schwartz. 1987. *Intercorporate Relations: The Structural Analysis of Business.* New York: Cambridge University Press.

Seidman, Steven B. 1981. "Structures Induced by Collections of Subsets: A Hypergraph Approach." *Mathematical Social Sciences* 1:381–96.

Stokman, Frans N., Rolf Ziegler, and John Scott. 1985. *Networks of Corporate Power.* Cambridge: Polity Press.

Taylor, A. M. 1971. *Imagination and the Growth of Science.* New York: Shocken.

Tufte, E. R. 1983. *The Visual Display of Quantitative Information.* Cheshire, Conn.: Graphics Press.

Tukey, John W. 1972. "Some Graphic and Semigraphic Displays. In *Statistical Papers in Honor of George W. Snedecor,* edited by T. A. Bancroft. Ames: Iowa State University Press.

Useem, Michael. 1984. *The Inner Circle: Large Corporations and the Rise of Business Political Activity.* New York: Oxford University Press.

Wasserman, Stanley, and Katherine Faust. 1993. *Social Network Analysis: Methods and Applications.* New York: Academic Press.

White, Douglas R. 1992. "On Lattice Approximations II: Statistical Interpretations from Entailment Analysis." *Social Networks,* forthcoming.

White, Douglas R., and Paul Jorion. 1993. "Representing and Analysing Kinship: A New Approach." *Current Anthropology,* forthcoming.

White, Douglas R., and Karl P. Reitz. 1983. "Graph and Semigroup Homomorphisms." *Social Networks* 5:193–234.

Wille, Rudolph. 1982. "Restructuring Lattice Theory: An Approach Based on

Hierarchies of Concepts." In *Ordered Sets,* edited by I. Rival. Boston: Reidel, Dordrecht.

———. 1984. "Line Diagrams of Hierarchical Concept Systems." *International Classification* 11:77–86.

Wilson, Thomas P. 1982. "Relational Networks: An Extension of Sociometric Concepts." *Social Networks* 4:105–16.

𝕩 5 𝕩

CONFIRMATORY TETRAD ANALYSIS

Kenneth A. Bollen*
Kwok-fai Ting*

A "tetrad" refers to the difference in the products of certain covariances (or correlations) among four random variables. A structural equation model often implies that some tetrads should be zero. These "vanishing tetrads" provide a means to test structural equation models. In this paper we develop confirmatory tetrad analysis (CTA). CTA applies a simultaneous test statistic for multiple vanishing tetrads developed by Bollen (1990). The simultaneous test statistic is available in asymptotically distribution-free or normal-distribution versions and applies to covariances or to correlations. We also offer new rules for determining the nonredundant vanishing tetrads implied by a model and develop a method to estimate the power of the statistical test for vanishing tetrads. Testing vanishing tetrads provides a test for model fit that can lead to results different from the usual likelihood-ratio (LR) test associated with the maximum likelihood methods that dominate the structural equation field. Also, the CTA technique applies to some underidentified models. Furthermore, some models that are not nested according to the traditional LR test are nested in terms of vanishing tetrads. Finally, CTA does not require numerical minimization and thus avoids the associated convergence problems that are present with other estimation approaches.

*University of North Carolina at Chapel Hill

An earlier version of this paper was presented in August 1991 at the annual meeting of the American Sociological Association in Cincinnati, Ohio. We thank Yu Xie, the referees, and Peter Marsden for their helpful comments.

147

In 1904 Spearman laid the groundwork for what was to become factor analysis. In this and more clearly in his later work (e.g., Spearman 1927), he demonstrated that a single factor underlying four or more observed variables implies that the difference in the products of certain pairs of the covariances (or correlations) of these variables must be zero. These came to be referred to as "vanishing tetrads." The use of vanishing tetrads to examine models with latent variables dominated the work on factor analysis for the first third of the twentieth century. This approach eventually gave way to other techniques such as principal components (Hotelling 1933) and later to the maximum likelihood (e.g., Lawley and Maxwell 1971) and weighted least squares (e.g., Browne 1984) estimators that dominate today's factor analyses. The general structural equation models (SEM) that have now swept through most of the social sciences initially also flirted with the tetrad approach to model testing (e.g., Costner 1969; Duncan 1972; Kenny 1974), but it has been replaced by the maximum likelihood method popularized by Jöreskog (1973) in the LISREL program (Jöreskog and Sörbom 1989).

The tetrad approach to SEM was all but forgotten until Glymour et al. (1987) proposed vanishing tetrads as a viable method to search for models that are consistent with the covariance matrix of observed variables. Their emphasis has been exploratory tetrad analysis (ETA) based on a computer intensive search algorithm to formulate models with a good match to the tetrads of the observed variables. In this paper we propose a confirmatory tetrad analysis (CTA) that tests one or several specific models. CTA is "confirmatory" in that models are specified in advance. The structure of each model often implies population tetrads that should be zero. A test of a model's vanishing tetrads is a test of the model's fit. Significant nonzero tetrads for the model implied vanishing tetrads cast doubt on the appropriateness of the model.

The relation between ETA and CTA is analogous to that between exploratory and confirmatory factor analysis. Our CTA approach differs from Glymour et al.'s ETA in several ways. First, CTA is meant to *test* rather than to generate models, the latter being the purpose of ETA. As such, CTA and ETA are not rival methods. Second, we employ a simultaneous test for vanishing tetrads that applies to normal or nonnormal variables (Bollen 1990). Glymour et al. (1987) use Wishart's (1928) *single* tetrad test that assumes multinormally distributed observed variables and that does not control for multiple testing problems. Third, we also provide a modification for the test statistic so that it applies to correlations as well as covariances. Fourth, we look only at the nonredundant vanishing tetrads whereas Glymour et al. (1987) examine all vanishing tetrads.

A natural question is why should we consider CTA when we already have confirmatory factor analysis and the other maximum likelihood (ML)/weighted least squares (WLS) approaches to the general SEM? There are several good reasons. First, testing vanishing tetrads provides a goodness-of-fit test for a model that can lead to results different from the usual likelihood-ratio (LR) test associated with the ML/WLS methods.[1] We do not claim that our test is superior to the LR test, but it may be possible to reveal specification errors that are not evident in the LR test. Second, the CTA technique applies to some underidentified models. We can have a test of model fit even if the parameters of the model cannot be uniquely determined.[2] Third, some models that are not nested according to the conventional LR test are nested in terms of vanishing tetrads.[3] CTA allows the overall fit of some "nonnested" models to be compared directly. Finally, as mentioned previously, we have asymptotically distribution-free tests that apply to covariances and correlations. Although distribution-free estimators also are available for SEM through the work of Browne (1984) and others, the main advantage of our technique is that CTA uses a

[1]We use the term "likelihood ratio (LR)" test here and throughout the paper to refer to the tests that are based on ML estimation as well as on WLS estimation. Strictly speaking, the LR test refers only to the test statistic from ML methods. However, Browne (1984), among others, justifies the usual ML fitting functions and test statistics under the less restrictive WLS family of estimators. Thus, for the sake of brevity, we use LR test to mean the overall fit tests derived from ML or WLS methods.

[2]Shapiro (1986) discusses the theoretical conditions where it is possible to have an LR or WLS test statistic that follows an asymptotic chi-square distribution for some underidentified models. We know of no empirical applications of this work.

[3]It is possible to compare the fit of nonnested models using some of the overall fit measures in structural equation models that take the degrees of freedom of a model into account (see, for example, Bollen 1989, pp. 256–81). However, these typically do not provide a test of the statistical significance of the differences in fit for nonnested models. A growing literature on significance testing for nonnested models is accumulating (e.g., MacKinnon 1983; Judge et al. 1985, pp. 881–85), but little of this work has penetrated the structural equation literature. On the other hand, this literature on nonnested models has not considered vanishing tetrads as a test for such models.

noniterative estimator that does not have nonconvergence problems as is sometimes true for the commonly used procedures.

In this paper we propose CTA and illustrate its application to the previously mentioned issues. We view CTA not as a replacement for the standard methods of SEM but rather as a technique that complements current methods of model evaluation. For models that are not easily testable under the conventional methods, CTA sometimes can be a useful tool for model evaluation. In the following sections, we will discuss the concept of vanishing tetrads, propose new rules for selecting nonredundant vanishing tetrads, provide a method of significance testing, and develop a method to estimate the power of the vanishing tetrad test. Finally, we will illustrate the applications of CTA with examples.

1. MODEL IMPLIED VANISHING TETRADS

The idea of vanishing tetrads is best introduced by way of examples. Figure 1(a) is a path diagram of a factor model with one latent variable (ξ_1) and four observed variables (x_1 to x_4). We use the usual path analysis conventions where an oval or circle signifies a latent variable and boxes denote observed variables. Disturbances (or errors) are not enclosed. A single-headed straight arrow indicates an effect of the variable from the base of the arrow to the variable at the head of the arrow. The equations corresponding to this diagram are of the form:

$$x_i = \lambda_{i1}\xi_1 + \delta_i \qquad (1)$$

where δ_i is the random measurement error (disturbance) term with $E(\delta_i) = 0$ for all i, $COV(\delta_i, \delta_j) = 0$ for $i \neq j$, and the $COV(\xi_1, \delta_i) = 0$ for all i. All variables are written as deviations from their means to simplify the algebra.

The population covariances (σ_{ij}) of the observed variables are of the following form:

$$\sigma_{ij} = \lambda_{i1}\lambda_{j1}\phi, \qquad (2)$$

where σ_{ij} is the population covariance of the i and j variables and ϕ is the variance of ξ_1. If the model is correct, then we can use covariance algebra (e.g., Bollen 1989, p. 21) to prove that the equalities below must hold:

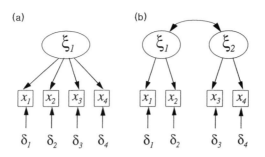

FIGURE 1. Two factor models.

$$\tau_{1234} = \sigma_{12}\sigma_{34} - \sigma_{13}\sigma_{24} = 0$$

$$\tau_{1342} = \sigma_{13}\sigma_{42} - \sigma_{14}\sigma_{32} = 0 \qquad (3)$$

$$\tau_{1423} = \sigma_{14}\sigma_{23} - \sigma_{12}\sigma_{43} = 0,$$

where τ_{ghij} is the population tetrad difference that equals the quantity to its right. We use the Kelley (1928) notation for tetrads, where τ_{ghij} refers to $\sigma_{gh}\sigma_{ij} - \sigma_{gi}\sigma_{hj}$. When τ_{ghij} is zero for a model, this is referred to as a vanishing tetrad. The model in Figure 1(a) implies the three vanishing tetrads in equation (3). Due to sampling errors, the sample counterpart, t_{ghij}, is likely to be nonzero. A simultaneous significance test described later can be used to determine whether the model in Figure 1(a) is consistent with the sample data. A nonsignificant test statistic means that the implied vanishing tetrads hold and the model is a legitimate candidate for consideration. If the significance test indicates otherwise, the one-factor model in Figure 1(a) would be rejected.

Figure 1(b) shows a two-factor model with two indicators for each latent variable. The only vanishing tetrad implied by this model is

$$\tau_{1342} = \sigma_{13}\sigma_{42} - \sigma_{14}\sigma_{32} = 0. \qquad (4)$$

A significance test of this vanishing tetrad provides a test of the model in Figure 1(b). Notice that the vanishing tetrad implied by the model in Figure 1(b) [see equation (4)] is a subset of the vanishing tetrads implied by the model in Figure 1(a) [see equation (3)]. Whenever the vanishing tetrads of one model are a subset of those in another, we refer to such models as having "nested tetrads." If the difference in the test statistics for the two models is not significant, this lends support to the model that implies the most vanishing tetrads. If the test result is significant, we would prefer the model with the fewest vanishing tetrads. In Figure 1 we would favor the one factor model if the test statistic for the vanishing tetrads in equation (3) is not significantly greater than the test statistic for the vanishing tetrads in equation (4).

2. IDENTIFYING VANISHING TETRADS

To perform significance tests, we need to identify the vanishing tetrads implied by a model. We propose three methods for this task: covariance algebra, a new rule for factor analysis models, and a new empirical method for general SEM.[4]

2.1. *Covariance Algebra*

The first method uses covariance algebra to show the vanishing tetrads for a model. The starting point is the structural equations and assumptions for a model (for example, see equation [1]). A few simple rules of covariance algebra (Bollen 1989, p. 21) allow us to express the covariance of any two variables in terms of the parameters of the model (for example, see equation [2]). A more general way of obtaining the covariances of the observed variables in terms of the model parameters is to use matrix methods to form the model implied covariance matrix for a model (see Jöreskog and Sörbom 1989, p. 5). We can then compare two pairs of covariances in a tetrad and conclude whether a vanishing tetrad is implied by the model. Whether a vanishing tetrad is implied does not depend on the value of the coefficients unless one or more have a trivial zero coefficient or the unlikely coincidence occurs that the combination of values of the parameters lead to zero. In other words, in practice the structure of a model determines the vanishing tetrads, not the specific values of the parameters.

---

[4]Another possibility is to use Glymour et al. (1987) computer algorithms to determine the vanishing tetrads of models.

2.2. *A Factor Analysis Rule*

Using covariance algebra, as we did for the models in Figure 1, becomes tedious for models with more than four variables. The second method, which can simplify the task, works for factor analysis models where each indicator is influenced only by one latent variable and an error variable, though this rule permits correlated errors of measurement. A vanishing tetrad is implied when two conditions are met: (1) none of the four covariances in a tetrad equation involve correlated error terms and (2) the two pairs of latent variables associated with the two covariances in the first term match those in the second term of the equation.

Regardless of the size of the model, we consider four variables at a time and repeat the process for every foursome of variables in the model. For every four variables, there are three possible vanishing tetrads, and each of them has to be checked regarding whether it fulfills the above two conditions. Suppose x_1, x_2, x_3, x_4 are four indicators in a factor model with each observed indicator affected only by one latent variable and an error variable. The four measurement equations are:

$$x_1 = \lambda_{1i}\xi_i + \delta_1, \qquad x_3 = \lambda_{3k}\xi_k + \delta_3,$$
$$\text{and}$$
$$x_2 = \lambda_{2j}\xi_j + \delta_2, \qquad x_4 = \lambda_{4l}\xi_l + \delta_4.$$

For instance, whether $\tau_{1234} = \sigma_{12}\sigma_{34} - \sigma_{13}\sigma_{24} = 0$ is implied by a model depends on $\sigma_{12}\sigma_{34}$ and $\sigma_{13}\sigma_{24}$. Each correlated error of COV(δ_1,δ_2), COV(δ_3,δ_4), COV(δ_1,δ_3), and COV(δ_2,δ_4) has a unique effect on the covariance of σ_{12}, σ_{34}, σ_{13}, and σ_{24} respectively. If any of the four correlated error terms is nonzero, $\sigma_{12}\sigma_{34}$ will not equal $\sigma_{13}\sigma_{24}$, except under the very unlikely case where the effects of correlated errors on the four covariances cancel each other out. A vanishing tetrad is implied only under the condition that none of the four covariances involves a correlated error term. (This condition can be used to rule out vanishing tetrads in models other than the one described here.)

If we assume that the latent variables do not correlate with the error terms and the correlated errors of COV(δ_1,δ_2), COV(δ_3,δ_4), COV(δ_1,δ_3), and COV(δ_2,δ_4) are zero, then $\sigma_{12}\sigma_{34}$ and $\sigma_{13}\sigma_{24}$ equal the following:

$$\sigma_{12}\sigma_{34} = \lambda_{1i}\lambda_{2j}\lambda_{3k}\lambda_{4l}\phi_{ij}\phi_{kl} \quad \text{and} \quad \sigma_{13}\sigma_{24} = \lambda_{1i}\lambda_{2j}\lambda_{3k}\lambda_{4l}\phi_{ik}\phi_{jl}.$$

It becomes obvious that $\sigma_{12}\sigma_{34} - \sigma_{13}\sigma_{24} = 0$ iff $\phi_{ij}\phi_{kl} = \phi_{ik}\phi_{jl}$, provided that none of the λ_{ij} is zero. This equality holds only if a vanishing tetrad satisfies the second condition that the two pairs of latent variables associated with $\sigma_{12}\sigma_{34}$ match with those associated with $\sigma_{13}\sigma_{24}$. In this example, $\xi_j = \xi_k$ is necessary and sufficient to make $\phi_{ij}\phi_{kl} = \phi_{ik}\phi_{jl}$.

We illustrate this rule with the four examples in Figure 2. In Figure 2(a), we add a correlated error between x_3 and x_4 to the two-factor model in Figure 1(b). Figure 2(a) becomes an underidentified model. The vanishing tetrad, $\tau_{1342} = 0$, is implied in Figure 1(b) and continues to be true in Figure 2(a). The correlated error term that appears in σ_{34} has no effects on this tetrad equation, and the two pairs

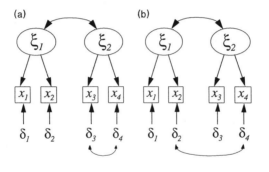

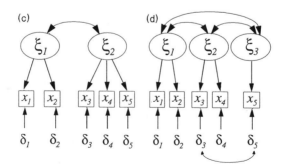

FIGURE 2. Four factor models.

of latent variables, (ξ_1,ξ_2) and (ξ_2,ξ_1), of $\sigma_{13}\sigma_{42}$ match those of $\sigma_{14}\sigma_{32}$. This vanishing tetrad is no longer implied in Figure 2(b), however, because a correlated error term appears in σ_{24}. The other two tetrad equations, $\tau_{1234} = 0$ and $\tau_{1423} = 0$, are not implied in the two-factor models in Figure 2(a) and 2(b) because the corresponding pairs of latent variables in the first and the second terms of the tetrad equations do not match each other. The correlated error term in Figure 2(a) alone is sufficient to rule out these two vanishing tetrads. Consequently, one tetrad is implied in Figure 2(a) and none is implied in Figure 2(b). As such, we have nested tetrads and we can compare the two models. Note that these two models are not nested in terms of an LR test, though they are nested for a tetrad test.

The same procedure applies to models with more variables. With five variables, such as the models in Figures 2(c) and 2(d), we have five sets (5!/1!4!) of tetrad equations. The task in Figure 2(c) is simplified because the model is composed of only two basic structures. Consider x_1, x_2, x_3, and x_4 with two indicators for each latent variable. This part of the model is identical to the model in Figure 1(b), and it implies the same vanishing tetrad, τ_{1342}. In an analogous fashion we can find the vanishing tetrads for x_1, x_2, x_3, and x_5, and for x_1, x_2, x_4, and x_5 since they share the same basic structure of two indicators per latent variable.

The second basic structure has one indicator for ξ_1 and three indicators for ξ_2. Consider x_1, x_3, x_4, and x_5. All three vanishing tetrads ($\tau_{1345} = 0$, $\tau_{1453} = 0$, and $\tau_{1534} = 0$) are implied. First, no correlated errors exist in any of the covariances, and second, (ξ_1,ξ_2) and (ξ_2,ξ_2) are the two pairs of latent variables in the first and the second terms of each tetrad equation. Similarly, the three vanishing tetrads among x_2, x_3, x_4, and x_5 are also implied for the same reasons.

We modify Figure 2(c) by adding one more latent variable and one correlated error term in Figure 2(d). The rule for determining implied vanishing tetrads is no different from that used in the previous three examples. If we consider x_1 to x_4, the model structure is identical to the one in Figure 1(b), and only $\tau_{1342} = 0$ is implied. For x_1, x_2, x_3, and x_5, $\tau_{1235} = 0$ and $\tau_{1523} = 0$ are not implied because σ_{35}, which is in both equations, has a correlated error term. The two pairs of latent variables associated with $\sigma_{13}\sigma_{52}$ and $\sigma_{15}\sigma_{32}$ are (ξ_1,ξ_2) and (ξ_3,ξ_1) and (ξ_1,ξ_3) and (ξ_2,ξ_1) respectively, and no correlated error term appears in the four covariances in this tetrad equation. As such, τ_{1352} = 0 is implied in the model. Among x_1, x_2, x_4, and x_5, only τ_{1452} = 0 is implied. Finally, application of our general rule to the set of x_1, x_3, x_4, and x_5 and the set of x_2 to x_5 shows no vanishing tetrads.

The same strategy for determining vanishing tetrads applies to other factor analysis models where each indicator is influenced by a single latent variable and an error term.

2.3. An Empirical Method

The covariance algebra technique for determining vanishing tetrads is perfectly general but too tedious to implement for complex models. The factor analysis rule is inapplicable to models with factor complexity greater than one or to general SEM. In this subsection we describe a simple but new empirical means to determine model implied vanishing tetrads. The procedure has four steps:

1. Arbitrarily specify the values of model parameters.
2. Use model parameters specified in step 1 to generate the implied covariance matrix through structural equation programs such as LISREL (Jöreskog and Sörbom 1989), EQS (Bentler 1989), or CALIS (Hartmann 1991).
3. Calculate all tetrads.
4. Take those tetrads within rounding of zero as the model implied vanishing tetrads.

In step 1 we recommend use of the parameter estimates for a model, if available, since the implied covariance matrix for step 2 is readily accessible in the above-mentioned programs. The essence of this method is to generate a covariance matrix that is consistent with the model so that when you calculate the tetrads, those that should be zero will be within rounding error of zero. Researchers having any doubt regarding whether a value is zero or not can apply the covariance algebra method to the specific tetrads that are in question as an additional check. Our experience suggests that this method is extremely accurate. Coupled with its generality, this makes it the method of choice for most models. We will illustrate the procedure in the examples section.

3. REDUNDANT VANISHING TETRADS

Previous tetrad analyses, such as those of Glymour et al. (1987), focused on tests of individual vanishing tetrads; redundancy was rarely a concern except in the simple case where all three vanishing tetrads are implied by a set of four variables. As a result, there is no guidance on how to select nonredundant vanishing tetrads among all those implied by a model. For a simultaneous test of a set of implied vanishing tetrads, we have to determine which vanishing tetrads are redundant and should be excluded from the test. Otherwise, the covariance matrix of the tetrads that is part of the test statistic can be singular, and its inverse will not exist. In the material that follows we develop a procedure to deal with this problem.[5]

Algebraic substitution between vanishing tetrads will show that some of the vanishing tetrads can be derived from the others and are redundant for the test. When none of the covariances are in common between vanishing tetrads, algebraic substitution is impossible. When two vanishing tetrads have three or more covariances in common, they must be identical. Therefore, we need to consider only two cases: those vanishing tetrads having either one or two covariances in common.

When two covariances in one vanishing tetrad are identical with the covariances in another vanishing tetrad, it is a sufficient condition that a third vanishing tetrad must be implied and should be eliminated in the simultaneous test. The simplest case is when all three vanishing tetrads are implied for a set of four variables, only two of them are needed for the simultaneous test due to redundancy. For instance, if

$$\tau_{abcd} = \sigma_{ab}\sigma_{cd} - \sigma_{ac}\sigma_{bd} = 0,$$
$$\tau_{acdb} = \sigma_{ac}\sigma_{db} - \sigma_{ad}\sigma_{cb} = 0, \quad \text{and}$$
$$\tau_{adbc} = \sigma_{ad}\sigma_{bc} - \sigma_{ab}\sigma_{cd} = 0,$$

then any two of them imply the third–that is, only two vanishing tetrads are independent. Suppose we have two vanishing tetrads

[5]In comments on this paper, Yu Xie suggested a method for determining the nonredundant vanishing tetrads by using an analogy to methods of determining the odds-ratios in a contingency table. However, the method was suggested for single factor models without correlated errors of measurement, and it is not clear whether the procedure generalizes to other models.

$$\tau_{acdb} = \sigma_{ac}\sigma_{db} - \sigma_{ad}\sigma_{cb} = 0 \text{ and} \qquad (5)$$

$$\tau_{adeb} = \sigma_{ad}\sigma_{eb} - \sigma_{ae}\sigma_{db} = 0, \qquad (6)$$

where σ_{ad} and σ_{db} appear in both vanishing tetrads. Algebraic manipulation between (5) and (6) will show that

$$\tau_{aceb} = \sigma_{ac}\sigma_{eb} - \sigma_{ae}\sigma_{cb} = 0 \qquad (7)$$

is implied.

In the case where there is only one common covariance between two vanishing tetrads, algebraic substitution will lead to a vanishing equation with six covariances, and no additional vanishing tetrad will be implied. For example,

$$\tau_{abcd} = \sigma_{ab}\sigma_{cd} - \sigma_{ac}\sigma_{bd} = 0 \text{ and} \qquad (8)$$

$$\tau_{abef} = \sigma_{ab}\sigma_{ef} - \sigma_{ae}\sigma_{bf} = 0 \qquad (9)$$

imply

$$\sigma_{ac}\sigma_{bd}\sigma_{ef} - \sigma_{ae}\sigma_{bf}\sigma_{cd} = 0. \qquad (10)$$

Introducing more vanishing tetrads with one common covariance with equation (10) only will further expand the equation. The single possibility is to have another vanishing tetrad that has three covariances in common with equation (10) such that three covariances can be eliminated and a new covariance term will be added to equation (10). Consider

$$\tau_{aecd} = \sigma_{ae}\sigma_{cd} - \sigma_{ac}\sigma_{ed} = 0. \qquad (11)$$

In vanishing tetrad (11), σ_{ac}, σ_{ae}, and σ_{cd} appear in equation (10). Equations (10) and (11) together imply a redundant vanishing tetrad,

$$\tau_{bfde} = \sigma_{bf}\sigma_{de} - \sigma_{bd}\sigma_{fe} = 0. \qquad (12)$$

That means given vanishing tetrads (8), (9), and (11), vanishing tetrad (12) should be excluded in the simultaneous test.

Alternatively, with the rule of two common covariances, vanishing tetrad (12) can be concluded from pairwise algebraic substitution between vanishing tetrads. Notice that σ_{ab}, σ_{ac}, σ_{ae}, and σ_{cd} appear twice in vanishing tetrads (8), (9), and (11). These four covariances can be eliminated through algebraic substitution and the remaining four covariances form vanishing tetrad (12). We begin with vanishing tetrads (8) and (11) because σ_{ac} and σ_{cd} appear in both equations. As a result, another vanishing tetrad

$$\tau_{aebd} = \sigma_{ae}\sigma_{bd} - \sigma_{ab}\sigma_{ed} = 0, \tag{13}$$

is implied. In vanishing tetrads (9) and (13), both have σ_{ab} and σ_{ae}, and (9) and (13) together lead to the redundant vanishing tetrad (12). This example illustrates that pairwise comparisons between those vanishing tetrads with two common covariances are an adequate means for identifying redundant vanishing tetrads.

The above example shows that vanishing tetrads (8), (9), (11), (12), and (13) are linearly dependent among each other; only three of them are needed for model testing. If the model is correct and the null hypothesis is true, then the choice of the three vanishing tetrads matters little. With an incorrect model and a false null hypothesis, it is possible that the selection might matter more. In our experience with the examples in the empirical example section, we found similar results regardless of the choice of the nonredundant vanishing tetrads. However, as a precaution one could select a different set of redundant vanishing tetrads to exclude and recalculate the test of significance. Since more than one significance test is being performed, the researcher should adjust the individual alpha levels for the significance tests to maintain an overall alpha level for the family of tests. A Bonferroni correction is probably the easiest one to implement. Consistent test results increase our confidence in the initial results while inconsistent test results indicate that the model is not correct.[6]

4. SIGNIFICANCE TESTING OF VANISHING TETRADS

Spearman and Holzinger (1924), Kelley (1928), Wishart (1928), and Kenny (1974) have proposed significance tests for a vanishing tetrad. All these tests are asymptotic, assume a multivariate normal distribution among the observed variables, and are not simultaneous tests for multiple vanishing tetrads. Bollen (1990) proposed a less restrictive

[6]There are two other possible sensitivity checks: (1) Take the pool of redundant tetrads and perform the simultaneous significance test on them, after eliminating any redundant tetrads in this group, and (2) perform individual vanishing tetrad tests on the redundant tetrads to see if any are significant. Use a Bonferroni correction to take into account the multiple tests that are performed.

test that evaluates multiple tetrads simultaneously, applies to normally or nonnormally distributed observed variables, and analyzes correlations or covariances. This test was originally proposed for ETA but is applicable to CTA as well. The null hypothesis is H_o: $\tau = \mathbf{0}$, and the alternative hypothesis is H_a: $\tau \neq \mathbf{0}$ where τ is a vector of the population tetrads that are implied to be zero for a specific model. A significant test statistic suggests that the model implied vanishing tetrads are not zero and casts doubt on the model's validity.

To derive the test statistic, we begin with a vector $\mathbf{S}$ that includes the nonredundant elements of $\mathbf{S}$, the unbiased sample covariance matrix of the observed variables.[7] Let σ be a similar vector formed from Σ, the population covariance matrix of the observed variables. We assume that the fourth-order moments of the observed variables exist and are finite. The $E(\mathbf{s})$ is σ. The distribution of $\sqrt{N}(s - \sigma)$ in finite samples is not always known but the limiting distribution is multivariate normal with a mean of zero and a covariance matrix of Σ_{ss} (e.g., see Browne 1984, p. 64):

$$\sqrt{N}(\mathbf{s} - \sigma) \xrightarrow{\text{D}} N(\mathbf{0}, \Sigma_{ss}). \qquad (14)$$

The elements of Σ_{ss} give the variances and covariances of the sample covariances. In general the elements of Σ_{ss} equal

$$[\Sigma_{ss}]_{ef,gh} = \sigma_{efgh} - \sigma_{ef}\sigma_{gh}, \qquad (15)$$

where σ_{efgh} is the fourth-order moment for the $e, f, g,$ and h variables. A sample estimator of σ_{efgh} is

$$s_{efgh} = N^{-1} [\Sigma (X_e - \bar{X}_e)(X_f - \bar{X}_f)(X_g - \bar{X}_g)(X_h - \bar{X}_h)]. \qquad (16)$$

If the observed variables are multinormally distributed, then the elements of Σ_{ss} are

$$\sigma_{eg}\sigma_{fh} + \sigma_{eh}\sigma_{fg}. \qquad (17)$$

Instead of the asymptotic covariance matrix of the sample covariances, we require the asymptotic variance of the sample tetrad differences. Define $\mathbf{t}$ as the column vector of the independent sample tetrad differences implied by a model, $\tau(\sigma)$ as the column vector of the population vanishing tetrads that is a function of σ, and σ as the

---

[7]The derivation of this test statistic is based on the description in Bollen (1990).

column vector of all σ_{ef} that appear in one or more of the vanishing tetrads. The tetrad differences, t, are nonlinear functions of the sample covariances. Assume that $\tau(\sigma)$ is a continuously differentiable function with respect to σ in a neighborhood of the true value of σ, say σ_o, that does not vanish at σ_o. In conjunction with equation (14), we can use the delta method (Rao 1973, 385–89; Bishop, Fienberg, and Holland 1975, 486–500) to estimate the asymptotic variance of t. Using this theorem, we have

$$\sqrt{N}t \xrightarrow{\text{D}} N(0, \Sigma_{tt}) \tag{18}$$

$$\Sigma_{tt} = (\partial \tau / \partial \sigma)' \, \Sigma_{ss} \, (\partial \tau / \partial \sigma), \tag{19}$$

where Σ_{tt} is the covariance matrix of the limiting distribution of the sample tetrad differences and Σ_{ss} is the covariance matrix of the limiting distribution of the sample covariances that appear in the sample tetrad differences. Assume that Σ_{ss} is continuous with respect to the fourth order moments and elements of σ of which it is a function in a neighborhood of the true values of the fourth order moments and σ_o. Then all the parameters in (19) can be estimated by replacing the population parameters by their sample counterparts. Note also that this can be made a distribution-free estimator of the asymptotic covariance matrix by the choice of Σ_{ss}. The main diagonal of Σ_{tt} contains the variances of the sample tetrad differences while the off-diagonal elements contain their covariances for the limiting distribution.

A test statistic of whether all tetrad differences are zero is

$$T = N \, t' \hat{\Sigma}_{tt}^{-1} t. \tag{20}$$

Asymptotically, T approximates a chi-square variate with df equal to the number of tetrad differences simultaneously examined. The H_o is that all tetrad differences implied by a model are zero (i.e., $\tau = 0$). Failure to reject H_o provides support for the model whereas rejection suggests that one or more tetrad differences are different from zero. When there is only one tetrad difference in t, then (20) equals:

$$(t_{1432})^2 / \text{AVAR}(t_{1432}). \tag{21}$$

Also, the test statistic generalizes to hypotheses of nonzero values of τ by replacing t with $(t - \tau)$ in equation (20), with τ containing the values of the population tetrads under H_o.

The results can be modified to apply to tetrad differences of correlation coefficients rather than covariances. The key change is to replace the covariance matrix of the covariances (i.e., Σ_{ss}) with the covariance matrix of the correlation coefficients (i.e., Σ_{rr}). The elements of Σ_{rr} for arbitrary distributions are (Isserlis 1916)

$$[\Sigma_{rr}]_{ef,gh} = \rho_{efgh} + (1/4)\rho_{ef}\rho_{gh}(\rho_{eegg} + \rho_{ffgg} + \rho_{eehh} + \rho_{ffhh})$$
$$- (1/2)\,\rho_{ef}(\rho_{eegh} + \rho_{ffgh}) \tag{22}$$
$$- (1/2)\,\rho_{gh}(\rho_{efgg} + \rho_{efhh}),$$

where ρ_{efgh} is the standardized fourth order moment and ρ_{ef} is the population correlation of variable e and f.

For a multinormal distribution, this simplifies to

$$[\Sigma_{rr}]_{ef,gh} = (1/2)\,\rho_{ef}\rho_{gh}(\rho_{eg}^2 + \rho_{eh}^2 + \rho_{fg}^2 + \rho_{fh}^2)$$
$$+ \rho_{eg}\rho_{fh} + \rho_{eh}\rho_{fg} - \rho_{ef}(\rho_{fg}\rho_{fh} + \rho_{eg}\rho_{eh}) \tag{23}$$
$$- \rho_{gh}(\rho_{fg}\rho_{eg} + \rho_{fh}\rho_{eh}).$$

Thus all of the above discussion applies to tetrad differences of correlations as well as of covariances.

5. POWER OF VANISHING TETRAD TEST

The power of a statistical test is the probability of rejecting a false null hypothesis when an alternative hypothesis is true. Recent research in SEM has provided ways to estimate the power of the chi-square likelihood ratio test of H_o: $\Sigma = \Sigma(\theta)$, where Σ is the population covariance matrix of the observed variables, $\Sigma(\theta)$ is the covariance matrix implied by the hypothesized model, and θ is the vector of free parameters in a model (Satorra and Saris 1985; Matsueda and Bielby 1986; Bollen 1989, pp. 338–49). It would be helpful to know the power of the simultaneous vanishing tetrad test of H_o: $\tau = 0$ for several reasons. One is that with it we could determine if a significant (nonsignificant) test statistic is due to too much (or too little) power. This information would aid our assessment of a tetrad test. For instance, if we find that a vanishing tetrad has low power, yet the test statistic is highly significant, this would cast serious doubt on any model that implies the set of vanishing tetrads that were tested. Alternatively, if a tetrad test had high power and the test statistic was not statistically significant, the plausibility of the vanishing tetrads would be increased. Second, the power estimate for the vanishing tetrad test would be helpful in the situation where conflicting results occur for the LR test and the tetrad test. Knowing the power of both tests could partially or totally explain the discrepancy.

The rationale for our method to assess the power of the vanishing tetrad test is as follows. Suppose that we replace (18) with the more general expression of

$$\sqrt{N}\mathbf{t} \xrightarrow{D} N(\tau_a, \Sigma_{tt}), \tag{24}$$

where τ_a is the column vector of the tetrads that are hypothesized to be zero for a specific model and all other symbols are defined as previously. Equation (24) equals equation (18) if we set τ_a to zero. However, in equation (24) we allow some or all of the population tetrads to be nonzero, an outcome that runs counter to the vanishing tetrads implied by the hypothesized model.

Under equation (24), the test statistic, T, in equation (20) asymptotically approximates a *noncentral* chi-square variate with df equal to the number of nonredundant tetrad differences simultaneously examined and with a noncentrality parameter of

$$\kappa = N\,\tau_a{}'\Sigma_{tt}^{-1}\tau_a. \tag{25}$$

By knowing the df, κ, and the Type I alpha level at which we test the vanishing tetrads, we can estimate the power of the simultaneous vanishing tetrad test. The df are obvious by counting the number of nonredundant vanishing tetrads implied by a model. The alpha value is the probability of a Type I error chosen by a researcher and is typically 0.05. The value of N is known and equation (19) enables us to get Σ_{tt}^{-1}.[8] The only remaining quantity in equation (25) is τ_a. To get τ_a, we must formulate an alternative model with respect to which we are testing the power.[9] Give values to all of the parameters in the alternative model and form the implied covariance matrix $[\Sigma(\theta_a)]$ for the observed variables at these values. Based on the tetrads that

---

[8]For variables with the same multivariate kurtosis as a normal distribution, the elements of Σ_{ss} that are needed to form Σ_{tt} can be taken from $\Sigma(\theta_a)$, which is the implied covariance matrix under the alternative model. For nonnormal data with excessive multivariate kurtosis, the elements of Σ_{ss} can be estimated from the sample data as described in the previous section.

[9]The same step of formulating an alternative model with all the parameter values is necessary in the usual power tests for structural equation models.

should be zero for the hypothesized (not the alternative) model and the implied covariance matrix, we can calculate the values of τ_a.
In brief, the steps to the procedure are:

1. Determine θ_a, the specific values for the parameters in the alternative model.
2. Generate the implied covariance matrix, $\Sigma(\theta_a)$.
3. Form τ_a, the vector of nonredundant tetrads implied under H_o using $\Sigma(\theta_a)$ instead of S.
4. Form $N\,\tau_a'\Sigma_{tt}^{-1}\tau_a$ as the noncentrality value.
5. Calculate the power of the tetrad test based on the df, the Type I probability, and the noncentrality value.

We will illustrate the procedure in the next section.

6. EXAMPLES

6.1. *Example 1: Sympathy and Anger Confirmatory Factor Analysis*

The first example illustrates the use of the CTA test statistic in testing the fit of a factor analysis model. Figure 3 is the path diagram for a two-factor model with each factor measured with three indicators.

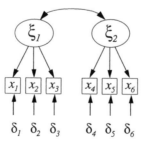

FIGURE 3. Sympathy and anger.

The data are taken from a social psychological experiment by Reisenzein (1986). As part of the experiment, he measures the feelings of sympathy and anger of 138 subjects. The covariance matrix for the six indicators is:

$$S = \begin{bmatrix} 6.982 & & & & & \\ 4.686 & 6.047 & & & & \\ 4.335 & 3.307 & 5.037 & & & \\ -2.294 & -1.453 & -1.979 & 5.569 & & \\ -2.209 & -1.262 & -1.738 & 3.931 & 5.328 & \\ -1.671 & -1.401 & -1.564 & 3.915 & 3.601 & 4.977 \end{bmatrix}$$

In Table 1, we use the sympathy and anger example of Figure 3 to illustrate the three methods of determining the vanishing tetrads. For the empirical method, the estimates of model parameters are used to generate the covariance matrix. This covariance matrix is used to calculate the tetrads. When comparing with the covariance algebra method and the factor model rules, it becomes apparent that the empirical method is effective in showing which vanishing tetrads are implied by the model. The model implied vanishing tetrads as determined by the covariance algebra and factor analysis analytic methods are virtually zero using the empirical method.

Eliminating the redundant vanishing tetrads, we identify eight independent vanishing tetrads ($\tau_{1234} = 0, \tau_{1235} = 0, \tau_{1236} = 0, \tau_{1456} = 0, \tau_{1423} = 0, \tau_{1523} = 0, \tau_{1623} = 0$, and $\tau_{1645} = 0$). With raw data kindly provided by Reisenzein, we tested for excessive multivariate kurtosis. Mardia and Foster's (1983) "normalized" estimate of multivariate kurtosis is 6.60 (Bollen 1989, p. 424), indicating substantial positive multivariate kurtosis. The simultaneous asymptotically distribution-free test of these eight tetrads results in a chi-square of 6.71 with 8 df and a p-value of 0.57. We cannot reject the null hypothesis that all eight population tetrads are zero. Thus the sample tetrads are consistent with this model structure. Using the usual structural equation procedures, the asymptotic distribution free test statistic (weighted least squares [WLS] estimator) for this model is 6.49 with 8 df ($p = 0.59$), which leads to the same conclusion.

The power of these statistical tests helps in evaluating model fit. As the alternative model, we take the WLS estimates of the parameters of the original model in Figure 3 and add to it three correlated errors of measurement. The covariances of these errors are set to be equivalent to correlations of 0.1 and we generated the implied covariance matrix. Following the power procedure described in the previous section, the noncentrality parameter is 1.45 with df of

TABLE 1
Model Implied Vanishing Tetrads for Sympathy and Anger Example

Tetrads	Cov. Algebra/ Factor Rules	Empirical Method
τ_{1234}	implied	-0.00000000
τ_{1423}	implied	-0.00000005
τ_{1342}	implied	0.00000006
τ_{1235}	implied	-0.00000004
τ_{1523}	implied	0.00000011
τ_{1352}	implied	-0.00000007
τ_{1236}	implied	0.00000003
τ_{1623}	implied	0.00000011
τ_{1362}	implied	-0.00000014
τ_{1245}		14.97524804
τ_{1524}		-14.97524810
τ_{1452}	implied	0.00000006
τ_{1246}		14.75163923
τ_{1624}		-14.75163932
τ_{1462}	implied	0.00000010
τ_{1256}		13.53462924
τ_{1625}		-13.53462927
τ_{1562}	implied	0.00000003
τ_{1345}		13.99787900
τ_{1534}		-13.99787907
τ_{1453}	implied	0.00000008
τ_{1346}		13.78886419
τ_{1634}		-13.78886426
τ_{1463}	implied	0.00000008
τ_{1356}		12.65128313
τ_{1635}		-12.65128313
τ_{1563}	implied	0.00000000
τ_{1456}	implied	-0.00000028
τ_{1645}	implied	0.00000024
τ_{1564}	implied	0.00000004
τ_{2345}		10.72377520
τ_{2534}		-10.72377521
τ_{2453}	implied	0.00000001
τ_{2346}		10.56364895
τ_{2634}		-10.56364894
τ_{2463}	implied	-0.00000001
τ_{2356}		9.69214805
τ_{2635}		-9.69214803
τ_{2563}	implied	-0.00000002
τ_{2456}	implied	-0.00000010
τ_{2645}	implied	0.00000001
τ_{2564}	implied	0.00000009
τ_{3456}	implied	-0.00000007
τ_{3645}	implied	0.00000003
τ_{3564}	implied	0.00000003

8. With a type I error of 0.05, the power of the tetrad test is 0.11. Using the same alternative model and estimating the power of the WLS-based test statistic, we find the same 0.11 value. Thus the tetrad test and the WLS test have low power to detect the correlated errors, and the fit of the model appears less ideal than an examination of p-value for the test of null hypothesis alone would lead one to believe. Though we found the power of the tetrad test and the WLS test to be the same in this example, this will not always be the case.

6.2. Example 2: Union Sentiment: An SEM Without Latent Variables

The second example illustrates that CTA also applies to SEM that do not contain any latent variables. Figure 4 is the path diagram for the model taken from Bollen (1989, pp. 82–83). The data are from a study of union sentiment among southern nonunion textile workers (McDonald and Clelland 1984). The variables are deference (or submissiveness) to managers (y_1), support for labor activism (y_2), sentiment toward unions (y_3), the logarithm of years in textile mill (x_1), and age (x_2). The sample covariance matrix $(N = 173)$ is (Bollen 1989, p. 120):

$$S = \begin{bmatrix} 14.610 & & & & \\ -5.250 & 11.017 & & & \\ -8.057 & 11.087 & 31.971 & & \\ -0.482 & 0.677 & 1.559 & 1.021 & \\ -18.857 & 17.861 & 28.250 & 7.139 & 215.662 \end{bmatrix}$$

The null hypothesis of multivariate normality could not be rejected for these data where the normalized test statistics for multivariate

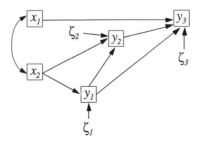

FIGURE 4. Union sentiment.

skewness was 0.74 and was −1.14 for multivariate kurtosis (Bollen 1989, p.424). Thus we use the CTA and LR test statistics that are based on the normality assumption.

With either covariance algebra or our empirical method, we find the only vanishing tetrad to be $\tau_{y1x1x2y2}$. The CTA test statistic is 0.73 with 1 df ($p = 0.39$). This excellent fit is consistent with the LR test statistic of 1.26 with 3 df ($p = 0.74$).

6.3. Example 3: Comparison of "Nonnested" Models with Simulated Data

Some models that are not nested for the usual SEM likelihood ratio (LR) test comparison of fit are nested in the implied vanishing tetrads. The implication is that model comparisons are possible for some models that we have traditionally believed to be nonnested. We take an example from Glymour et al. (1987) to illustrate this. The three models in Figure 5 differ in the relation between the x_3 and y_1 variables. In Figure 5(a), x_3 affects y_1, while in 5(b) the opposite relation holds. Figure 5(c) shows only correlated errors between these two variables. Clearly, from the perspective of LR test comparisons, these models are nonnested. However, the implied vanishing tetrads in Figures 5(a) and 5(b) are subsets of those implied in Figure 5(c). Figure 5(c), which has the most implied vanishing tetrads, is the most restrictive model of the three, and we can compare whether this more restrictive model fits as well as the less restrictive ones in Figures 5(a) and 5(b). We use the simulated "Data Set 2, Study 1" ($N = 2000$) from Glymour et al. (1987, p. 128). The correlation matrix

$$
S = \begin{bmatrix}
1 \\
0.73218 & 1 \\
0.71263 & 0.61605 & 1 \\
0.65140 & 0.56910 & 0.88900 & 1 \\
0.75321 & 0.65899 & 0.64722 & 0.82760 & 1 \\
0.69263 & 0.60523 & 0.60106 & 0.76872 & 0.87026 & 1
\end{bmatrix}
$$

is generated from the model in Figure 5(c). The models in Figures 5(a) and 5(b) have 6 df and chi-squares of 2.76 and 3.26 (p-values of 0.84 and 0.78) respectively. The model in Figure 5(c) has 7 df and a chi-square value of 3.39 (p-value of 0.85). Chi-square difference tests of the first two models compared to Figure 5(c) reveal no significant differences, lending support to the validity of Figure 5(c); therefore

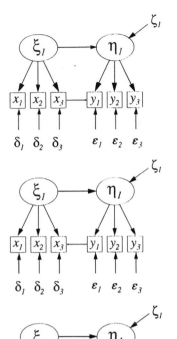

(a)

(b)

(c)

FIGURE 5. Simulated data.

we retain the model with a correlated error and select the true model. Note also that this example illustrates how the simultaneous test statistic developed here can be applied in the exploratory tetrad analyses proposed by Glymour et al. (1987) to compare alternative models that have nested vanishing tetrads.

6.4. *Example 4: Four-Wave Developmental Model*

McArdle and Epstein (1987) introduce the path model in Figure 6 to study the developmental changes in intelligence measured by the

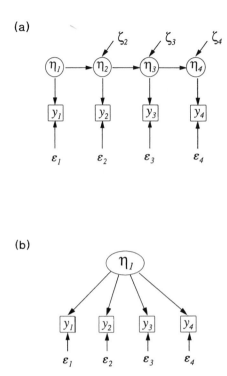

FIGURE 6. Four-wave developmental model.

Wechsler Scale in a four-wave study of 204 children. The covariance matrix is ($N = 204$):

$$S = \begin{bmatrix} 40.628 & & & \\ 37.741 & 53.568 & & \\ 40.051 & 48.500 & 60.778 & \\ 50.643 & 63.169 & 70.200 & 107.869 \end{bmatrix}$$

The model has four latent variables, each of which has one indicator. Each latent variable is determined only by the immediately preceding latent variable. This is commonly known as the "autoregressive" or the "simplex" model. The authors did not evaluate this model against the data partly because without further restrictions this is an underidentified model. Such a model can be tested with CTA. One vanishing tetrad, $\tau_{1342} = 0$, is implied by the model, and the CTA test statistic is a chi-square estimate of 1.12 with 1 df and a p-value of

0.29. The CTA results suggest a good fit for the four-wave path model. We are encouraged to explore this model with the conventional ML method by constraining $\beta_{21} = \beta_{32} = \beta_{43}$ and $VAR(\delta_1) = VAR(\delta_2) = VAR(\delta_3) = VAR(\delta_4)$. The model with these equality constraints has an excellent fit with a chi-square of 2.93 with 4 df and a p-value of 0.57. This example shows that multiwave single indicator panel models can be tested with CTA procedures even when the model is underidentified.

Dimensionality tests are also possible with CTA. Suppose we wish to test whether intelligence is a stable latent variable that influences all four tests. Figure 6(b) contains the path diagram for this alternative model. Compared to Figure 6(a), this model assumes a one latent-variable solution rather than a four latent-variable one. The model in Figure 6(b) implies two independent vanishing tetrads. The CTA test statistic is 5.42 with 2 df and a p-value of 0.07. The vanishing tetrad for the four-wave simplex model shown in Figure 6(a) is nested in those implied in the one latent-variable model. The chi-square difference between these two models is 4.30 with 1 df. The p-value is less than 0.05, which suggests that the four-wave model in Figure 6(a) is preferable. Thus this example illustrates a tetrad test for dimensionality.

7. CONCLUSIONS

Confirmatory Tetrad Analysis holds promise as a model testing procedure in SEM. At a minimum, it provides a check on the LR test results. When both test statistics agree, it increases our confidence in a model's match to the data. Disagreements suggest potential specification errors or differences in the power of the tests. In addition, CTA applies in some situations where the LR test statistic is inapplicable or is more complicated to apply. We gave examples of models that were not nested for LR tests but were nested in their vanishing tetrads. Thus we can compare and test some models that have long been considered nonnested. Furthermore, the fit of some under-identified models can be assessed with the CTA test statistic. This could help researchers to determine whether it is worth looking for further restrictions that would help to identify a model. Finally, the test statistic we have used could also be helpful in ETA when comparing alternative models that have nested vanishing tetrads.

The characteristics of CTA may be made clearer by contrasting it with the more common maximum likelihood (ML) and weighted least squares (WLS) approaches to SEM. In ML/WLS approaches, the null hypothesis is H_o: $\Sigma = \Sigma(\theta)$, where Σ is the population covariance matrix of the observed variables and $\Sigma(\theta)$ is the model implied covariance matrix with θ the vector of free parameters in the model. We have a test statistic that has an asymptotic chi-square distribution when H_o is valid. In CTA the null hypothesis is H_o: $\tau = 0$ where τ is the vector of vanishing tetrads implied by the model. Here, too, we have a test statistic that has an asymptotic chi-square distribution when H_o is valid. In both cases the chi-square distribution is a large sample result; the small sample properties require further study. This suggests the need for Monte Carlo simulation experiments to explore the behavior of the test statistics in commonly used sample sizes.

Nesting of models in the ML/WLS approach occurs when the parameters of one model are a restricted version of the parameters in another model. Nesting in CTA exists when the vanishing tetrads of one model are a restricted version, typically a subset, of the vanishing tetrads of another model. As we illustrated here, a set of models can be nested in their vanishing tetrads but not nested in their parameters, and this allows a test of some models that are nonnested in their structural parameters.

With ML/WLS methods, it is possible that multiple models have identical values for the implied covariance matrix and for the test statistic. The equivalent models are indistinguishable in terms of their overall fit to the data (Jöreskog and Sörbom 1989, pp. 221–24). Similarly, we can have the same vanishing tetrads implied by multiple models. These "tetrad equivalent" models are indistinguishable in fit using our test statistic. Thus with both the ML/WLS and CTA approaches we should not confuse a favorable test statistic with proof of the validity of a model since other models can have a fit as good as or better than the ones tested.

The idea of tetrad equivalent models can help explain why it is possible for models to have tetrads that are nested but parameters that are not. A given set of vanishing tetrads can be implied by more than one model. The same is true for a second set of vanishing tetrads that is nested in the first. A test statistic for the nested tetrads provides a test of the relative fit of all models that imply the one set of vanishing tetrads to all models that imply the other set. Some of the models in the two sets may be nested in their parameters, but, as we illustrated, this need not be true. And this leads to situations where we can compare the fit of models not nested in their parameters.

An important difference in methodologies is that ML/WLS is a structural parameter estimator, while CTA tests only model fit and does not estimate structural parameters.[10] For this reason, CTA clearly is a complement, not a replacement, for the traditional procedures. Largely because it is not a structural parameter estimator, CTA does not require iterative methods as do the ML/WLS methods.

We close by pointing out that CTA is in the original spirit of Spearman's work of determining the vanishing tetrads implied by a model and assessing whether they hold. It also is consistent with the early work on SEM that attempted to test models by examining the implied vanishing tetrads. This paper furthers the work of Spearman and others by providing a general simultaneous test of vanishing tetrads to evaluate models, by giving new rules for determining the vanishing tetrads implied by a model and eliminating the redundant ones, and by providing a method to estimate the power of the vanishing tetrad test.

REFERENCES

Bentler, P. M. 1989. *EQS: Structural Equations Program Manual.* Los Angeles: BMDP Statistical Software.

Bishop, T. S., S. E. Fienberg, and P. Holland. 1975. *Discrete Multivariate Analysis.* Cambridge, Mass.: MIT Press.

Bollen, K. A. 1989. *Structural Equations with Latent Variables.* New York: Wiley.

———. 1990. "Outlier Screening and a Distribution-Free Test for Vanishing Tetrads." *Sociological Methodology and Research* 19:80–92.

Browne, M. W. 1984. "Asymptotic Distribution Free Methods in Analysis of Covariance Structures." *British Journal of Mathematical and Statistical Psychology* 37:62–83.

Costner, H. L. 1969. "Theory, Deduction, and Rules of Correspondence." *American Journal of Sociology* 75:245–63.

Duncan, O. D. 1972. "Unmeasured Variables in Linear Models for Panel Analysis." In *Sociological Methodology 1972,* edited by H. L. Costner, 36–82. San Francisco: Jossey-Bass.

---

[10]Of course, the vanishing tetrads, τ, are parameters that are estimated with CTA, but by structural parameters we are referring to the coefficients, variances, and covariances parameters that are part of the model structure.

174   KENNETH A. BOLLEN AND KWOK-FAI TING

Glymour, C., R. Scheines, P. Spirtes, and K. Kelly. 1987. *Discovering Causal Structure*. Orlando, Fla.: Academic Press.

Hartmann, W. M. 1991. *The CALIS Procedure Extended User's Guide*. Cary, N.C.: SAS Institute.

Hotelling, H. 1933. "Analysis of a Complex of Statistical Variables into Principal Components." *Journal of Educational Psychology* 24:417–41, 498–520.

Isserlis, L. 1916. "On Certain Probable Errors and Correlation Coefficients of Multiple Frequency Distributions with Skew Regression." *Biometrika* 11:185–90.

Jöreskog, K. G. 1973. "A General Method for Estimating a Linear Structural Equation System." In *Structural Equation Models in the Social Sciences*, edited by A. S. Goldberger and O. D. Duncan, 85–112. New York: Academic Press.

Jöreskog, K. G., and D. Sörbom. 1989. *LISREL 7: A Guide to the Program and Applications*. Chicago: SPSS.

Judge, G., W. E. Griffiths, R. C. Hill, H. Lütkepohl, T. C. Lee. 1985. *The Theory and Practice of Econometrics*, 2d ed. New York: Wiley.

Kelley, T. L. 1928. *Crossroads in the Mind of Man*. Stanford, Calif.: Stanford University.

Kenny, D. A. 1974. "A test for Vanishing Tetrad: The Second Canonical Correlation Equals Zero." *Social Science Research* 3:83–87.

Lawley, D. N., and A. E. Maxwell. 1971. *Factor Analysis as a Statistical Method*. London: Butterworth.

MacKinnon, J. G. 1983. "Model Specification Tests Against Nonnested Alternatives." *Econometric Review* 2:85–110.

McArdle, J. J., and D. Epstein. 1987. "Latent Growth Curves Within Developmental Structural Equation Models." *Child Development* 58:110–33.

McDonald, J. A., and D. A. Clelland. 1984. "Textile Workers and Union Sentiment." *Social Forces* 63:502–21.

Mardia, K. V., and K. Foster. 1983. "Omnibus Tests of Multinormality Based on Skewness and Kurtosis." *Communication in Statistics* 12:207–21.

Matsueda, R. L., and W. T. Bielby. 1986. "Statistical Power in Covariance Structure Models." In *Sociological Methodology 1986*, edited by N. B. Tuma, Washington, D.C.: American Sociological Association.

Rao, C. R. 1973. *Linear Statistical Inference and Its Applications*, 2d ed. New York: Wiley.

Reisenzein, R. 1986. "A Structural Equation Analysis of Weiner's Attribution-Affect Model of Helping Behavior." *Journal of Personality and Social Psychology* 50:1123–33.

Satorra, A., and W. E. Saris. 1985. "Power of the Likelihood Ratio Test in Covariance Structure Analysis." *Psychometrika* 50:83–90.

Shapiro, A. 1986. "Asymptotic Theory of Overparameterized Structural Models." *Journal of the American Statistical Association* 81:142–49.

Spearman, C. 1904. "General Intelligence Objectively Determined and Measured." *American Journal of Psychology* 15:201–93.

———. 1927. *The Abilities of Man.* New York: Macmillan.

Spearman, C., and K. Holzinger. 1924. "The Sampling Error in the Theory of Two Factors." *British Journal of Psychology* 15:17–19.

Wishart, J. 1928. "Sampling Errors in the Theory of Two Factors." *British Journal of Psychology* 19:180–87.

6

CORRELATION AND ASSOCIATION MODELS FOR STUDYING MEASUREMENTS ON ORDINAL RELATIONS

Katherine Faust*
Stanley Wasserman†

This paper describes and illustrates correlation models (correspondence analysis and canonical correlation analysis) and association models for studying the order and spacing of categories of ordinal relational variables. Both correlation models and association models study departures from independence in two-way contingency tables. One result of fitting these models is the possibility of assignment of scores to the categories of the row and/or the column variables to reflect the relative spacing of these categories. If the model fitting is done using statistical procedures, then restricted versions of these models allow one to test hypotheses about the spacing, linearity, or equality of the categories. Correlation and association models are especially useful for studying discrete ordinal variables, which arise quite frequently in the social and behavioral sciences.

We illustrate correlation and association models using two empirical examples in which respondents used ordered

*University of South Carolina
†University of Illinois
This paper was presented at the Conference on Measurement Theory and Social Networks, University of California, Irvine, August, 1991. We would like to thank Carolyn Anderson, Clifford Clogg, Linton Freeman, Peter Marsden, James A. McRae, Alaina Michaelson, and several anonymous reviewers for helpful comments. Special thanks go to Carolyn Anderson for computational assistance.

177

categories to rate the strength of their liking for, or acquaintance with, others in a social network. In this paper we describe how to use both correlation models and association models to test specific hypotheses about the spacing of these response categories.

1. INTRODUCTION

This paper describes and illustrates correlation and association models for studying the order and spacing of categories on ordinal relational variables. Both correlation and association models study the nature and strength of the relationship between rows and columns in a contingency table. Correlation models (including correspondence analysis and canonical correlation models) and association models have been the focus of considerable research in the last decade or so (Anderson 1992; Becker and Clogg 1989; Becker 1990; Böckenholt and Böckenholt 1990; Clogg 1982a, 1982b, 1986; Gilula 1986; Gilula and Haberman 1986, 1988; Goodman 1979, 1981a, 1981b, 1985, 1986, 1991; Greenacre 1984; Haberman 1981; Nishisato 1980; van der Heijden and de Leeuw 1985, 1989; van der Heijden and Meijerink 1989).

   Correlation and association models both study departures from independence in contingency tables; however, the models differ in how they measure the strength and nature of the relationship between the rows and columns. Correlation models focus on departures from independence using the correlations between row categories and column categories. Both correspondence analysis and canonical correlation analysis are often referred to as *correlation* models. Alternatively, one could study departure from independence using other measures of the relationship between rows and columns, such as odd ratios for two-by-two subtables in a two-way cross-classification. Such models are referred to as *association* models. We describe both correlation and association models in detail below.

   Correlation models and association models involve the assignment of scores to the categories of the row and column variables in order to maximize the relevant measure of relationship (the correlation coefficient in the correlation models or the measure of intrinsic association in association models). One can then use the scores pertaining to the row or column categories to study the order and spacing of these categories. Both models are especially interesting when the row and/or column variables are ordinal. A few examples of substantive problems for which these models have been used to study ordinal variables include: measures of well-being or happiness (Clogg 1982*a*, 1982*b*; Goodman 1985, 1986) attitudes toward treatment of criminals (Clogg 1982*b*), socioeconomic status (Goodman 1985; 1991), and levels of donations from corporations to not-for-profit agencies (Wasserman, Faust, and Galaskiewicz 1990).

Restricted versions of correlation and association models place constraints on the values of the scores assigned to the row and/ or the column categories. If the model fitting is done using statistical procedures, one can then use the restricted models to test specific hypotheses about the dimensionality of the solution (the number of sets of scores needed), and about the spacing of row and/or column categories (such as their equality, uniform spacing, or other a priori spacing).

In this paper we describe and illustrate both correlation models and association models, including versions of these models that place restrictions on the scores for the row and/or column categories. The specific problem that we focus on is the assignment of scores to peoples' ratings of the strength of their acquaintance or friendship with others in a social network. The goal is to use models of correlation and association to study the order, spacing and equality of response categories that respondents use to indicate their degree of acquaintance or friendship. We use two social network data sets: one on observed and reported interactions among members of a fraternity (Bernard, Killworth, and Sailer 1979–80) and the second on friendship and message sending among members of a computer network (S. Freeman and L. Freeman 1979; L. Freeman and S. Freeman 1980; L. Freeman 1986). In both cases we use the measures of interactions among people as predictors of the strength of their friendship or acquaintance. We conclude the paper with a general comparison of correlation and association models.

Our illustrations use the specific example of ordered relational variables measuring the strength of ties among actors in a social network. However, it is important to note that the correlation and association models described here are applicable to any two-way contingency table of counts or frequencies, not just to social network data. We begin by describing our application before moving on to a discussion of the models.

2. ORDERED RELATIONAL VARIABLES

In recent decades social network analysis has become widely accepted as an approach for modeling social systems as collections of relational ties linking actors. The actors in the network are social units (such as people, nations, corporations, and so on), and the relational ties are substantive connections among the actors (such as friendships among people, imports and exports among nations, or interlocking boards of directors among corporations). The ties among actors may have values or strengths indicating the intensity, frequency, closeness, or amount of the relational tie between a pair of actors. Valued relational variables are almost always discrete and are often measured on an ordinal scale.

When actors are people in a group, relational ties can be measured by having people evaluate the strength of their ties to others within the group. An important question is how the various responses people give in evaluating the strength of their relational ties to others indicate the relative intensity of the relational ties. In this paper we describe models for studying these responses directly.

Researchers have considered the strength of network ties from several perspectives. Authors such as Granovetter (1973), Winship (1977), and more recently Freeman (1992), among others, consider the implications of the distribution of strong and weak ties for social structural patterns and processes. Other authors, notably Marsden and Campbell (1984) and Friedkin (1990) have considered factors that influence whether strong versus weak ties will occur between people. Relatively less attention has been paid to studying the strength of ties directly (however, see Burt and Guilarte 1986). In this paper we take this third perspective, by proposing and illustrating models to assign scores to categories of tie strength so that we can study directly the strength of relational ties.

Granovetter (1973) was among the first to discuss the theoretical importance of tie strength, distinguishing between strong, weak, and absent ties. He argued that

The strength of a tie is a (probably linear) combination of the amount of time, the emotional intensity, the intimacy (mutual confiding), and the reciprocal services which characterize the tie. (1973, p. 348)

Granovetter also discussed the implications of tie strength for social
structural processes such as the diffusion of novel information and
community integration. Following the arguments of Granovetter,
certain patterns of strong and weak ties are permitted, or forbidden
within a network. For example, if actor i has a strong tie to actor j,
and actor j in turn has a strong tie to actor k, then the tie from actor i
to actor k should not be absent. Freeman (1992) argues that one way
to determine which level of tie is strong versus weak is to describe
properties of networks that hold at each level of a valued relation.
Theoretically important properties (for example, transitivity) should
hold for strong ties but not necessarily for weak ties.

In their discussion of how to measure the strength of relational
ties, Marsden and Campbell (1984) distinguish between *indicators*
and *predictors* of tie strength. Indicators are "actual components of
tie strength" (p. 485) as specified by Granovetter, whereas predictors
are variables such as context and attribute similarity that are related
to the strength of ties. Friedkin (1990) argues that components of tie
strength (discussion, seeking help, and friendship) form a Guttman
scale, rather than an additive function (as argued by Granovetter) in
that "the claim of friendship implies the claims of help seeking and
frequent discussion; the claim of help seeking implies the claim of
frequent discussion" (p. 250).

Few studies have focused directly on the strength of relational
ties linking pairs of individuals. A notable exception is Burt and
Guilarte (1986), who studied tie strength in the General Social Survey ego-centered network data by looking at reported properties of
ties from respondent to the alters named, and among pairs of alters
named by the respondent. In these data, respondents evaluated the
relational tie between each pair of alters named as "especially close,"
"acquainted," or "strangers."

Burt and Guilarte (1986) propose that response categories
indicating the strength of relational ties can be scaled by considering
how the probability of a given level of a second variable changes

across categories of the relational variable that is being scaled. For example, if one is scaling categories of friendship strength, then one could compare the probability of a specific amount of behavioral interaction across the several categories of friendship. In Burt and Guilarte's model, the spacing between two friendship categories would be proportional to the difference in the probabilities of a specific level of interaction between the friendship categories. Their paper includes details on how to estimate these values.

Using this method to scale response categories for acquaintanceship in the General Social Survey network data, Burt and Guilarte concluded that "the middle category of interalter relations lies about 0.2 of the distance from total strangers to people being especially close" (p. 391). On the other hand, they found that respondents make no distinction between alters with whom they are "especially close" and alters to whom they are "equally close," whereas alters who are "less close" are about 0.7 the strength of "especially close" or "equally close" (p. 395). Thus their method results in a set of scale values describing the spacing or intervals between response categories on an ordinal relational variable. The models we describe in this paper provide an alternative method for assigning scores to the categories of an ordinal relational variable.

An important property of a relational variable is whether it is dichotomous (taking on only two values) or whether it is valued. Valued relational variables usually have values indicating the strength, intensity, or frequency of the relational tie.

Social network data are often collected by asking respondents to *rate* the strength or intensity of their relational ties to others in the group (for example, their degree of friendship or respect for each person in the group). Responses may take the form of labeled categories, for example "close personal friend," "friend," "acquaintance," "someone I have met," "someone I have heard of but not met," "someone I have not heard of" (for example, see S. Freeman and L. Freeman 1979; L. Freeman and S. Freeman 1980). Or, the responses may be numerical values indicating the intensity of the relational tie. Whether verbal labels or numerical values are used, the resulting relation is measured by responses on a number of ordered response categories.

It is important to contrast the *rating* response format, where respondents use a limited number of response categories, with a *complete rank order* format. In a complete rank order format, respondents typically are asked to rank order the other people in the network from most to least in terms of the intensity of the respondent's relational tie to each other person. If there are g people in the group, then respondents are asked to use all integers from 1 to $g - 1$ to rank order the strength of their ties to others. By contrast, in a rating format the response categories may be reused by a respondent. In fact, if the number of response categories, C, is less than the number of other people in the group, $g - 1$, then a respondent must reuse some response categories.[1]

Consider the example of the five ordered response categories for measuring friendship that we described above. Although it seems likely that degree of friendship is ordered from "close personal friend" through "someone I have met" to "someone I have not heard of," it is important to study the relative spacing of these categories. It might be the case that respondents see very little difference between "a friend" and "a close personal friend" but both responses are quite different from "a person I have met." One of the results of the models described here is the assignment of scores to response categories of ordinal relational variables to reflect the order and spacing of the categories.

Let us consider a respondent choosing among the response categories on a given relation to indicate the strength of her relational tie to each other person in the group. In complete social network studies, each respondent judges her own relational ties to all other people in the group. For example, each respondent judges her degree of friendship with each member of the group. We assume that individuals are presented with stimuli (relational ties) that vary in terms of important determinants of degree of the response relation

---

[1]In order to aggregate responses across people, we are assuming that all respondents use the response categories in the same way. For example, if a rating of "1" means that a person is disliked by the respondent, then this response should tend to go with infrequent interactions for all respondents who use the response category "1." However, in a full rank order format all respondents are forced to use the category "1" for their least-liked person in the group, regardless of their absolute degree of liking for, or frequency of interaction with, that person. Thus responses from a full rank order format are not expected to be associated with predictor relational variables in the ways required by our approach. In a more general context, Nishisato (1980) discusses correspondence analysis models for rank order data coded as paired comparisons.

(say friendship). A given respondent, when presented the list of others in the group, is faced with people whom they have known a long time, people they have met recently, and others they have never met (ties vary in duration). In addition, there are some people whom the respondent sees quite often, and others whom the respondent sees only occasionally (ties vary in frequency of contact). Also, some of the people may be the respondent's family members, coworkers, or neighbors (ties vary in context). Thus duration, frequency, and context are also properties of the relational ties to which the respondent is assigning an evaluation of strength of friendship.

We assume that a respondent's assessment of strength of a relational tie depends primarily on properties of the relational tie from respondent to alter, and not on the attributes of the respondent or of the alter. Thus the response category that is used by a respondent to describe the strength of their relational tie should be associated with other aspects of the relationship from respondent to alter. For example, the degree of friendship expressed by a respondent for alter is likely to be associated with the length of time they have known each other, the frequency with which they interact, and so on (see Marsden and Campbell 1984).

It seems unreasonable to assume that all respondents have the same degree of friendship with a specific other person. Thus we do not assume that all respondents will use the same response category (for example, "friend") for a given person. Rather, we assume that in general people use the same response category on a relational variable to describe *relational ties* that are similar on other relational variables. These other relational variables are considered to be *predictors* of the strength or value of a relational tie (Marsden and Campbell 1984). Therefore, in order to study response categories on a given relation, we must have (at least) a second relational variable measured on the same pairs of actors. We will distinguish between the *relational response* variable (whose categories we are attempting to scale), and the *relational predictor* variable(s) that we use to understand the response categories on the response relation.

For example, we can study response categories for different degrees of friendship by examining how the categories are associated with categories for other predictor relations, such as the frequency, duration, intensity, and context of the relational tie.

3. NOTATION AND DATA ARRAYS

Both correlation and association models study contingency tables. We will denote the contingency table as $\mathbf{F}$, where f_{kl} is the observed frequency in row k column l of $\mathbf{F}$. Commonly, the frequencies in $\mathbf{F}$ record the responses from g respondents to two (or more) question- naire items. All of the models described in this paper can be used to study such a contingency table. However, to study social network data, the particular example we will use, it is necessary to focus on *pairs* of people, rather than individual respondents. In this section we describe the particular data arrays that are required to study social network data.

We begin with a set of g actors, and two (or more) relations X_1, $X_2, \ldots, X_R$, defined on these actors. We will designate X_1 as the relational response variable, whose response categories we are study- ing. In addition we will have X_2 (and possibly other Xs) as relational predictor variable(s). There are R relations in total. Let x_{ijr} be the value of the relational tie from actor i to actor j on relation X_r. We will assume that these values are ordered and discrete. In general, we let C_r be the number of levels of relational variable X_r.

The most common data representation for social network data is a *sociomatrix*. A sociomatrix for a single relation, $\mathbf{X} = \{x_{ij}\}$, is a matrix with g rows and g columns, indexing actors and partners. The (i, j)th entry of $\mathbf{X}$ codes the value of the tie from row actor i to column actor j. However, when the focus of the analysis is the strengths or values of the relational ties, a sociomatrix is not the appropriate data array to analyze. In this section we describe a two- way array that codes the relational ties among a set of actors on two or more relations, which will allow us to fit proper models. (The appendix to this chapter describes in detail the relationship between this array and other common data arrays that are used for fitting the models that we describe in later sections.)

We are interested in studying the distribution of relational response categories for ties defined on ordered pairs of actors, across different levels of one (or possibly more) predictor relations. The idea is to code the state of each of the $g(g - 1)$ dyads (or ordered pairs of actors) defining the relational ties in a network data set. This state is defined by two quantities: the category (or strength) of the relational response variable and the combination of categories of the relational predictor variables.

First, consider the state of an ordered pair of actors on the relational response variable, X_1. Since this variable has C_1 categories, each ordered pair of actors can be in one of C_1 states on this variable. Now consider the number of states for the relational predictor variable(s). This number depends on the number of relational predictor variables that are included and the number of categories of each. We will let L be the total number of states on the relational predictor variables. In the simplest case there is a single relational predictor variable, X_2, with C_2 levels, and there are as many possible states as there are levels of X_2: namely, $L = C_2$. If there is more than one relational predictor variable, then we consider the combination of possible states on all predictor variables. This state can be coded by the cross-classification of these predictor variables. In general, there are $R - 1$ relational predictor variables, $X_2, X_3, \ldots, X_R$, with C_2, $C_3, \ldots, C_R$ categories, respectively. The state of an ordered pair of actors on these variables is given by the cross-classification of these variables, and the number of possible states is equal to the number of entries in the cross-classification. Since there are $C_2 \times C_3 \times \ldots \times C_R$ cells in this cross-classification, there are $L = C_2 \times C_3 \times \ldots \times C_R$ possible states for an ordered pair of actors on the relational predictor variables.

To study the state of an ordered pair of actors on both the relational response variable and the relational predictor variable(s), we focus on the cross-classification of the relational variable whose response categories we are studying, with one or more other relational predictor variables. For example, we can look at the cross-classification of level of friendship and frequency of contact for pairs of actors in a group. This cross-classification, which we denote by $\mathbf{F}$, has C_1 rows coding the state of the ordered pair on the relational response variable and L columns coding the state of the ordered pair on the relational predictor variable(s).

The $\mathbf{F}$ array is a C_1 by L table, whose entries code the state of each ordered pair of actors. Since there are $g(g - 1)$ ordered pairs of actors, there are $g(g - 1)$ observations classified in $\mathbf{F}$. For a single relational predictor variable, the entry in cell (k,l) of $\mathbf{F}$ counts the number of times $x_{ij1} = k$ and $x_{ij2} = l$, for $i,j = 1,2 \ldots ,g$, and $i \neq j$: the number of times response category k is used at level l of the relational predictor variables. For $R - 1$ relational predictor variables with $L = C_2 \times C_3 \times \ldots \times C_R$ states, each entry in **F** counts the number of times category k of the relational response variable is used for each state of the combined relational predictor variables.

We will now describe correlation models (correspondence analysis and canonical correlation analysis), including restricted versions of these models, and illustrate how these models can be used to study the spacing, linearity, and equality of relational response categories. We then describe and illustrate association models.

4. CORRELATION MODELS: CORRESPONDENCE AND CANONICAL CORRELATION ANALYSIS

In this section we present a general description of the mathematics of correlation models, including both canonical correlation analysis and correspondence analysis for a two-way contingency table. More extensive discussions of correspondence analysis and canonical correlation analysis can be found in Gilula and Haberman (1986, 1988), Goodman (1985, 1986), Greenacre (1984), van der Heijden and de Leeuw (1985, 1989), van der Heijden and Meijerink (1989), Wasserman and Faust (1989), and Wasserman, Faust, and Galaskiewicz (1990).

We define:

- $\mathbf{F} = \{f_{kl}\}$ a two-way cross-classification, with C_1 rows and L columns,

- $P_{kl} = \dfrac{f_{kl}}{f_{++}}$ the probability that an observation is in row k, column l,

- $P_{k\bullet} = \dfrac{f_{k+}}{f_{++}}$ the probability that an observation is row k,

- $P_{\bullet l} = \dfrac{f_{+l}}{f_{++}}$ the probability that an observation is in column l,

- $t = \min(C_1 - 1, L - 1)$.

The $\{P_{kl}\}$ probabilities are observed, rather than theoretical probabilities. The *canonical decomposition* of **F** is defined as:

$$P_{kl} = P_{k\bullet}P_{\bullet l}\left[1 + \sum_{m=1}^{t}p_m u_{km} v_{lm}\right]. \qquad (1)$$

We will refer to this as the $C(t)$ model. Goodman (1986) refers to the theoretical version of this as the *saturated RC canonical correlation* model.

Canonical correlation analysis of **F** results in three sets of information:

- A set of C_1 row scores, $\{u_{km}\}$ for $m = 1,2, \ldots t$,
- A set of L column scores, $\{v_{lm}\}$ for $m = 1,2, \ldots t$,
- A set of t principal inertias (squared canonical correlations), $\{\rho_m^2\}$ for $m = 1,2, \ldots t$; ρ_m measures the correlation between the row scores, u_{km}, and the column scores, v_{lm}.

The canonical variables $\mathbf{u}_m$ and $\mathbf{v}_m$ are constrained as follows:

$$\sum_{k=1}^{C_1} u_{km} P_{k\bullet} = \sum_{l=1}^{L} v_{lm} P_{\bullet l} = 0 \qquad (2)$$

$$\sum_{k=1}^{C_1} u_{km}^2 P_{k\bullet} = \sum_{l=1}^{L} v_{lm}^2 P_{\bullet l} = 1. \qquad (3)$$

When scaled in this way, the **u**'s and **v**'s are referred to as *standard coordinates* (Greenacre 1984). For distinct m and m', $\mathbf{u}_m$ and $\mathbf{u}_{m'}$ are uncorrelated, as are $\mathbf{v}_m$ and $\mathbf{v}_{m'}$:

$$\sum_{k=1}^{C_1} u_{km} u_{km'} P_{k\bullet} = \sum_{l=1}^{L} v_{lm} v_{lm'} P_{\bullet l} = 0, \qquad \text{for } m \neq m'. \qquad (4)$$

For a given m, the correlation between canonical variables $\mathbf{u}_m$ and $\mathbf{v}_m$ is equal to the canonical correlation ρ_m. The canonical correlation, ρ_m, can be expressed as:

$$\rho_m = \sum_{k=1}^{C_1} \sum_{l=1}^{L} P_{kl} u_{km} v_{lm}. \qquad (5)$$

The canonical variables $\mathbf{u}_m$ and $\mathbf{v}_m$ are the scores for the rows and columns, respectively, that maximize the correlation, ρ_m, in equation (5). It is important to note that the scores for the row categories are optimal with respect to maximizing the correlation with the specific column variable being studied, and vice versa.

A rescaling of the canonical scores in equation (1) is equivalent to Goodman's (1986) *saturated RC correspondence analysis model*. We will denote these rescaled canonical scores by $\bar{u}$ and $\bar{v}$, where:

$$\sum_{k=1}^{C_1} \bar{u}_{km} P_{k\bullet} = \sum_{l=1}^{L} \bar{v}_{lm} P_{\bullet l} = 0 \tag{6}$$

$$\sum_{k=1}^{C_1} \bar{u}_{km}^2 P_{k\bullet} = \sum_{l=1}^{L} \bar{v}_{lm}^2 P_{\bullet l} = \rho_m^2 \tag{7}$$

for each set $m = 1,2, \ldots ,t$. When the row and column scores are scaled as in equations (6) and (7), they are referred to as *principal coordinates* (Greenacre 1986, 1984). The relationship between the principal coordinates and the standard coordinates is straightforward:

$$\bar{u}_{km} = u_{km} \rho_m$$
$$\bar{v}_{jm} = v_{jm} \rho_m. \tag{8}$$

Therefore equation (1) can be rewritten in terms of principal coordinates as:

$$P_{kl} = P_{k\bullet} P_{\bullet l} \left[1 + \sum_{m=1}^{t} \bar{u}_{km} \bar{v}_{lm} / \rho_m \right]. \tag{9}$$

The advantage of the principal coordinates scaling is that the variance of each set of scores, within each of the t sets, is equal to the principal inertia, ρ_m^2, for that dimension. This scaling is standard output of Greenacre's correspondence analysis program, *SIMCA* (Greenacre 1986).

Correspondence analysis or canonical correlation analysis of the **F** array results in scores that pertain directly to the categories of the row and column variables. When the rows of **F** code the state of the relational response variable and the columns code the state of the relational predictor variable(s), then the row scores, u_{km} for $k = 1,2, \ldots ,C_1$ and $m = 1,2, \ldots ,t$ pertain to the C_1 categories of the relational response variable and the column scores, v_{lm} for $l = 1,2, \ldots ,L$ and $m = 1,2, \ldots ,t$ pertain to the L states of the relational predictor variable(s). The canonical correlations, ρ_m, describe the correlation between the scores for the relational response categories and the scores for the relational predictor categories.

5. AN EXAMPLE

We illustrate correspondence analysis for studying the response categories on an ordinal relational variable using a data set collected by
Bernard, Killworth, and Sailer (1979–80). Bernard et al. measured
liking, observed interactions, and reported interactions among 58
students in a fraternity. There are three relations in this data set:

- X_1—*liking:* rating by a fraternity member of how well he likes each
  person in the group, on an 11-point scale, where 11 means most
  liked, and 1 means least liked; $C_1 = 11$.
- X_2—*observed interactions:* recorded as the number of times each
  pair of actors was observed interacting over a several week period.
  The modal number of interactions is 0, the median is 1, and 75
  percent of all pairs of actors were observed interacting 2 times or
  less. We have recoded this variable to $C_2 = 5$ levels:
  - 0
  - 1
  - 2
  - 3 or 4
  - 5 or more.
- X_3—*reported interactions:* rating by each fraternity member of their
  recalled amount of interaction with each member of the group,
  measured on a five-point scale, where 5 means most and 1 means
  least amount of interaction; $C_3 = 5$.

We will focus on the 11-point rating of liking as the relational
response variable. We would like to study how people use these 11
categories of liking, across the combined levels of observed and reported interactions. For this analysis, $L = 5 \times 5 = 25$—the cross-
classification of observed and reported interactions. The F array for
this example is the 11 by 25 cross-classification of liking by the combination of observed and reported interactions. This array is given in
Table 1.

   Results of correspondence analysis of the data in Table 1 (us-
ing *SIMCA*, Greenacre 1986) give $\rho_1^2 = 0.4917$, $\rho_2^2 = 0.1915$, and $\rho_3^2 = 0.0652$, and account for 59.90, 23.32, and 7.95 percent of the total
inertia, respectively. The complete model has $t = 11 - 1 = 10$ sets of

TABLE 1
Fraternity Liking by Reported and Observed Interactions

Reported Interaction	Observed Interaction																								
	0					1					2					3 or 4					5 or more				
	1	2	3	4	5	1	2	3	4	5	1	2	3	4	5	1	2	3	4	5	1	2	3	4	5
LIKING																									
1	20	2	3	0	0	6	4	0	0	0	1	4	0	0	0	3	2	0	0	0	1	2	1	0	0
2	15	6	1	0	0	10	2	0	0	0	1	2	0	0	0	0	0	0	0	0	0	2	0	0	0
3	8	5	0	0	0	8	1	3	0	0	0	3	0	0	0	0	0	0	0	0	3	1	2	0	0
4	16	7	4	0	0	2	5	1	0	0	1	3	2	0	0	2	1	1	0	0	2	3	0	1	0
5	28	30	9	0	0	8	17	6	0	1	3	4	2	0	0	1	6	2	1	0	1	3	2	0	0
6	88	124	83	9	1	24	44	26	7	2	9	28	15	5	0	4	15	12	2	1	6	12	10	3	2
7	28	105	65	7	1	7	48	36	8	0	1	19	25	5	0	0	7	13	0	2	0	18	24	8	1
8	25	92	92	8	1	8	46	42	20	3	0	17	44	9	0	1	9	12	8	0	0	8	29	13	1
9	18	55	93	36	8	5	22	59	42	8	2	9	30	34	8	0	1	18	24	7	0	6	30	44	12
10	3	27	81	56	9	1	8	41	49	14	0	2	22	31	12	0	4	18	20	9	0	2	29	43	40
11	2	8	17	33	43	1	7	13	29	48	0	2	8	18	27	0	0	4	9	25	0	1	5	37	132

TABLE 2
First Set of Scores from Correspondence Analysis Correlation Model for
Fraternity Data

Liking	u_1
1	1.10085
2	1.11731
3	1.01451
4	0.91727
5	0.81895
6	0.64371
7	0.45940
8	0.32805
9	−0.15377
10	−0.50014
11	−1.34569

	Observed Interactions				
	0	1	2	3 to 4	5 or more
Reported					
1	0.88209	0.94399	0.91409	1.14852	1.16942
2	0.52737	0.52306	0.65881	0.68777	0.63951
3	0.16311	0.05563	0.12204	0.05411	0.06372
4	−0.63474	−0.50832	−0.51014	−0.46958	−0.64389
5	−1.40720	−1.30854	−1.32189	−1.22053	−1.49746

scores; however, the last seven sets of scores account for only 8.83 percent of the total inertia. Table 2 presents only the first set of scores (corresponding to ρ_1^2) for the 11 categories of liking, and the 25 categories of the cross-classification of observed and reported interactions. Although these results show negative scores for high levels of liking and high levels of reported interactions (and positive scores for low levels of these variables), equivalent solutions exist in which the signs of all scores are reversed. The first set of scores for the 11 categories of liking is displayed in Figure 1, where it is clear that the 11 levels of liking are, with one reversal, ordered from most to least. However, they are not equally spaced. There are relatively small distinctions among the lowest levels of liking (levels 1, 2, 3, 4 and 5) and there are larger distinctions among the higher levels (9, 10, and 11).

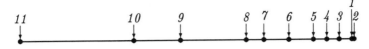

FIGURE 1. Scores for fraternity liking response categories, from correspondence analysis.

The canonical correlation, ρ_m, measures the correlation between the friendship response categories and the combination of observed and reported interactions. For this fraternity example, higher levels of liking are associated with higher levels of reported interaction and with higher levels of observed interaction, but liking appears to be more strongly related to reported interaction than to observed interaction.

In this example we used correspondence analysis to study a two-way table constructed by "stacking" levels of a three-way array. As van der Heijden and de Leeuw (1985) have noted, there are many ways to use correspondence analysis to study three-way problems by analyzing two-way tables derived from the three-way array by different aggregations. As they note, some of these approaches are equivalent, or are equivalent when the derived row/column scores are appropriately rescaled. Other methods are difficult to compare.

Consider the C_1 by $L = C_2 \times C_3$ array, **F**. This array is identical to "stacking" the C_1 by C_2 cross-classification of variables X_1 by X_2 next to each other for each of the C_3 levels of variable X_3. Correspondence analysis of this array gives scores for the C_1 categories of variable X_1, and the $L = C_2 \times C_3$ categories of the cross-classification of variables X_2 and X_3. As van der Heijden and de Leeuw (1985) and van der Heijden and Meijerink (1989) have observed, correspondence analysis of this array can be interpreted as a decomposition of the residuals from the log-linear model of the independence of variable X_1 from X_2 and X_3 jointly: [1][23].

Thus we can interpret correspondence analysis of the relationship between liking response categories and the cross-classification of observed and reported interactions (Table 2) as a decomposition of the residuals from the log-linear model of the independence of liking ratings and the joint effects of observed and reported interactions.

Now let us turn to more parsimonious versions of correlation models.

6. RESTRICTED CANONICAL CORRELATION ANALYSIS

The canonical decomposition described in equation (1) completely describes the data in $\mathbf{F}$. It is a saturated model and uses all available degrees of freedom. As noted above, we refer to this as the $C(t)$ model. Goodman (1985) refers to theoretical versions of this model as the *saturated RC(t) canonical correlation model*.

In this section we will consider restricted versions of $C(t)$ that describe $\mathbf{F}$ in a considerably more parsimonious manner. First, we will describe models that use fewer than t dimensions (or sets of scores). We will then describe models that place restrictions on the scores for the categories of the row and/or column variables. These restricted models have natural and interesting interpretations, and they are most useful for studying the order, spacing, equality, and linearity of the response categories on ordinal relations. Restricted correspondence analysis and restricted correlation models are described in Gilula (1986), Gilula and Haberman (1986, 1988), Böckenholt and Böckenholt (1990), and Takane, Yanai, and Mayekawa (1991). Theoretical versions of these models can be fit using statistical methods, such as maximum likelihood estimation as in Gilula and Haberman's program *CANON*, (Gilula and Haberman, 1986; Gilula 1986). One can then compare the fit of these restricted models with the saturated model, to see whether the more restricted model provides an adequate description of the data.

Standard statistical theory, including the use of maximum likelihood estimation, assumes that observations are independent and identically distributed. Thus, as is standard in many statistical analyses of social network data (Holland and Leinhardt 1975; Fienberg and Wasserman 1981, and so on), we assume that dyads (ordered pairs of actors along with the relational ties between them) are independent. In the following sections we report parameter estimates and goodness-of-fit statistics (X^2 and G^2), but not the p-values for the hypotheses tested by these statistics. Researchers who are uncomfortable with the assumption of dyadic independence can, nevertheless, use correspondence analysis and related approaches to study network data in an exploratory vein (as in Gifi 1990).

First, let us consider models with fewer than the full t sets of scores in the saturated model $C(t)$ presented in equation (1).

6.1. *Fewer Than* t *Dimensions*

The simplest restricted models take equation (1), but they include fewer than the full set of t canonical correlations. So, for $w < t$ we have model $C(w)$:

$$P_{kl} = P_{k\bullet}P_{\bullet l}\left[1 + \sum_{m=1}^{w}\rho_m u_{km}v_{lm}\right]. \qquad (10)$$

$C(w)$ has $(C_1 - 1 - w)(L - 1 - w)$ degrees of freedom. Canonical correlations $\rho_{w+1}, \ldots, \rho_t$ are equal to 0 in this model. The same conditions and interpretations of the canonical correlations and canonical scores hold as in the saturated model $C(t)$ (see equations (2) and (3)). The model $C(0)$ implies independence of the rows and columns.

When statistical procedures, such as the maximum likelihood estimation procedure described by Gilula and Haberman (1986, 1988) and Goodman (1987), are used to fit $C(w)$, one gets the usual goodness-of-fit statistics, Pearson's X^2 and the likelihood-ratio test statistic G^2. One can then test whether the data may be modeled by the more parsimonious model, $C(w)$, compared to $C(t)$.

Of more interest for studying response categories on ordinal variables are models that place restrictions on the scores associated with the response categories. We will describe three such models: equality of response categories, uniform spacing (linearity) of categories, and a priori scores for categories.

6.2. *Equality of Response Categories*

The model for equality of response categories examines whether two (or more) categories of the row (or column) variables are equivalent in terms of the conditional distributions within the equivalent rows (or columns). This model stipulates that the canonical scores for equivalent row categories (k and k'), or column categories (l and l'), are equal. Specifically, for $m = 1, 2, \ldots, w$, we have for row categories

$$u_{km} = u_{k'm} \qquad k \neq k', \qquad (11)$$

and for column categories

$$v_{lm} = v_{l'm} \qquad l \neq l'. \qquad (12)$$

This restriction (equating two categories on w sets of scores) has w degrees of freedom associated with it. In terms of the probabilities of observations in F, stating that two rows, k and k', have equivalent scores, $u_{km} = u_{k'm}$, stipulates that for a given column, say l, differences between cell probabilities, P_{kl} and $P_{k'l}$, are attributable to differences in marginal row probabilities, $P_{k\bullet}$ and $P_{k'\bullet}$. If row categories k and k' have equivalent scores, then $P_{kl}/P_{k\bullet} = P_{k'l}/P_{k'\bullet}$ for $l = 1,2, \ldots ,L$. For example, a model equating two categories of friendship ratings would stipulate that a difference in probabilities of levels of interaction (a predictor relation) across equivalent friendship categories is due to different marginal probabilities of the friendship response categories.

Goodman (1981b) and Gilula (1986) have used this model to study the *homogeneity* of rows or columns in a table.

6.3. Uniform Spacing (Linearity) of Response Categories

This model states that the interval between adjacent row (or column) categories is constant. For rows

$$u_{mk} - u_{m,k+1} = d_u \qquad (k = 1,2, \ldots ,C_1 - 1), \qquad (13)$$

or for columns,

$$v_{ml} - v_{m,l+1} = d_v \qquad (l = 1,2, \ldots ,L - 1), \qquad (14)$$

where d_u and d_v are constants. For restrictions on the rows, this model has $(C_1 - 1 - w)(L - 2 - w) + (C_1 - 2)$ degrees of freedom; for restrictions on the columns, it has $(C_1 - 1 - w)(L - 2 - w) + (L - 2)$ degrees of freedom; and for restrictions on both rows and columns, it has $(C_1 - 1 - w)(L - 2 - w) + (C_1 - 2) + (L - 2)$ degrees of freedom.

Uniform spacing of both row and column canonical scores implies that $C(w)$ (equation (10)) may be restated as:

$$P_{kl} = P_{k\bullet}P_{\bullet l}\left[1 + \sum_{m=1}^{w} \rho_m kld_u d_v\right]. \qquad (15)$$

Goodman (1987) refers to this as the U or *uniform RC correlation model*. One could use this model to test whether response categories on an ordinal variable are equally spaced.

6.4. A priori *Scores for Response Categories*

Instead of equal spacing between row (column) scores, one might have a prior hypothesis about the spacing. In this model a priori scores are proposed for row (and/or column) categories to reflect the relative spacing of these categories. For example, scores $\dot{u}_{km}$ and $\dot{u}_{k'm}$ can be assigned to row categories k and k' respectively so that

$$u_{km} = a + b\dot{u}_{km} \quad \text{and} \quad u_{k'm} = a + b\dot{u}_{k'm} \ (2 \le k \le C_1, k \ne k'). \quad (16)$$

There are $C_1 - 2$ degrees of freedom associated with the restrictions on the C_1 row scores. This model implies that

$$\frac{u_{km} - u_{1m}}{u_{k'm} - u_{1m}} = \frac{\dot{u}_{km} - \dot{u}_{1m}}{\dot{u}_{k'm} - \dot{u}_{1m}}. \quad (17)$$

The model of uniform spacing, described above, is a special case of the model of a priori scores in which all intervals between adjacent categories are specified to be equal.

One could use the model of a priori scores to study hypotheses about the intervals among relational response categories. For example, we illustrate this model by evaluating both suggestions by Burt and Guilarte (1986) about the spacing: first, that a relational tie described as "less close" is about 0.7 the strength of the relational tie described as "especially close"; and second, that the middle level of ties between alters is 0.2 of the distance from "strangers" to "especially close."

Restricted versions of correlation models place constraints on the values of the canonical scores in equations (1) and (10). These models are more parsimonious than unrestricted correlation models in that they use fewer degrees of freedom. If one model is a restricted version of another, then the fit of the more restricted model may be compared with the fit of the less restricted model in order to assess whether the restricted model provides an adequate description of the data. Using maximum likelihood estimation techniques, the associated goodness-of-fit statistics from the more and less restricted models can be compared (with the degrees of freedom equal to the difference between the degrees of freedom associated with the two models). We have found Gilula and Haberman's (1986) program *CANON* to be useful for fitting restricted correlation models.

7. AN EXAMPLE

Now let us consider a different example to illustrate restricted versions of correlation models. We will illustrate these models using data collected by Freeman from a computer conference among social science researchers, the Electronic Information Exchange System (EIES) (S. Freeman and L. Freeman 1979; L. Freeman and S. Freeman 1980; Freeman 1986). There are two relations measured on 32 people in this group:

- X_1–*friendship:* a person's reported friendship with each member of the group on a five-point scale:
  - "Unknown"
  - "Person I've heard of"
  - "Person I've met"
  - "Friend"
  - "Close personal friend."
- X_2–messages: the number of messages sent from a person to each other person. The median number of messages is 0, and 75 percent of all ordered pairs of people sent 12 or fewer messages. We have recoded this to three levels:
  - 0
  - 1 to 11
  - 12 or more.

Table 3 presents the cross-classification of Friendship and Message sending for Freeman's EIES data (the **F** array). Since there are $L = 3$ levels of message sending, and $C_1 = 5$ levels of friendship, this

TABLE 3
EIES Messages and Friendship

Friendship	Messages		
	0	1 to 11	12 or more
Unknown	228	68	46
Heard of	96	25	16
Met	168	70	122
Friend	51	24	36
Close personal friend	9	4	29

TABLE 4
Correlation Models for EIES Messages and Friendship

MODEL	X^2	G^2	df	ρ_1	ρ_2
(1) C(2) (saturated)	0	0	0	0.322	0.049
Restrict number of dimensions					
(2a) C(1)	2.647	2.775	3	0.313	–
(2b) C(0) (independence)	105.153	102.337	8	–	–
Restrict canonical scores C(1)					
(3) Uniform spacing of response categories	20.603	22.040	6	0.274	–
Equality of response categories C(1)					
(4a) *Unknown = Heard of*	2.991	3.113	4	0.313	–
(4b) *Met = Friend*	2.675	2.805	4	0.313	–
(4c) *Unknown = Heard of* and *Met = Friend*	3.020	3.143	5	0.313	–
A priori scores C(1)					
(5a) A priori scores (0 0 .7 .7 1)	11.102	11.266	6	0.296	–
(5b) A priori scores (0 0 .2 .2 1)	17.054	16.812	6	0.301	–

5×3 table is completely explained by $t = 3 - 1$ sets of scores. Thus C(2) is a saturated model for this table.

Table 4 presents the results of several restricted correlation models of the relationship between friendship and message sending from Table 3. We first consider models that include fewer than the full $t = 2$ sets of scores. The independence model, C(0), does not fit these data; therefore, there is some relationship between friendship and message sending in this group. The model with a single set of scores, C(1), does fit these data.

Scores for the friendship response categories, and message sending levels for C(1) (model 2a in Table 4) are presented in Table 5. The scores for the Friendship response categories from this model are displayed in Figure 2.

Now, consider placing restrictions on the set of scores for the relational response categories from C(1). We present the goodness-of-fit statistics for several models in Table 4 (even though a glance at Figure 2 leads us to expect that some of these are unlikely to fit well). First, consider uniform (equal) spacing of the response categories. This model stipulates that the interval between adjacent categories is a constant. This model (model 3) does not fit these data.

TABLE 5
Scores from Correlation Model C(1) of EIES
Messages and Friendship

Friendship	$\mathbf{u}_1$
Unknown	−0.8761
Heard of	−1.0200
Met	0.6808
Friend	0.6149
Close personal friend	3.0006

Messages	$\mathbf{v}_1$
0	−0.6934
1 to 11	−0.2100
12 or more	1.6983

Some models for equality of response categories fit quite well. Model (4a) equating *Unknown* with *Heard of,* model (4b) equating *Met* with *Friend,* and model (4c) equating *Unknown* with *Heard of* and *Met* with *Friend* at the same time, all seem to fit these data quite well. Model (4c) suggests that the five response categories of friendship can be summarized in three levels: {*Unknown* or *Heard of*}, {*Met* or *Friend*}, and {*Close personal friend*}. In addition, collapsing the five levels of friendship to three levels suggests that we could combine the corresponding rows in **F**, and represent the frequencies in a smaller, 3 × 3 table (see Gilula 1986). However, model (4c) does not specify the relative spacing of these three levels of friendship.

The spacing of the response categories, shown in Figure 2, suggests that the middle level of friendship (*Met* and *Friend*) is about midway between the lower level (*Unknown* and *Heard of*) and the higher level (*Close personal friend*). We thus fit both of the models of a priori scores suggested by Burt and Guilarte:(0, 0, 0.7, 0.7, 1); and (0, 0, 0.2, 0.2, 1). These models both equate the two lowest categories of friendship (*Unknown* and *Heard of*), and the two middle

FIGURE 2. Scores for EIES friendship response categories, from correlation model C(1).

categories (*Met* and *Friend*). The first model proposes that the middle level of friendship is 0.7 of the distance from the lowest to the highest level; the second model proposes that the middle level of friendship is 0.2 of the distance from the lowest to the highest. Models (5a) and (5b) in Table 4 show that neither set of a priori scores provides a good fit for these data.

The next section describes association models and restricted association models. Following that, we return to the EIES data and illustrate these models.

8. ASSOCIATION MODELS

Models of association study the relationship between rows and columns in a cross-classification using odds-ratios. We let F_{kl} be the expected frequency under the model, and denote the odds-ratio by θ, where:

$$\theta_{kl,k'l'} = \frac{F_{kl}F_{k'l'}}{F_{k'l}F_{kl'}}. \qquad (18)$$

This focus on odds-ratios (rather than the correlation ρ) gives rise to models of *association*. There has been considerable research on models of association since the late 1970s (Goodman 1979, 1985, 1986, 1991; Haberman 1981; Clogg 1982*a*, 1982*b*, 1986; Gilula and Haberman 1988; Becker and Clogg 1989; Becker 1990).

As above, we have the cross-classification of observed frequencies, $\mathbf{F} = \{f_{kl}\}$. In addition, for association models, we define:

- $\tau_k^{(R)}$, for $k = 1,2,\ldots,C_1$, a set of row effects,
- $\tau_l^{(C)}$, for $l = 1,2,\ldots,L$, a set of column effects,
- τ, an "overall" effect.

The τ's are main effects for the rows, the columns, and the sample size, respectively, and are of little substantive interest. The model of association for $\mathbf{F}$ is defined as:

$$F_{kl} = \tau\tau_k^{(R)}\tau_l^{(C)}\exp(\sum_{m=1}^{t} \phi_m\mu_{km}\nu_{lm}). \qquad (19)$$

One can also express the model in equation (19) in terms of the natural logarithm of F_{kl}. Letting $\lambda_k^{(R)} = \log\tau_k^{(R)}$, $\lambda_l^{(C)} = \log\tau_l^{(C)}$, and $\lambda = \log \tau$, and taking natural logarithms of both sides of equation (19), gives:

$$\log F_{kl} = \lambda + \lambda_k^{(R)} + \lambda_l^{(C)} + \sum_{m=1}^{t} \phi_m \mu_{km} \nu_{lm}. \tag{20}$$

We will refer to either model (19) or model (20) as the A(t) association model.

Association analysis of **F** results in three important sets of information:

- A set of C_1 row scores, $\{\mu_{km}\}$ for $m = 1,2, \ldots, t$,
- A set of L column scores, $\{\nu_{lm}\}$ for $m = 1,2, \ldots, t$,
- A set of t measures of intrinsic association, ϕ_m for $m = 1,2, \ldots, t$, that measure the association between the row scores μ_{km}, and the column scores, ν_{lm}.

The row and column variables $\boldsymbol{\mu}_m$ and $\boldsymbol{\nu}_m$ are scaled as follows:

$$\sum_{k=1}^{C_1} \mu_{km} P_{k\bullet} = \sum_{l=1}^{L} \nu_{lm} P_{\bullet l} = 0 \tag{21}$$

$$\sum_{k=1}^{C_1} \mu_{km}^2 P_{k\bullet} = \sum_{l=1}^{L} \nu_{lm}^2 P_{\bullet l} = 1, \tag{22}$$

for all m. In addition, for distinct m and m', $\boldsymbol{\mu}_m$ and $\boldsymbol{\mu}_{m'}$ are uncorrelated, as are $\boldsymbol{\nu}_m$ and $\boldsymbol{\nu}_{m'}$:

$$\sum_{k=1}^{C_1} \mu_{km} \mu_{km'} P_{k\bullet} = \sum_{l=1}^{L} \nu_{lm} \nu_{lm'} P_{\bullet l} = 0, \quad \text{for } m \neq m'. \tag{23}$$

Goodman (1991) refers to the theoretical version of the association model with row and column scores scaled as in equations (21) and (22) as the *weighted association model,* where the weights are the marginal row and column proportions ($P_{k\bullet}$ and $P_{\bullet l}$). Association models with other weights are also possible (see Becker and Clogg 1989 and Anderson 1992, for example). The scaling in equations (21) and

(22) is most useful for comparing results of correlation and association models.

The intrinsic association, ϕ_m, can be expressed as:

$$\phi_m = \sum_{k=1}^{C_1} \sum_{l=1}^{L} (\log P_{kl}) P_{k\bullet} P_{\bullet l} \mu_{km} \nu_{lm}. \tag{24}$$

Scores ν_m and μ_m, for rows and columns respectively, maximize the intrinsic association ϕ_m in equation (24).

One can also consider the natural logarithm of the odds-ratio as a function of the intrinsic association, ϕ_m, and the relevant row and column scores. For the two-by-two subtable of rows k and k' and columns l and l', $\log \theta_{kl,k'l'}$ can be expressed as a function of the intrinsic association, ϕ_m, and the differences between the row category scores for rows k and k' and between the column category scores for columns l and l':

$$\log \theta_{kl,k'l'} = \sum_{m=1}^{t} \phi_m (\mu_{km} - \mu_{k'm})(\nu_{lm} - \nu_{l'm}). \tag{25}$$

From equation (25) we see that the intrinsic association, ϕ_m, can be interpreted as the expected log-odds-ratio for the two-by-two subtable comparing rows and columns that are one unit apart (Goodman 1986).

The A(t) model, equations (19) or (20), is a saturated model. As with the correlation models, we can consider more parsimonious versions of A(t) that either include fewer than the full set of t sets of scores, or place restrictions on the row scores, the μ_m's, and/or the column scores, the ν_m's. These models are parallel to the restricted correlation models that we described in Section 6. More extensive discussion of restricted association models can be found in Clogg (1982a, 1982b), Goodman (1981a, 1985, 1986, 1991), Gilula (1986), and Gilula and Haberman (1988).

When statistical procedures, such as maximum likelihood estimation described by Gilula and Haberman (1986, 1988) and Goodman (1987), are used to fit restricted association models, one obtains the usual goodness-of-fit statistics, Pearson's X^2, and the likelihood-ratio test statistic G^2. One can then test whether the data may be fit by more parsimonious models.

8.1. *Fewer Than* t *Dimensions*

The simplest restricted association models take equation (19), but include fewer than the full set of t dimensions. For $w < t$, we have model A(w):

$$F_{kl} = \tau \tau_k^{(R)} \tau_l^{(C)} \exp\left(\sum_{m=1}^{w} \phi_m \mu_{km} \nu_{lm}\right). \qquad (26)$$

Model A(w) has $(C_1 - 1 - w)(L - 1 - w)$ degrees of freedom. Intrinsic associations $\phi_{w+1}, \ldots, \phi_t$ are equal to 0 in this model. The model A(0) is the model of independence.

Now let us consider models that place restrictions on the row and/or the column scores. We will describe three models that are parallel to restricted correlation models described above: equality of response categories, uniform spacing (linearity) of categories, and a priori scores for categories. It is important to note that the interpretations of these restricted association models are similar to, but not identical to, the restricted correlation models. (We discuss these differences below.)

8.2. *Equality of Response Categories*

The model for equality of response categories examines whether two (or more) categories of the row (or column) variables are equivalent in terms of their odds-ratios. This model stipulates that the scores for equivalent categories are equal. Specifically, for row categories,

$$\mu_{km} = \mu_{k'm} \quad k \neq k', \qquad (27)$$

and for column categories,

$$\nu_{lm} = \nu_{l'm} \quad l \neq l', \qquad (28)$$

for all m. A restriction such as one of the two above, equating two categories across w sets of scores, has w degrees of freedom associated with it. Goodman (1981*b*) has used this model to study the homogeneity of row (or column) categories in a cross-classification.

Returning to equation (25), we can see that stating that two rows, k and k', have equivalent scores, $\mu_{km} = \mu_{k'm}$, stipulates that all odds-ratios involving rows k and k', $\theta_{kl,k'l'}$, are equal to one, for columns $l = 1,2, \ldots ,L - 1$.

A model equating two categories, k and k', of a relational response variable stipulates that the odds of response k to response k' is the same for all values of the predictor relational variable(s), l and l'; $F_{kl}/F_{k'l} = F_{kl'}/F_{k'l'}$ for $l = 1,2, \ldots ,L - 1$. For example, a model equating two categories of friendship ratings with respect to a relational predictor variable (for example, amount of interaction) would stipulate that the odds of using one friendship response category to the other equivalent friendship response category is the same across all levels of interaction.

8.3. *Uniform Spacing (Linearity) of Response Categories*

This model states that the interval between adjacent row (or column) categories is equal to a constant. For rows,

$$\mu_{mk} - \mu_{m,k+1} = d_\mu \qquad (k = 1,2, \ldots C_1 - 1), \qquad (29)$$

or for columns,

$$\nu_{ml} - \nu_{m,l+1} = d_\nu \qquad (l = 1,2, \ldots ,L - 1) \qquad (30)$$

for all m. For restrictions on the rows, this model has $(C_1 - 1 - w)(L - 2 - w) + (C_1 - 2)$ degrees of freedom. For restrictions on the columns, this model has $(C_1 - 1 - w)(L - 2 - w) + (L - 2)$ degrees of freedom. And, for restrictions on both rows and columns, this model has $(C_1 - 1 - w)(L - 2 - w) + (C_1 - 2) + (L - 2)$ degrees of freedom. Uniform spacing of both row and column scores in the association model constrains odds ratios between adjacent rows/columns to be a constant: $\theta_{kl,k+1l+1} = \theta$ for $k = 1, \ldots ,C_1 - 1$, and $l = 1, \ldots ,L - 1$.

For uniform spacing of *both* row and column scores, A(w) (equation 19) may be restated as:

$$F_{kl} = \tau \tau_k^{(R)} \tau_l^{(C)} \exp(\sum_{m=1}^{w} \phi_m kl d_\mu d_\nu). \qquad (31)$$

This model has been referred to as the U, or *uniform RC association model* (Goodman 1986, 1987; Clogg 1982a).

8.4. A Priori *Scores for Response Categories*

A priori scores can also be proposed for the row and/or column category scores to reflect the relative spacing of these categories (for example, see Clogg 1982*b*). We will let scores $\dot{\mu}_{km}$ and $\dot{\mu}_{k'm}$ be assigned to row categories k and k', respectively, so that

$$\mu_{km} = a + b\dot{\mu}_{km} \quad \text{and} \quad \mu_{k'm} = a + b\dot{\mu}_{k'm} \ (2 \le k \le C_1, k \ne k'). \quad (32)$$

There are $C_1 - 2$ degrees of freedom associated with the restrictions on the C_1 row scores.

The association model with these a priori scores assigned to row categories k and k' implies that ratios of differences of scores are fixed; that is,

$$\frac{\mu_{km} - \mu_{1m}}{\mu_{k'm} - \mu_{1m}} = \frac{\dot{\mu}_{km} - \dot{\mu}_{1m}}{\dot{\mu}_{k'm} - \dot{\mu}_{1m}} \quad (33)$$

for all k, l, and m. Such constraints affect the interpretation of fitted models.

As with the correlation models, restricted versions of association models place constraints on the values of the row and column category scores in equations (19), (20), or (26). These models are more parsimonious than unrestricted association models in that they use fewer degrees of freedom, so that conditional tests can be made to test for parsimonious, nested models. For fitting these models, we have found Gilula and Haberman's program ASSOC (Gilula and Haberman 1986) and Eliason's program CDAS (Eliason 1990) to be quite useful.

9. EXAMPLE

Let us return to Freeman's EIES example of friendship and message sending (the cross-classification in Table 3) to illustrate association models. Table 6 presents results of restricted versions of association models. From the analysis of these data using the correlation model, we already know that the model of independence does not fit these data ($C(0)$ and $A(0)$ give identical results). The association model with a single dimension, $A(1)$, (model 2a in Table 6) does fit these data. The scores for row categories, the μ_m's, and the scores for the

TABLE 6
Association Models for EIES Messages and Friendship

MODEL	X^2	G^2	df	ϕ_1	ϕ_2
(1) A(2) (saturated)	0	0	0	0.327	0.033
Restrict number of dimensions					
(2a) A(1)	0.791	0.804	3	0.331	–
(2b) A(0) (independence)	105.153	102.337	8	–	–
Restrict canonical scores A(1)					
(3) Uniform spacing of response categories	17.865	18.731	6	0.301	–
Equality of response categories A(1)					
(4a) Unknown = Heard of	1.231	1.245	4	0.330	–
(4b) Met = Friend	0.827	0.837	4	0.332	–
(4c) Unknown = Heard of and Met = Friend	1.265	1.281	5	0.329	–
A priori scores A(1)					
(5a) A priori scores (0 0 0.7 0.7 1)	8.197	8.362	6	0.326	–
(5b) A priori scores (0 0 0.2 0.2 1)	21.972	20.562	6	0.297	–

column categories, the ν_m's, are presented in Table 7. The scores for the friendship response categories from model A(1) are displayed in Figure 3.

Comparing the results of the association models (Table 6) with the results of correlation models (Table 4), we can see that for this

TABLE 7
Scores from Association Model A(1) of EIES
Messages and Friendship

Friendship	μ_1
Unknown	−0.8736
Heard of	−1.1311
Met	0.7338
Friend	0.6785
Close personal friend	2.7203

Messages	ν_1
0	−0.7266
1 to 11	−0.0848
12 or more	1.6757

FIGURE 3. Scores for EIES friendship response categories, from association model A(1).

example the results are quite similar. The model with a single dimension fits these data using either the association model, A(1), or the correlation model, C(1). In addition, the model that equates the friendship responses *Unknown* with *Heard of*, and *Met* with *Friend*, fits these data, using either the asociation model or the correlation model. Neither set of a priori scores fits these data, using either the correlation or the association model.

We turn now to some general comparisons of correlation and association models.

10. COMPARISON OF CORRELATION AND ASSOCIATION MODELS

Several recent papers have compared models for association and models for correlation (including correspondence analysis and canonical correlation analysis), and they have commented on situations in which the two models would be expected to give similar results, and situations in which the two models would be expected to give different results (Goodman 1981*a*, 1985, 1986, 1991; Clogg 1986; Gilula and Haberman 1988; Gilula, Krieger, and Ritov 1988; Haberman 1981). We summarize some of these comparisons in this section.

First, consider the parameters in each model. The ρ_m in the correlation model, equation (1), measures the correlation between row variables and column variables in terms of the Pearson product moment correlation coefficient. As Goodman (1991) shows, for a two-by-two table, ρ_1 is equal to the correlation between the variables:

$$\rho_1 = \frac{F_{11}F_{22} - F_{12}F_{21}}{\sqrt{F_{1\bullet}F_{2\bullet}F_{\bullet1}F_{\bullet2}}}. \tag{34}$$

In the correlation model, the row scores $\{u_m\}$ and the column scores $\{v_m\}$ maximize the correlations ρ_m, defined in equation (5).

On the other hand, the measure of intrinsic association, ϕ, in the association model, equation (19) or (20), is based on the log-odds-ratio for the two-by-two subtables within the table. For a two-by-two table, Goodman (1991) shows that:

$$\phi_1 = \frac{|\log \theta_{11,22}|}{2}. \tag{35}$$

Goodman (1991) gives examples of tables that have the same value of ϕ_1 but different values of ρ_1, and of tables that have the same value of ρ_1 but different values of ϕ_1.

Both the correlation models and the weighted association model are sensitive to marginal distributions; ϕ and ρ are not invariant under multiplicative changes in row/column marginal totals. However, *unweighted* association models—in which $P_{k\bullet}$ and $P_{\bullet l}$ in equations 19 and 20 are replaced by unity—are "margin free" (Goodman 1991; Clogg 1986; Clogg and Rao 1991).

Consider the models of independence, C(0) and A(0). In the association model, $\phi_m = 0$ for $m = 1, 2, \ldots, t$, and similarly in the correlation model, $\rho_m = 0$ for $m = 1, 2, \ldots, t$. Models C(0) and A(0) are identical.

If we now consider models C(w) and A(w), with $1 \le w < t$, both association models and correlation models study departures from independence (Clogg 1986; Clogg and Rao 1991; Goodman 1985, 1986, 1991). However, the two models represent this departure in different ways. The correlation model focuses on the residuals from the model of independence (van der Heijden and de Leeuw 1985; Goodman 1991 and commentary following). On the other hand, association models represent the "intrinsic" association present in the entire table using odds-ratios (Clogg 1986; Goodman 1991).

Goodman (1991) describes conditions under which the association model is especially appropriate. If the row and column variables are assumed to adhere to a bivariate normal distribution (or one that can be transformed to a joint normal distribution by separately transforming the marginal distributions), and if the "discretizations" of the row and column variables are not too coarse, then the association model gives a better approximation to this distribution than does the correlation model.

Several authors have noted that fitting the association model is somewhat easier than fitting the correlation models, in that the asso-

ciation model cannot give rise to negative fitted values. Certain constraints on the $\mathbf{u}_m$ and $\mathbf{v}_m$, equation (10), are necessary in order to
avoid negative fitted values in the correlation models (Goodman
1985).

Finally, in practice, association models often seem to give better fits (lower G^2 and X^2) than do correlation models. For example,
our results on the EIES data on friendship and message sending
show slightly better fits for the association models for all but model
(5b) specifying a priori scores (0, 0, 0.2, 0.2, 1) (compare Tables 4
and 6).

On the other hand, computer programs for correspondence
analysis are more readily available than are computer programs for
association models. In addition, correspondence analysis (a correlation model) is widely used in exploratory analysis. In this context,
correspondence analysis can be used to study many different kinds of
data arrays, including data arrays that are not contingency tables of
counts or frequencies (such as incidence matrices, response pattern
matrices, and so on; see Nishisato 1980, Greenacre 1984, and Weller
and Romney 1990, for example). Correspondence analysis results
are also more likely to be used for graphical displays of the row and
column scores (see Carroll, Green, and Schaeffer 1986; and Greenacre and Hastie 1987, for example). Association models are less
widely used for graphical display (but see Goodman 1991; Clogg
1986; and Clogg and Rao 1991).

11. DISCUSSION

In this paper we have described the use of correlation models, including both correspondence analysis and restricted versions of canonical
correlation analysis and association and restricted association models
for directly studying the order and spacing of response categories of
ordinal relational variables. These models were illustrated on two
social network data sets. Correspondence analysis of the 11-point
rating scale of liking from Bernard et al.'s (1979–80, 1982) study of a
fraternity showed that respondents make greater distinctions among
the higher levels of liking than among lower levels of liking. In the
second example, restricted versions of correlation models and restricted versions of association models using maximum likelihood
estimation on ratings of friendship from Freeman and Freeman's

(Freeman 1986; S. Freeman and L. Freeman 1979; L. Freeman and S. Freeman 1980) study of an electronic information exchange network, showed that five levels of friendship could be well represented by just three levels.

APPENDIX

In this paper we have described correspondence and canonical correlation analysis of the matrix F, the cross-classification of the relational response variable, and the relational predictor variable(s). However, in previous papers we have argued that the most appropriate array for (multiple) correspondence analysis of social network data is a *response pattern matrix,* also called an *indicator matrix,* that codes the state of each of the dyads in a network data set (Wasserman and Faust 1989; Wasserman, Faust and Galaskiewicz 1990). In addition, many general discussions of multiple correspondence analysis use the indicator matrix (Greenacre 1984; van der Heijden and de Leeuw 1989; van der Heijden and Meijerink 1989). Thus it is important to note that correspondence analysis and canonical correlation analysis of the F array are equivalent to analysis of a specific indicator matrix coding the state of each case in a data set.

An indicator matrix, denoted M, has cases (here ordered pairs of actors) defining the rows and indicator variables defining the columns. The appropriate indicator matrix for a social network with g actors has $g(g - 1)$ rows, and two sets of columns. The first set of columns is a collection of C_1 indicator variables, coding the state of the relational tie from actor i to actor j on the relational response variable. A single entry of "1" in the appropriate column codes the level of the relational tie from actor i to actor j on the relational response variable (there are "0"'s in the remaining $C_1 - 1$ columns). The second set of columns codes the state of the ordered pair of actors on the relational predictor variable(s). As described above, the state of an ordered pair of actors on these variables is given by the cross-classification of the $R - 1$ relational predictor variables, with $L = C_2 \times C_3 \times \ldots \times C_R$ cells. Thus the second set of columns in the indicator matrix is a collection of L indicator variables. A single "1" in this set of columns codes the state of the ordered pair of actors on the relational predictor variables.

Thus there are $C_1 + L$ columns in M. The state of each ordered pair of actors is coded by two entries in its corresponding row of $\mathbf{M}$. All row marginal totals of $\mathbf{M}$ are equal to 2. The column marginal totals indicate the total number of ordered pairs of actors in each state or level of the relational variables.

The matrix $\mathbf{M}$ consists of two submatrices: $\mathbf{M}_1$, a $g(g-1) \times C_1$ matrix coding the state of the relational response variable, and $\mathbf{M}_2$, a $g(g-1) \times L$ matrix coding the state of the relational predictor variables. Schematically, we can represent this matrix as:

$$\mathbf{M} = [\mathbf{M}_1 | \mathbf{M}_2].$$

Occasionally correspondence analysis is described for a "Burt" matrix, which we denote by $\mathbf{B}$. There are simple relationships among the indicator matrix, $\mathbf{M}$, with submatrices $\mathbf{M}_1$ and $\mathbf{M}_2$, the "Burt" matrix, $\mathbf{B}$, and the cross-classification, $\mathbf{F}$:

- Indicator matrix, $\mathbf{M} = [\mathbf{M}_1 | \mathbf{M}_2]$, of size $g(g-1) \times (C_1 + L)$,
- Cross-classification, $\mathbf{F} = \mathbf{M}_1' \mathbf{M}_2$, of size $C_1 \times L$,
- "Burt matrix", $\mathbf{B} = \mathbf{M}'\mathbf{M}$, of size $(C_1 + L) \times (C_1 + L)$.

In addition, if we denote the row and column marginal totals of $\mathbf{F}$ as f_{i+}, and f_{+j}, respectively, we can then construct two diagonal matrices: a $C_1 \times C_1$ matrix $\mathbf{C} = \mathrm{diag}(f_{i+})$, with row totals of $\mathbf{F}$ on the diagonal and zeroes elsewhere, and an $L \times L$ matrix $\mathbf{L} = \mathrm{diag}(f_{+j})$, with column totals of $\mathbf{F}$ on the diagonal and zeroes elsewhere. The "Burt" matrix has the form:

$$\begin{bmatrix} \mathbf{C} & \mathbf{F} \\ \mathbf{F}' & \mathbf{L} \end{bmatrix}.$$

The indicator matrix, $\mathbf{M}$, or some function of it, is one of the most common data arrays for multiple correspondence analysis (van der Heijden and de Leeuw 1989; van der Heijden and Meijerink 1989), and it is useful when one is interested in studying individual cases (here, ordered pairs of actors). However, when one is not interested in individual cases, equivalent scores are obtained from correspondence analysis or canonical correlation analysis of $\mathbf{F}$, $\mathbf{M}$, or $\mathbf{B}$ (once scores are appropriately scaled).

Correspondence analysis (or canonical correlation analysis), of $\mathbf{F}$, $\mathbf{M}$, or $\mathbf{B}$ results in equivalent sets of scores for the C_1 categories of the relational response variable, and the L states of the relational predictor variable(s), once scores are rescaled within sets. Thus, when one is not interested in scores for the individual cases (here the ordered pairs of actors), analyzing the $C_1 \times L$ array **F** is likely to be more efficient than analyzing the $g(g - 1) \times (C_1 + L)$ array, **M**.

REFERENCES

Anderson, C. J. 1992. "The Analysis of Multivariate Categorical Data by Canonical Correlation and Association Models." Ph.D. diss., University of Illinois.

Becker, M. P. 1990. "Maximum Likelihood Estimation of the RC(M) Association Model." *Applied Statistics* 39:152–67.

Becker, M. P., and C. C. Clogg. 1989. "Analysis of Sets of Two-Way Contingency Tables Using Association Models." *Journal of the American Statistical Association,* 84:142–51.

Bernard, H. R., P. D. Killworth, and L. Sailer. 1979–80. "Informant Accuracy in Social-Network Data IV: A Comparison of Clique-Level Structure in Behavioral and Cognitive Network Data." *Social Networks* 2:191–218.

———. 1982. "Informant Accuracy in Social-Network Data V: An Experimental Attempt to Predict Actual Communication from Recall Data." *Social Science Research* 11:30–66.

Böckenholt, U., and I. Böckenholt. 1990. "Canonical Analysis of Contingency Tables with Linear Constraints." *Psychometrika* 55:633–39.

Burt, R. S., and M. G. Guilarte. 1986. "A Note on Scaling the General Social Survey Network Item Response Categories." *Social Networks* 8:387–96.

Carroll, D. C., P. E. Green, and C. M. Schaffer. 1986. "Interpoint Distance Comparisons in Corresponding Analysis." *Journal of Marketing Research* 24:271–80.

Clogg, C. C. 1982*a*. "Some Models for the Analysis of Association in Multiway Cross-Classifications Having Ordered Categories." *Journal of the American Statistical Association* 77:803–15.

———. 1982*b*. "Using Association Models in Sociological Research: Some Examples." *American Journal of Sociology* 88:114–34.

———. 1986. "Statistical Modelling Versus Singular Value Decomposition." *International Statistical Review* 54:284–88.

Clogg, C. C., and C. R. Rao. 1991. "Comment." *Journal of the American Statistical Association* 86:1118–20.

Eliason, S. R. 1990. *Categorical Data Analysis System: User's Manual.* University of Iowa, Department of Sociology.

Fienberg, S. E., and S. Wasserman. 1981. "Categorical Data Analysis of Single Sociometric Relations." In *Sociological Methodology 1981,* edited by S. Leinhardt, 156–92. San Francisco: Jossey-Bass.

Freeman, L. C. 1986. "The Impact of Computer-Based Communication on the Social Structure of an Emerging Scientific Specialty." *Social Networks* 6:201–22.

————. 1992. "The Sociological Concept of "Group": An Empirical Test of Two Models." *American Journal of Sociology* 98:55–79.

Freeman, L. C., and S. C. Freeman. 1980. "A Semi-Visible College: Structural Effects of Seven Months of *EIES* Participation by a Social Networks Community. In *Electronic Communication: Technology and Impacts,* edited by M. M. Henderson and M. J. MacNaughton, 77–85, AAAS Symposium 53. Washington, D.C.: American Association for the Advancement of Science.

Freeman, S. C., and L. C. Freeman. 1979. "The Networkers Network: A Study of the Impact of a New Communications Medium on Sociometric Structure." Social Science Research Reports No. 46. Irvine, Calif.: University of California.

Friedkin, N. E. 1990. "A Guttman Scale for the Strength of an Interpersonal Tie." *Social Networks* 12:239–52.

Gifi, A. 1990. *Nonlinear Multivariate Analysis.* New York: Wiley.

Gilula, Z. 1986. "Grouping and Association in Contingency Tables: An Exploratory Canonical Correlation Approach. *Journal of the American Statistical Association* 81:773–79.

Gilula, Z., and S. J. Haberman. 1986. "Canonical Analysis of Contingency Tables by Maximum Likelihood." *Journal of the American Statistical Association* 81:780–88.

————. 1988. "Analysis of Multivariate Contingency Tables by Restricted Canonical and Restricted Association Models." *Journal of the American Statistical Association* 83:760–71.

Gilula, Z., A. M. Krieger, and Y. Ritov. 1988. "Ordinal Association in Contingency Tables: Some Interpretative Aspects." *Journal of the American Statistical Association* 83:540–45.

Goodman, L. A. 1979 "Simple Models for the Analysis of Association in Cross-classifications Having Ordered Categories." *Journal of the American Statistical Association* 74:537–52.

————. 1981*a*. "Association Models and Canonical Correlation in the Analysis of Cross-Classifications Having Ordered Categories." *Journal of the American Statistical Association* 76:320–34.

————. 1981*b*. "Criteria for Determining Whether Certain Categories in a Cross-Classification Table Should Be Combined, with Special Reference to Occupational Categories in an Occupational Mobility Table." *American Journal of Sociology* 87:612–50.

————. 1985. "The Analysis of Cross-Classified Data Having Ordered and/or Unordered Categories: Association Models, Correlation Models, and Asymmetry Models for Contingency Tables with or without Missing Entries." *Annals of Statistics* 13:10–69.

————. 1986. "Some Useful Extensions of the Usual Correspondence Analysis Approach and the Usual Log-Linear Models Approach in the Analysis of Contingency Tables." *International Statistical Review* 54:243–309.

————. 1987. "New Methods for Analyzing the Intrinsic Character of Qualitative Variables Using Cross-Classified Data." *American Journal of Sociology* 529–83.

————. 1991. Measures, Models, and Graphical Displays in the Analysis of Cross-Classified Data." *Journal of the American Statistical Association* 86: 1085–138.

Granovetter, M. S. 1973. "The Strength of Weak Ties." *American Journal of Sociology* 78:1360–80.

Greenacre, M. J. 1984. *Theory and Application of Correspondence Analysis.* New York: Academic Press.

————. 1986. "*SIMCA:* A Program to Perform Simple Correspondence Analysis." *Psychometrika* 51:172–73.

Greenacre, M. J., and T. Hastie. 1987. "The Geometric Interpretation of Correspondence Analysis." *Journal of the American Statistical Association* 82:437–47.

Haberman, S. J. 1981. "Tests for Independence in Two-Way Contingency Tables Based on Canonical Correlation and on Linear-by-Linear Interaction." *The Annals of Statistics* 9:1178–86.

Holland, P. W., and S. Leinhardt. 1975. "Local Structure in Social Networks." In *Sociological Methodology 1976,* edited by D. R. Heise, 1–45. San Francisco: Jossey-Bass.

Marsden, P. V., and K. E. Campbell. 1984. "Measuring Tie Strength." *Social Forces* 63:482–501.

Nishisato, S. 1980. *Analysis of Categorical Data: Dual Scaling and Its Applications.* Toronto: University of Toronto Press.

Takane, Y., H. Yanai, and S. Mayekawa. 1991. "Relationships Among Several Methods of Linearly Constrained Correspondence Analysis." *Psychometrika* 56:667–84.

van der Heijden, P. G. M., and J. de Leeuw. 1985. "Correspondence Analysis Used Complementary to Loglinear Analysis." *Psychometrika* 50:429–47.

————. 1989. "Correspondence Analysis, with Special Attention to the Analysis of Panel Data and Event History Data." *Sociological Methodology, 1989,* 43–87. Cambridge, Mass.: Basil Blackwell.

van der Heijden, P. G. M., and F. Meijerink. 1989. "Generalized Correspondence Analysis of Multi-way Contingency Tables and Multi-way (Super-) Indicator Matrices." In *Multiway Data Analysis,* edited by R. Coppi and S. Bolasco, 185–202. Amsterdam: North-Holland.

Wasserman, S., and K. Faust. 1989. "Canonical Analysis of the Composition and Structure of Social Networks." In *Sociological Methodology, 1989,* edited by C. C. Clogg, 1–42. Cambridge, Mass.: Basil Blackwell.

Wasserman, S., K. Faust, and J. Galaskiewicz. 1990. "Correspondence and Canonical Analysis of Relational Data." *Journal of Mathematical Sociology* 15:11–64.

Weller, S. C., and A. K. Romney. 1990. *Metric Scaling: Correspondence Analysis.* Newbury Park, Calif.: Sage.

Winship, C. 1977. "A Distance Model for Sociometric Structure." *Journal of Mathematical Sociology* 5:21–39.

7

EVENT-HISTORY ANALYSIS FOR LEFT-TRUNCATED DATA

Guang Guo*

A subject is left-truncated when it comes under observation after having been exposed to the risk of an event for some time. Left-truncated subjects tend to have lower risks at shorter durations than those in a normal sample because high-risk subjects tend to experience the event and drop out before reaching the point at which observation begins. When start times are unknown, left truncation is practically intractable unless the hazard rate is constant or all left-truncated subjects are discarded. When start times are known, left-truncated data can be handled by the conditional likelihood approach. The critical information on the start time of a left-truncated subject can be frequently obtained from human subjects. The concentration of covariate information in the observation period in a longitudinal social survey is well-suited for the conditional approach. We show that a piece-wise exponential hazard model and a discrete-time model based on the conditional likelihood approach can be readily estimated by extant packages like SAS. We also describe an alternative conditional partial likelihood approach. An empirical example of marital dissolution in the United States is provided.

*University of North Carolina at Chapel Hill
I am indebted to Sanders Korenman for involving me in his research and for many helpful comments. The work was supported by the Department of Sociology and the Office of Population Research at Princeton University. Additional support was provided by the Carolina Population Center at the University of North Carolina at Chapel Hill. The paper has benefited from comments by David Guilkey, Lorenzo Moreno, Thomas Mroz, and Germán Rodríguez. I also thank the editor, Peter Marsden, and the anonymous reviewers for many helpful suggestions.

1. INTRODUCTION

Social scientists' event-history data are almost never complete. Frequently, an event history is right-censored, meaning that the length of the survival time is observed to be greater than a certain value, but the precise length is unknown. For instance, in a study of divorce rates, a subject is right-censored if the subject's marriage remains intact at the end of an observation period. The subject's marriage may dissolve in the future, but we do not know when. Statistical procedures for right-censored data have been developed and used routinely (Cox and Oakes 1984; Tuma and Hannan 1984; Allison 1984; Yamaguchi 1991).

Sometimes, event-history data are left-truncated, meaning that a subject has been exposed to the risk of an event for a while when it comes under observation; the length of exposure prior to observation may or may not be known. In contrast to the clear-cut statistical solutions for right-censored event-history data, there is considerable confusion surrounding the solutions for the data that are left-truncated. Even the definitions of left censoring and left truncation in the literature can be quite puzzling. This paper aims at providing a practical guidance for coping with social science event-history data that are left-truncated, especially when the length of exposure prior to observation is known. Only the case of single events is treated, although much of the discussion should be applicable to the case of repeated events, in which only the first spell is likely to be left-truncated. Marital dissolution data from the Panel Study of Income Dynamics (PSID) are used as an example throughout the paper (Survey Research Center 1989).

1.1. *Characterization of Incomplete Data*

Figure 1 illustrates various complete and incomplete event histories. The horizontal axis indicates the calendar time denoted by τ. The observation period is usually of finite length, with the beginning and ending marked by τ_0 and τ_1. For convenience and without loss of generality, the start time of the observation window is assumed to be zero. A lowercase e for *event* at the right end of a line indicates the exact time at which an event occurs is observed. A lowercase s for *start time* at the left end of a line indicates that the start time is

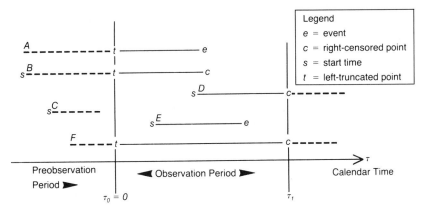

FIGURE 1. Complete and incomplete event-history observations.

known. A lowercase c for *censored* indicates that the subject is right censored at that point. Right censoring may arise from the termination of the observation period (subject D) or the loss to follow-up (subject B). The right-censored subject D can be handled routinely by conventional methods. A lowercase t for *truncated* at τ_0 signifies that the subjects A and B have been exposed to the risk for some time. Subject E is the only complete event history described in Figure 1. Subject F is both left-truncated and right-censored.

Both subjects A and B are left-truncated, but the start time is known only for the latter. An example of subject A arises in the use of longitudinal social survey data such as those collected in the PSID. The PSID began collecting information from a nationally representative sample of households in the United States in 1968 (τ_0), and the respondents were interviewed each year thereafter. For illustrative purposes, we consider 1987 as the end of the observation window (τ_1). If we are interested in the event of first marital dissolution for women, we need to know the start time of a marriage as well as the time of dissolution or censoring. Left truncation arises when a woman married some time before 1968 and entered the observation period in 1968. She might or might not have divorced after 1968. For many years before the 1985 wave of the survey that collected information on retrospective marital history, the exact length of exposure to divorce before 1968 could not be identified.

1.2. *Definitions of Left Censoring and Left Truncation*

While we consider subjects that enter the observation period after having been exposed to the risk for a while as left-truncated, some social scientists consider them as left-censored or partially left-censored (Tuma and Hannan 1984 and Yamaguchi 1991). Their definition is intuitive in that it defines the lack of information on the left and right symmetrically as left and right censoring. Econometricians usually treat this situation as a part of the problems caused by "sampling of duration data" (Ridder 1984) or "the initial conditions" (Heckman and Singer 1986) in event-history analysis.

Our definition of left truncation is drawn from the work of Cox and Oakes (1984, pp. 177–78), Miller (1981, p. 7), Trussell and Guinnane (1991), Keiding (1986), Hald (1952), and Turnbull (1974). They distinguish two kinds of data: truncated and censored. Truncation arises when sampling from an incomplete population. Left truncated event-history data are incomplete because they do not include those subjects that have not survived long enough to be observed.[1] As Keiding (1986, p. 357) explained: "On the other hand censoring occurs when we are able to sample the complete population but the individual values of observations below (or above) a given value are not specified." A left-censored subject is known to have experienced the event, but the exact failure time is unknown. In Figure 1, subject C is left-censored. The absence of e at the right end of the time line for subject C in Figure 1 signifies the lack of knowledge about the exact time at which the event occurs. Note the symmetry in the definitions of left and right censoring here. In both left and right censoring, the exact length of time until the event is unknown, but we know that the event occurs before the start of the observation window in the case of left censoring and after the end of the observation window in the case of right censoring.

----

[1]It should be emphasized that, unlike censoring, truncation is a characteristic of a *sample*, rather than of an individual subject. Suppose that we observe a sample of subjects A, B, D, E, and F in the observation period (Figure 1). The *sample* is left-truncated because it has left out the high-risk subject C. In this paper, however, we sometimes refer to *subjects* such as A, B, and F as left-truncated when the sample is already known to be left-truncated for convenience. Fixing a left-truncated sample usually amounts to a special treatment of the standard likelihood function of the left-truncated subjects A, B, and F while leaving the likelihood function of the subjects such as D and E unchanged.

Turnbull (1974) provides an example of left censoring that Leiderman et al. (1973) came across in a study of African infant precocity. The 65 children in the sample were born between July 1 and December 31, 1969. Starting in January 1970, each child was given a test every month to see if he or she had learned to perform a particular task. The start time is birth and the event is accomplishing the task. Left censoring occurred when some children were found to be able to perform the task at the very first test (i.e., they had experienced the event before the observation period). Sample selection is absent since these left-censored children remained in the sample after they had experienced the event.

1.3. *Problems of Left Truncation*

The characteristic problem of left truncation is sample selection, whether or not the start time is known. The left-truncated cases sampled at the beginning of the observation period tend to over-represent low-risk cases among any given cohort. For instance, the couples sampled in 1968 in the PSID can be viewed as survivors of their marriage cohorts. The original size of a marriage cohort must be bigger than what is observed in 1968 though the exact size is unknown, because many in the original cohort did not stay in the first marriage long enough to be sampled in 1968.

The problem of sample selection can be illustrated more formally. Define the length of time from τ_0 to the start of exposure as T_r, with r standing for *retrospective*, and define the length of time from τ_0 to the time the subject is last observed as T_p, with p standing for *prospective* (Figure 2). Define T, which is the sum of T_r and T_p, as the survival time of the population in whose parameters we are interested. Let the density of the subjects that start t_r periods before τ_0 be expressed as $h(-t_r)$. The probability of these subjects surviving t_r periods must be $S_T(t_r)$, the survivor function of the population. Then the proportion of those that start t_r periods before τ_0 and have made it to τ_0 is $h(-t_r)S_T(t_r)$. Integrating over all cohorts, we obtain the probability of those that start before τ_0 and have survived to τ_0

$$P_0(\tau_0 \in T) = \int_0 h(-t_r) \, S_T(t_r) \, dt_r, \qquad (1)$$

where $\tau_0 \in T$ means that the duration time t includes the calendar time $\tau_0 = 0$ as an element. Dividing the surviving cohort by the surviving population, we obtain

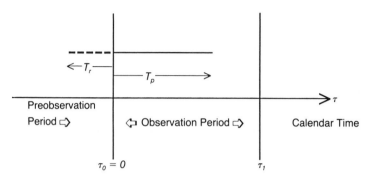

FIGURE 2. T_r and T_p.

$$f(t_r) = \frac{h(-t_r) \, S_T(t_r)}{P_0 \, (\tau_0 \in T)}, \qquad (2)$$

which is the density of those cases that start some time before τ_0 and have made it at least to τ_0. Assuming a constant entry rate $h(-t_r) = h$ over time, this density (2) would correspond to Cox's (1962) equilibrium density of the backward recurrence-time distribution. Due to sample selection, $f_{T_r}(t_r)$ (the density of left-truncated subjects) is quite different from $f_T(t)$ (the density of the population) and cannot be used as if it were $f_T(t)$ for the estimation of the parameters of the population.

2. SOME SOLUTIONS TO LEFT TRUNCATION WITH UNKNOWN START TIMES

The previous work on the "initial conditions problems" (Heckman and Singer 1986) and the distribution of event-history data (Ridder 1984) provides an important framework within which various solutions to left truncation can be better understood. In this paper, we give only a brief review of the results. For more details, see also Hamerle's (1991) exposition. Ridder shows that the density of the joint distribution of T_r and T_p, given covariates x and the condition that T starts at the calendar time $-t_r$ and has survived beyond τ_0, is

$$g(t_r, t_p | x, \tau_0 \in T) = \frac{h(-t_r | x) f(t_r + t_p | x)}{\int_0^\infty h(-t_r | x) S_T(t_r | x) dt_r}. \qquad (3)$$

Integrating (3) over t_r, the unobserved part of T, we obtain the density of a left-truncated case (observation A in Figure 1)

$$f(t_p|x,\tau_0 \in T) = \frac{\int_0^\infty h(-t_r|x) f(t_r + t_p|x) \, dt_r}{\int_0^\infty h(-t_r|x) S_T(t_r|x) dt_r}. \tag{4}$$

Expression (4), however, is intractable. The term $h(-t_r|x)$, the proportion of the population that starts being exposed to the risk at time $-t_r$, is almost never known.

An easy solution to left truncation is available, however, if one is willing to assume that the survival time T has an exponential distribution with the density $f_T(t) = \lambda e^{-\lambda t}$. Under this assumption, expression (4) for left-truncated observations simplifies to

$$f(t_p|\tau_0 \in T) = \lambda e^{-\lambda t_p}. \tag{5}$$

Expression (5) is in itself the density of an exponential distribution, as if the exposure of the observation started at τ_0, rather than the calendar time $-t_r$. The left-truncated observation simply *forgets* its experience before τ_0. This result comes directly from the property of *memorylessness* of the exponential distribution. Unfortunately, the assumption of a constant hazard $\lambda(t) = \lambda$ is often unrealistic. Erroneously assuming an exponential distribution may lead to severe bias in parameter estimates (Heckman and Singer 1986).

Another simple solution is to discard all left-truncated cases from analysis as Allison suggests (1984). Ridder's (1984) distribution theory shows that the resulting sample is not biased. The loss of information, however, can be huge. For example, in the first marital dissolution data of the PSID we have described, 49 percent of white women and 39 percent of black women, whose first marriages began prior to 1968, would have to be discarded if we are to follow this strategy. Moreover, some of the lost information is unique. Suppose that we are interested in the differential impact of the "no fault" divorce laws on divorce rates of the women who have been married for 20 years or less and the women who have been married for more than 20 years. In the PSID, we have observed the women for only 20 years (1968–1987). Then the use of left-truncated cases is the only way to answer questions concerning divorce rates at durations longer than 20 years.

We have mentioned that one major obstacle to the direct use of (4) as the likelihood function for left-truncated cases is the unavailability of the entry rate $h(-t_r)$. The easiest solution is to make a time homogeneity assumption: $h(-t_r) = h$. Under this assumption, which allows the cancellation of the entry rate, the density for left-truncated cases (4) becomes

$$f(t_p|x, \tau_0 \in T) = \frac{S(t_p|x)}{\int_0^\infty S_T(t_r|x)dr}. \tag{6}$$

The denominator of (6) yields $E(T|x)$, the expected value of the distribution. With further parametric assumptions on the distribution of T, (6) can be used to estimate the parameters related to the population distribution T.

The problem of unobserved entry rates is merely circumvented rather than confronted in (6). Under certain circumstances, external data sources (external to data analyzed) may be used to estimate entry rates empirically. See Tuma and Hannan (1984, pp. 131–32) for a similar argument. In the case of women's marital dissolution in the PSID, the aggregate data from the census may be used to establish the probabilities of marriage during the years before 1968. The difficulty of this strategy is the need to calculate the probabilities of marriage during those years for every possible combination of covariates x. Chances are that no external data source can match the large number of combinations of covariates, which is typical in social scientists' work today. In general, the density for left-truncated subjects (4) remains intractable.

The unknown entry rate is not the only problem for (4). The usage of time-varying covariates is a major feature of event-history analysis. Time-varying covariates offer an opportunity to examine the relation between the risk of an event and the *changing* conditions under which the event occurs. For a left-truncated subject, however, the values of time-varying covariates before τ_0 are almost always unobserved. When density (4) is used, we are forced to abandon basically all time-varying covariates even though these covariates are observed during the observation period.

In summary, when the start time is not known, left truncation remains a very difficult problem unless we are willing to assume a constant hazard rate or to delete all left-truncated subjects. The problem becomes much easier, however, when the start time is known. In the rest of this paper, we focus on a conditional likelihood approach to left truncation when start times are known. The conditional approach does not have the drawbacks of the approaches we have described in this section. We will show that many flexible hazard models based on the approach can be easily estimated with commercial statistical packages that are widely available. We believe that the conditional approach deserves special attention from social scientists because of the distinctive characteristics of social scientists' event-history data that we will describe in the next section.

3. SOCIAL SCIENTISTS' EVENT-HISTORY DATA

3.1. *Longitudinal Surveys*

Event-history analysis was originally developed in the biomedical sciences and engineering. Typical data in these fields consist of the survival times of cancer patients or the failure times of equipment components. In social sciences, the typical data are the waiting times of social and economic events in the life of human subjects. In the present context, at least two characteristics of social scientists' event-history data should be taken into consideration when statistical methods are selected. First, when start times fall before the observation period, social scientists' human subjects are much more likely to be aware of the start of the exposure to a life event (date of marriage in the PSID example) than cancer patients, for example, to be aware of the beginning date of their cancer. Second, social scientists' event-history data are often collected by a longitudinal survey that follows a respondent for many years. Before discussing these characteristics in detail, we give a brief description of several major longitudinal social surveys.

The past 25 years have seen the start and growth of several nationally representative longitudinal surveys of households and individuals. Two of the most important ones were initiated in the 1960s: the National Longitudinal Surveys of Labor Market Experience (NLS) and the Panel Study of Income Dynamics (PSID) (Center for Human Resources Research 1991). The NLS has collected five separate longitudinal data bases: men aged 45 to 59 in 1966, young men aged 14 to 24 in 1966, women aged 30 to 40 in 1967, young women aged 14 to 24 in 1968, and youth aged 14 to 21 in 1979. Each of the first four data bases contains approximately 5,000 individuals and the last one contains more than 10,000 young men and young women. The PSID data set contained about 6,000 households and 15,000 individuals at the beginning of the survey in 1968. With a few exceptions, annual interviews were conducted. Most of the surveys have continued to the present. More recent years saw the start of the U.S. Survey of Income and Program Participation (SIPP) and the German Socio-Economic Panel (SOEP) (U.S. Department of Commerce 1987; Deutsches Institut 1991). Both have been conducted much the same way as the NLS and the PSID. The results are a wealth of information on the respondent's history of marriage, fertility, labor force participation, education, personal income, health, and so on.

Taken together, these and other longitudinal surveys have been and will probably remain primary data sources for social scientists' event-history analysis.

3.2. Acquiring Start Times

The conditional approach requires that the start time of a left-truncated case be known—that is, that we have data like subject B rather than A in Figure 1. It is often difficult to ascertain the outset of a cancer, for instance, in an analysis of cancer patients. The situation changes radically, however, when human individuals and their important life events are the subjects of event-history analysis.

The date of an important life event can be recalled even years after it occurred. Moreover, the dates of the past events should be recalled relatively accurately in social surveys because social scientists tend to be interested in only well-defined, important social and economic occurrences. Freedman et al. (1988) report a remarkable correspondence between the data acquired in 1980 about current life events and the data about these events recalled retrospectively in 1985 via the life-history-calendar technique. It has often been suggested that the social scientists' task is more complicated because their subjects are people. But in this case, human subjects work to our advantage: People have memories.

When the PSID started in 1968, the start times of most first marriages were not collected. This was the case until 1985 when retrospective marital histories were taken, which naturally include the start date of the first marriage. Subject A in Figure 1 thus becomes subject B, a left-truncated case with known start time. In fact, this information could have been acquired in any of the 17 yearly surveys conducted between 1968 and 1985. We have checked the reliability of the retrospective information by comparing the date of the first marriage reported retrospectively in 1985 against the date reported in the yearly surveys among those who married after 1968. The two sets of reports are quite consistent. In the more recent SIPP and SOEP, retrospective questions on dates of past events were administered much earlier during the observation period than they were in the PSID.

It should be recognized that a substantial amount of event-history data is from archival sources from which acquiring start times is more difficult. Unlike the observations in an ongoing survey, the archival subjects usually cannot be reached again for more information. Nevertheless, researchers working with left-truncated archival data should be aware that start times are sometimes available.

One such example arises from the official data on the life insurance industry in New York (Lehrman 1989). Most of the data come from the *Annual Report of the Superintendent of the Insurance Department*. These annual reports include abstracts of the annual financial statements of all assessment companies and fraternal societies actively selling life insurance in New York state from 1881 onward. The event of interest here is the failure of these insurance businesses. The problematic or left-truncated subjects are those that started operating before 1881, the beginning of the observation period. These businesses tend to be more successful. The less successful ones tend to fail before 1881 and thus are excluded from the official reports. Analyzing the left-truncated businesses as if they were regular subjects would lead to an underestimation of failure rates. Fortunately, the annual reports contain the date of creation, or start time, for each business, which can be used in the conditional likelihood approach to address the problem of sample selection.

3.3. Asymetry of the Preobservation and Observation Periods

Previous work on left truncation tends to view the preobservation and observation periods as more or less symmetrical with respect to the amount of information they contain. In the development of equation (6), a left-truncated case is considered to consist of the information (t_r) from the preobservation period and the information (t_p) from the observation period. Then, the joint distribution of T_r and T_p is sought for the construction of the likelihood function. The unobservability of T_r requires integration of the joint distribution under parametric assumptions. The inclusion of t_r in this manner is preferred because it increases the statistical efficiency of the estimation.

In longitudinal social surveys, however, the distribution of information between the preobservation and observation periods is heavily skewed to the latter. During the observation period, the respondents are interviewed year after year, even three times a year in the SIPP. Not surprisingly, an enormous amount of information would accumulate on the respondent's changing social, economic, and personal circumstances during the observation period. By 1988, the PSID had accumulated nearly 15,000 variables, almost all of which are concerned with the observation period. Although dates of important life events before the observation period can be retrieved quite accurately through retrospective questions, the possibility of obtaining information such as detailed income and employment history from the distant past is extremely slim.

One's objectives may be limited to estimating the parameters in the distribution of the survival time and its relation to covariates, such as gender, that do not change in a respondent's lifetime. In that case, the preobservation and observation periods may well be viewed as symmetrical. But social scientists are usually interested in much more complex questions, the answers to which demand detailed information over time. In some recent studies on the relationship between individual divorce rates over time and women's economic status, for instance, an examination of the detailed income history of women is essential (e.g., Korenman, Guo, and Geronimus 1991; Dechter 1992).

4. A CONDITIONAL LIKELIHOOD APPROACH

4.1. *Conditional Likelihood*

The examination of longitudinal social surveys reveals that most complications occur before the observation period, and most information is contained in the observation period. In this section, we describe an approach of conditional likelihood that avoids the complications in the preobservation period and maximizes the use of the available information in the observation period.

Recall the two problems of left truncation: unknown start time and sample selection. Availability of start times removes the first, but the second remains. Treating a left-truncated subject with a known start time as if it were a standard subject still leads to an underestimation of hazard rates at shorter durations (to be illustrated by an example in Section 6). The conditional likelihood approach addresses the problem of sample selection by conditioning the density of a left-truncated case on the case's having survived to t_r, the amount of time the case spends in the preobservation period. The idea is to use only those pieces of exposure that have not been selected.

The idea has been around for many years. Schoen (1975) studied increment-decrement life tables that a subject can enter at different durations, so that the selection bias can be eliminated. The increments mean entrants here. Thompson (1977) suggests that observations be grouped into intervals when ties are present and that the likelihood function be constructed for each interval conditionally on having made it to the beginning of the interval. Lancaster (1979) and Elandt-Johnson and Johnson (1980, p. 349) also describe the conditional likelihood.

The conditional density of a left-truncated case is defined as

$$f_T[t|T>t_r, x(t)] = \frac{\lambda[t|x(t)]\, S_T\, [t|\, \{x(u)\}_{u=0}^{u=t}]}{S_T[t_r|\{x(u)\}_{u=0}^{u=t_r}]}, \tag{7}$$

$$= \lambda[t|x(t)]\, exp\, [-\int_{t_r}^{t}\lambda(u)\, e^{x(u)'\beta}du], \tag{8}$$

where $\{x(u)\}_{u=0}^{u=t_r}$ and $\{x(u)\}_{u=0}^{u=t}$ stand for the time-varying covariates from 0 to t_r and from 0 to t, respectively. Note that u in (7) is used in exactly the same way as that in the integral in (8) to represent the points along t. The second term in (8) can be interpreted as the survivor function of T given having survived from $t=0$ to $t=t_r$. The values of time-varying covariates need to be observed only in the observation period from t_r to t. This implies that all information required in the conditional likelihood approach is supplied from the observation period except the start time of t. Note that model (8) assumes that the covariates act multiplicatively on the hazard function.

Except for t_r, the information required by the conditional approach amounts to the collection of all the solid lines (both exposure and accompanying covariates) within the observation period in Figure 1. The interrupted lines that extend to the left of τ_0 or to the right of τ_1 are excluded. These required data correspond almost exactly to the data normally collected during an observation period by a longitudinal social survey. In this sense, the conditional approach is probably the most effective way of using the collected information. In contrast, discarding left-truncated cases equals wasting the solid parts of subjects A, B, and F in Figure 1. The data collected in the observation period in a social survey bear a resemblance to those for the construction of a period life table. The estimates from analyzing these data via the conditional approach can be readily interpreted in terms of a calendar period. On the other hand, the same data with left-truncated subjects excluded resemble those for the construction of a cohort life table. An analysis of these data is relevant only to the cohort that starts in the observation period.

The conditional likelihood (8) can be alternatively derived by conditioning $f(t_p)$ (4), the density for left-truncated cases with unknown start times, on t_r. The resulting conditional density (8) is much simpler than (4) and does not depend on the entry rate $h(-t_r)$. The conditional likelihood approach has been compared with approach (6), and criticized for being less efficient than (6), since the information contained in t_r is used only for eliminating the complications caused by left truncation and not for estimating parameters β (Hamerle 1991). There seems to be more, however, to the comparison of the two approaches than efficiency. Whereas the more efficient approach (6) depends on the convenient assumption of time homogeneity, the less efficient conditional likelihood does not. Besides, approach (6) is more efficient only in the use of information on the distribution of time. When time-varying covariates are available, the conditional likelihood approach is much more "efficient" than approach (6), which is usually compelled to give up the use of any time-varying covariates collected in the observation period because these covariates are almost never observed before the observation period.

4.2. Continuous-Time Piece-Wise Exponential Models

A key issue for most data analysts is the accessibility of the estimation methods. The maximum likelihood estimates from this conditional likelihood function are, in general, different from those yielded by the methods for conventional event-history data. For instance, when T has a Weibull distribution with density $f(t) = \lambda p(\lambda t)^{p-1} exp[-(\lambda t)^p]$, the cumulative hazard functions $\int_0^t \lambda(u;x)\, du$ and $\int_{t_r}^t \lambda(u;x)\, du$ yield different expressions of $(\lambda t)^p e^{x'\beta}$ and $(\lambda)^p [t^p - (t_r)^p] e^{x'\beta}$ respectively. This means that software developed for standard event-history analysis cannot be used for the type of data under consideration unless the more general form of the cumulative hazard function $[\int_{t_r}^t \lambda(u;x)\, du$, which includes $\int_0^t \lambda(u;x)\, du$ as a special case] is a built-in feature in the software.

In this and the next sections, we will show that piece-wise exponential hazard models based on the conditional approach can be estimated by any package estimating a Poisson regression and that the conditional discrete-time models can be estimated by any package estimating a logistic regression. The important point is that these results are not package-specific. A data analyst has to know only how to estimate a Poisson model or a logistic model, which can be estimated by almost any general commercial statistical package.

Because of its flexible functional form, the piece-wise exponential model is one of the most widely used hazard models in the social sciences. The basic idea is simple. We divide the maximum duration into a number of intervals. The baseline hazard within each interval is assumed to be constant, but the baseline hazards are allowed to vary across intervals. The baseline hazards are a vector of parameters that determine the shape of hazard rate over time.

We first consider data that are not left-truncated. We construct J duration intervals with $J+1$ cut points $0 = \tau_1 < \tau_2 < \ldots < \tau_{J+1} = \infty$ and assume that the baseline hazard $\lambda(t)$ takes the value λ_j when t is in interval j–that is, $\tau_j < t < \tau_{j+1}$. Define t_j as the exposure time spent in the j-th interval by a subject. Define δ_j as one if the subject experiences the event in the interval and as zero otherwise.

Holford (1980) shows that the log-likelihood of the above model is equivalent to the kernel of the log-likelihood that treats the event indicators $\delta_j s$ as if they were independent Poisson random variables with means $\mu_j = t_j \lambda_j e^{x'\beta}$. Note that the means depend on a proportional hazards assumption. We point out that this result holds for left-truncated data with known start time as well. We write the conditional log-likelihood of a piece-wise exponential hazard model for subject i as

$$logL_i = \sum_{j=j_i}^{m_i} \delta_{ij}(log\lambda_j + x_i'\beta) - \sum_{j=j_i}^{m_i} \lambda_j t_{ij} e^{x_i'\beta}, \qquad (9)$$

where interval m_i is the interval in which subject i is last observed with $m_i = J$ as a special case when subject i is last observed in interval J and interval j_i is the interval in which subject i is first observed with j_i taking the value 1 as a special case when the first interval starts within the observation period. Adding to and subtracting from (9) the quantity $\sum_{j=j_i}^{m_i} \delta_{ij}logt_{ij}$ yield

$$\log L_i = \sum_{j=j_i}^{m_i} [\delta_{ij}\log(\lambda_j t_{ij} e^{x_i'\beta}) - \lambda_j t_{ij} e^{x_i'\beta}] - \sum_{j=j_i}^{m_i} \delta_{ij}\log t_{ij}. \qquad (10)$$

The first summation term can, again, be considered equivalent to the kernel of the log-likelihood of independent Poisson random variables with the log of exposure $\log t_{ij}$ and linear predictors $\alpha_j + x_i'\beta$, where $\alpha_j = \log \lambda_j$. This differs from the case Holford (1980) considered in that the summation now can start from any interval. But this difference is of no consequence for using Poisson regression routines in standard statistical software. The routines treat each interval as if it were an independent observation without regard to whether its previous interval is observed or not. The second summation term is a constant and therefore may be ignored in the maximization of the likelihood. An empirical example is provided in Section 6 to show how estimation based on (10) can be accomplished in practice. When the explanatory variables are constant over time, a piece-wise exponential hazard model can also be estimated with a program for exponential accelerated life models.[2]

4.3. Discrete-time Models

Discrete-time models have become one of the most popular class of hazard models for social scientists since Allison's (1982) work, because of their connection in conceptualization with the familiar statistical models for binary data, their uncomplicated way of incorporating time-varying covariates, and their ease of estimation via standard software developed for binary data. In this section, we point out that

[2]Pointed out by an anonymous reviewer.

the whole class of discrete-time models based on the conditional likelihood can be estimated by the same standard software for binary data.

The discrete-time models arise when the random variable T takes values at distinct $t_1 < t_2 < \ldots < t_J$ with the corresponding probability function

$$f(t) = Pr(T=t) = \lambda_J \prod_{j=1}^{J-1} (1-\lambda_j), \qquad (11)$$

and survivor function

$$S(t) = Pr(T > t) = \prod_{j=1}^{J} (1-\lambda_j), \qquad (12)$$

where the discrete-time hazard rate $\lambda_j = Pr(T=t_j|T \geq t_j)$ is the conditional probability of experiencing the event at t_j.

To develop the conditional likelihood, we again use t_r (Figure 2) to represent the length of exposure before the observation period with $t_r \leq \tau_0 < t_{r+1}$, where t_r and t_{r+1} are two adjacent distinct survival times. Using δ_i again as the event indicator, conditioning the likelihood on having survived to t_r, taking logs, and multiplying over the sample, we obtain the conditional log-likelihood for the discrete-time models

$$\log L = \sum_{i=1}^{n} \sum_{j=1}^{J} \delta_{ij} \log \left(\frac{\lambda_{ij}}{1-\lambda_{ij}} \right) + \sum_{i=1}^{n} \sum_{j=r+1}^{J} \log (1-\lambda_{ij}). \qquad (13)$$

Since the hazard rate $\lambda_j = 1 - S(t_{j+1})/S(t_j)$ can be treated as a probability, (13) can be considered the log-likelihood of binomial data except that the second summation in the second term sums from $r+1$, rather than 1. Whenever $\log(1-\lambda_{ij})$ in the second term is conditioned away (when $j \leq r$), however, its corresponding part in the first term of (13) is always zero, since by definition only the last of the series of trials may be a success in a discrete-time model. Thus the conditional log-likelihood (13) remains a binomial log-likelihood.

The hazard rate λ_{ij} for observation i at time j may, in turn, be linked to the observation's covariates through one of the four link functions: the logistic, probit, complementary log-log, and log-log functions (McCullagh and Nelder 1989; Kalbfleisch and Prentice

1980, ch. 2). The logistic link function is by far the most popular choice for discrete-time models partly because the software for logistic regressions is widely available. The empirical example in Section 6 will demonstrate how a model based on (13) can be estimated.

5. CONDITIONAL PARTIAL LIKELIHOOD

The methods discussed so far all need parametric assumptions on the functional form of the baseline hazards. The information on which such assumptions are made is often scarce. In standard event-history analysis, Cox's (1972) partial likelihood hazard model has been used extensively to avoid making such assumptions. In this section, we describe an extension of Cox's partial likelihood, so that it can be used for left-truncated event-history data with known start times. See Helsen (1990) for another discussion of this approach.

Consider a situation in which there are J observed events among a total of K survival times and in which events occur at distinct ordered $\tau_1 < \tau_2 < \ldots < \tau_J$. The extension to Cox's partial likelihood is based on the same idea as that behind the conditional likelihood, hence the term conditional partial likelihood. We start from the full conditional likelihood (7). Following Cox's original development, we factorize the full likelihood into two products. Retaining only the product of the likelihood that contains the information on the order, rather than the exact time, of events, and canceling baseline hazards, we obtain the conditional partial likelihood function

$$L_P = \prod_{j \in J} \frac{e^{x_j' \beta}}{\sum\limits_{k: \, t_k \geq \tau_j \, , \, t_r \leq \tau_j} e^{x_k' \beta}}. \tag{14}$$

This differs from the standard partial likelihood in that the summation space in the denominator is restricted by one additional condition, $t_r \leq \tau_j$, where t_r is again the length of time that has elapsed before the observation period. This restriction ensures that all the left-truncated cases are excluded from the risk set at τ_j if they have not entered the observation period at τ_j, even though the total length of the survival time of this left-truncated case is longer than τ_j.

Figure 3 illustrates the conditional partial likelihood. Unlike that in Figure 1, the axis indicates duration time. All event histories are left-aligned. The peculiar feature of the conditional partial likeli-

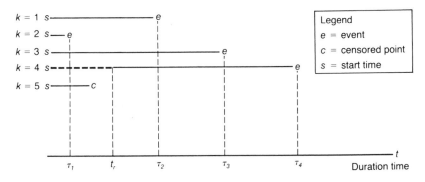

FIGURE 3. The conditional partial likelihood.

hood is illustrated by case $k=4$. Case 4 comes into observation after having spent t_r periods of time. As in (7), the length of t_r is used to determine the position of the observed part of case 4 along t. The important point is that, at τ_1, the risk set is $\Re_1 = \{1, 2, 3, 5\}$ rather than $\Re_1 = \{1, 2, 3, 4, 5\}$. Case 4 has yet to be under observation to be included in the risk set. The conditional partial likelihood can then be treated as an ordinary likelihood exactly as Cox's (1972) partial likelihood is. Helsen (1990) shows that a program for a partial likelihood model such as BMDP2L can be manipulated to estimate a conditional partial likelihood model.

6. AN EMPIRICAL EXAMPLE OF MARITAL DISSOLUTION IN THE U.S.

In this section we provide an empirical example of marital dissolution in the United States, using the PSID data that we have referred to frequently. This example tries to achieve two objectives. First, the example demonstrates how standard statistical packages may be used to estimate a conditional likelihood piece-wise exponential model and a conditional likelihood discrete-time model. A conditional partial likelihood model will also be estimated. Second, the example shows the consequences of ignoring left truncation when the start time is known.

The event of interest is first divorce over the period between 1970 and 1987. We select those women who were aged 65 or younger in 1970, who had married at least once by 1985, and who reported

positive durations married. This sample includes 3701 first marriages. We rely on the 1985 retrospective questions to construct marital histories. Marital duration is calculated from the start of the first
marriage to the date of the first separation. About 28 percent of the
sample are blacks.

We first describe the procedures of estimating a conventional
piece-wise exponential hazard model (model 1b in Tables 1 and 2) via
a Poisson regression. To prepare data for a Poisson regression, we

TABLE 1

Estimates of the Baseline Hazard Rates or Odds Ratios of First Divorce in the
U.S. from a Piece-wise Exponential Model (1a and 1b) and a Discrete-time
Model (2a and 2b).[a]

	A Conditional Likelihood Approach			
	(1a)		(2a)	
	$exp(\beta)$[b]	$|t|$[c]	$exp(\beta)$	$|t|$
Baseline hazards or odds ratios (years)				
0–3	0.0035[d]	88.4	0.0423[f]	48.5
4–8	0.0025	3.6[e]	0.0301	3.6
9–15	0.0016	7.5	0.0190	7.7
16–40	0.0006	16.1	0.0075	16.3
	Standard Models Ignoring Left Truncation			
	(1b)		(2b)	
Baseline hazards or odds ratios (years)				
0–3	0.0019	98.0	0.0235	58.3
4–8	0.0014	3.4	0.0170	3.5
9–15	0.0008	7.7	0.0105	7.9
16–40	0.0004	14.1	0.0052	14.3

[a]Models (1a) and (2a) are based on a conditional likelihood approach. Models
(1b) and (2b) show the consequences of ignoring left truncation. N = 3701.
[b]Relative risks.
[c]Absolute values of t statistics.
[d]Monthly rate of divorce.
[e]The t-statistics for the second through the fourth intervals test whether the baseline hazard rates in these intervals are significantly different from the rate for the first
interval. The same can be said for the discrete-time model.
[f]Yearly odds ratio of divorce.

TABLE 2

Estimates of Cohort and Race Effects on First Divorce Rates in the U.S. from a Piece-wise Exponential Model (1a and 1b), a Discrete-time Model (2a and 2b), and a Partial Likelihood Model (3a and 3b).[a]

	A Conditional Likelihood Approach					
	(1a)		(2a)		(3a)	
	$exp(\beta)$[b]	$|t|$[c]	$exp(\beta)$	$|t|$	$exp(\beta)$	$|t|$
Baseline hazards or odds ratios (years)						
0–3	0.016[d]	22.8	0.187[f]	9.2	na[q]	na
4–8	0.013	2.3[e]	0.149	2.4	na	na
9–15	0.010	4.2	0.113	4.6	na	na
16–40	0.008	4.3	0.088	4.8	na	na
Age in 1970	0.961	7.5	0.960	7.4	0.977	3.8
Black	1.000		1.000		1.000	
White	0.665	5.6	0.663	5.6	0.666	5.6

	Standard Models Ignoring Left Truncation					
	(1b)		(2b)		(3b)	
Baseline hazards or odds ratios (years)						
0–3	0.064	18.3	0.723	2.1	na	na
4–8	0.059	0.8	0.663	1.0	na	na
9–15	0.056	1.2	0.602	1.7	na	na
16–40	0.088	2.4	0.907	1.7	na	na
Age in 1970	0.913	21.9	0.915	21.4	0.913	20.9
Black	1.000		1.000		1.000	
White	0.661	5.7	0.659	5.7	0.660	5.7

[a]Models (1a), (2a), and (3a) are based on a conditional likelihood approach. Models (1b), (2b), and (3b) show the consequences of ignoring left truncation. N = 3701.
[b]Relative risks.
[c]Absolute values of t statistics.
[d]Monthly rate of divorce.
[e]The t-statistics for the second through the fourth intervals test whether the baseline hazard rates in these intervals are significantly different from the rate for the first interval. The same can be said for the discrete-time model.
[f]Yearly odds ratio of divorce.
[g]Not applicable.

break the observed duration time into pieces of exposure according to the specified intervals: 0–3, 4–8, 9–15, and 16–40 years. The resulting pieces of exposure are treated as independent cases of a Poisson regression. For a woman who divorces at the end of the nineteenth year of marriage, we would have four pieces of exposure with lengths of 3, 5, 7, and 4 years. The last piece of four years is the amount of time the woman spends in marriage during the fourth interval of 16 to 40 years. A set of dummy variables needs to be created to index the four pieces of exposure and capture interval effects. Corresponding to each of the four pieces of exposure is a divorce indicator and covariates. Divorce indicators are usually coded as 1 if the woman divorces during the exposure or 0 if the marriage remains intact. Only the last indicator can be 1. For this woman, the divorce indicators are 0, 0, 0, and 1 for the four pieces of exposure, respectively.

In this example, we consider only two variables: age in 1970 and race. Age in 1970 is expected to capture the cohort effect of rising divorce rate over the past 20 years. The values of the covariates such as race and age in 1970 are the same for the four pieces of exposure unless the covariates are time-dependent. A Poisson regression procedure treats the divorce indicator as the dependent variable and pieces of exposure as a fixed intercept to be included as part of the linear predictor. The resulting parameter estimates can be interpreted as those of a piece-wise exponential hazard model. The set of dummy variables gives the baseline hazards.

When a case is left-truncated, only slightly more data work is needed for estimating a piece-wise exponential model using the conditional approach (model 1a in Tables 1 and 2). Suppose that the woman still divorced at the end of the nineteenth year, but did not enter the observation period until the end of the fifth year of marriage. We would then have three pieces of exposure with lengths of 3, 7, and 4 years for intervals 2, 3, and 4, respectively. Discarded is the exposure of three years in the first interval and the first two years of exposure in the second interval. The remaining three pieces of exposure with their corresponding divorce indicators and covariates can then be treated as independent cases. The rest remains the same. Model (1a) in Tables 1 and 2 are estimated using a Poisson regression procedure in SAS (SAS Institute 1990, p. 224).

The data preparation for a standard discrete-time model

(model 2b in Tables 1 and 2) is very similar to that for a piece-wise exponential model. We use year as the unit of discrete time. Each time unit is viewed as an independent Bernoulli trial. A woman who divorces at the end of the nineteenth year of marriage is considered having experienced 19 trials. Corresponding to these 19 trials are 19 trial success indicators, which are defined as 1 if a divorce occurs and 0 otherwise. Only the indicator for the last trial can possibly be one. Accompanying each trial is one or more covariates. Time-varying covariates can be easily incorporated by changing the value of a covariate at each time unit. Dummy variables can be used to capture duration effects. The same specifications of duration effects as those in model (1a) in Tables 1 and 2 amount to assigning the first three trials to group 1, the next five trials to group 2, the next seven trials to group 3, and the last 25 trials to group 4. Alternatively, duration effects can be captured by a linear or quadratic function of time since the beginning of marriage (Allison 1982).

For a left-truncated subject first observed at τ_0 at the end of the fifth year of marriage, the only additional thing that a conditional discrete-time model (model 2a in Tables 1 and 2) requires is to drop the first five trials from the analysis. The results are obtained using the logistic procedures in SAS (SAS Institute 1990, p. 175). The default logit link function is used in this example. SAS (p. 190) and GLIM (Payne 1986) also offer the option of the complementary log-log link function.

Models (3a) and (3b) in Table 2 present estimates from a conditional partial likelihood hazard model. We estimate the model by maximizing the conditional partial likelihood function (14), using a general purpose numerical optimization package (Quant and Goldfeld 1989).

Table 1 compares the baseline risks of marital dissolution esti-mated by the conditional approach with those estimated by standard event-history analysis. Models (1a)—piece-wise exponential—and (2a)—discrete-time—are based on the conditional approach. The risk of divorce is assumed to be constant within each of the four marital durations: 0–3 years, 4–8 years, 9–15 years, and 16–40 years, but the levels of the risk across the four durations are allowed to vary. Marital durations longer than 40 years are censored at the end of the fortieth year. Both models (1a) and (2a) show a monotonically declining risk of divorce over marital duration. In contrast, models

(1b) and (2b) are estimated by standard event-history analysis that makes use of the information on start time but ignores sample selection due to left truncation. As we predicted in Section 1.3, ignoring sample selection has led to an underestimation of the risks of marital dissolution. The risks of divorce estimated by models (1b) and (2b) are much lower than those estimated by models (1a) and (2a).

Table 2 examines the impact of ignoring sample selection on the effects of covariates. According to the conditional approach, shown by models (1a) and (2a), the rate of divorce is negatively correlated with duration, implying that the longer the woman has been married, the less likely she experiences a divorce. Age in 1970 is negatively related to risk of divorce, confirming our expectation that an older cohort tends to experience lower divorce rates. White Americans experienced divorce rates about 34 percent lower than Black Americans from 1970 to 1987. The three sets of results from models (1a), (2a), and (3a) are very similar except that the age effect estimated by the conditional partial likelihood hazard model (3a) is somewhat smaller than those estimated by models (1a) and (2a).

The three standard hazard models (1b, 2b, and 3b) that ignore left truncation also yield very similar results among themselves (Table 2). These results, however, are very different from those estimated by the three conditional hazard models (1a, 2a, and 3a). In contrast to the monotonically declining baseline risks of divorce in models (1a) and (2a), the baseline risks of divorce in the first three intervals (0–3, 4–8, and 9–15) in models (1b) and (2b) are not significantly different from one another and the baseline risk in the last interval (16–40) is the highest of all. Moreover, the age effects estimated in models (1b), (2b), and (3b) are much larger (0.91 vs. 0.96). than those estimated in models (1a), (2a), and (3a). Considering that age is used as a continuous variable, these differences are quite large.

The problems with models (1b), (2b), and (3b) are directly related to sample selection. The sample selection occurs when some high-risk women divorced and dropped out of the sample before 1968. As a result, women with left-truncated marriage histories (those who married before 1968 and whose marriage remained intact beyond 1968) tend to have lower rates of divorce. The problem is that the left-truncated women also tend to be older, resulting in an exaggeration of age effect. Apparently, the age variable in models

(1b), (2b), and (3b) has picked up some of the effect of sample selection.

7. SUMMARY AND CONCLUSIONS

A subject is left-truncated when it comes under observation after having been exposed to the risk of an event for some time; the amount of time may or may not be known. The characteristic problem of left truncation is sample selection. Left truncated subjects tend to have lower risks at shorter durations than do subjects in a normal sample.

When the length of exposure before a left-truncated subject comes under observation is unknown, left truncation is practically intractable except for the special cases in which the hazard rate is constant or all left-truncated subjects are discarded. When the length of exposure or start time is known, left-truncated data can be handled by the conditional likelihood approach. This approach conditions the likelihood function on the subject's having survived to the start of the observation period. We believe that the conditional approach deserves special attention from social scientists not only because it is free from the complications caused by left truncation but also because of the characteristics of social scientists' event-history data. The critical information on the start time of a left-truncated subject can be frequently obtained from human subjects in social surveys even years after the event occurs. The concentration of covariate information in the observation period in a longitudinal social survey is also well-suited for the conditional approach.

An important practical issue is how to estimate a model based on the conditional approach since the software designed for conventional event-history analysis can no longer be used in general. We show that a piece-wise exponential hazard model can still be estimated readily using any software that estimates a Poisson regression, and that a discrete-time model can still be calculated easily via any package designed for binary data.

Additionally, we describe a conditional partial likelihood approach that combines Cox's partial likelihood and the conditional likelihood. The advantage is that no parametric assumption on the functional form of the baseline hazard is needed.

REFERENCES

Allison, Paul D. 1982. "Discrete-Time Methods for the Analysis of Event Histories." In *Sociological Methodology 1982*, edited by S. Leinhardt, 61–98. San Francisco: Jossey-Bass.

———. 1984. *Event History Analysis, Regression for Longitudinal Event Data.* Beverly Hills, Calif.: Sage.

Center for Human Resources Research. 1991. *NLS Handbook 1991.* Columbus: Center for Human Resources Research, Ohio State University.

Cox, David R. 1962. *Renewal Theory.* London: Methuen.

———. 1972. "Regression Models and Life-tables (with Discussion)." *Journal of the Royal Statistical Society B* 34:187–220.

Cox, David R., and D. Oakes. 1984. *Analysis of Survival Data.* New York: Chapman and Hall.

Dechter, Aimée R. 1992. "The Effect of Women's Economic Independence on Marital Dissolution." Paper presented at the 1992 annual meeting of the Population Association of America, Denver.

Deutsches Institut für Wirtschaftsforschung. 1991. *Das Sozio-ökonomische Panel (SOEP): Benutzerhandbuch.* Berlin.

Elandt-Johnson, Regina C., and Norman L. Johnson. 1980. *Survival Models and Data Analysis.* New York: Wiley.

Freedman, Deborah, Arland Thornton, Donald Camburn, Duane Alwin, and Linda Young-DeMarco, 1988. "*The Life History Calendar: A Technique for Collecting Retrospective Data.*" In *Sociological Methodology 1988*, edited by Clifford Clogg, 37–68. Washington, DC: American Sociological Association.

Hald, A. 1952. *Statistical Theory with Engineering Applications.* New York: Wiley.

Hamerle, A. 1991. "On the Treatment of Interrupted Spells and Initial Conditions in Event History Analysis." *Sociological Methods and Research* 19: 388–414.

Heckman, James, and B. Singer. 1986. "Econometric Analysis of Longitudinal Data." In *Handbook of Econometrics,* vol. 3, edited by Z. Griliches and M.D. Intriligator, 1689–1763. Amsterdam: North-Holland.

Helsen, Kristiaan. 1990. "New Developments in Duration Time Modeling with Applications to Marketing." Ph.D. diss., University of Pennsylvania.

Holford, T. R. 1980. "The Analysis of Rates and Survivorship Using Log-linear Models." *Biometrics* 36:299–305.

Kalbfleisch, J. D., and R. L. Prentice. 1980. *The Statistical Analysis of Failure Time Data.* New York: Wiley.

Keiding, Niels. 1986. "Nonparametric Estimation Under Truncation." In *Encyclopedia of Statistical Sciences,* vol. 9, edited by Samuel Kotz and Norman L. Johnson, 357–59. New York: Wiley.

Korenman, Sanders, Guang Guo, and Arline T. Geronimus. 1991. "Relative Wage and Marital Separation." Paper prepared for the PSID Event History Conference, Stanford University, June.

Lancaster, T. 1979. "Econometric Methods for the Duration of Unemployment." *Econometrica* 47:939–56.

Lehrman, William G. 1989. "Organizational Form and Failure in the Life Insurance Industry." Ph.D. diss., Princeton University.

Leiderman, P. H., D. Babu, J. Kagia, H.C. Kraemer, and G.F. Leiderman. 1973. "African Infant Precocity and Some Social Influences during the First Year." *Nature* 242:247–49.

McCullagh, P., and J. A. Nelder. 1989. *Generalized Linear Models.* London: Chapman and Hall.

Miller, Rupert G., Jr. 1981. *Survival Analysis.* New York: Wiley.

Payne, C. D., ed. 1986. *The GLIM System, Release 3.77.* Oxford: Numerical Algorithms Group.

Quant, R. E., and S. M. Goldfeld. 1989. *GQOPT/I.* (Version 5.00). Princeton: Department of Economics, Princeton University.

Ridder, G. 1984. "The Distribution of Single Spell Duration Data." In *Studies in Labor Market Dynamics,* edited by G. R. Neumann and N. C. Westergard-Nielsen, 45–73. New York: Springer.

SAS Institute. 1990. *SAS Technical Report P-200, SAS/STAT Software: CALIS and LOGISTIC Procedures, Release 6.04.* Cary, N.C.

Schoen, Robert. 1975. "Constructing Increment-Decrement Life Tables." *Demography* 12:313–24.

Survey Research Center. 1989. *A Panel Study of Income Dynamics: Procedures and Tape Codes.* Ann Arbor: Institute for Social Research, University of Michigan.

Thompson, W. A., Jr. 1977. "On the Treatment of Grouped Observations in Life Studies." *Biometrics* 33:463–70.

Trussell, James, and Timothy Guinnane. 1991. "Techniques of Event History Analysis." Paper prepared for an IUSSP seminar on Old and New Methods in Historical Demography, Palma de Mallorca, Spain, June.

Tuma, Nancy B., and Michael T. Hannan. 1984. *Social Dynamics, Models and Methods.* New York: Academic Press.

Turnbull, B. W. 1974. "Nonparametric Estimation of a Survivorship Function with Doubly Censored Data." *Journal of the American Statistical Association* 69:169–73.

U.S. Department of Commerce and Bureau of the Census. 1987. *Survey of Income and Program Participation: Users' Guide.* Washington, D.C.

Yamaguchi, Kazuo. 1991. *Event History Analysis.* Newbury Park, Calif.: Sage Publications.

℀ 8 ℀

COMPETING HAZARDS WITH SHARED UNMEASURED RISK FACTORS

*Daniel H. Hill**
William G. Axinn†
Arland Thornton‡

Most competing hazards models are based on the rather strong assumption that alternative destinations are stochastically independent. Individual-specific unmeasured risk factors that are shared by two or more alternatives are, as a result, ruled out. The present paper develops a generalization of the standard discrete-time competing hazards model that allows for the types of stochastic dependencies resulting from shared unmeasured risk factors. An empirical example is provided using the process by which young women form their first conjugal residential union, with married and unmarried cohabitation representing the competing alternatives. The results suggest considerable and significant similarity of the alternatives in terms of the unmeasurables. It is also shown that, as a result, the independence assumption leads to substantially biased estimates of the

*University of Toledo
†University of Chicago
‡University of Michigan
The authors are, respectively, Director of the Survey Research Institute and Associate Professor of Economics at the University of Toledo; Assistant Professor of Sociology at the University of Chicago; and Research Scientist at the Institute for Social Research and Professor of Sociology at the University of Michigan. We would like to thank Professors Kazuo Yamaguchi, Jay Teachman, Steven Marsden and anonymous referees for their many helpful comments on earlier versions of this paper. Any errors are the responsibility of the authors.

245

net marriage and net cohabitation survival functions. While the model does require a temporal independence assumption, Monte Carlo simulations indicate that the biases introduced by violations of this assumption are confined primarily to the estimates for time-varying covariates. Estimates for other covariates and the cross-destination correlation coefficient, itself, are relatively robust.

Event-history analysis using varying forms of hazard rate models has become commonplace in the social sciences (Teachman 1983). Many applications of these methods in a wide range of substantive fields focus on problems that involve competing risks. For example, in analyzing rates of death by cause, dying of one cause removes an individual from the risk of dying by another cause. Likewise, in analyzing rates of premarital cohabitation, marrying removes one from the risk of cohabiting. Unfortunately, most competing hazards models are based on the rather strong assumption that alternative destinations are stochastically independent. Aside from systematic elements controlled by the inclusion of covariates, these alternative states are assumed to be distinct. While the propensity to exit via each state may be affected by unmeasured factors, these factors are assumed to be unique to each state (Petersen 1991, p. 303). As a result, such models ignore the possibility that alternative destination states may be linked by unmeasured factors. These include individual-specific factors like physical frailty in analyses of mortality and morbidity, or the presence of a romantic partner in analyses of cohabitation and marriage.

A number of methods have been developed to deal with shared unmeasured risk factors, but they are all quite computationally intensive and/or require special algorithms that are beyond the scope of many social researchers. Flinn and Heckman (1982), for instance, address the problem by specifying the competing hazards as conditional on unmeasured heterogeneity and then "integrate it out" as a nuisance parameter (see also Lancaster 1990, pp. 59–62). A similar approach is exemplified in the recent work in biometrics that addresses the problem by assuming each hazard is affected by a common underlying frailty factor and employs EM estimation methods. Finally, in an approach more in the spirit of our own, Hann and Hausman (1988) deal with shared unmeasured risk factors by formulating the two-alternative case as a bivariate ordered probit model in which the correlation coefficient captures their net effects. This approach, while quite feasible for the two-alternative case, is not yet practical for problems involving more alternatives.[1]

In this paper we present a relatively simple method of testing the independence assumption and correcting for correlations if they exist. We apply a well-known maximum-likelihood technique, nested multinomial-logit (McFadden 1981; Amemiya 1985), to the discrete-time formulation of the competing hazards model. The technique is attractive, in part, because it can be implemented with even the most rudimentary of maximum likelihood software.[2] This procedure provides a measure of the shared unmeasured risk factors (SURF). In this respect, our paper is as much about error-correlated latent-variable formulations of models for discrete dependent variables as it is about survival analysis. There are many other potential applications of such models in the social sciences (e.g., see Duncan and Hoffman 1990).

After developing our model, we provide an empirical example of the technique by analyzing cohabitation and marriage in the competing risks format. The results demonstrate that correcting for SURF can dramatically alter estimates of the net survival functions. While the results of this empirical example are dependent on model specification, we also provide, in an appendix, examples from Monte Carlo experiments in order to gauge the accuracy of the new estimating procedure. These results indicate that taking SURF into account provides more accurate estimates than ignoring such factors. The implication of this finding is that competing hazards models that ignore SURF may provide inaccurate estimates of base hazard rates or parameters.

While we are forced to assume temporal independence of the unmeasured risk factors, Monte Carlo experiments suggest that the primary effects of violations of this assumption are to bias the parame-

[1]Some recent advances in numerical methods such as Gibbs sampling and Monte Carlo integration (see McFadden 1989), as well as advances in computer speed and capacity, may make this technique practical for larger problems in the future.
[2]See Appendix A. Implementation of the procedure is, of course, facilitated by more sophisticated software such as LIMDEP's nested multinomial logit procedure, but it can be accomplished with OSIRIS's DREG program.

ters relating to time varying covariates and to increase the variance of the other parameters. The estimated effects for time-invariant covariates, as well as the estimated level of cross-destination stochastic correlation, are relatively unaffected by temporal stochastic dependence.

1. DISCRETE-TIME COMPETING HAZARDS MODELS

Following Allison (1982), we consider the situation in which there are 'm' possible alternative ways of exiting the base state. Including the base state, there are $m + 1$ alternative states and they are indexed by $j = 0, . . , m$. We can define J as a random variable indicating the particular state in time T. The discrete time hazard rate for exiting the base state by means j at time t can be defined as:

$$P_{tj} = Pr(T=t, J=j | T \geq t) \qquad j>0. \qquad (1)$$

Equation (1) states that the hazard of exiting via means J at time T is the probability of doing so given survival up to at least time T. Defining δ_{ji} as a dummy variable equaling 1 if individual i exits via means j (and 0 otherwise), the likelihood function for a sample of n individuals can be expressed as:

$$\mathbf{L} = \prod_{i=1}^{n} \prod_{j=1}^{m} [P_{t_i j_i}/(1 - P_t)]^{\delta_{ji}} \prod_{k=1}^{t_i} (1 - P_k), \qquad (2)$$

where $P_t = \Sigma_{j>0} P_{tj} = 1 - P_{t0}$ is the hazard of exiting the base state by any means. The model is completed by specifying the form of P_{tj} and, assuming the m alternatives are uncorrelated, Allison suggested the multinomial logit model:

$$P_{tj} = exp(\beta_j' X_{jt})/(1 + \sum_{q=1}^{m} exp(\beta_q' X_{qt})), \qquad (3)$$

where X_{qt} is a vector of explanatory variables (including a column of ones for the constant term), which may or may not vary with time.

Full information maximum likelihood estimates can be obtained by substituting equation (3) into equation (2) and maximizing the result with respect to the β's.

2. INDEPENDENCE OF IRRELEVANT ALTERNATIVES

The independence assumption of the multinomial logit specification is actually a rather strong one and deserves more detailed attention. First, for each individual i let us define a "state propensity index" for each time period and for each state, including the base state, according to:

$$
\begin{aligned}
S_{t0i} &= \beta_0^{*\prime} X_{t0i} + \epsilon_{t0i} \\
S_{t1i} &= \beta_1^{*\prime} X_{t1i} + \epsilon_{t1i} \\
&\vdots \qquad \vdots \qquad \vdots \\
S_{tmi} &= \beta_m^{*\prime} X_{tmi} + \epsilon_{tmi,}
\end{aligned}
\tag{4}
$$

in which the state propensity index (S_{tj}) is composed of a systematic portion $(\beta_j^{*\prime} X_{tji})$ and a random portion (ϵ_{tji})—the latter representing the net effect of all unmeasured risk factors. Note that equation (4) is a latent variable formulation of the discrete dependent variable problem of explaining the destination state. The individual is assumed to choose the state with the highest propensity—i.e., we observe state j for individual i in period t if and only if $S_{tji} > S_{tki}$ for all k not equal to j.

For discrete-time hazards models, we can imagine a dynamic in which the ϵ_{tji} are determined by $m + 1$ independent draws from some probability distribution in each time period. The base state propensity index (S_{t0i}) is assumed to start out higher than any of the alternative indices, and the individual as a result stays in the base state until one or more of the alternative indices exceeds it—something that could occur either by luck of the draw or as a consequence of changes in covariates (X_{tji}) or both.[3]

The multinomial logit model of equation (3) is a particular form of the latent variable formulation that results when the $m + 1$ random errors (ϵ_{tji}) are the result of *independent* draws from the extreme value or log-Weibull distribution. This independence assumption is known in the literature as the Independence of Irrelevant Alternatives (IIA) assumption because the ratio of the probabilities of any two alterna-

---

[3]If only individual-varying X's are present, then $\beta_m X_{tmi}$ reduces to $\beta_m X_{ti}$. If only state-varying X's are present, then $\beta_m X_{tmi}$ reduces to βX_{tmi}, where X_{tmi} depends on characteristics of the state "m." If both individual- and state-varying characteristics are present, then we can decompose $\beta_m X_{tmi}$ into $\beta Z_{tmi} + \beta_m Y_{ti}$, where Z_{tmi} are the state-varying and Y_{ti} are the individual-varying characteristics.

tives is independent of all other state propensities.[4] To see this, first
note that as a general matter, the probability of staying in the base
state in period t, given survival up to $t-1$, is:

$$P_{t0i|t_i \geq t-1} = Pr(S_{t0i} > S_{tji} \mid t_i \geq t-1) \; \forall j \neq 0. \tag{5}$$

Under the assumption that the ϵ_{tj} are independent log Weibull, this
can be shown to reduce to:[5]

$$P_{t0i|t_i \geq t-1} = \exp(S_{t0i}) - \epsilon_{t0i}) \sum_{j=0}^{m} \exp(S_{tji} - \epsilon_{toi})$$

$$= \exp(\beta_0^{*'} X_{t0i}) \Big/ \sum_{j=0}^{m} \exp(\beta_j^{*'} X_{tji}) \tag{6}$$

$$= 1 \Big/ \left[1 + \sum_{j=1}^{m} \exp\!\left(\beta_j' X_{tji} \right) \right],$$

where the final equality is obtained from the second by dividing the
numerator and denominator by $\exp(\beta_0' X_{t0i})$ and defining $\beta_j =
\beta_j^* - \beta_0^*$.[6] The probability of exiting in period t to alternative state j,
given survival to period $t-1$ (and the distributional assumptions)
can be shown, analogously, to be equation (3) from the preceding
section.

The ratio of the hazard of exiting via j and the hazard of
remaining in the base state is simply:

$$P_{tji}/P_{t0i} = \exp\,(\beta_j' X_{tji}), \tag{7}$$

which is unaffected by any of the other state propensities.

To see why this might not be plausible, it is useful to consider a
substantive example. Suppose we are interested in the process by
which young adults form conjugal residential relationships. The base
state is "single" and the alternatives are married or unmarried cohabi-

---

[4] The IIA restriction is not so much a result of the multinomial logit specification in equation (3) as it is of the assumption implicit in equation (4)–that the
state propensities for the various states are independent. If S_{tji} were a function of
the other state propensities, as in McFadden's "Universal Logit" model, then the
IIA restriction would not hold (see McFadden 1983, pp. 1414–15).

[5] See Amemiya 1985, pp. 296–97.

[6] This transformation converts our model into the familiar form in which
the base state is the "contrast."

tation. The independence of irrelevant alternatives assumption requires that the hazard of unmarried cohabitation relative to remaining single is uncorrelated with the corresponding relative marriage hazard. This means that if something, not reflected in the X's, happened to make marriage infeasible (e.g., a million dollar marriage tax), those who would otherwise have married during the period would now distribute themselves between cohabitating and remaining single in the same proportions as those who originally chose not to marry. However, to the extent that married and unmarried cohabitation are similar in unmeasured respects, it would be more reasonable to expect proportionately more of those precluded from marriage to choose cohabitation.[7]

3. A SHARED UNMEASURED RISK FACTOR (SURF) MODEL

The problem with the IIA assumption noted above is that there may be unobserved factors common to competing alternatives, which act as correlating influences in the ϵ_{tji}. For concreteness, let us continue with the marriage/cohabitation example and assume that the ϵ can be expressed as:

$$\epsilon_{tsi} = \mu_{tsi}$$
$$\epsilon_{tci} = \nu_{ti} + \mu_{tci} \qquad (8)$$
$$\epsilon_{tmi} = \nu_{ti} + \nu_{tmi},$$

where the subscripts s, c, and m correspond to the single, cohabitating and married states, respectively, the ν_{ti} represent the unmeasured factors common to cohabitation and marriage, and the μ_{tji} are independent (both of the ν and across alternatives) log-Weibull disturbances. The correlation of the ϵ_{tci} and ϵ_{tmi} can be shown to be:

---

[7]A second example may be helpful. Suppose people died of one of two causes—heart failure or pneumonia. Under the IIA assumption, the probability of dying of heart failure in period t relative to surviving would be unaffected by the introduction of a totally effective pneumonia vaccine. If, however, both causes of death are manifestations of the same underlying condition (e.g., congestive heart disease), then the hazard of dying of heart failure would increase upon introduction of the vaccine since relatively more of those saved from pneumonia would now die of heart failure than would survive the period.

$$I_{\epsilon_{tci}\epsilon_{tmi}} = \sum_{i=1}^{n} \nu^2_{ti}/\sigma_{\epsilon_{tc}}\sigma_{\epsilon_{tm}} \qquad (9)$$

An alternative to multinomial logit, which does explicitly allow such correlations, is McFadden's (1981) nested logit model.[8] The nested model assumes that all the alternatives (including the base state) can be grouped into stochastically independent sets, the individual members of which may be correlated. In our example, remaining single during a period may comprise one set, and marriage and cohabitation the other. These two sets are assumed to be independent but the alternatives in the second set are assumed to follow the bivariate distribution:

$$F(\epsilon_{tm},\epsilon_{tc}) = \exp\left(-[\exp(-\epsilon_{tm}/\rho_t)+\exp(-\epsilon_{tc}/\rho_t)]^{\rho_t}\right) \qquad (10)$$

for ρ_t, known as the index of dissimilarity,[9] confined to the half-open interval $(0,1]$. This distribution is known as Gumbel's Type B bivariate extreme-value distribution. The correlation of the ϵ's can be shown to be, at least approximately:[10]

$$r_{\epsilon_{tci}\epsilon_{tmi}} = 1-\rho_t^2. \qquad (11)$$

Within this framework, the hazard of marrying, given that the individual either married or cohabited during the period, can be expressed as:

$$Pr(J=m_t|J=m_t\cup c_t,T=t) = \frac{\exp(\beta'_m X_{tmi}/\rho_t)}{\exp(\beta'_c X_{tci}/\rho_t) + \exp(\beta'_m X_{tmi}/\rho_t)}. \qquad (12)$$

The hazard of exiting at time t via either married or unmarried cohabitation is:

[8]As noted in the introduction, another alternative would be to formulate the model as a multivariate temporally ordered probit. With m exit alternatives, this would involve m-dimensional integration of the multivariate normal density function–something which, at present, is very intensive computationally for $m > 2$. For an application of the bivariate ordered probit approach to correlated latent variables, see Hill 1990.

[9]Not to be confused with the index of dissimilarity used in segregation research. Our exposition of the nested logit model closely follows that of Amemiya (1985). Other excellent expositions of the model are those of Ben-Akiva and Lerman (1985), and Maddala (1983).

[10]See Johnson and Kotz 1972, pp. 254–56. There appears to be some confusion in the literature about whether this is an exact or an approximate result (e.g., see Maddala 1983, p. 71).

$$Pr(m_t \cup C_t | T \geq t) = \frac{[\exp(\beta'_c X_{tci}/\rho_t) + \exp(\beta'_m X_{tmi}/\rho_t)]^{\rho_t}}{1 + [\exp(\beta'_c X_{tci}/\rho_t) + \exp(\beta'_m X_{tmi}/\rho_t)]^{\rho_t}}$$

$$= \frac{\exp(\rho_t \ln(I_{ti}))}{1 + \exp(\rho_t \ln(I_{ti}))} \qquad (13)$$

$$= \frac{I_{ti}^{\rho_t}}{1 + I_{ti}^{\rho_t}},$$

where $I^{\rho} = [\exp(\beta_c' X_{tci}/\rho_t) + \exp(\beta_m' X_{tmi}/\rho_t)]^{\rho_t}$ can be defined as the "inclusive" exit propensity which is, as Amemiya (1985) puts it, "a kind of weighted average" of the individual exit propensities.[11] It represents the combined exit propensity when the individual propensities are stochastically dependent. While it might appear a strange type of weighted average, it is actually one with which we are all familiar. If we define $a = \exp(\beta_c' X_{tci})$ and $b = \exp(\beta_m' X_{tmi})$, then at $\rho_t = 0.5$:

$$I^{\rho_t} = \sqrt{a^2 + b^2}, \qquad (14)$$

which is simply the Pythagorean formula for the length of the hypotenuse of a right triangle with sides of length a and b. If ϵ_m and ϵ_c are uncorrelated, then ρ will equal 1 and I^ρ will be $a + b$—the ordinary combined hazard of the competing proportional hazards model. In general, ρ will be less than 1 and I^ρ will be less than $a + b$—which is the natural consequence of alternative exit states being similar in some unmeasured respects. In other words, with correlated unmeasured risk factors the sum of the parts is greater than the whole.

Full information maximum likelihood estimates of the β's and ρ can be obtained by first substituting equation (13) for P_t in equation (2), and the product of equations (13) and (12) (and its counterpart for unmarried cohabitation) for P_{tj}. The resulting likelihood function then becomes:

$$L = \prod_{i=1}^{n} \left[\prod_{j=1}^{m} \left[\frac{\exp(\beta_j' X_{tji}/\rho_t)}{I_{ti}} I_{ti}^{\rho_t} \right] \delta_{ji} \prod_{k=1}^{t_i} \frac{1}{1 + I_{ti}^{\rho_t}} \right], \qquad (15)$$

the natural log of which can be maximized with respect to β and ρ_t.

It is important to note that the IIA restriction that the ratio of

[11]Most econometric developments of discrete choice models define the inclusive value as the natural logarithm of our I.

the hazard of exiting via j to the hazard of remaining in the base state is now:

$$P_{tji} / P_{t0i} = \exp\left(\beta'_j X_{tji}\right) I^{\rho_t^{-1}}, \qquad (16)$$

which, so long as $\rho_t < 1$, is affected by all those factors affecting any of the alternatives in I.

This result is important enough to deserve some elaboration. Suppose we begin with IIA and in an "even money" situation in which an individual is equally likely to stay in the base state, to exit to the cohabiting state, or to exit to the married state (i.e., $P_{t0i} = P_{tci} = P_{tmi} = \frac{1}{3}$). Under IIA, this could occur if and only if $\beta_c X_{tci} = \beta_m X_{tmi} = 0$. Since, in this case $\rho_t = 1$, equation (16) implies that $P_{tci}/P_{t0i} = 1$. Now suppose a very stiff marriage tax were imposed and included as a predictor. This would drive $\beta_m X_{tmi}$ strongly negative—say to -4. Under IIA, ρ_t would still equal 1 and so would P_{tci}/P_{t0i}, the reason being that those people driven away from marriage by the tax will split evenly between remaining single and cohabitating.

Now suppose that cohabitation and marriage have many common unmeasured characteristics and as a result $\rho_t = 0.5$. Beginning with $\beta_c X_{tci} = \beta_m X_{tmi} = 0$, equation (16) states that $P_{tci}/P_{t0i} = 1*[1+1]^{-0.5} = 0.707$. After the marriage tax is imposed, however, this increases to $0.991 = 1*[1+\exp(-4)]^{-0.5} = 1.018^{-0.5}$. Since cohabitation provides many of the same unmeasured benefits as marriage, more of the people driven from marriage by the tax will cohabit than remain single.

3.1. Many Competing Hazards

When there are more than two competing hazards, the estimation problem becomes somewhat more complex, but the same general principles apply.[12] Returning to the notation of Section 1 where there were m possible methods of exiting the base state, the first step is to partition these m into S mutually exclusive, exhaustive, and indepen-

---

[12]For a more complete exposition of the model see Amemiya (1985), upon which we draw heavily here. The only substantive differences in our specification and his is that (1) we make the systematic portion of the exit propensities (and their dependence on time) explicit; (2) our exit probabilities are conditional on survival up to the period in question; and (3) our model is normalized by setting propensity to remain single to zero (hence the 1 in the denominator of equation (18)).

dent subsets $(G_1, \ldots, G_s)$, the individual members of which (i.e., $j \in G_s$) may be subject to correlated unmeasured risk factors. Since the number of possible partitions increases factorially with m, as a practical matter we must rely on theory to suggest which partitions are substantively reasonable. Once the partition is identified, the individual probabilities of exiting via means j, given exit to a member of j's group ($j \in G_s$) can be estimated using:

$$Pr(y{=}j, T{=}t | j \epsilon G_s) = \frac{\exp(\beta_j' X_{jt}/\rho_s)}{\sum\limits_{k \in G_s} \exp(\beta_k' X_{kt}/\rho_s)}, \tag{17}$$

where the individual subscripts (i) have been suppressed for clarity, and ρ_s is the index of dissimilarity for the competing hazards in group s. The probability that choice j will be in group s is then obtained via:

$$\sum_{j \in G_s} P_j = \frac{\alpha_s \left[\sum\limits_{k \in G_s} \exp\left(\beta_j' X_{jt}/\rho_s\right) \right]^{\rho_s}}{1 + \sum\limits_{\tau=1}^{S} \alpha_\tau \left[\sum\limits_{k \in G_\tau} \exp(\beta'_j X_{jt}/\rho_\tau) \right]^{\rho_\tau}}, \tag{18}$$

where the α_θ are group specific shift parameters.

The product of equations (17) and (18) can then be substituted for P_j in equation (3) and the likelihood function formed via equation (2).

3.2. Prior Knowledge and Identification

Use of the SURF model does require considerable prior knowledge on the part of the researcher. First, researchers must know a priori which alternatives "belong" together—i.e., they must know the appropriate nesting. When the number of competing alternatives is small, it is possible to estimate the model with alternative nestings and see which nesting conforms best to the data. The number of possible unique nestings, however, increases so quickly with the number of alternatives that such an empirical strategy is often impractical with more than about three competing alternatives. Thus prior knowledge must be drawn upon.

Identification of the competing hazards SURF model also requires prior knowledge. As with all competing hazards models, the existence of covariates allows us to relate the set of empirical survival functions to a single theoretical survival function (see Heckman and

Honore 1989; and Elbers and Ridder 1982). This aspect of identification requires us to know which covariates belong in the systematic
portions of equation (4).

Prior knowledge and theory must also be drawn upon with the
SURF model for practical reasons. Specifically, while ρ may be theoretically identified in equation (15), as a practical matter it can sometimes be difficult to estimate precisely. To see why, note that the first
bracketed term in equation (15) is:

$$\frac{\exp(\beta_j' X_{tji}/\rho)}{I_{ti}} I_{ti}^\rho = \exp\left[\beta_j' X_{tji} + (\rho-1)\ln(I_{ti})\right]. \quad (19)$$

A change in a particular variable x_{jk} will affect the right-hand side
both directly via $\beta_j X$ and indirectly via $(\rho-1)\ln(I_{ti})$, since I_{ti} is a function of the X's. The form of the latter is sufficiently different from
the former to theoretically identify β and ρ. But, when ρ is allowed to
depart from 1 (its value under the independence assumption), x_k and
$\ln(I)$ will be so highly collinear as to allow only the most imprecise
estimates of β and ρ. Again, what is needed in this case is the imposition of some further restrictions on the exit propensities. Depending
on the type of data employed, the most reasonable restrictions take
the form of excluding some x from all but one of the exit propensities, or constraining the coefficients for other x's to be the same for
all competing hazards.

In many applications, the competing hazards transition process can be thought of as a sequential one in which one set of covariates affects the propensity to leave the base state, while another set
affects the relative propensities of exiting to specific alternatives.
Prior knowledge of which covariates belong in which set is sufficient
to identify the model because it implies a set of variable exclusions. It
is this type of knowledge which we draw upon in our empirical example below to identify the model.

3.3. Independence Across Time

While the SURF model allows correlations of unmeasured risk factors across choices and is quite flexible with respect to the treatment
of time-varying covariates, it must be noted that, like the original
discrete-time competing risks model (Allison 1982), it still assumes

independence of the ϵ_{tji} across time. If correlations of the stochastic elements are due to unmeasured risk factors, then it seems only reasonable that they would be correlated across time as well. Indeed, most treatments of unmeasured heterogeneity are concerned primarily with these temporal correlations and their relation to state-dependence.

Modeling competing hazards with both temporal and destination correlations is sufficiently difficult that we will not attempt it here. Since we are concerned with the potential effects of violations of the temporal independence assumption on our estimates, however, we investigate the issue numerically using Monte Carlo methods in Appendix B.

4. AN EMPIRICAL EXAMPLE

4.1. *Data and Assumed Dynamic Process*

To illustrate the shared unmeasured risk factors competing hazards model, we will analyze the dynamics of the first conjugal residential relationship (marriage versus unmarried cohabitation) behavior of young women, using data from an intergenerational panel study of mothers and children. These data follow a cohort of white children born in 1961 in the Detroit metropolitan area and their mothers for 23.5 years (through 1985). They include a life-history calendar measuring monthly timing of nonmarital cohabitation and marriage from age 15 to age 23.5 (Freedman et al. 1988). To reduce the computational burden, we define the time unit as the three-month season and examine the experiences of the young people born in 1961 from their sixteenth birthday until the date of the 1985 interview (at roughly age 23.5).[13] Note that our main purpose is to provide an empirical example of the SURF competing-hazards technique, *not* to provide a definitive theoretical or empirical examination of cohabitation and marriage.

We assume that the dynamic process is one in which the timing of formation of conjugal residential relationships is affected by one

---

[13]For a descriptive analysis of the rates of cohabiting and marrying in this cohort, see Thornton (1988).

set of characteristics and the type of conjugal relationship chosen by another. Specifically, following Thornton (1991), we argue that mothers' premarital pregnancy and marital timing influence the rate of the formation of conjugal relationships. This is consistent with the hypothesis that intergenerational effects are transmitted via sexual maturation.[14] On the other hand, we expect the type of relationship to be a function of the child's religion and religiosity (Thornton, Axinn, and Hill 1992) and the divorce or widowhood experiences of her mother (Thornton 1991).[15]

Furthermore, we assume that the occurrence of any one event removes the individual from risk of the other event.[16] In this respect, our model is similar to what Yamaguchi (1991) terms an "Ideal Type 2 Model." The difference is that here we relax the assumption of *independent* censoring by allowing for stochastic interdependence in the competing risks.

4.1.1. Results Under Constant SURF

We begin our empirical analysis by assuming the level of correlation of unmeasured risk factors is the same in each period t. While this is a rather restrictive assumption, the resulting model has a number of things to recommend it—for one thing, it can be estimated in a two-step fashion using packaged logit algorithms (see Appendix A). For another, it provides more stable estimates of the effect of time-varying covariates that are components of the SURF (discussed in Section 5.1.2 below).

Table 1 presents the estimates for the resulting married/ unmarried cohabitation competing hazards model obtained with and

[14]Note that intergenerational effects on sexual maturation may be the result of family context rather than biological factors (Kahn and Anderson 1992).

[15]Note that a more realistic model might include more covariates and covariates that affect both the timing of union formation *and* the type of union chosen. Also note that our model does not assume sequential decision making, but only that different factors affect the timing of exits and choice of exit modes. Similarly, the multinomial procedures on which our technique is based do not imply a sequence of decision making but only the range of alternatives available (Train 1986, p. 72).

[16]This formulation may seem somewhat strained in the sense that cohabitation does not preclude marriage or vice versa. Our interest here is in the nature of the *initial* conjugal relationship—of which there can be but one.

COMPETING HAZARDS WITH SURF   259

TABLE 1
Married and Unmarried Cohabitation: SURF Hazards Model[a]

	IIA	ML SURF
ρ	{1.0}	0.44*
		(0.18)
Leave single		
Union constant	−6.22**	−5.74**
	(0.60)[b]	(0.63)
Mother's age at marriage	−0.48*	−0.55*
	(0.24)	(0.15)
Mother pregnant at marriage	0.26	0.27
	(0.17)	(0.17)
Time	0.11**	0.11**
	(0.01)	(0.01)
Spring[c]	1.15**	1.15**
	(0.22)	(0.22)
Summer[c]	1.04**	1.03**
	(0.22)	(0.22)
Fall[c]	−0.17	−0.17
	(0.28)	(0.28)
Choose cohabit or marry		
Constant	−5.15**	−5.09**
	(0.63)	(0.61)
Church attendance	−0.40**	−0.24**
	(0.09)	(0.09)
Whether Catholic	−0.33	−0.09
	(0.22)	(0.13)
Mother divorced or widowed	0.78**	0.53**
	(0.23)	(0.20)
Sample size	381	381
ln(L)	−1021.62	−1019.31

*p < 0.05 **p < 0.01

[a]Sample represents 381 females from the 1961 birth cohort.
[b]Standard errors in parentheses.
[c]Omitted category for these comparisons is winter.

without the IIA assumption.[17] The first column contains the estimates obtained under the independence (IIA) assumption. The estimates indicate that children of women who marry young will themselves tend to form conjugal relationships at a younger age (significant negative effect of mothers' age at marriage). Furthermore, the hazard rate of conjugal relationships increases with age throughout the observation period (as indicated by the positive and significant coefficient on the "Time" variable). Finally, the formation of relationships appears to be a warm weather phenomenon in as much as the hazard rate is significantly higher for the spring and summer months than for either fall or winter (the omitted season).

With respect to type of conjugal residential relationship chosen, the estimates from Table 1 indicate that religiosity, as measured by frequency of church attendance, has a strongly negative effect on the hazard of unmarried cohabitation. The mother's divorce and widowhood experiences also have a strong impact, with the hazard of unmarried cohabitation being significantly higher for those children whose mothers suffered a marital disruption. All of these results are consistent with findings from previous studies (Thornton 1991; Thornton, Axinn, and Hill 1992).

The second column of estimates in Table 1 are those obtained when the independence assumption is dropped and the logarithm of equation (15) is maximized in a single step. The χ^2 of the model is slightly but significantly better under the SURF specification.[18] The point estimate of 0.44 for ρ, which is significantly different from both zero and one (the value under IIA), suggests that the correlation of ϵ_c

---

[17]The models were estimated using Pascal programs written by Hill. The David-Fletcher-Reeves version of the Davidson-Fletcher-Powell algorithm contained in Press, et al. (1986) was used for optimization with modifications to eliminate excessive line searches incorporating the stopping rules of Berndt, et al. (1974). Standard errors are obtained from the diagonal elements of the inverse of the matrix of outer products of first derivatives. While this method is computationally efficient, it is also possible to estimate the models using standard packaged programs such as LIMDEP or SAS (see Appendix A for details).

[18]Some authors have argued that cohabitation may be more like remaining single than it is like marriage (Davis 1985; Rindfuss and VandenHeuval 1990). The consequences of marriage and cohabitation may be quite different in relation to factors like home ownership and fertility. However, that is not necessarily inconsistent with our finding that the timing of entrances into a first marriage or first cohabitation in early adulthood is quite similar with respect to unmeasured variables.

and ϵ_m is about 0.81 ($= 1 - (0.44)^2$). Additionally, the size of the effects of religiosity and mother's marital experiences on the hazard of unmarried cohabitation decreases. This suggests that at least part of the apparent effect of religiosity and mother's marital experiences on child's cohabitation hazards is due to correlated unmeasured attributes of married and unmarried cohabitation. Relaxing the independence assumption has the effect of purging β of this spurious effect.[19]

Aside from these differences, the parameter estimates from the independent and correlated competing hazard's models are remarkably similar. Indeed, as we will see in the following section, the parameter estimates obtained with and without the IIA assumption are deceptively similar, but their predictive implications are actually quite different. Before exploring these differences, however, we need to see to what extent our results are sensitive to the time-constant SURF assumption.

4.1.2. Results Under Time-Varying SURF–A Digression
In order to examine the effects of the time-constant SURF assumption, we must make ρ a function of the time-varying covariates. Although the specification we employ is completely arbitrary and is not directly derivable from equation (8), it is sufficiently general as to provide some indication of the potential of the SURF model in estimating time-varying correlations. The specific functional form we examine is

$$\rho_t = \rho_0 + \rho_{t'} + \rho_q Q_t , \tag{20}$$

where ρ_0 is the intercept, $\rho_{t'}$ is the time slope, and ρ_q is a vector of seasonal parameters relating the seasonal or "quarter" dummy variables (Q) to the level of the correlation of the unmeasured risk factors.

Before presenting the empirical results, a few words of caution regarding the time-varying SURF model are in order. First, it may or may not be estimable. Identification depends on the functional relationship chosen for ρ and the time-varying covariates included in it and in the basic model. Second, even if identified, estimation may be quite computationally intesive. In our case, estimation took approxi-

---

[19]Note that different model specifications result both in different estimates of ρ and in different parameter estimates.

mately 90 minutes on a 40486-33–based machine for the models presented in Tables 1 and 2 combined. Finally, Monte Carlo simulations, similar to those presented in Appendix B, indicate that when the same predictors are included in both the systematic and stochastic portions of the state propensities, the estimates (especially for the time-varying components of ρ) tend to become unstable.

Table 2 presents the results obtained for the time-varying covariates when the SURF model is estimated with this specification of ρ (the estimated parameters for the time-invariant factors have been suppressed but are very similar to those in the second column of Table 1). The first column reproduces the parameter estimates of the second column of Table 1 for the time-varying covariates along with the log-

TABLE 2

Married and Unmarried Cohabitation Competing Hazards Model: Time-Varying Correlation of Unmeasured Risk Factors[a]

Effect on Hazard of	Correlation Constant	Correlation Dependent on All Time Covariates
Time	0.11**	0.11**
	(11.00)[b]	(7.58)
Spring	1.15**	1.19**
	(5.23)	(5.10)
Summer	1.04**	0.30
	(4.73)	(0.33)
Fall	−0.17	−0.32
	(0.61)	(−0.84)
Effect on Correlation of		
Time		−0.00
		(−0.22)
Spring		−0.07
		{0.19}
Summer		1.14+
		{3.26}
Fall		0.25
		{0.56}
Log Likelihood	−1019.31	−1014.433

+ p < 0.10 * p < 0.05 **p < 0.01

[a]Estimates taken from models including the time-constant covariates in Table 1.
[b]t-ratios in parentheses; likelihood ratio X^2 in braces.

likelihood value. The second column presents the parameter estimates for the more general model. Comparison of the log-likelihood
values with and without the additional parameters indicates that as a
set the four new parameters are significant with a likelihood-ratio X^2
of 9.75. This implies that the SURF correlations do vary systematically with the time-varying components of our model.

4.2. Predictive Differences Between Shared and Independent Unmeasured Risk Factors Models

As noted above, the similarity of the estimates obtained with and
without the IIA assumption is somewhat deceptive. While it is true
that both sets of estimates will do just about as well in describing the
crude hazard or survival probabilities for average individuals, there
are major differences in their implications for predicted survival
probabilities when exogenous factors are assumed to change, or
when we examine sample members with less typical characteristics.

Estimation of the net survival probability of one hazard is,
perhaps, the most common example of a "predictive" use of the
estimates in event-history analysis. The net survival probability of
one hazard (e.g., marriage) is the probability of surviving *if the competing hazard* (e.g., unmarried cohabitation) *were eliminated.* While
this may seem an extreme application of the estimated parameters,[20]
calculating net survival probabilities is standard practice in event-
history analysis, and analysts need to be aware of the effects of the
IIA assumption on them. The crude predicted marriage survival
probabilities for individual i can be obtained via the recursion:[21]

$$S_{m,t_i} = S_{m,t_i-1} [1 - Pr(m_{ti})], \qquad (21)$$

[20]Indeed, net survival probabilities implicitly involve extrapolations well
beyond the bounds of the sample and, depending on the nature of the problem,
one can question whether the structure of the problem remains meaningful in
such terra incognita. Predictive differences between the IIA and SURF estimates also appear, however, for more modest departures of the X's from the
sample averages.

[21]The crude marriage survival probability can also be thought of as a
single decrement survival probability, where single is the base state and marriage
is the exit state of interest. Cohabitation is treated as a competing risk, with
those who cohabit being censored at the time of cohabitation. The crude marriage and cohabitation survival probability can be thought of as a double decrement survival probability, again with single as the base state but with individuals
exiting the single state to either marriage or cohabitation.

264   HILL, AXINN, AND THORNTON

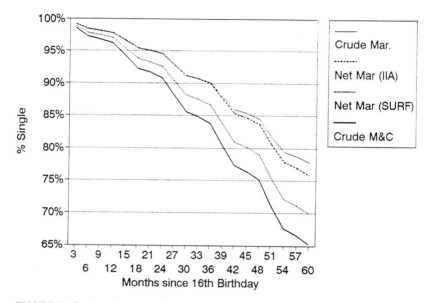

FIGURE 1. Crude and net marriage survival for IIA and SURF models.

where $S_{m,0} = 1$ and $Pr(m_t)$ is obtained by multiplying the product of
equations (12) and (13) by the probability of surviving both marriage
and cohabitation up to period t. The parameter estimates from Table
1 for the IIA and ML SURF models can be used for the β's in the
equations. The net survival probabilities can be obtained in the same
manner by replacing $\beta_c X_{ti}$ in equations (12) and (13) with a large
negative number—effectively eliminating cohabitation as a choice.

Figure 1 presents these estimated marriage survival probabilities with and without the IIA assumption. The top line in the figure
represents the crude marriage survival curve for a hypothetical
young woman with average characteristics, and the bottom line the
crude total union formation survival curve.[22] These two curves are
not visually affected by whether or not one uses the IIA or correlated
estimates. The general concavity (from below) of these survival
curves is a reflection of the fact that the hazard rate is increasing
throughout the sample period, and the sawtooth nature of the profile
is a reflection of the seasonality of relationship formation.

[22]Because of the nonlinearity of the logit model, this is not the same as
the average survival probability. To obtain this, we would need to do a full
sample enumeration in which the survival probabilities are estimated for each
individual separately and the results averaged.

The middle two survival curves in Figure 1 represent the predicted marriage survival probabilities, assuming that cohabitation were eliminated as an option (i.e., the net marriage survival). The curves differ because the two models differ in how potential cohabitors are apportioned between single and married states. The upper curve is that obtained under the IIA assumption. It clings closely to the crude marriage survival curve because the independence assumption assigns most of the women who would be cohabitating to the single status. It does so because marriage and cohabitation are assumed to be completely distinct, and the cohabitors are divided between marriage and single in proportion to the fraction of the noncohabiting in each state. In these early adult years, most of the noncohabiting women are single.

The predicted net marriage survival curve under the shared unmeasured risk factors (SURF) assumption is represented by the next to lowest curve in Figure 1. It follows the combined marriage and cohabitation survival curve more closely than the IIA net survival curve because far more of the cohabitors are apportioned to the married status. This is a reflection of the fact that, in terms of the unmeasurables, marriage and cohabitation are "similar." These differences in predicted net marriage survival from the different assumptions are substantively very large. By age 21 (i.e., the sixtieth month after the sixteenth birthday) the net marriage survival is some seven percentage points higher with the IIA assumption. This phenomenon occurs because the SURF model indicates that approximately one-half of those who would cohabit choose marriage if cohabitation is eliminated.

Note that these results are consistent with the fact that the dramatic rise in rates of premarital cohabitation in recent years has not dramatically changed the total union formation rate. Instead, it is more likely that cohabitation has acted at least partially as a substitute for marriage, thereby keeping the total union formation rates relatively steady as rates of marriage have declined (Bumpass and Sweet 1989; Bumpass et al. 1991).

5. CONCLUSIONS

As event-history analysis grows more common in the social sciences, many such analyses focus on problems that involve competing risks. The hazard models usually employed in such analyses generally treat the competing risks as stochastically independent. In this paper we have examined the assumption that competing hazards do not share common unmeasured risk factors. We argue that this is an unreasonable assumption in many applications, which results in the predicted ratio of any two hazards being structurally independent of all other hazards.

We propose a method of testing the assumption and correcting for the effects of correlations in the unmeasured risk factors across alternative exit states. This method, what we call the shared unmeasured risk factors (or SURF) model, can be applied to a wide variety of competing hazards models. We apply the method to two variants of an event-history analysis of the union formation behavior of young women in which marriage and premarital cohabitation are treated as two competing means of exiting the single state. The results show that there is significant correlation in the unmeasured risk factors for marriage and premarital cohabitation—that is, with respect to the unmeasurables, the timing of entrance into marriage and premarital cohabitation is similar. One result of this correlation is that the estimated net hazard function, under the independence assumption, substantially overstates the survival rates of one hazard when the other hazard is removed. Correcting for this correlation also results in different parameter estimates for important predictor variables.

Estimates of the true level of SURF and the impact of SURF on parameter estimates may vary with different specifications of the SURF model, just as with many other statistical techniques. However, the computational ease of the SURF model will allow researchers to examine many alternative models to judge the robustness of their specification. This provides researchers an opportunity to estimate the level of independence among competing risks. In many applications we expect that the level of correlation among competing alternatives is not negligible.

APPENDIX A: A TWO-STEP BINARY LOGIT METHOD OF ESTIMATING THE SURF MODEL

The models presented in the main text were estimated using special algorithms developed by Hill. It is possible, however, to estimate SURF models with time-constant correlations via a two-step method using packaged binary logit programs. Since the time-varying SURF estimates can be quite imprecise, as a practical matter, little is likely to be lost by restricting analysis to time-constant SURF specifications.

The two-step SURF procedure for estimating with two competing destinations using packaged binary logit programs is as follows:

1. Estimate a logit regression predicting which type of exit is chosen among those that exit the base state. The independent variables consist of all those factors affecting the type of exit chosen.

2(a) Construct a discrete-time person-period data file with t_i records per individual and a dependent variable equaling 0 for all records prior to t_i and 1 for record t_i if the individual exited the base state (0 if the spell is right-censored).

2(b) Use the coefficients estimated in (1) to construct an estimate of the I_{ti} for every record in (2a) via:

$$I_{ti} = 1 + \exp(a + b_1 X_{tli} + \ldots + b_k X_{tki}).$$

2(c) Use logit regression to estimate the model of leaving the base state including the natural logarithm of the estimated inclusive value $\ln(I_t)$ as a predictor along with those independent variables which affect the *timing* of exits.

The coefficient obtained on $\ln(I_{ti})$ in step (2c) is the estimated index of dissimilarity ρ. If it is significantly less than 1, then the IIA assumption must be rejected. As noted in section A.2, the coefficients (b_k) obtained in step (1) are simple transformations of the structural coefficients β_c, β_m, and ρ.

A.1. *An Example*

We implemented the two-step procedure using the logit regression routines in SAS. Columns 2 and 3 of Table A.1 present the first and second stage estimates, respectively, of the two-step procedure, while column 1 shows the corresponding estimates for the direct maximum likelihood method.

The step (1) logit regression consisted of the estimating of a model predicting which of the 207 women who exited the single state chose cohabitation. Step (2a) consisted of creating a dataset with one

TABLE A.1
Married and Unmarried Cohabitation Correlated Competing Hazards Model[a]

	ML SURF	Step 1	Step 2
ρ	0.44*		0.36**
	(0.18)[b]		(0.13)
Leave single			
Union constant	−5.74**		−5.64**
	(0.63)		(0.63)
Mother's age at marriage	−0.55*		−0.57*
	(0.15)		(0.25)
Mother pregnant at marriage	0.27		0.27
	(0.17)		(0.17)
Time	0.11**		0.11**
	(0.01)		(0.01)
Spring	1.15**		1.15**
	(0.22)		(0.22)
Summer	1.03**		1.03**
	(0.22)		(0.22)
Fall	−0.17		−0.17
	(0.28)		(0.28)
Chose cohabitation			$\rho b_{1k} + b_{2k}$
Constant	−5.09**	1.37**	[−5.15]
	(0.61)	(0.39)	
Church attendance	−0.24**	−0.56**	[−0.20]
	(0.09)	(0.11)	
Whether Catholic	−0.09	0.10	[0.04]
	(0.13)	(0.31)	
Mother divorced or widowed	0.53**	1.28**	[0.46]
	(0.20)	(0.45)	
Sample size	381	207	6,234
ln(L)	−1019.31	−121.74	−898.08

*$p < 0.05$ **$p < 0.01$ two-tail

[a]Sample represents 381 females from the 1961 birth cohort.
[b]Standard errors in parentheses.

record for each of the 6,234 person-periods of exposure time among
the 381 women in the sample. For the non-right censored spells, a
value of 1 was assigned for the dependent variable in the last record
while the value of zero was assigned for all prior records and for the
right-censored observations. The time-varying covariates were also
transferred to the 6,234 records at this time. Step (2b) consisted of

creating the estimated inclusive value I_{ti} for each of the 6,234 records from the step (1) coefficients–e.g., I_{ti} for a (four times per month) church-going daughter of a non-Catholic divorced woman would be 2.51 (= 1 + exp[1.37 − 0.56*4 + 0.1 * 0 + 1.28*1]). Finally, step (2c) consisted of including the natural logarithm of these inclusive values along with the other covariates in the logit regression to predict which of the 6,234 person-periods of exposure represented exits from the single state.

The bracketed numbers in column 3 represent the β_c calculated from the first and second stage estimates via the formula $\beta_c = \rho b_1 + b_2$, where b_1 and b_2 are the coefficients from the first and second step logits respectively. In our example, b_2 equaled zero for all the first stage predictors (except the constant). This is because, in our model, none of the predictors used in the first stage are also used in the second stage. Also note that these procedures do not provide a standard error for testing the significance of parameters included in the first stage. To test the statistical significance of any of these parameters, simply reestimate both steps excluding the variable in question. The log-likelihood from this reestimate can be compared to that of the original model to test the significance of the parameter from the omitted variable. Twice the difference in these log-likelihoods is X^2 with one degree of freedom for this test.

There are three interesting things to note about the direct ML estimates of column 1 and the second stage estimates from the two stage procedure in column 3. First, while not identical, the estimates are very close. Second, the sum of the log-likelihoods of the first and second stage equals the log-likelihood of the direct ML procedure. This means that any likelihood-ratio tests based on the log-likelihood of the direct procedure can be implemented using the sum of the log-likelihoods from the two-step procedure. Third, the two-step procedure is much more computationally efficient than the direct ML procedure. Using an Intel-based 80486 microcomputer operating at 33 mHz, and using the IIA estimates as starting values, the direct estimation method requires seven minutes to attain convergence. This compares with just over one-half minute (32 seconds) for the two stages of the two-stage procedure combined. This savings in computational time comes at notable costs in terms of the amount of human setup time, data storage, and the lack of appropriate standard errors for testing the β_{ck} of the first-stage parameters. However, this two-stage procedure is an easily applicable method of testing hazard models with competing risks for violations of the IIA assumption.

A.2. Rationale for the Two-step Procedure

The two-step method requires some minor reformulation of the model. First of all, equation (12), which is the basis of the first step logit, is not in a form which can be estimated by ordinary logit. This is easily remedied, however, by dividing both numerator and denominator by $\exp(\beta_m'X/\rho)$ which yields:

$$Pr(J=c|T=t,c \cup m) = \frac{\exp[(\beta_c-\beta_m)'X_{ti}/\rho]}{1 + \exp[(\beta_c-\beta_m)'X_{ti}/\rho]}, \tag{22}$$

in which only the difference in effects $(\beta_c-\beta_m)/\rho$ can be identified.[23] The hazard of exiting for the base state at time t can be expressed as:

$$Pr(c \cup m|T \geq t_i) = \frac{\exp[\beta_m'X_{ti} + \rho\ln(I_{ti})]}{1+\exp[\beta_m'X_{ti}+\rho\ln(I_{ti})]}, \tag{23}$$

where I_{ti} is defined as $1 + \exp[(\beta_c-\beta_m)'X_{ti}]$. Similarly, the probability of survival until time t can be expressed as:

$$Pr(T \geq t_i) = \prod_{j_i=1}^{t_i-1} \frac{1}{1+\exp[\beta_m'X_{j_i}+\rho\ln(I_{j_i})]}. \tag{24}$$

Equation (23) is the basis for including the logarithm of the inclusive value in the second stage logit–i.e., for step (2c)–while equation (24) is the basis for pooling person-periods—i.e., step (2a).

Note that the β_c can be obtained from the step 1 coefficients, denoted for clarity as b_1, via: $\beta_c = \rho b_1 + \beta_m$. If a predictor appears only in the step (1) portion of the model, then $\beta_m = 0$.

APPENDIX B: SIMULATION EXAMPLES OF SURF MODELS

The results of empirical examples depend, at least in part, on the model specification chosen for the example. Alternative covariates

[23]We should note that in what Yamaguchi (1991) calls type 1 models only those factors that affect the type of exit appear in the first-step estimation. The other factors (i.e., those affecting the timing of exit irrespective of type) fall out of the first-stage estimation because β_c is constrained to equal β_m.

or specifications that allow the same covariates to predict different transitions result in different parameter estimates and different estimates of SURF. In order to examine the SURF competing hazards model on a data set for which the true parameters are known, we conducted several Monte Carlo experiments. The basic idea is to create data sets with known systematic and stochastic structures and then see how well the SURF model detects and estimates these structures. Although in this section the data will be manufactured rather than actual, we will continue to talk in terms of the marriage-cohabitation example.

The systematic and stochastic structure we investigate is a simplified version of the actual model we investigated above. To be most informative, the specification should incorporate all of the major elements of the full model, including time-varying covariates and time-varying SURF. This can be done by specifying the marriage-cohabitation state propensities of equation (8) as:

$$
\begin{aligned}
S_{ict} &= \alpha_c + \beta_c X_{i1} + \beta_{cm} X_{i2} + \beta_t t + a_{1t}(b_1 \nu_{it} + b_2 \nu_i) + a_{2t}\mu_{ict} \\
S_{imt} &= \alpha_m \qquad\quad + \beta_{cm} X_{i2} + \beta_t t + a_{1t}(b_1 \nu_{it} + b_2 \nu_i) + a_{2t}\mu_{imt},
\end{aligned}
\tag{25}
$$

where the ν_{it} represent the effects of individual-specific time-independent shared risk factors, the ν_i represent the effects of individual-specific time-invariant unmeasured shared risk factors, and μ_{ict} and μ_{imt} represent white noise.

The constants a_{1t}, a_{2t}, b_1, and b_2 can be manipulated to produce varying degrees of SURF with varying amounts of time dependence. For simplicity, we choose values for these constants such that $a_{1t}^2 + a_{2t}^2 = 1$ and $b_1^2 + b_2^2 = 1$. The cross destination correlation of the resulting composite error term is, as a result, simply a_{1t}^2. The IIA model of Allison (1982) results when $a_1 = 0$, while when a_1 is set to 0.9 the expected SURF model ρ is 0.436 ($= [1-(0.9)^2]^{\frac{1}{2}}$).[24] Furthermore, ρ can be made a function of time by varying a_{1t}–specifically, we will set $a_{1t} = 0$ for the summer months to correspond approximately to the situation found with our actual data. The results of those experiments indicate the extent to which the SURF technique provides a

---

[24]Note that the stochastic structure is not the same as Gumble's type 2 extreme value distribution, upon which the nested logit model is based. Instead, it is more in line with the error components approach to unmeasured heterogeneity. Part of our purpose here, however, is to assess the extent to which the nested logit approach approximates the unmeasured heterogeneity parameters.

closer estimate of the true parameters than a competing hazards approach that ignores the possibility of SURF.

Our Monte Carlo approach consists of repeatedly constructing statistically independent data sets with known values of the parameters of equation (25) and estimating the SURF model on them. The resulting parameter estimates are then averaged across these repetitions, and these average estimates are evaluated relative to the known parameter values. Individual event-history records for each of these replicates are constructed by:

1. Calculating the systematic portions of S_{i0}, S_{ic}, and S_{im}, using the predetermined α's, β's, X's and t;
2. Adding a randomly selected value for ν_i to S_{ic} and S_{im};
3. Repeatedly drawing independent random ν^{jt} and μ_{ijt} and combining them with the corresponding state propensities from step 2 until:

   a) $S_{ict} > S_{i0t}$–in which case cohabitation is entered at time t;
   b) $S_{imt} > S_{i0t}$–in which case marriage is entered at time t; or
   c) $t > 99$–in which case the observation is right-censored.

The unstandardized type 1 extreme value distribution is used for all the stochastic components. Deviates are derived from uniform deviates (x) using the transformation method–for example, $\epsilon = -\ln[-\ln(x)]$.

B.1. *IIA vs. SURF*

The first order of numerical business is to see what happens when the model based on the IIA assumption is used on data that contains significant amounts of SURF. Column 2 of Table B.1 presents the average IIA estimates for 20 repetitions of 400 cases per repetition when the true level of stochastic correlation is 0.81. The numbers in braces below the parameter labels in column 1 represent the true parameter values used in creating the data. An estimate of the standard error of the estimates can be derived from their Monte Carlo standard deviation (in parentheses) by dividing the latter by the square root of 20 (=4.4). Using these standard errors, we can easily test for the significance of the difference between the estimates and their known true values. With the exception of the time rate of growth of the hazard β_t, all the IIA estimates are substantially and

TABLE B.1
Monte Carlo Estimates of IIA and SURF Models
When SURF Is Present in the Data

	IIA Estimator	SURF Estimator
ρ	1.00	0.467
{0.436}		(0.104)
	[0.318][a]	[0.012]
ρ_s	0.00	0.456*
{$1-\rho$}		(0.159)
	[0.318]	[0.037]
β_c	−0.361**	−0.315*
{−0.3}	(0.029)	(0.033)
	[4.56e−3]	[1.31e−3]
β_{cm}	−3.190**	−3.139**
{−3}	(0.207)	(0.209)
	[7.89e−2]	[6.30e−2]
β_t	0.011	0.010
{0.01}	(0.003)	(0.003)
	[1.00e−5]	[0.90e−5]

*p < 0.05 **p < 0.01

[a]Standard errors in parentheses; MSE in brackets.

significantly biased. The IIA estimate of β_c (analogous to church attendance in the example) is more than 20 percent higher than its true value of −0.3. Even more severe, of course, is the bias of the assumed value of 1.0 for ρ relative to its true value of 0.436 (= $[1-0.81]^{1/2}$) and, correspondingly, the assumed value of 0 for ρ_s.

Column 3 of Table B.1 presents the Monte Carlo results obtained when the SURF estimator is employed on the same data. The estimates are substantially and significantly closer to the true values used in creating the pseudo data and the goodness of fit of the model (not shown) is greatly improved. The mean squared error of β_c (1.31e−3) for the SURF estimator is only about a third as large as that of the IIA estimator (3.56e−3). The mean squared error for the ρ parameters are roughly an order of magnitude higher for the IIA than for the SURF estimator.

Having said this, we should note that there are still small but marginally significant biases in the estimates. The source of these small biases is that the stochastic structure of equation (25) is not identical to that assumed in equation (10) for the nested logit model.

It is comforting that the biases are small even when the stochastic
structure is not as assumed by the model.

B.2. Time-Varying SURF

As noted in Section 3.4, the most dubious assumption of the SURF
model is that while unmeasured risk factors can be correlated across
competing destinations, we must assume that they are not correlated
across time. Assessing the importance of violations of this time-
independence assumption analytically is a daunting task. Instead,
therefore, we provide some insight into the likely effects of time
dependence in correlated risk factors on SURF estimates using numerical methods.

The amount of time dependence in the state propensities is
determined by the weights b_1 and b_2 in equation (22)—with zero
time-dependence resulting when $b_1 = 1$, and complete time-
dependence when $b_1 = 0$.

Table B.2 presents the Monte Carlo results obtained for 20
repetitions of 400 observations using the SURF model with four
combinations of time-dependent SURF. The first column of numbers
represents the results obtained under the IIA structure that results
when a_{1t} is set to zero for all t. The Monte Carlo point estimates for
all of the parameters are extremely close to their true values. Indeed,
none of the parameters are biased when the SURF model is estimated on data that contains no true SURF. This is an important
finding since it suggests that using the SURF estimator will "do no
harm" even if it is not required.

A main purpose of the Monte Carlo exercise is to examine the
effects of violations of the time-independence assumption of the
SURF model. Columns 3 and 4 present the results obtained with the
SURF model when time-invariant shared unmeasured risk factors
account for half ($b_1 = b_2 = 0.71$) and all ($b_1 = 1$, $b_2 = 0$) of the
correlated variance of the unmeasured risk factors, respectively. (Column 2 provides reference values by reproducing the estimates when
the SURF model is estimated on pure SURF data.) As suggested by
the literature on true versus spurious state dependence, the most
important effects of time-dependence on the SURF estimates is with
respect to the time-related parameters β_t and ρ_s. Specifically, time-
dependence in SURF attenuates the estimated effect of time on the

COMPETING HAZARDS WITH SURF   275

TABLE B.2
SURF Model Estimates with Varying Degrees of Dependence in Data

	Type of Data			
	No SURF	Time-Independent SURF	Partly Time-Dependent SURF	Fully Time-Dependent SURF
ρ	1.041	0.467	0.449	0.623**
{1.0}	(0.180)	(0.104)	(0.116)	(0.194)
{0.436}	[3.40e−2]	[1.18e−2]	[1.36e−2]	[7.26e−2]
ρ_s	−0.003	0.456*	0.897**	2.566**
{1−ρ}	(0.199)	(0.159)	(0.156)	(0.161)
	[3.96e−2]	[2.96e−2]	[14.4e−2]	[4820e−2]
β_c	−0.295	−0.315*	−0.332**	−0.387**
{−0.3}	(0.041)	(0.033)	(0.033)	(0.049)
	[1.71e−3]	[1.31e−3]	[2.11e−3]	[9.97e−3]
β_{cm}	−2.993	−3.139**	−3.171*	−3.219**
{−3.0}	(0.161)	(0.209)	(0.184)	(0.224)
	[2.60e−2]	[6.30e−2]	[6.30e−2]	[9.81e−2]
β_t	0.010	0.010	0.005**	0.002**
{0.01}	(0.002)	(0.003)	(0.003)	(0.003)
	[4.00e−6]	[9.00e−6]	[34.0e−6]	[73.0e−6]

* $p < 0.05$ ** $p < 0.01$

[a]Standard errors in parentheses; MSE in brackets.

hazard rate. If all the SURF is time-invariant, the estimated effect of time on the hazard of exiting the single state is only one-fifth its true value, and the MSE of β_t is some seven-times its value under time-independent SURF. Even more dramatically, the introduction of time-dependence in the v's results in the time-varying portion of error correlation (ρ_s) being grossly overestimated. While the increase in MSE of ρ_s associated with partial time-dependence in the v is substantial, with full dependence it is enormous–some three orders of magnitude higher than with time-independent SURF. This suggests that time-varying SURF specifications should be interpreted with extreme caution.

In contrast to the estimated effects of the time-varying measures, the estimates for the time-invariant covariates, and for the error correlation itself, are relatively robust with respect to moderate amounts of temporal stochastic dependence. The precision with which they are estimated is reduced substantially (especially for ρ), but the additional bias introduced is relatively small. Time-dependence does tend to bias the estimate of ρ_0 toward one (i.e., the estimated correlation toward zero)—something that would lead us to reject the hypothesis of correlated unmeasured risk factors even when they are present. This is important since it means that when we do find evidence of significant SURF under the assumption of no time-dependence, the true level of SURF is likely to be even higher. It also suggests that when we fail to find evidence of SURF there is still a possibility that some SURF exists.

REFERENCES

Allison, P. 1982. "Discrete-Time Methods for the Analysis of Event Histories." In *Sociological Methodology 1982,* edited by S. Leinhardt, 61–98. San Francisco: Jossey-Bass.

Amemiya, T. 1985. *Advanced Econometrics.* Cambridge: Harvard University Press.

Ben-Akiva, M., and S. Lerman. 1985. *Discrete Choice Analysis: Theory and Application to Travel Demand.* Cambridge: MIT Press.

Brendt, E., B. Hall, R. Hall, and J. Hausman. 1974. "Estimation and Inference in Nonlinear Structural Models." *Annals of Economic and Social Measurement 3*(4), 653–66.

Bumpass, L., and J. Sweet. 1989. "National Estimates of Cohabitation." *Demography 26,* 615–25.

Bumpass, L., J. Sweet, and A. Cherlin. 1991. "The Role of Cohabitation in Declining Rates of Marriage." *Journal of Marriage and the Family,* 53: 913–927.

Davis, K. 1985. "The Meaning and Significance of Marriage in Contemporary Society." In *Contemporary Society,* edited by K. Davis, 1–21. New York: Russell Sage.

Duncan, G., and S. Hoffman. 1990. "Welfare Benefits, Economic Opportunities, and Out-of-Wedlock Births Among Black Teenage Girls." *Demography 27*(4): 519–63.

Elbers, C., and G. Ridder. 1982. "True and Spurious Duration Dependence: The Identifiability of the Proportional Hazard Model." *Review of Economic Studies,* 49:403–409.

Flinn, C. J., and J.J. Heckman. 1982. "Models for the Analysis of Labor Force Dynamics. In *Advances in Econometrics,* vol. 1, edited by R. Bassman and G. Rhodes, 35–95. Greenwich, Conn.: JAI Press.

Freedman, D., A. Thornton, D. Camburn, and L. Young-DeMarco. 1988. "The Life History Calendar: A Technique for Collecting Retrospective Data." In *Sociological Methodology,* vol. 18, edited by C. Clogg, 37–68. San Francisco: Jossey-Bass.

Hann, A., and J. Hausman. 1988. *Semi-Parametric Estimators of Duration and Competing Risk Models*. Cambridge: Department of Economics, M.I.T.

Heckman, J., and B. Honore. 1989. "The Identifiability of the Competing Risks Model." *Biometrika* 76(2): 325–30.

Hill, D. 1990. "An Endogenously-Switching Ordered-Response Model of Information, Eligibility and Participation in SSI." *Review of Economics and Statistics* 72(2): 368–71.

Johnson, N., and S. Kotz. 1972. *Distributions in Statistics: Continuous Multivariate Distributions*. New York: Wiley.

Kahn, J., and K. Anderson. 1992. "Intergenerational Patterns of Teenage Fertility." *Demography* 29(1) 39–57.

Lancaster, T. 1990. *The Econometric Analysis of Transition Data*. New York: Cambridge University Press.

Maddala, G. S. 1983. *Limited Dependent and Qualitative Variables in Econometrics*. Econometric Society Monograph No. 3. Cambridge: Cambridge University Press.

McFadden, D. 1981. "Econometric Models of Probabilistic Choice." In *Structural Analysis of Discrete Data: With Econometric Applications,* edited by C. Manski and D. McFadden, 198–272. Cambridge: MIT Press.

———. 1983. "Econometric Analysis of Qualitative Response Models." In *Handbook of Econometrics,* vol. 2, edited by Z. Griliches and M. Intriligator, 1395–457. New York: Elsevier Science.

———. 1989. "A Method of Simulated Moments for Estimation of Discrete Response Models Without Numerical Integration." *Econometrica* 57(5)995–1026.

Petersen, T. 1991. "The Statistical Analysis of Event Histories." *Sociological Methods and Research* 19: 270–323.

Press, W., B. Flannery, S. Teukolsky, and W. Vetterling. 1986. *Numerical Recipes*. Cambridge: Cambridge University Press.

Rindfuss, R., and A. VandenHeuval. 1990. "Cohabitation: A Precursor to Marriage or an Alternative to Being Single." *Population and Development Review* 16(4): 703–26.

Teachman, J. 1983. "Analyzing Social Processes: Life Tables and Proportional Hazards Models." *Social Science Research* 12: 263–301.

Thornton, A. 1988. "Cohabitation and Marriage in the 1980s." *Demography* 25: 497–508.

———. 1991. "Influence of the Marital History of Parents on the Marital and Cohabitation Experiences of Children." *American Journal of Sociology* 96: 868–94.

Thornton, A., W. Axinn, and D. Hill. 1992. "Reciprocal Effects of Religiosity, Cohabitation, and Marriage." *American Journal of Sociology* 98: 628–51.

Train, K. 1986. *Qualitative Choice Analysis*. Cambridge: MIT Press.

Yamaguchi, K. 1991. *Event-History Analysis*. (Applied Research Methods Monograph No. 28, pp. 169–71). Newbury Park, Calif.: Sage.

𝕏 9 𝕏

MODELING TIME-VARYING EFFECTS OF COVARIATES IN EVENT-HISTORY ANALYSIS USING STATISTICS FROM THE SATURATED HAZARD RATE MODEL

Kazuo Yamaguchi*

This paper presents a method for modeling time-varying effects of categorical covariates in event-history analysis using statistics obtained from the saturated hazard rate model. First, the closed-form solution for the maximum likelihood estimators of parameters and their variance-covariance matrix for general saturated models of hazard rates are presented. The paper then presents methods that use statistics obtained from the saturated model to conduct (1) a proportionality test of the covariate effect for multiplicative hazard rate models and a linear-additivity test of the covariate effect for additive hazard rate models; (2) a goodness of fit test for various parametric models for time variations in the covariate effects; and (3) a test for comparing the relative goodness of fit among alternative parametric models. This paper also discusses the advantages and

*University of Chicago
This research is partially supported by a UCLA Academic Senate grant, a University of Chicago Social Science Division research grant, and a National Science Foundation grant SES-9008163. The author wishes to thank the editor and anonymous reviewers of *Sociological Methodology* for helpful comments, and is grateful to the research and editorial assistance of Linda R. Ferguson. Address correspondence to Kazuo Yamaguchi, Department of Sociology, The University of Chicago, 1126 E. 59th Street, Chicago, IL 60637.

279

limitations of the proposed methods compared with other methods for modeling time variations in the covariate effects, and the choice between additive versus multiplicative hazard rate models. An application analyzes the rate of first marriage as a function of age and employment using data from the 1973 Occupational Changes in a Generation Survey.

INTRODUCTION

This paper is concerned with modeling time-varying effects of covariates in event-history analysis for categorical covariates using statistics obtained from *saturated hazard rate models.* Here, a saturated model is defined as a model with a categorical time variable, categorical covariates, and a full set of interactions among them. The saturated model can be formulated for any *piecewise constant rate model with categorical covariates* or *discrete-time model with categorical covariates.* Hazard rates in piecewise constant-rate models are defined for continuous time but are assumed to be constant within each time interval for a given set of time intervals and vary only across time intervals. In discrete-time models, hazard rates are defined at discrete time points.

Time dependence in the use of covariates in event-history analysis has two aspects. First, covariates' values may vary with time, as in the case of employment status as a time-dependent covariate for the rate of marriage. Second, covariate effects–i.e., the regression coefficients of covariates—may vary with time. Nonproportionality of covariate effects in the Cox model is an example. This paper is concerned with the second aspect of time dependence.

However, these two aspects of time dependence overlap conceptually. For example, if a model includes a covariate and its interaction with time t–i.e., $b_1X + b_2tX$–there are two acceptable interpretations: (1) the effect of covariate X is time-varying and is equal to $b_1 + b_2t$; or (2) the interaction term tX is a time-dependent covariate and its coefficient b_2 is a time-constant effect. In other cases, only one of the two interpretations is appropriate. For example, if a hazard rate model includes $bX(t)$ in the regression equation where the values of $X(t)$ are determined according to a stochastic process, then only the first interpretation is possible. On the other hand, if the model includes the term $[A\exp(Bt)]X$ or $[A/(B+t)]X$ in the regression equation where A and B are parameters, then we should interpret $A\exp(Bt)$ or $A/(B+t)$ as a time-varying effect of covariate X. However, if the value of B is given and only A is a parameter, we can also interpret $X/(B+t)$ or $\exp(Bt)X$ as a time-dependent covariate and A as its time-constant effect. We can utilize this "dual" characteristic of time dependence for certain cases in parameter estimation, as discussed later.

The estimation of parameters is complicated for a general multivariate model that includes a covariate with a nonlinear parametric expression for its time-varying effect. As a basis of comparison, consider the generalized linear model (McCullagh and Nelder 1989). Nonlinearity appears here only in the form of a link function that relates a *linear* function of covariates' parameters to the dependent variable. In contrast, the hazard rate model with a covariate whose effect becomes a nonlinear parametric function of time involves nonlinearity not only in the link function (e.g., complementary log-log function) for the sum of covariate effects but also in characterizing the effect of the *particular* covariate. However, a much simpler method for parameter estimation becomes possible if models include only a few categorical covariates and a categorical time variable. This method uses statistics obtained from the saturated hazard rate model, as described in this paper. Since this method is practically applicable to models with only a few categorical covariates, its primary application is in the preliminary analysis of time-varying effects for some key covariates. This paper also discusses a possible use of the method presented in this paper for the application of general multivariate models.

The analysis of time-varying covariate effects is often narrowly conceptualized and equated with the proportionality test in proportional hazards models. A number of methods have been proposed to assess proportionality, including: (1) a test of an interaction effect between the covariate and time (and/or between the covariate and a fixed function of time) (e.g., Cox and Oakes 1984, ch. 8); (2) a test based on the autocovariance of the residuals proposed by Nagelkerke et al. (1984); (3) a related test based on the linear correlation between the residuals, which is employed in the procedure PHGLM in the SAS package (SAS Institute 1985); and less formally, (4) a graphical examination of parallelism of log minus log survival curves (Kalbfleisch and Prentice 1980). See Blossfeld et al. (1989) and

Yamaguchi (1991) for empirical examples of (1) and (4); see Schoenfeld (1982) for a graphical analysis related to test (2).

The last three methods are concerned with a test of deviation from proportionality in the covariate effects rather than with modeling time-varying covariate effects. The first method involves both the test of proportionality and, implicitly, a modeling of time-varying covariate effects. This method, however, is useful only if time variation in the covariate effects can be expressed by a sum of interaction effects between covariate X and some fixed functions of time, as in the case of $(a + bt + ct^2)X$ for which parameters a, b and c can be estimated as the effects of X, tX, and t^2X.

More general strategies for modeling time-varying covariate effects have been discussed in recent literature. One general strategy is the use of "local hazard models" for time-varying covariate effects as well as for the baseline hazard function (Wu and Tuma 1990, 1991), using local likelihood estimation proposed by Tibshirani and Hastie (1987). A second related method is the use of smoothing splines for time-varying covariate effects in the Cox model (Sleeper and Harrington 1990). These two methods share a *semiparametric* approach to modeling time-varying covariate effects. This approach is particularly useful when there is little or no guidance regarding the shape of time-varying covariate effects and, therefore, the modeling of time variations in the covariate effects is exploratory in nature.

This paper introduces an alternative method that is useful in situations when we have some prior expectations about how covariate effects vary with time. The method is concerned with testing various *parametric* specifications for time-varying covariate effects. We consider a wider range of parametric models than can be tested with readily available computer software for multivariate rate models. As mentioned above, however, this method is limited in the type and number of covariates that can be employed in the model because it uses statistics estimated from the saturated model.

In the following sections, this paper first introduces closed-form solutions for the maximum likelihood estimators of parameters and their variance-covariance matrix for saturated models of hazard rates without specifying the link function. The solutions are then applied to selected models with a specified link function, including (1) exponential and (2) linear models, among continuous-time models; (3) complementary log-log and (4) complementary log models, among discrete-time models. Models (3) and (4) are obtained when the speci-fication of the hazard rate is the same as that employed in continuous-time models (1) and (2), respectively, but the measurements of time are discrete (Prentice and Gloeckler 1978; Allison 1982).

When the saturated model is parameterized in a specific way, the time-specific parameter estimates for covariates become asymp-totically independent. Utilizing this asymptotic independence, this paper introduces a method (1) to test the goodness of fit of various parametric models for time variations in the covariate effects and (2) to compare among alternative parametric models—while retaining a nonparametric treatment for the baseline time effects. Specifically, this method provides a proportionality test of covariate effects in multiplicative hazard rate models (such as the exponential and com-plementary log-log models) and a linear-additivity test of covariate effects in additive hazard rate models (such as the linear and comple-mentary log models).

This paper further discusses how results from an analysis may depend on the choice between additive versus multiplicative hazard rate models. Few empirical applications have examined whether the results are sensitive to this choice. The parameters of multiplicative models reflect differences in the *relative risk* while those of additive models reflect differences in the *absolute risk*. Although multiplica-tive models are dominant in empirical research because they always generate positive estimates for rates, additive models are possible alternatives (Coleman 1981) and may provide substantively impor-tant information, though they usually require certain constraints on parameter estimation to generate positive estimates for rates.

2. THE MAXIMUM LIKELIHOOD ESTIMATORS OF PARAMETERS AND THE VARIANCE-COVARIANCE MATRIX OF PARAMETER ESTIMATES FOR THE SATURATED MODEL

2.1. *A Review of Basic Formulas*

In the following discussion, we assume the use of (1) a categorical time variable in hazard rate models, which implies either piecewise constant-rate models or discrete-time models, and (2) categorical covariates. Let t_i be the observed duration of the risk period for person i, and d_i be a dummy variable which indicates whether or not the observation is terminated by an occurrence of the event ($d_i=1$) or by censoring ($d_i=0$). Then given the hazard rate for person i, $\alpha_i(t)$, the likelihood function for the continuous-time model is given as:

$$L = \Pi_i \, \alpha_i(t_i)^{d_i} S_i(t_i), \tag{1}$$

where $S_i(t)$ is the survivor function at time t for person i and is given as:

$$S_i(t) = \exp\!\left(-\int_0^t \alpha_i(u)\,du\right). \tag{2}$$

Suppose we denote by c a covariate pattern that is defined as a distinct combination of the values of the time variable and all covariates employed in the model. It follows that for a given function of the hazard rate such that $\alpha_i(t) = f(\mathbf{b}'\mathbf{X_i}(t))$, where $\mathbf{b}$ and $\mathbf{X}$ are respectively the parameter and covariate vectors, the log-likelihood function, $L \equiv \ln L$, can be expressed as:

$$L = \Sigma_i \, d_i \ln[f(\mathbf{b}'\mathbf{X_i}(t_i))] - \Sigma_i \Sigma_c \, U_{ic} f(\mathbf{b}'\mathbf{X_c}), \tag{3}$$

where $\mathbf{X_c}$ is the value of $\mathbf{X}$ when the covariate pattern is c, and U_{ic} is the total amount of time that person i was observed with covariate pattern c during the period of risk.

As for discrete-time models, the likelihood function is given in general as:

$$L = \prod_i \prod_{t=1}^{t_i} P_i(t)^{d_i(t)} (1-P_i(t))^{(1-d_i(t))}, \tag{4}$$

where $P_i(t)$ is the probability that person i in the risk set has the event at discrete time t; $d_i(t)$ is a dummy variable that indicates an occurrence ($=1$) or a nonoccurrence ($=0$) of the event at time t for person i; and t_i denotes the same thing as above.

It follows that for a given hazard function such that $P_i(t)=f(\mathbf{b}'\mathbf{X_i}(t))$, the log-likelihood function is expressed as:

$$L = \Sigma_i \Sigma_t \, d_i(t) \ln[f(\mathbf{b}'\mathbf{X_i}(t))/(1-f(\mathbf{b}'\mathbf{X_i}(t)))] + \Sigma_i \Sigma_c \, U_{ic} \ln(1-f(\mathbf{b}'\mathbf{X_c})), \tag{5}$$

where X_c and U_{ic} denote the same things as in formula (3).

For both the continuous-time and discrete-time models, the

maximum likelihood estimates of parameters for a given data set are obtained by solving the equations, $\partial L/\partial \mathbf{b}=\mathbf{0}$. Given the parameter estimates from these equations, the variance-covariance matrix of parameter estimates can be obtained as minus the inverse of the second-order derivative matrix of the log-likelihood function, i.e., $V \equiv -(L'')^{-1}$.

2.2. Maximum Likelihood Estimators of Parameters for the Saturated Model with a Categorical Time Variable and a Single Categorical Covariate

In the following discussion, we employ the saturated model with a categorical time variable with T states and a categorical covariate with K states. A generalization of the results for the saturated model with a few categorical covariates, which is omitted here, is obtained by treating a full cross-classification of all covariates' states as categories of a single categorical variable.

We employ the following specific parameterization for the saturated hazard rate model:

$$\alpha_i(t) = f[a_1 + \sum_{t=2}^{T} a_t D_{it} + \sum_{t=1}^{T} \sum_{k=2}^{K} b_{tk} D_{it} D_{ik}(t)], \qquad (6)$$

where f is any function that satisfies certain conditions that are described later; D_{it}, for $t=1, \ldots, T$, are the dummy variables for time categories where $D_{it}=1$ if and only if person i is at time t; $D_{ik}(t)$, for $k=2, \ldots, K$, are the dummy variables for the covariate $X_i(t)$ using state $k=1$ as the baseline state; a_1 is the parameter for the constant term; a_t, $t=2, \ldots, T$, represents the effect of time t (versus time 1) when the covariate has the baseline category ($X=1$); and b_{tk}, $t=1, \ldots, T$, $k=2, \ldots, K$, represents the effect of state k (versus state 1) of the covariate X when the time variable has state t. Here the baseline category 1 for the time variable need not be real time 1. Any value of the time variable can be specified as the baseline category.

The following notations are used: N_{tk} denotes the total number of occurrences of the event for all units under study when the time variable has state t and the covariate has state k; and U_{tk} denotes the total amount of time spent in state (t,k) during the period of risk for all units under study. The amount of exposure to risk U_{tk} includes periods that end in censoring as well as those that end with an occurrence of the event.

It is also assumed that the function $f(x)$ used in formula (6) satisfies the following conditions:

1. $f(x)$ is a strongly monotonic function of x. Without loss of generality, $f(x)$ is also assumed to be an increasing function of x.
2. $f(x)$ is a smooth continuous function for which the first and the second derivatives, $f'(x)$ and $f''(x)$, both exist for all x at which $f(x)$ is defined.

It follows from (1) and (2) that $f'(x)$ is positive and the inverse function $f^{-1}(y)$ can be defined within the domain of the values of $y=f(x)$.

Then the log-likelihood function of the continuous-time model given in formula (3) can be simplified as:

$$L = N_{11}\ln(f(a_1)) + \sum_{t=2}^{T} N_{t1}\ln(f(a_1+a_t)) + \sum_{k=2}^{K} N_{1k}\ln(f(a_1+b_{1k}))$$
$$+ \sum_{t=2}^{T}\sum_{k=2}^{K} N_{tk}\ln(f(a_1+a_t+b_{tk})) - U_{11}f(a_1) - \sum_{t=2}^{T} U_{t1}f(a_1+a_t)$$
$$- \sum_{k=2}^{K} U_{1k}f(a_1+b_{1k}) - \sum_{t=2}^{T}\sum_{k=2}^{K} U_{tk}f(a_1+a_t+b_{tk}). \qquad (7)$$

The log-likelihood function of the discrete-time model in formula (5) thus becomes:

$$L = N_{11}\ln[f(a_1)/(1-f(a_1))]) + \sum_{t=2}^{T} N_{t1}\ln[f(a_1+a_t)/(1-f(a_1+a_t))]$$
$$+ \sum_{k=2}^{K} N_{1k}\ln[f(a_1+b_{1k})/(1-f(a_1+b_{1k}))]$$
$$\sum_{t=2}^{T}+\sum_{k=2}^{K} N_{tk}\ln[f(a_1+a_t+b_{tk})/(1-f(a_1+a_t+b_{tk}))] + U_{11}\ln[1-f(a_1)]$$
$$+ \sum_{t=2}^{T} U_{t1}\ln[1-f(a_1+a_t)] + \sum_{k=2}^{K} U_{1k}\ln[1-f(a_1+b_{1k})] +$$
$$\sum_{t=2}^{T}\sum_{k=2}^{K} U_{tk}\ln[1-f(a_1+a_t+b_{tk})] \qquad (8)$$

For both cases, it can be easily shown that the set of equations, $\partial L/\partial \mathbf{a} = 0$ and $\partial L/\partial \mathbf{b} = 0$, leads to the following set of equations for parameter estimates $\hat{a}_t, t=1, \ldots, T$ and $\hat{b}_{tk}, t=1, \ldots, T; k=1, \ldots, K$:

$$f(\hat{a}_1) = N_{11}/U_{11}$$
$$f(\hat{a}_1+\hat{a}_t) = N_{t1}/U_{t1}, \ t=2, \ldots, T$$
$$f(\hat{a}_1+\hat{b}_{1k}) = N_{1k}/U_{1k}, \ k=2, \ldots, K$$
$$f(\hat{a}_1+\hat{a}_t+\hat{b}_{tk}) = N_{tk}/U_{tk}, \ t=2, \ldots, T; \ k=2, \ldots, K. \qquad (9)$$

It follows that the maximum likelihood estimates of parameters permit an identical expression for the continuous-time and discrete-time models such that:

$$\hat{a}_1 = f^{-1}(N_{11}/U_{11})$$
$$\hat{a}_t = f^{-1}(N_{t1}/U_{t1}) - f^{-1}(N_{11}/U_{11}), \ t=2, \ldots, T$$
$$\hat{b}_{tk} = f^{-1}(N_{tk}/U_{tk}) - f^{-1}(N_{t1}/U_{t1}), \ t=1, \ldots, T, \qquad (10)$$
$$k=2, \ldots, K$$

The ratio of the number of events to the amount of exposure to risk—i.e., N_{tk}/U_{tk}—expresses the estimated *rate* of occurrences of the event at each group level, (t,k). Formula (10) describes how these rate estimates are related to parameter estimates from a general saturated model of the hazard rate given in formula (6). From formula (10) we can obtain the closed-form solution for the constant, time effects and covariate effects for selected models. These models differ only in the *link function*, f^{-1}, that relates rates estimated at the group level, N_{tk}/U_{tk}, to parameter estimates. The selected models and their equations for parameter estimates follow.

1. Continuous-time exponential model: $f(x)=\exp(x)$

$$\hat{a}_1 = \ln(N_{11}/U_{11})$$
$$\hat{a}_t = \ln(N_{t1}/U_{t1}) - \ln(N_{11}/U_{11}) \qquad \text{for}$$
$$t=2, \ldots, T$$
$$\hat{b}_{tk} = \ln(N_{tk}/U_{tk}) - \ln(N_{t1}/U_{t1}) \qquad \text{for} \qquad (11.1)$$
$$t=1, \ldots, T; k=2, \ldots, K$$

2. Continuous-time linear model: $f(x)=x$

$$\hat{a}_1 = N_{11}/U_{11}$$

$$\hat{a}_t = (N_{t1}/U_{t1}) - (N_{11}/U_{11})$$
$$\text{for } t=2, \ldots, T$$

$$\hat{b}_{tk} = (N_{tk}/U_{tk}) - (N_{t1}/U_{t1}) \qquad (11.2)$$
$$\text{for } t=1, \ldots, T; k=2, \ldots, K$$

3. Discrete-time complementary log-log model:
   $f(x)=1-\exp(-\exp(x))$

$$\hat{a}_1 = \ln[-\ln(1-(N_{11}/U_{11}))]$$

$$\hat{a}_t = \ln[-\ln(1-(N_{t1}/U_{t1}))]-\ln[-\ln(1-(N_{11}/U_{11}))]$$
$$\text{for } t=2, \ldots, T$$

$$\hat{b}_{tk} = \ln[-\ln(1-(N_{tk}/U_{tk}))]-\ln[-\ln(1-(N_{t1}/U_{t1}))] \qquad (11.3)$$
$$\text{for } t=1, \ldots, T; k=2, \ldots, K$$

4. Discrete-time complementary log model: $f(x)=1-\exp(-x)$

$$\hat{a}_1 = -\ln(1-(N_{11}/U_{11}))$$

$$\hat{a}_t = -\ln(1-(N_{t1}/U_{t1}))+\ln(1-(N_{11}/U_{11}))$$
$$\text{for } t=2, \ldots, T$$

$$\hat{b}_{tk} = -\ln(1-(N_{tk}/U_{tk}))+\ln(1-(N_{t1}/U_{t1})) \qquad (11.4)$$
$$\text{for } t=1, \ldots, T; k=2, \ldots, K.$$

2.3. *Variance-Covariance Matrix*

Given the solution for parameter estimates in formula (10), the second-order derivatives of the log-likelihood function L'' and the variance-covariance matrix of parameters estimates $V=-(L'')^{-1}$ can be obtained for the saturated model defined in formula (6). (See the appendix to this chapter for their derivations.) Unlike parameter estimates, the solutions differ between the continuous-time and discrete-time models. Hence, they are given separately below.

2.3.1. *Continuous-time Models*
For the continuous-time model, the *diagonal* entries in the variance-covariate matrix of parameter estimates become (see appendix):

$$V(\hat{a}_1,\hat{a}_1) = N_{11}/[U_{11}{}^2 f'(\hat{a}_1)^2]$$

$$V(\hat{a}_t,\hat{a}_t) = N_{11}/[U_{11}{}^2 f'(\hat{a}_1)^2] + N_{t1}/[U_{t1}{}^2 f'(\hat{a}_1+\hat{a}_t)^2]\ t\geq 2$$

$$V(\hat{b}_{1k},\hat{b}_{1k}) = N_{11}/[U_{11}{}^2 f'(\hat{a}_1)^2] + N_{1k}/[U_{1k}{}^2 f'(\hat{a}_1+\hat{b}_{1k})^2]\ k\geq 2$$

$$V(\hat{b}_{tk},\hat{b}_{tk}) = N_{t1}/[U_{t1}{}^2 f'(\hat{a}_1+\hat{a}_t)^2] + N_{tk}/[U_{tk}{}^2 f'(\hat{a}_1+\hat{a}_t+\hat{b}_{tk})^2]\ t\geq 2, k\geq 2 \quad (12)$$

Off-diagonal entries that represent the covariance of parameter estimates across time for each given state k of the covariate become:

$$V(\hat{a}_t,\hat{a}_s) = N_{11}/[U_{11}{}^2 f'(\hat{a}_1)^2] \qquad t\geq 2,\ s\neq t.$$

$$V(\hat{b}_{tk},\hat{b}_{sk}) = 0 \qquad t,s\geq 1,\ s\neq t,\ k\geq 2 \qquad (13)$$

The standard errors of parameter estimates are given as the square root of the diagonal elements of the variance-covariance matrix. Hence, from formula (12), we obtain the following solutions for standard errors in specific continuous-time models. These formulas illustrate how the precision of parameter estimates depends on the numbers of events (equation 14.1) and both the number of events and rates (equation 14.2).

1. Continuous-time exponential model: $f(x)=\exp(x)$

$$\text{S.E.}(\hat{a}_1) = 1/\sqrt{N_{11}}$$

$$\text{S.E.}\,(\hat{a}_t) = \sqrt{(1/N_{t1}) + (1/N_{11})} \qquad \text{for } t=2,\ldots,T.$$

$$\text{S.E.}(\hat{b}_{tk}) = \sqrt{(1/N_{tk}) + (1/N_{t1})} \qquad \text{for } t=1,\ldots,T; k=2,\ldots,K. \quad (14.1)$$

2. Continuous-time linear model: $f(x)=x$

$$\text{S.E.}(\hat{a}_1) = \sqrt{N_{11}/U_{11}}=R_{11}/\sqrt{N_{11}}$$

$$\text{S.E.}(\hat{a}_t) = \sqrt{(N_{t1}/U_{t1}{}^2)+(N_{11}/U_{11}{}^2)}$$

$$= \sqrt{R_{t1}{}^2/N_{t1}+R_{11}{}^2/N_{11}} \qquad \text{for } t=2,\ldots,T.$$

$$\text{S.E.}(\hat{b}_{tk}) = \sqrt{(N_{tk}/U_{tk}{}^2)+(N_{t1}/U_{t1}{}^2)}$$

$$= \sqrt{R_{tk}/N_{tk}+R_{t1}{}^2/N_{t1}} \qquad \text{for } t=1,\ldots,T; k=2,\ldots,K.$$

where $R_{tk} \equiv N_{tk}/U_{tk}$ for $t=1,\ldots,T;$

$$k=1,\ldots,K. \qquad (14.2)$$

2.3.2. *Discrete-time Models*

Similarly, we obtain the closed-form solution for the variance-covariance matrix of parameter estimates for the discrete-time model (see appendix). Its *diagonal* entries are:

$$V(\hat{a}_1,\hat{a}_1) = N_{11}(U_{11}-N_{11})/[U_{11}{}^3f'(\hat{a}_1)^2]$$

$$V(\hat{a}_t,\hat{a}_t) = N_{11}(U_{11}-N_{11})/[U_{11}{}^3f'(\hat{a}_1)^2]+N_{t1}(U_{t1}-N_{t1})/[U_{t1}{}^3f'(\hat{a}_1+\hat{a}_t)^2]\, t{\geq}2$$

$$V(\hat{b}_{1k},\hat{b}_{1k}) = N_{11}(U_{11}-N_{11})/[U_{11}{}^3f'(\hat{a}_1)^2] + N_{1k}(U_{1k}-N_{1k})/[U_{1k}{}^3f'(\hat{a}_1+\hat{b}_{1k})^2]$$
$$k{\geq}2$$

$$V(\hat{b}_{tk},\hat{b}_{tk}) = N_{t1}(U_{t1}-N_{t1})/[U_{t1}{}^3f'(\hat{a}_1+\hat{a}_t)^2] + N_{tk}(U_{tk}-N_{tk})/$$
$$[U_{tk}{}^3f'(\hat{a}_1+\hat{a}_t+\hat{b}_{tk})^2]$$
$$t{\geq}2,\, k{\geq}2 \tag{15}$$

The off-diagonal entries for the covariance of parameter estimates across time for a given state k of the covariates are:

$$V(\hat{a}_t,\hat{a}_s) = N_{11}(U_{11}-N_{11})/[U_{11}{}^3f'(\hat{a}_1)^2] \quad t{\geq}1,\, s{\neq}t.$$
$$V(\hat{b}_{tk},\hat{b}_{sk}) = 0 \quad s,t{\geq}1,\, s{\neq}t,\, k{\geq}2 \tag{16}$$

The following solutions for standard errors in specific discrete-time models are obtained from formula (15).

1. Discrete-time complementary log-log model:
$f(x)=1-\exp(-\exp(x))$

$$\text{S.E.}(\hat{a}_1) = -R_{11}/[\ln(1-R_{11})\sqrt{N_{11}(1-R_{11})}]$$

$$\text{S.E.}(\hat{a}_t) = \sqrt{R_{t1}{}^2/[N_{t1}(1-R_{t1})(1n(1-R_{t1}))^2]}$$
$$\overline{+\ R_{11}{}^2/[N_{11}(1-R_{11})(1n(1-R_{11}))^2]}$$
$$\text{for } t{=}2,\ldots,T.$$

$$\text{S.E.}(\hat{b}_{tk}) = \sqrt{R_{tk}{}^2/[N_{tk}(1-R_{tk})(1n(1-R_{tk}))^2]}$$
$$\overline{+\ R_{t1}{}^2/[N_{t1}(1-R_{t1})(1n(1-R_{t1}))^2]}$$

for $t{=}1,\ldots,T;k{=}2,\ldots,K$, where $R_{tk}{\equiv}N_{tk}/U_{tk},$ (17.1)
$t{=}1,\ldots,T;\, k{=}1,\ldots,K.$

2. Discrete-time complementary log model: $f(x)=1-\exp(-x)$

$$\text{S.E.}(\hat{a}_1) = \sqrt{N_{11}/[U_{11}(U_{11}-N_{11})]} = R_{11}/\sqrt{N_{11}(1-R_{11})}$$

$$\text{S.E.}(\hat{a}_t) = \sqrt{R_{t1}{}^2/[N_{t1}(1-R_{t1})] + R_{11}{}^2/[N_{11}(1-R_{11})]} \text{ for } t{=}2,\ldots,T.$$

$$\text{S.E.}(\hat{b}_{tk}) = \sqrt{R_{tk}^2/[N_{tk}(1-R_{tk})] + R_{t1}^2/[N_{t1}(1-R_{t1})]}$$
for $t=1, \ldots, T; k=2, \ldots, K,$

where $R_{tk} \equiv N_{tk}/U_{tk}$ for $t=1, \ldots, T; k=1, \ldots, K.$ \hfill (17.2)

2.3.3. A Note on Zero Covariance of Covariate Effects Across Time

An important characteristic of the variance-covariance matrix of parameter estimates is that $V(\hat{b}_{tk}, \hat{b}_{sk})=0$ holds true for any pair of t and $s (\neq t)$, for each given k, $k=2, \ldots, K$ (formulas 13, 16). In other words, *the covariance between parameter estimates for covariate effects at two distinct time points, for each given state k ($k \geq 2$) of the covariate, always becomes zero* for any saturated model in formula (6).

This characteristic does not hold true for time effects–that is, among the estimates of a_t parameters in the model (formulas 13, 16). Note also that in order for the covariance of the covariate effects across time to become zero, it is required that the time-varying covariate effects be expressed, as in formula (6), *at every time point separately*. On the other hand, if the covariate effect at a particular time point is specified as the "main effect," and its effects at other time points are specified as interaction effects of time and the covariate, then the covariances among the latter parameter estimates do not become zero. The characteristic of zero correlations among parameter estimates for the saturated model of formula (6) is utilized for the parametric modeling of time-varying covariate effects as described below.

3. A GOODNESS-OF-FIT TEST OF PARAMETRIC MODELS FOR COVARIATE EFFECTS, AND A TEST FOR COMPARING MODELS

The following discussion is concerned with statistical tests for time-varying covariate effects in the saturated hazard rate model, namely: (1) a proportionality test of covariate effects for multiplicative rate models, and a linear-additivity test for additive rate models; (2) a method of fitting various parametric models for time-varying covariate effects and the related goodness of fit test; and (3) a test for comparing alternative parametric models. The baseline time effects—

that is, parameters a_t—are treated nonparametrically. This strategy parallels the use of Cox's proportional hazards models where the baseline hazard function is not parametrically specified. We base the following discussion on the saturated model of formula (6).

For each parameter estimate $\hat{b}_{tk}$, we can estimate its variance from formulas (12) and (15), respectively, for the continuous-time and discrete-time models. Let's denote $\hat{b}_{tk}$ by $\hat{b}_t$ for simplicity and denote the estimate of its variance by $\hat{\sigma}_t^2$. The tests described below are based on the following two assumptions, both of which hold true asymptotically under certain regularity conditions. It is assumed that (i) $\hat{b}_t$, $t=1, \ldots ,T$, are multivariate normally distributed and (ii) the variance of $\hat{b}_t$ is known and is given by $\hat{\sigma}_t^2$. Since $\hat{b}_t$, $t=1, \ldots ,T$, are uncorrelated regardless of sample size (from formulas 13 and 16), it follows from assumption (i) that $\hat{b}_t$, $t=1, \ldots ,T$, are *independent* observations.

Under these two assumptions, we can formulate a null hypothesis for a parametric model of the population mean of $\hat{b}_t$ as a function of time t for $t=1, \ldots ,T$ such that $E(\hat{b}_t)=g(t,\boldsymbol{\theta})$, where $\boldsymbol{\theta}$ is a set of n_θ parameters. Then, we obtain the following:

1. Under the null hypothesis, we obtain a heteroskedastic equation of $\hat{b}_t$ with the following known entries in the variance-covariance matrix of the error term:

$$\hat{b}_t = g(t,\boldsymbol{\theta}) + \epsilon_t \qquad (18.1)$$

$$V(\epsilon_t) = V(\hat{b}_t - g(t,\boldsymbol{\theta})) = \hat{\sigma}_t^2 \qquad (18.2)$$

$$COV(\epsilon_t, \epsilon_s) = 0 \text{ for } s \neq t. \qquad (18.3)$$

2. Since ϵ_t $(=\hat{b}_t - g(t,\boldsymbol{\theta}))$ are normally distributed and independent under the null hypothesis (due to normality and independence of $\hat{b}_t$), the quantity given below

$$L^2(\boldsymbol{\theta}) \equiv \Sigma_t(\hat{b}_t - g(t,\boldsymbol{\theta}))^2/\hat{\sigma}_t^2 \qquad (19)$$

becomes a chi-squared statistic with T degrees of freedom. When the population parameters $\boldsymbol{\theta}$ are replaced by their estimates $\hat{\boldsymbol{\theta}}$ in formula (19), we obtain a chi-square statistic $L^2(\hat{\boldsymbol{\theta}})$ with $T-n_\theta$ degrees of freedom such that:

$$L^2(\hat{\boldsymbol{\theta}}) \equiv \Sigma_t(\hat{b}_t - g(t,\hat{\boldsymbol{\theta}}))^2/\hat{\sigma}_t^2 \qquad (20)$$

This statistic can be used to test the goodness of fit of model $g(t,\boldsymbol{\theta})$ with the data.

3. Due to the normality and independence of $\hat{b}_t$, the log-like likelihood function of the set of observations $\hat{b}_t$, $t=1, \ldots, T$ becomes:

$$-(\tfrac{1}{2})\ln(2\pi)T - \Sigma_t\ln(\hat{\sigma}_t) - (\tfrac{1}{2})\Sigma_t(\hat{b}_t - g(t,\boldsymbol{\theta}))^2/\hat{\sigma}_t^2 \qquad (21)$$

Therefore, the maximum likelihood (ML) estimate of $\boldsymbol{\theta}$ minimizes $L^2(\boldsymbol{\theta})$ defined in formula (19). Since the last component of formula (21) becomes zero for the saturated model (for which $\hat{b}_t=g(t,\hat{\boldsymbol{\theta}})$ for all t), the test statistic $L^2(\hat{\boldsymbol{\theta}})$ in formula (20) is identical to the likelihood-ratio chi-squared for comparing model $E(\hat{b}_t)=g(t,\boldsymbol{\theta})$ with the saturated model.

4. In particular, the ML estimate for parameter $\boldsymbol{\theta}$ under the hypothesis of constancy of $g(t,\boldsymbol{\theta})$–that is, $E(\hat{b}_t)=\boldsymbol{\theta}$–becomes a weighted mean of $\hat{b}_t$ with $1/\hat{\sigma}_t^2$ as weights, i.e.,

$$\hat{\boldsymbol{\theta}}=(\Sigma_t\hat{b}_t/\hat{\sigma}_t^2)/\Sigma_t(1/\hat{\sigma}_t^2) \qquad (22)$$

We obtain this by solving $\partial L^2/\partial\boldsymbol{\theta}=0$ for $L^2(\boldsymbol{\theta})=\Sigma_t(\hat{b}_t - \boldsymbol{\theta})^2/\hat{\sigma}_t^2$.

5. It follows that $L^2(\hat{\boldsymbol{\theta}})=\Sigma_t(\hat{b}_t - \hat{\boldsymbol{\theta}})^2/\hat{\sigma}_t^2$ is a chi-squared statistic (with $T-1$ degrees of freedom) for the test of either proportionality (in the case of multiplicative hazard rate models) or linear additivity (in the case of additive hazard rate models) of covariate effects.

6. If two parametric models for $E(\hat{b}_t)$ are nested, twice the difference in the chi-squared statistics ($L^2(\hat{\boldsymbol{\theta}})$) of the two models provides a likelihood ratio test for comparing their relative goodness of fit. The BIC statistic (Raftery 1986a,1986b), defined as $\mathrm{BIC}\equiv L^2(\hat{\boldsymbol{\theta}})-(T-n_\theta)\ln(T)$, can be used for comparing nonnested models. A model with a negative BIC is better than the saturated model, and the model with the smallest BIC value is the best model.

An additional note is worthy from a practical point of view. If the model $g(t,\boldsymbol{\theta})$ specifies a polynomial function, such as $E(\hat{b}_t)=A+Bt+Ct^2$ where $\boldsymbol{\theta}=(A,B,C)$, then the regression parameters can be estimated from the generalized least square method by using $V(\boldsymbol{\epsilon})=Q\sigma^2$, where Q is the diagonal matrix whose t-th diagonal element is $\hat{\sigma}_t^2$. Since matrix Q is diagonal, the parameter estimates can be obtained from a weighted least square solution, with weight$=1/\hat{\sigma}_t^2$ for the t-th observation. These estimates can be obtained using econometric software such as LIMDEP (Green 1990). However, the standard errors of the parameter estimates are biased because the weighted LS method (1) assumes $V(\epsilon)=Q\sigma^2$–that is, the correlation matrix of the error term is proportional to Q, and (2) estimates σ^2 from the sample data. In fact, the correlation matrix of the error term should be Q itself in the present case. Since the weighted least square method calculates the weighted sum of squared errors (i.e., the SS residual) as $(\hat{b}_t - g(t,\hat{\theta}))'Q^{-1}(\hat{b}_t - g(t,\hat{\theta}))$, the SS residual becomes the chi-squared statistic for the goodness-of-fit test. For nonpolynomial models, the Newton Raphson algorithm can be effectively used for the ML estimation of θ parameters—though its convergence requires reasonably good initial values for $\hat{\theta}$.[1]

4. ILLUSTRATIVE ANALYSIS

4.1. *Data*

The illustrative analysis employs data for males aged 25–64 in the 1973 Occupational Changes in a Generation Survey (OCG-II). Major results from the analysis of this data set are reported by Featherman and Hauser (1978). Hogan (1978) employed this data set to analyze the timing and sequencing of life events that include employment and marriage. The latter study is substantively related to the present application, which analyzes the rates of first marriage during ages 14–40.[2] Quite a few studies have applied event-history analysis

---

[1] The use of a nonlinear regression program in a standard statistical package, such as the procedure NLR in SPSS, provides a reasonably good estimate for θ when each observation is weighted by $1/\hat{\sigma}_t^2$. The set of predicted values for $\hat{b}_t$ can be used for calculating the chi-squared statistic. However, the goodness-of-fit chi-square statistics estimated by SPSS-NLR tend to be slightly larger than those of the ML estimates and, therefore, provide conservative tests. But the algorithm employed in SPSS-NLR seems to attain a convergence of parameter estimates for a wide range of initial values. Hence, I employed the estimates from SPSS-NLR as initial values in the FORTRAN program, which was written to obtain the ML solutions based on the Newton-Raphson algorithm, for specific nonlinear models employed in the application section of this paper. This FORTRAN program is available on request.

[2] Marriages at age 13 *or under* are coded in the data set as marriages at age 13. Hence, we do not know exactly when these marriages occurred and, therefore, cannot correctly estimate the amount of exposure to risk that corresponds to these marriages. Hence, we omitted from the analysis cases with

for the study of marriage timing (e.g., Michael and Tuma 1985; Teachman 1982; Trussell and Bloom 1983; Yamaguchi and Kandel 1985). This section examines the pattern of time-varying employment effects on the rate of getting married.

The OCG-II survey contains data on the age of subjects at (1) marriage and (2) first full-time employment after leaving school, both of which are measured in single years. As time-dependent covariates, the present analysis employs (1) age and (2) a dummy variable that distinguishes between having ever entered full-time employment after leaving school or not. The baseline category for age is 21, and the baseline category for employment is never employed full-time before.

We are interested here in time variations of employment effects on the rate of marriage. Since marriage is more likely to occur after rather than before entry into employment, we expect positive effects of employment on the rate of marriage, controlling for age. However, we also expect that the positive effects of employment will decrease with age. There are several reasons for this expectation. As age increases, fewer years remain to get married within a desirable (or normative) age range; therefore, people will be more inclined to marry even though they have not entered full-time employment. Second, as age increases, people mature emotionally and behaviorally. Hence, men who are not economically ready for marriage may still be considered, and consider themselves, ready for marriage because of this maturity. The following analysis examines how employment effects change with age.

4.2. Results from Saturated Models

For each age and employment state, Table 1 presents the data for the number of events and the number of person-years at risk (columns B and C). In the calculation of these data, the individual sampling weight and the design effect were used to adjust these data to their effective sample size (Featherman and Hauser 1978). The results of four saturated models—exponential, complementary log-log, linear, and complementary log models—are presented in the table (columns

marriages at age 13 or under. Since saturated models do not employ a parametric characterization for age effects, this omission does not affect the results for the saturated models presented in the paper.

TABLE 1
Getting Married as a Function of Age and Employment

Age (A)	Data		Multiplicative Models		Additive Models	
	N(t,1) (B)	U(t,1) (C)	Exponential (D)	Complementary log-log (E)	Linear (F)	Complementary log (G)
			Age Effects ($\hat{a}_t$)			
14	8	16667	−5.262 (14.8)	−5.310 (14.9)	−0.0921 (22.3)	−0.0967 (22.4)
15	17	15645	−4.445 (18.0)	−4.493 (18.2)	−0.0915 (22.2)	−0.0961 (22.2)
16	32	14268	−3.720 (20.4)	−3.768 (20.7)	−0.0903 (21.9)	−0.0949 (21.9)
17	92	12151	−2.504 (22.1)	−2.548 (22.5)	−0.0850 (20.3)	−0.0896 (20.4)
18	183	9854	−1.607 (18.6)	−1.645 (19.1)	−0.0740 (17.1)	−0.0784 (17.3)
19	326	8247	−0.851 (12.0)	−0.879 (12.4)	−0.0531 (11.4)	−0.0568 (11.7)
20	402	6874	−0.459 (6.9)	−0.478 (7.1)	−0.0341 (6.8)	−0.0369 (7.0)
21	506	5465	[0.000]	[0.000]	[0.0000]	[0.0000]
22	522	4190	0.297 (4.8)	0.314 (5.0)	0.0320 (4.7)	0.0359 (4.9)
23	374	3086	0.269 (3.9)	0.285 (4.2)	0.0286 (3.8)	0.0320 (4.0)
24	293	2293	0.322 (4.4)	0.342 (4.6)	0.0352 (4.1)	0.0396 (4.4)
25	231	1671	0.401 (5.0)	0.426 (5.4)	0.0457 (4.6)	0.0516 (4.8)
26	137	1192	0.216 (2.2)	0.228 (2.4)	0.0223 (2.1)	0.0249 (2.2)
27	109	890	0.280 (2.7)	0.296 (2.8)	0.0299 (2.4)	0.0335 (2.5)
28	76	673	0.199 (1.6)	0.210 (1.7)	0.0203 (1.5)	0.0227 (1.6)
29	49	521	0.016 (0.1)	0.016 (0.1)	0.0015 (0.1)	0.0016 (0.1)

30	39	431	−0.023	(0.1)	−0.024	(0.1)	−0.0021	(0.1)	−0.0023	(0.1)
31	23	351	−0.346	(1.6)	−0.360	(1.7)	−0.0271	(1.9)	−0.0294	(2.0)
32	16	300	−0.552	(2.2)	−0.573	(2.3)	−0.0393	(2.8)	−0.0424*	(2.9)
33	13	259	−0.612	(2.2)	−0.635	(2.3)	−0.0424	(2.9)	−0.0457	(3.1)
34	15	235	−0.372	(1.4)	−0.387	(1.5)	−0.0288	(1.7)	−0.0312	(1.8)
35	8	200	−0.839	(2.4)	−0.867	(2.4)	−0.0526	(3.6)	−0.0563	(3.7)
36	4	184	−1.449	(2.9)	−1.486	(3.0)	−0.0709	(6.1)	−0.0752	(6.4)
37	9	170	−0.559	(1.7)	−0.580	(1.7)	−0.0396	(2.2)	−0.0428	(2.3)
38	6	155	−0.872	(2.1)	−0.901	(2.2)	−0.0539	(3.3)	−0.0577	(3.5)
39	8	142	−0.497	(1.4)	−0.516	(1.4)	−0.0363	(1.8)	−0.0392	(1.9)
40	6	129	−0.688	(1.7)	−0.713	(1.7)	−0.0461	(2.4)	−0.0495	(2.5)

Age-Specific Employment Effects ($\hat{b}_t$)

	$N(t,2)$	$U(t,2)$					$\hat{b}_t$			
14	8	1775	2.240	(4.5)	2.242	(4.5)	0.0040	(2.5)	0.0040	(2.5)
15	26	2780	2.153	(6.9)	2.157	(6.9)	0.0083	(4.5)	0.0083	(4.5)
16	66	4115	1.967	(9.1)	1.974	(9.2)	0.0138	(6.9)	0.0139	(6.9)
17	220	6135	1.555	(12.5)	1.570	(12.6)	0.0283	(11.1)	0.0289	(11.2)
18	526	8121	1.249	(14.6)	1.273	(14.8)	0.0462	(14.7)	0.0482	(14.9)
19	922	9022	0.950	(14.7)	0.983	(15.3)	0.0627	(15.6)	0.0675	(16.1)
20	1210	9146	0.816	(14.2)	0.856	(14.9)	0.0738	(15.4)	0.0816	(16.1)
21	1405	8944	0.529	(10.2)	0.565	(10.9)	0.0645	(11.0)	0.0737	(11.7)
22	1469	8310	0.350	(6.9)	0.380	(7.4)	0.0522	(7.3)	0.0615	(7.9)
23	1375	7423	0.424	(7.3)	0.461	(7.9)	0.0640	(8.0)	0.0757	(8.7)
24	1201	6466	0.374	(5.7)	0.407	(6.2)	0.0580	(6.3)	0.0688	(6.9)
25	1042	5592	0.299	(4.1)	0.326	(4.5)	0.0481	(4.5)	0.0574	(4.9)

KAZUO YAMAGUCHI

TABLE 1 (cont.)

Age (A)	Data		Multiplicative Models		Additive Models	
	N(t,1) (B)	U(t,1) (C)	Exponential (D)	Complementary log-log (E)	Linear (F)	Complementary log (G)
			Age Effects ($\hat{a}_i$)			
26	867	4660	0.482 (5.2)	0.522 (5.7)	0.0711 (6.1)	0.0838 (6.7)
27	662	3821	0.347 (3.4)	0.376 (3.6)	0.0508 (3.8)	0.0596 (4.1)
28	535	3181	0.398 (3.2)	0.430 (3.5)	0.0553 (3.7)	0.0643 (4.0)
29	413	2655	0.503 (3.2)	0.538 (3.6)	0.0615 (4.0)	0.0703 (4.3)
30	317	2217	0.458 (2.7)	0.487 (2.9)	0.0525 (3.2)	0.0595 (3.4)
31	251	1906	0.698 (3.2)	0.734 (3.4)	0.0662 (4.1)	0.0734 (4.4)
32	185	1638	0.750 (2.9)	0.782 (3.0)	0.0596 (3.8)	0.0650 (4.0)
33	144	1440	0.689 (2.4)	0.716 (2.5)	0.0498 (3.1)	0.0539 (3.2)
34	114	1277	0.335 (1.2)	0.349 (1.3)	0.0254 (1.4)	0.0276 (1.4)
35	96	1142	0.743 (2.0)	0.766 (2.1)	0.0441 (2.7)	0.0470 (2.8)
36	92	1029	1.414 (2.8)	1.450 (2.8)	0.0677 (4.7)	0.0717 (4.9)
37	68	914	0.340 (1.0)	0.352 (1.0)	0.0215 (1.1)	0.0229 (1.1)
38	54	829	0.520 (1.2)	0.534 (1.2)	0.0264 (1.5)	0.0279 (1.5)
39	44	758	0.030 (0.1)	0.031 (0.1)	0.0017 (0.1)	0.0018 (0.1)
40	36	704	0.095 (0.2)	0.097 (0.2)	0.0046 (0.2)	0.0049 (0.2)
Constant			-2.380	-2.331	0.0926	0.0972

The ratio $|b/\text{s.e.}(b)|$ is in parentheses.

D–G). The hazard rate for all models takes the following saturated form:

$$\alpha_i(t) = f(a_0 + \Sigma_{t \neq 21}\, a_t D_t + \Sigma_t b_t D_t X_i(t)), \qquad (23)$$

where D_t are the age dummy variables and $X_i(t)$ is the time-dependent dummy variable that takes 1 if person i has entered full-time employment by age t. The design matrix for this saturated model is given in Table 2.

Parameter estimates for all models in Column D–G of Table 1 are calculated from the event/risk data in columns B and C. For example, for the *exponential model* in column D, the age effect at age 18 and the employment effect at age 18 respectively are given by:

$$\hat{a}_{18} = \ln(N_{18,1}/U_{18,1}) - \ln(N_{21,1}/U_{21,1}) = \ln(183/9854) - \ln(506/5465) = -1.607$$

$$\hat{b}_{18} = \ln(N_{18,2}/U_{18,2}) - \ln(N_{18,1}/U_{18,1}) = \ln(526/8121) - \ln(183/9854) = 1.249,$$

using formula (11.1). Their standard errors are given respectively by:

$$\sqrt{1/183 + 1/506} = 0.0863; \quad \sqrt{1/526 + 1/183} = 0.0858,$$

using Formula (14.1). Subsequently, we obtain the ratio of the parameter estimate to its standard error, as presented in Table 1. Similarly, the results for each model can be calculated using formulas (11), (14), and (17) and the data of N_{tk} and U_{tk}, for $k=1,2$, presented in columns B and C of Table 1.

The scaling of parameter estimates in Table 1 differs between the first two multiplicative rate models (columns D–E) and the last two additive rate models (columns F–G). The parameter estimates for the first two models are dimension-free measures of *relative risk* (except for the parameter estimate for the constant term). The parameter estimates for the last two models measure *absolute risk* and have dimensions identical to the hazard rate—that is, 1/[time]. Nevertheless, the four models generate quite similar *qualitative* results for age effects: The hazard rate almost monotonically increases from age 14 to 25, peaks at age 25, then steadily decreases during ages 26–33. It fluctuates for the remaining ages due to the small number of subjects who have not entered employment. This correspondence of age effects among the four models is not a coincidence because they all employ a simple monotonic transformation of age effects estimated from the exponential model.

TABLE 2
Design Matrix for the Saturated Model[a]

The Values of Age and Employment Variables

Parameters	Before Employment X = 0 Age (base = 21)										After Employment X = 1 Age (base = 21)									
	14	15	16	—	20	21	22	—	39	40	14	15	16	—	20	21	22	—	39	40
1. Constant																				
a_0	1	1	1	—	1	1	1	—	1	1	1	1	1	—	1	1	1	—	1	1
2. Age effects (there is no a_{21})																				
a_{14}	1	0	0	—	0	0	0	—	0	0	1	0	0	—	0	0	0	—	0	0
a_{15}	0	1	0	—	0	0	0	—	0	0	0	1	0	—	0	0	0	—	0	0
a_{16}	0	0	1	—	0	0	0	—	0	0	0	0	1	—	0	0	0	—	0	0
a_{20}	0	0	0	—	1	0	0	—	0	0	0	0	0	—	1	0	0	—	0	0
a_{22}	0	0	0	—	0	0	1	—	0	0	0	0	0	—	0	0	1	—	0	0
a_{39}	0	0	0	—	0	0	0	—	1	0	0	0	0	—	0	0	0	—	1	0
a_{40}	0	0	0	—	0	0	0	—	0	1	0	0	0	—	0	0	0	—	0	1
3. Employment effects																				
b_{14}	0	0	0	—	0	0	0	—	0	0	1	0	0	—	0	0	0	—	0	0
b_{15}	0	0	0	—	0	0	0	—	0	0	0	1	0	—	0	0	0	—	0	0
b_{16}	0	0	0	—	0	0	0	—	0	0	0	0	1	—	0	0	0	—	0	0
b_{20}	0	0	0	—	0	0	0	—	0	0	0	0	0	—	1	0	0	—	0	0
b_{21}	0	0	0	—	0	0	0	—	0	0	0	0	0	—	0	1	0	—	0	0
b_{22}	0	0	0	—	0	0	0	—	0	0	0	0	0	—	0	0	1	—	0	0
b_{39}	0	0	0	—	0	0	0	—	0	0	0	0	0	—	0	0	0	—	1	0
b_{40}	0	0	0	—	0	0	0	—	0	0	0	0	0	—	0	0	0	—	0	1

[a]The saturated model is defined as:

As for the effects of employment, however, there are substantial qualitative differences between the results of the first two models
and those of the last two models. If we rely on the results from the
multiplicative rate models, the hypothesis about employment effects
is supported: These two models consistently show that employment
effects monotonically *decrease* during ages 14–22 and fluctuate for
ages above 22. On the other hand, the results from the additive rate
models consistently show that the employment effects *increase* during ages 14–20, fluctuate at around the level of 0.05–0.08 for ages
21–33, and then tend to decline for ages above 33. Hence, depending
on whether relative or absolute risk is analyzed, opposite trends in
the employment effects are found as a function of age.

The differences between the multiplicative rate models and
the additive rate models become clearer when we depict estimated
rates and log-rates. Figures 1 and 2 respectively present log-rates and
rates as a function of age and employment using the complementary
log-log and complementary log models. For both models, the de-
picted pattern for the "before employment" state characterizes the
age effects, and the differences between "after" and "before" employ-

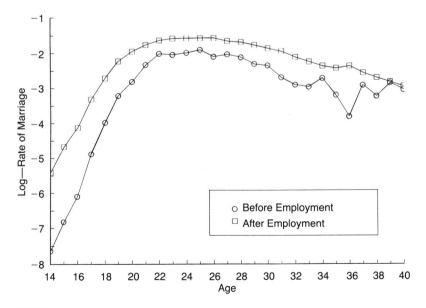

FIGURE 1. Becoming married, complementary log-log model.

302				KAZUO YAMAGUCHI

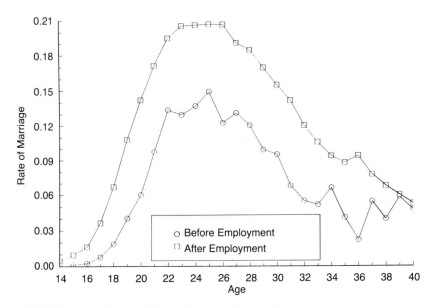

FIGURE 2. Becoming married, complementary log model.

ment characterize the age-specific employment effects. The complementary log-log and complementary log models are obtained when we assume that hazard rates follow the exponential and linear models, respectively, but the observations for events are grouped into discrete time intervals. The results for the former two models eliminate the "time aggregation bias" (Petersen 1991) which is present in the estimates from the latter two models.

These two figures clearly show differences in the employment effects between the two models, one of which characterizes changes in the relative risk (i.e., log-rates) and the other in the absolute risk (i.e., rates) as a function of age. The differences are analyzed further later. The results for relative risk need to be interpreted carefully because when the absolute level of rates is small, as in the case of rates of marriage during adolescence, a large difference in the relative risk can imply a very small difference in the absolute risk.

Whether or not we should analyze relative or absolute risk is mainly a theoretical issue. For example, if we are concerned with the effects of various states of a covariate on subjects' *relative propensities* to have the event compared with the propensity under a particular state, the analysis of relative risk will be appropriate. On the other hand, if we are concerned with the determinants of variations in the prevalence of the event, an analysis of absolute risk will be more informative. As in a comparison between the use of raw income and the logarithm of income as the dependent variable in regression analysis (Hauser 1980), the analysis of relative risk will be useful to compare differences in "the rate of return" associated with a change in the value of independent variables among groups. On the other hand, an analysis of absolute risk is better suited to comparing differences in rates themselves given a change in the value of independent variables among groups.

In practice, the relative-risk models dominate research mainly because of their technical convenience: The absolute-risk models usually require certain constraints on parameters in order not to have negative estimates for rates. However, these constraints do not have to be imposed in the current application, which is based on saturated models since rates estimated from saturated models are always nonnegative.

4.3. The Test of Proportionality/Linearity and Parametric Models for the Time-Varying Covariate Effects

The results from saturated models presented in the last subsection have one major limitation: They may obscure the pattern of employment effects because the models may have used an unnecessarily large number of parameters. But as described in the methods section, the results for the employment effects and their standard errors from a saturated model can be used (1) to test proportionality/ linearity and (2) to test and compare various parametric models for time-varying effects of employment. If a parametric model fits the data, it has a more parsimonious use of parameters than the saturated model.

Table 3 presents the results from applying polynomial and selected nonlinear parametric models to the employment effects estimated from the saturated complementary log-log and complementary log models. Here, the dependent variable is the employment effects for which we have 27 observations—that is, from age 14 to age 40—or each of these two saturated models. The independent variable X is equal to $t-13$, where t represents age, for all parametric

TABLE 3
Parametric Models for Time-Varying Employment Effects[a]

I. Employment Effects b_t, Estimated from the Complementary Log-log Model

Models ($X = t-13$)	L^2	df	BIC	A	B	C	D
1. Constant $E(\hat{b}_t)=A$	315.38	26	229.69	0.6339 (9.47)	—	—	—
2. Linear $E(\hat{b}_t)=A+BX$	197.10	25	114.70	1.1749 (7.85)	−0.0563 (−3.87)	—	—
3. Quadratic $E(\hat{b}_t)=A+BX+CX^2$	81.77	24	2.67	2.1849 (10.92)	−0.2533 (−7.20)	0.0082 (5.82)	—
4. Cubic $E(\hat{b}_t)=A+BX+CX^2+DX^3$	20.32	23	−55.49	3.5698 (18.40)	−0.6646 (−12.67)	0.0439 (10.13)	−0.0009 (−8.34)
5. Exponential $E(\hat{b}_t)=B\exp(CX)$	82.19	25	−0.20	—	3.0696 (11.68)	−0.1893 (−15.07)	—
6. Generalized Expon. $E(\hat{b}_t)=A+B\exp(CX)$	48.03	24	−31.07	0.3155 (7.67)	4.0824 (9.68)	−0.3169 (−12.07)	—
7. Pareto $E(\hat{b}_t)=B/(X+C)$	82.59	25	0.20	—	5.8689 (22.36)	0.6884 (3.17)	—
8. Generalized Pareto $E(\hat{b}_t)=A+B/(X+C)$	76.58	24	−2.52	−0.1876 (−2.26)	8.0269 (7.18)	1.2949 (3.03)	—

II. Employment Effects b_t, Estimated from the Complementary Log Model

Models ($X \equiv t-13$)	L^2	df	BIC	A	B	C	D
1. Constant $\quad$ E($\hat{b}_t$)	773.09	26	687.40	0.02254 (4.86)	—	—	—
2. Linear $\quad$ E($\hat{b}_t$)=$A+BX$	411.48	25	329.08	0.00720 (1.51)	0.00419 (4.69)	—	—
3. Quadratic $\quad$ E($\hat{b}_t$)=$A+BX+CX^2$	94.65	24	15.55	-0.01411 (-4.24)	0.01387 (11.90)	-0.00050 (-8.96)	—
4. Cubic $\quad$ E($\hat{b}_t$)=$A+BX+CX^2+DX^3$	94.52	23	18.72	-0.01465 (-3.21)	0.01425 (5.86)	-0.00055 (-1.87)	0.00000 (0.18)
5. Generalized Expon. $\quad$ E($\hat{b}_t$)=$A+B\exp(CX)$	162.87	24	83.77	0.07494 (20.13)	-0.09308 (-23.47)	-0.21158 (-11.32)	—
6. Generalized Pareto $\quad$ E($\hat{b}_t$)=$A+B/(X+C)$	192.17	24	113.07	0.10160 (15.10)	-0.61999 (-5.46)	5.05840 (6.57)	—
7. Log-logistic $\quad$ E($\hat{b}_t$)=$A(BX)^{C-1}/[(BX)^C+1]$	34.49	24	-44.61	0.94333 (13.55)	0.14980 (20.37)	3.67903 (16.15)	—

[a] t-statistics are in parentheses.

models of $E(\hat{b}_t)$. In addition to the constant effects model, the linear, quadratic, and cubic models are tested as hierarchical polynomial models. Furthermore, three groups of nonlinear models are applied. One group includes the exponential model, where $g(t,\theta) = B\exp(CX)$, and the generalized exponential model with a nonzero threshold–that is, $g(t,\theta) = A+B\exp(CX)$. The second group includes the Pareto model, where $g(t,\theta) = B/(X+C)$, and the generalized Pareto with a nonzero threshold–that is, $g(t,\theta) = A+B/(X+C)$. Both the exponential and Pareto groups represent $E(\hat{b}_t)$ as a monotonic function of time t. Only the generalized versions are applied when a negative estimate of B is anticipated. The last model is the log-logistic model with an additional scaling parameter A, where $g(t,\theta) = A(BX)^{C-1}/[(BX)^C+1]$. It is employed as a representative model with an inverse-U shape.

First of all, the results of the chi-squared test in Table 3 show that the constant effects model does not fit with either of the two data sets, one from the complementary log-log model and the other from the complementary log model. Hence, the employment effects are neither proportional nor linearly additive.

Regarding parametric models for the employment effects estimated from the complementary log-log model, the results in Table 3 show that according to the BIC statistic, two models (the cubic and the generalized exponential) are much better than the saturated model, and two other models (the exponential and the generalized Pareto) are almost as good as the saturated model. Between the first two, the cubic model is better. Since the BIC statistic penalizes for a large number of parameters more than the likelihood-ratio test does, comparisons with the saturated model give somewhat different results if we use the LR test: Only the cubic model fits the data well and the generalized exponential model has only a marginal fit $(0.001<P<0.01)$.

For the employment effects estimated from the complementary log-log model, Figure 3 depicts the original non-parametric estimates, $\hat{b}_t$, with their upper and lower 95 percent confidence limits, and their reestimates, $g(t,\hat{\theta})$, from the cubic and the generalized exponential models.

Figure 3 shows that the predicted values from both the cubic model and the generalized exponential model almost consistently lie within the 95 percent confidence intervals of the nonparametric esti-

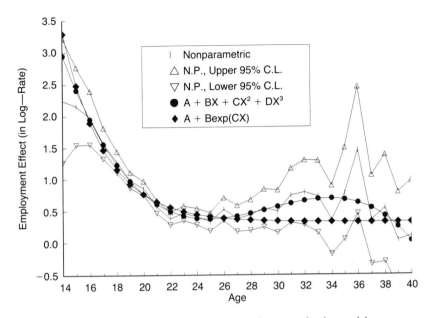

FIGURE 3. Time varying employment effects, complementary log-log model.

mates. Further, the employment effects monotonically decrease from age 14 to 25 (which is the age at which the marriage rate reaches its peak). However, the predictions from the two models differ slightly for older ages. Since the cubic model is better according to the BIC criterion, we should regard its results for ages 26–40 as more reliable: The employment effects increase slightly until about age 34, followed by another decline.

Substantively, the results are consistent with the following speculation. People who have not entered employment face an increasing risk of passing over the desirable (or "normative") ages of marriage as they approach the age with the modal marriage rate (i.e., age 25). They thereby increase their propensities to marry even though they have not entered full-time employment, over and beyond the age effects. This tendency accounts for the decrease in the positive employment effects from age 14 to 25. However, as age increases further, the employment effect will increase slightly. This occurs because among persons who have not entered employment, those who have a strong tendency to retain a desirable timing of marriage rather than the work-before-marriage sequence are increasingly and selectively removed from the risk set—thereby leaving a larger proportion of persons who wish to retain the work-before-marriage sequence in the risk set.

As for the employment effects estimated from the complementary log model, the results in Table 3 show that only the log-logistic model is better than the saturated model according to the BIC criterion. The log-logistic model attains an adequate fit with the data by the LR test as well ($P>0.05$). Among the group of polynomial models, the quadratic model is the best but this model is significantly worse than the log-logistic model and does not fit the data well.

For the employment effects estimated from the complementary log model, Figure 4 presents the original nonparametric estimates $\hat{b}_t$, its upper and lower 95 percent confidence limits, and their reestimates from the log-logistic and quadratic models.

Figure 4 shows that the predicted values from the log-logistic model lie almost consistently within the 95 percent confidence intervals of the nonparametric estimates. The worse fit of the quadratic model compared with the log-logistic model is due primarily to its

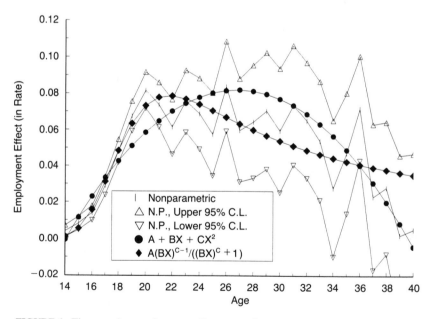

FIGURE 4. Time-varying employment effects, complementary log model.

poorer prediction for young ages (14–20). It can be seen that the pre-dicted values from the quadratic model often deviate from the 95 per-cent confidence interval at this age range. The log-logistic model shows that the employment effects from age 14 to 21 take a S-shape—that is, a gradual increase followed by a sharper increase and then a gradual increase again. The good fit of the log-logistic model also indicates that the employment effects decrease monotonically after they reach a peak (at around ages 21–22). The effects are positively skewed.

The implications of the results from the complementary log model are not clear if we try to relate the results to the substantive hypothesis given before. The pattern of initial increases in the em-ployment effects looks quite similar to that in the rate of marriage itself. However, it is not clear in Figure 4 whether the employment effects are proportional to the rate or not. We know from Figure 3 that they are in fact not proportional. The employment effects in Figure 4 reach their peak earlier (age 21) than the peak rate of marriage (age 25) because of the age-dependent decrease in the positive employment effects on the relative risk, as shown in Figure 3. However, without an additional analysis of relative risk, these patterns are rather difficult to explain.

The results presented in Figures 3 and 4 suggest that the analy-sis of relative risk permits a greater interpretability compared with the analysis of absolute risk—at least for the test of the particular substantive hypothesis described before. At the same time, a com-parison of the two results clearly shows that we should not confuse time-varying covariate effects on relative risk with those on absolute risk. In particular, the declining positive employment effects on rela-tive risk during ages 14–20 do not mean that the rate of marriage narrows between those who have and have not entered employment. In fact, it widens, as shown in the analysis of absolute risk.

5. CONCLUSION AND DISCUSSION

While the saturated models of hazard rates may have limited use by themselves because of potential redundancy in parameters, this pa-per shows that the results for covariate effects from the saturated model may be employed usefully in secondary analyses for (1) tests of proportionality/linearity and (2) tests and comparisons of paramet-ric models for time variations in the covariate effects, while treating the baseline time effects nonparametrically. These secondary analyses are possible because the parameter estimates for covariate effects based on the saturated models are, with the particular parameterization employed in this paper, uncorrelated across time points and, therefore, become asymptotically independent, given the multivariate normality of parameter estimates that is asymptotically satisfied under certain regularity conditions.

The major limitation of the method presented in this paper is that it can be of practical use only for a model with, at most, a few categorical covariates. In this regard, the method can be applied mostly to two situations—namely (1) where either a nonparametric method (Miller 1981) or the life-table technique (Namboodiri and Suchindran 1987) has been used for comparing groups,[3] or (2) where a preliminary analysis of time-varying covariate effects for selected key covariates is undertaken.

However, the results from such an analysis may be used further for a general multivariate analysis in certain cases. If the model that fits the data becomes a linear function of parameters when one parameter is fixed, then the model can be easily incorporated into a multivariate framework by fixing one parameter based on its prior estimate. For example, if the model that fits the data of covariate effects is either the generalized exponential, $A + B\exp(Ct)$, or the generalized Pareto, $A + B/(t + C)$, then the model becomes a linear function of parameters A and B, *if parameter* C *is given*. It follows that we may conduct a two-step analysis. First, we model the time-

---

[3]A proportionality test may be conducted in a regression analysis based on "model life tables" that Brass et al. (1968) proposed (see also Brass 1974; Coale and Demeny 1983; Namboodiri and Suchindran 1987, ch. 12). They proposed the following regression analysis:

$$\ln[l_c(x)/(1 - l_c(x))] = \alpha + \beta\ln[l_b(x)/(1 - l_b(x))],$$

where $l_c(x)$ and $l_b(x)$, given in the life-table notation, are survivor functions at age x, respectively, for any comparison group and the baseline group. Then the significance test of $\beta = 1$ provides a proportionality test for the odds of the survivor functions between the comparison and baseline groups. This test is quite similar to a proportionality test of a dummy covariate in proportional hazard models because the latter proportionality test is obtained when we employ the complementary log-log function $-\ln(-\ln(l))$ instead of the logit function $\ln[l/(1 - l)]$ in the above formula, and these two functions have similar shapes. This method, however, can be applied only for comparing groups—for the effects of a time-constant categorical variable—and it is rather specific regarding the hypothesized form of deviation from proportionality.

varying effects of a particular covariate, say X, based on the method presented in this paper. Second, we use the results of the first step for multivariate models that include covariate X, and fix parameter C using its estimate from the first step. Parameters A and B for the effects of X and either $X\exp(Ct)$ or $X/(t+C)$ can then be simultaneously estimated with parameters for other covariates. A caveat offered here is that the estimates of parameters for other covariates as well as A and B are conditional upon the prior estimate of parameter C. However, fixing some parameters with their reasonably good prior estimates is quite common in the use of complicated nonlinear models, such as the Coale-McNeil model of marriage rate (Coale and McNeil 1972; Bennett et al., 1989; Bloom and Bennett 1990).

The method presented in this paper has advantages and disadvantages compared with other methods. Semiparametric approaches such as the use of local likelihood estimation or smoothing splines for covariate effects are useful when the shape of the covariate effects is too complicated to be fitted effectively by parametric models. Similar to the method presented in this paper, however, the use of these alternative methods is limited in general multivariate models. The methods are exploratory in nature, such that a series of models differing in the number of time intervals and cutting positions of time intervals need to be tested to find the best-fitting model. They therefore best serve for an analysis of a single time-varying covariate. However, unlike the method presented in this paper, they can handle time-varying effects of continuous as well as categorical covariates. The method presented in this paper requires that continuous variables be categorized using some cutoff points.

The test of proportionality in Cox's regression model can be performed in a variety of ways, as described in the introductory section. However, the method introduced in this paper can perform similar tests for many more kinds of models, including additive as well as multiplicative hazard rate models. Furthermore, the method can be extended effectively to a test of various parametric models for time-varying covariate effects.

Finally, although I have given concrete closed-form solutions for only four representative saturated models, the general solutions given in equation (10), which do not specify the link function, can be applied to various other kinds of specific hazard rate models, such as discrete-time logit and probit models.

APPENDIX: THE VARIANCE-COVARIANCE MATRIX OF PARAMETER ESTIMATES

In the following discussion, it is first assumed that the hazard-rate model includes a single categorical covariate and a constant term, and that the covariate has TK categories with state 1 as the baseline category. Given the solution for this model, the solution for the saturated model of formula (6) described in the text is obtained by a simple reparameterization. The hazard rate is now assumed to be:

$$\alpha_i(t) = f(c_{11} + \sum_{(t,k)\neq(1,1)} c_{tk}D_{itk}),\qquad (A1)$$

where D_{itk} is the dummy variable for state (t,k) of the covariate against state $(1,1)$ for person i, and c_{tk}, $t=1,\ldots,T, k=1,\ldots,K$ are parameters. Then from formulas (3) and (5) in the text, the log-likelihood function for the continuous-time model becomes:

$$L = N_{11}\ln(f(c_{11})) + \sum_{(t,k)\neq(1,1)} N_{tk}\ln(f(c_{11}+c_{tk})) - U_{11}f(c_{11})$$
$$- \sum_{(t,k)\neq(1,1)} U_{tk}f(c_{11}+c_{tk}),\qquad (A2)$$

and for the discrete-time model it becomes:

$$L = N_{11}\ln[f(c_{11})/(1-f(c_{11}))] + \sum_{(t,k)\neq(1,1)} N_{tk}\ln[f(c_{11}+c_{tk})/(1-f(c_{11}+c_{tk}))]$$
$$+ U_{11}\ln(1-f(c_{11})) + \sum_{(t,k)\neq(1,1)} U_{tk}\ln(1-f(c_{11}+c_{tk})).\qquad (A3)$$

Here as in the text, notations N_{tk} and U_{tk} respectively indicate the number of events and the amount of exposure to risk at state (t,k). For both cases, the set of equations, $\partial L/\partial \mathbf{c}=\mathbf{0}$, leads to the following set of equations for parameter estimate $\hat{c}_{tk}$:

$$f(\hat{c}_{11}) = N_{11}/U_{11}$$
$$f(\hat{c}_{11}+\hat{c}_{tk}) = N_{tk}/U_{tk}, (t,k)\neq(1,1)\qquad (A4)$$

It follows that the maximum likelihood estimates of parameters permit an identical expression for the continuous-time and discrete-time models such that:

$$\hat{c}_{11} = f^{-1}(N_{11}/U_{11})$$
$$\hat{c}_{tk} = f^{-1}(N_{tk}/U_{tk}) - f^{-1}(N_{11}/U_{11}), \quad (t,k)\neq(1,1).\qquad (A5)$$

Given the likelihood functions in formulas (A2) and the solution for parameter estimates in formula (A5), it can be easily shown that the value of the second-order derivatives of the log-likelihood function, $L''(m,n)$, $m,n=1, \ldots ,TK$ for the *continuous-time model* with a single categorical covariate with TK states has the following entries:

$$L''(1,1) \;=\; -\,(U_{11}^{\,2}/N_{11})f'(\hat{c}_{11})^2 - \sum_{m=2}^{TK}(U_m^{\,2}/N_m)f'(\hat{c}_{11}+\hat{c}_m)^2$$

$$L''(1,m) \;=\; L''(m,1) = -\,(U_m^{\,2}/N_m)f'(\hat{c}_{11}+\hat{c}_m)^2 \qquad m\ge2$$

$$L''(m,m) \;=\; -\,(U_m^{\,2}/N_m)f'(\hat{c}_{11}+\hat{c}_m)^2 \qquad\qquad m\ge2$$

$$L''(m,n) \;=\; 0 \qquad\qquad\qquad\qquad m,n\ge2;\; m\ne n. \quad \text{(A6)}$$

Here m and n denote states (t,k) other than $(1,1)$. A matrix expression can be obtained by replacing A_1 by $(U_{11}^{\,2}/N_{11})f'(\hat{c}_{11})^2$ and A_m, $m=2, \ldots ,TK$, by $(U_m^{\,2}/N_m)f'(\hat{c}_{11}+\hat{c}_m)^2$ in matrix 1 of Figure A1.

For a general form of L'' expressed as matrix 1 of Figure A1, the variance-covariance matrix of parameter estimates, which is minus the inverse of L'', becomes Matrix 2 of Figure A1. A direct proof of this is the fact that the product of matrices 1 and 2 becomes minus the unit matrix. It follows that the variance-covariance matrix, V, has the following entries:

$$V(1,1) \;=\; N_{11}/[U_{11}^{\,2}f'(\hat{c}_{11})^2]$$

$$V(1,m) \;=\; V(m,1) = -\,N_{11}/[U_{11}^{\,2}f'(\hat{c}_{11})^2] \qquad m\ge2$$

$$V(m,m) \;=\; N_{11}/[U_{11}^{\,2}f'(\hat{c}_{11})^2] + N_m/[U_m^{\,2}f'(\hat{c}_{11}+\hat{c}_m)^2] \quad m\ge2$$

$$V(m,n) \;=\; N_{11}/[U_{11}^{\,2}f'(\hat{c}_{11})^2] \qquad\qquad m,n\ge2;\; m\ne n. \quad \text{(A7)}$$

The second-order derivative matrix of the log-likelihood function for the *discrete-time* model with a single categorical covariate with TK categories and a constant term is given, using formulas (A3) and (A5), as:

$$L''(1,1) \;=\; -\,U_{11}^{\,3}f'(\hat{c}_{11})^2/[N_{11}(U_{11}-N_{11})] - \sum_{m=2}^{TK} u_m^{\,3}f'(\hat{c}_{11}+\hat{c}_m)^2/[N_m(U_m-N_m)]$$

$$L''(1,m) \;=\; L''(m,1) = -\,U_m^{\,3}f'(\hat{c}_{11}+\hat{c}_m)^2/[N_m(U_m-N_m)] \quad m\ge2$$

$$L''(m,m) \;=\; -\,U_m^{\,3}f'(\hat{c}_{11}+\hat{c}_m)^2/[N_m(U_m-N_m)] \qquad\qquad m\ge2$$

$$L''(m,n) \;=\; 0 \qquad\qquad\qquad\qquad m,n\ge2;\; m\ne n. \quad \text{(A8)}$$

A matrix expression can be obtained by replacing A_1 by $U_{11}^{\,3}f'(\hat{c}_{11})^2/[N_{11}(U_{11}-N_{11})]$ and A_m, $m=2, \ldots ,TK$, by $U_k^{\,3}f'(\hat{c}_{11}+\hat{c}_m)^2/[N_m$

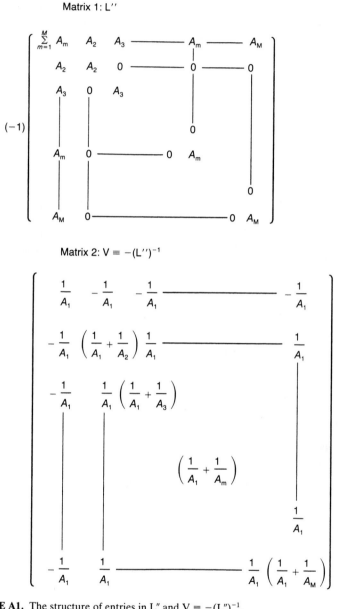

FIGURE A1. The structure of entries in L'' and $V \equiv -(L'')^{-1}$.

$(U_m - N_m)]$ in matrix 1 of Figure A1. Note that although A_m, $m=1, \ldots, TK$, represent different factors for the continuous-time and discrete-time models, the same matrix expression—that is, matrix 1 of Figure A1—applies to both. It follows that the entries of the variance-covariance matrix are given in this case as follows:

$$V(1,1) = N_{11}(U_{11} - N_{11})/[U_{11}{}^3 f'(\hat{c}_{11})^2]$$

$$V(1,m) = V(m,1) = -N_{11}(U_{11} - N_{11})/[U_{11}{}^3 f'(\hat{c}_{11})^2] \qquad m \geq 2$$

$$V(m,m) = N_{11}(U_{11} - N_{11})/[U_{11}{}^3 f'(\hat{c}_{11})^2]$$
$$\quad + N_m(U_m - N_m)/[U_m{}^3 f'(\hat{c}_{11} + \hat{c}_m)^2] \qquad m \geq 2$$

$$V(m,n) = N_{11}(U_{11} - N_{11})/[U_{11}{}^3 f'(\hat{c}_{11})^2] \qquad m,n \geq 2; \ m \neq n. \qquad (A9)$$

Given these solutions for the variance-covariance matrix for continuous-time and discrete-time models with the saturated model of formula (A1), the variance-covariance matrix for the saturated model defined in formula (6) in the text is given by using the following relationships:

$$\hat{a}_t = \hat{c}_{1t} \qquad \text{for } t=1, \ldots, T$$

$$\hat{b}_{1k} = \hat{c}_{1k} \qquad \text{for } k=2, \ldots, K$$

$$\hat{b}_{tk} = \hat{c}_{tk} - \hat{c}_{t1} \qquad \text{for } t=2, \ldots, T, k=2, \ldots, K \qquad (A10)$$

For example, it follows from formulas (A7) and (A10) that for the continuous-time model, we obtain:

$$V(\hat{a}_t, \hat{a}_t) = V(\hat{c}_{t1}, \hat{c}_{t1}) = N_{11}/[U_{11}{}^2 f'(\hat{c}_{11})^2] + N_{t1}/[U_{t1}{}^2 f'(\hat{c}_{11} + \hat{c}_{t1})^2]$$
$$= N_{11}/[U_{11}{}^2 f'(\hat{a}_1)^2] + N_{t1}/[U_{t1}{}^2 f'(\hat{a}_1 + \hat{a}_t)^2]$$
$$t \geq 2$$

$$V(\hat{b}_{tk}, \hat{b}_{tk}) = V(\hat{c}_{tk} - \hat{c}_{t1}, \hat{c}_{tk} - \hat{c}_{t1}) = V(\hat{c}_{tk}, \hat{c}_{tk}) + V(\hat{c}_{t1}, \hat{c}_{t1}) - 2V(\hat{c}_{tk}, \hat{c}_{t1})$$
$$= N_{tk}/[U_{tk}{}^2 f'(\hat{c}_{11} + \hat{c}_{tk})^2] + N_{t1}/[U_{t1}{}^2 f'(\hat{c}_{11} + \hat{c}_{t1})^2]$$
$$= N_{tk}/[U_{tk}{}^2 f'(\hat{a}_1 + \hat{a}_t + \hat{b}_{tk})^2 + N_{t1}/[U_{t1}{}^2 f'(\hat{a}_1 + \hat{a}_t)^2]$$
$$t \geq 2$$

$$V(\hat{b}_{tk}, \hat{b}_{sk}) = V(\hat{c}_{tk} - \hat{c}_{t1}, \hat{c}_{sk} - \hat{c}_{s1})$$
$$= V(\hat{c}_{tk}, \hat{c}_{sk}) + V(\hat{c}_{t1}, \hat{c}_{s1}) - V(\hat{c}_{tk}, \hat{c}_{s1}) - V(\hat{c}_{sk}, \hat{c}_{t1})$$
$$= 2N_{11}/[U_{11}{}^2 f'(\hat{c}_{11})^2] - 2N_{11}/[U_{11}{}^2 f'(\hat{c}_{11})^2] = 0$$
$$\text{for } s \neq t$$

Similarly, other elements of V for the continuous-time model and elements of V for the discrete-time model, both with the saturated model defined in formula (6) in the text, can be obtained using the relationship between the two sets of parameter estimates described in formula (A10).

REFERENCES

Allison, P. D. 1982. "Discrete-time Methods for the Analysis of Event Histories." In *Sociological Methodology 1982,* edited by S. Leinhardt, 61–98. San Francisco: Jossey-Bass.

Bennett, N. G., D. B. Bloom, and P. A. Craig. 1989. "The Divergence of Black and White Marriage Patterns." *American Journal of Sociology* 95:692–722.

Bloom, D. E., and N. G. Bennett. 1990. "Modeling American Marriage Patterns." *Journal of the American Statistical Association* 85:1009–1017.

Blossfeld, H., A. Hermerle, and K.U. Mayer. 1989. *Event History Analysis.* Hilldale, N.J.: Lawrence Erlbaum Associates.

Brass, W. 1974. "Perspectives in Population Prediction, Illustrated by the Statistics of England and Wales." *Journal of the Royal Statistical Society,* Series A. General 137: 532–83.

Brass, W., A. J., Coale, P. Demeny, D. F. Heisel, F. Lorimer, A. Rumanik, and E. van de Walle. 1968. *The Demography of Tropical Africa.* Princeton: Princeton University Press.

Coale, A. J., and P. Demeny. 1983. *Regional Model Life Tables and Stable Populations,* 2d ed. New York: Academic Press.

Coale, A. J., and D. R. McNeil. 1972. "The Distribution by Age of the Frequency of First Marriage in a Female Cohort." *Journal of the American Statistical Association* 67:743–48.

Coleman, J. S. 1981. *Longitudinal Data Analysis.* New York: Basic.

Cox, D. R., and D. Oakes. 1984. *Analysis of Survival Data.* New York: Chapman and Hill.

Featherman, D. L., and Hauser, R. M. 1978. *Opportunity and Change.* New York: Academic Press.

Green, W. H. 1990. *LIMDEP* (revised version). New York: Econometric Software, Inc.

Hauser, R. M. 1980. "On 'Stratification in a Dual Economy' (Comments on Beck et al., *ASR,* October, 1978)." *American Sociological Review* 45:702–12.

Hogan, D. P. 1978. "The Variable Order of Events in the Life Course." *American Sociological Review* 43:573–86.

Kalbfleisch, J. D., and R. L. Prentice, 1980. *The Statistical Analysis of Failure Time Data.* New York: Wiley.

McCullagh, P., and J. S. Nelder, 1989. *Generalized Linear Models,* 2d ed. New York: Chapman and Hall.

Michael, R. T., and N. B. Tuma, 1985. "Entry into Marriage and Parenthood by Young Men and Women." *Demography* 22:309–52.

Miller, R. G. 1981. *Survival Analysis*. New York: Wiley.

Nagelkerke, N.J.D., J. Oosting, and A.A.M. Hart. 1984. "A Simple Test for Goodness-of-Fit of Cox's Proportional Hazards Regression Model." *Biometrics* 40: 483–86.

Namboodiri, K., and C. M. Suchindran. 1987. *Life Table Techniques and Their Applications*. New York: Academic.

Petersen, T. 1991. "Time Aggregation Bias in Continuous-Time Hazard-Rate Models." In *Sociological Methodology 1991*, edited by P.V. Marsden, 263–90. Oxford: Blackwell Publishers.

Prentice, R. L., and L. A. Gloeckler. 1978. "Regression Analysis of Grouped Survival Data with Application to Breast Cancer Data." *Biometrics* 29:57–67.

Raftery, A. E. 1986a. "A Note on the Bayes Factors for Log-linear Contingency Table Models with Vague Prior Information." *Journal of the Royal Statistical Society*, Series B, 48:249–50.

———. 1986b. "Choosing Models for Cross-Classifications." *American Sociological Review* 51:145–46.

SAS Institute, 1985. *SAS User's Guide: Statistics*, version 5. Cary, N.C.

Schoenfeld, D. 1982. "Partial Residuals for the Proportional Hazards Regression Model." *Biometrika* 69:239–41.

Sleeper, L. A., and D. P. Harrington, 1990. "Regression Splines in the Cox model with Applications to Covariate Effects in Liver Disease." *Journal of the American Statistical Association* 85:941–49.

Teachman, J.D. 1982. "Methodological Issues in the Analysis of Family Formation and Dissolution." *Journal of Marriage and the Family* 44:1037–1053.

Tibshirani, R., and T. Hastie. 1987. "Local Likelihood Estimation." *Journal of the American Statistical Association* 82:559–67.

Trussell, J., and D. E. Bloom. 1983. "Estimating the Covariates of Age at Marriage and the First Birth." *Population Studies* 37:403–16.

Wu, L.L., and N.B. Tuma. 1990. "Local Hazard Models." In *Sociological Methodology 1990*, edited by C. C. Clogg. Oxford: Basil Blackwell.

———. 1991. "Assessing Bias and Fit of Global and Local Hazard Models." *Sociological Methods & Research* 19:354–87.

Yamaguchi, K. 1991. *Event History Analysis*. Beverly Hills, Calif.: Sage.

Yamaguchi, K., and D. B. Kandel. 1985. "On the Resolution of Role Incompatibility: A Life Event History Analysis of Family Roles and Marijuana Use." *American Journal of Sociology* 90:1284–325.

NAME INDEX

SUBJECT INDEX